★ ★ ★ ★ OLD-TIME ★ ★ ★ ★
COUNTRY
WISDOM & LORE

Voyageur Press

OLD-TIME ★ ★ ★ ★ ★
COUNTRY
WISDOM & LORE
1000ˢ ★ ★
OF ★ ★
TRADITIONAL SKILLS FOR SIMPLE LIVING

JERRY MACK JOHNSON

Voyageur Press

First published in 2011 by
Voyageur Press, an imprint of
MBI Publishing Company,
400 First Avenue North, Suite 300,
Minneapolis, MN 55401 USA

IMPORTANT, PLEASE READ:
Any recipes or "health cures" are intended as a historical reference only. They are NOT recommended by the editors or publisher of this book. They have been compiled as a historical narrative for historical purposes only. The publisher assumes no responsibility whatsoever for any injury or damage resulting from reader's use of any of the material or information contained in this book.

We recognize, further, that some words, model names, and designations mentioned herein are the property of the trademark holder. We use them for identification purposes only. This is not an official publication.

Voyageur Press titles are also available at discounts in
bulk quantity for industrial or sales-promotional use.
For details write to Special Sales Manager at
MBI Publishing Company, 400 First Avenue North, Suite 300,
Minneapolis, MN 55401 USA.

To find out more about our books,
visit us online at www.voyageurpress.com.

ISBN-13: 978-0-7603-4001-1

Editor: Margret Aldrich
Design Manager: LeAnn Kuhlmann
Designed by: Rick Korab, Korab Company Design
Cover designed by: Matthew Simmons

Image Credits—Images are from the Voyageur Press Archive and the following sources: Clipart.com: 185 (bottom);
Florida Center for Instructional Technology: 86, 96, 116, 117, 170 (top right), 173, 185 (top), 186 (top),
188, 189, 190, 192, 193, 197, 208, 243, 269, 339 (left), 340; *Graphic Ornaments* by The Pepin Press: 6–8 (banner),
9 (banner), 153, 167 (banner), 259 (banner), 260–269 (banner), 339–352 (banner);
Library of Congress: 45, 47, 48, 256 (bottom left); Shutterstock: 111 (top right); Eric Sloane: 2.

Printed in China

Preface

Maple leaves stained gold and crimson, sent by friends from the Northeast, brightened our home. A visitor, unaccustomed to leaves of such vivid hues here in West Texas, remarked on their beauty— adding, however: "I don't know what kind they are, but as far as I'm concerned, leaves are just leaves." That commentary set me to recalling the varied roles leaves had played in my boyhood, valid evidence that leaves were more than "just leaves."

At the first signs of spring, shoes were kicked aside, and boys ran barefoot. By midsummer, quite a callused pad had built up on the bottoms of our feet. The roughest terrain of stones, stubble, or even nettles scarcely caused us to wince, so protected were we by our leathery soles. But feet at summer's start were tender, having been pampered through the winter months by such civilized gear as socks and boots or brogans. As a consequence, many a foot suffered from bruising. Grandfather had a sure-fire remedy for this. He gathered Madeira vine and bound the mashed leaves around each stone bruise. By next morning I'd be off and running, the cure complete.

We didn't have bottled air fresheners in those days; instead, they sprang from the ground. I remember Mother picking mint sprigs from around an old water spigot, drying them, and crumbling their brittle leaves into small china pots, placed strategically throughout the house.

I accepted as fact that Nature could satisfy almost any need, if we but had the knowledge of her secrets. My elders appeared to exhibit an unending supply of that vital knowledge with their ability to heal with herbs, to predict weather and animal behavior, and to locate underground water with a forked twig.

Such reminiscences of my country boyhood led to others: my string of pets. While city boys might cherish their pedigreed dogs, my pets came to me from the surrounding fields and range—without credentials as to genteel genealogy, but each winning my affection in its own unique way. I wondered how many folks had a firsthand acquaintance with possums, armadillos, and other small country creatures. (Not all animals are to be recommended as pets, however, as my interesting and odoriferous possum soon proved when he sank his needle-sharp teeth through my hand.)

Pets weren't our only diversion. Outings to medicine shows, tent circuses, Wild West shows and rodeos, horse races, brush-arbor camp-meeting preachings, and the simple but enjoyable games we indulged in after school were deeply satisfying forms of entertainment.

I can't forget the way our house gleamed, despite the lack of today's highly touted cleansers. Homemade soap and plenty of elbow grease kept both clothes and home sparkling.

Many an old recipe handed down from before Grandma's time was responsible for the tantalizing smells that permeated our kitchen.

My friend's observation that "leaves are just leaves" sparked the thought that perhaps we need to be reminded of the bounty of Nature's offerings. Her riches are all around us; yet so often they are taken for granted. With such feelings and memories in mind, I wrote this volume as a means of sharing them with others. And so maple leaves, not the Muses, inspired this book.

CONTENTS

PART II | HEARTH AND HOMESTEAD   167

CONTENTS

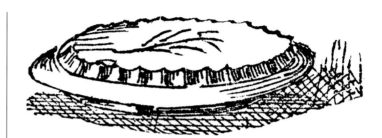

PART I

NATURE TRAIL

1 | WEATHER WISDOM

Over the ages, country people developed an oral catalogue of weather wisdom through their observation of weather patterns, atmospheric conditions, and their consequences on living creatures and inanimate objects. Each generation handed down its accumulated knowledge to the next, new information being added with the years. Such knowledge, both inherited and gleaned from experience, was relied upon in daily life by farmers, cattlemen, sheepherders, and navigators. Gradually, oft-noted weather sequences and their effects became incorporated into sayings, frequently based on dependable lore but sometimes solely on superstition.

At times it is nice to have advance knowledge of what Mother Nature has in mind for tomorrow's weather. By reading her weather signs you can become a fairly reliable weather forecaster.

What follows is a gathering of many of nature's weather's signs that have been handed down for many generations. These signs were learned on the range, prairie, mountains, and sea. We have gathered them over many years and many miles.

Clouds

The hooded clouds, like friars,
Tell their beads in drops of rain.
—Longfellow

Clouds are so often with us we usually overlook them unless a storm is on the way. Mother Nature has a habit of using clouds to write messages in the sky, plain enough for all to see, about what She plans to do with the weather. There are two basic cloud formations; "cumulus" clouds, which are puffy or piled up, and are formed by rising air currents, and "stratus," which are layered or sheet-like clouds. Stratus clouds are formed when a layer of air is cooled below saturation level without any vertical movement. There are also four families of clouds: high, middle, low, and towering clouds.

The "Summary of Cloud Types" that follows will help you identify the major cloud types and better understand their relationship to the weather.

Forecasting Weather by the Clouds

High Clouds

If clouds are white and thin and scattered across the sky with mostly west winds, the weather will be fair with little change.

It is a strong indication of rain if clouds turn gray or show yellow coloring and thicken, seemingly moving together; if they gradually drop and thick clouds develop beneath them; if the high clouds move from the south or from the southwest with surface winds prevailing from the east. There will be some wind and visibility will be reduced; rain will begin in six to twenty-four hours. Winds will usually shift to the southwest and will be warmer.

Cirrostratus are responsible for "halo rings" around the sun or moon. If they thicken it is a strong indication of coming snow or rain.

Middle Clouds

There is a good possibility of rain within six to twelve hours

Summary of Cloud Types	Height	Cloud Name and Symbol	Description
High Clouds	(16,500 to 45,000 ft.)	Cirrus (Ci)	Thin, feathery, white, wispy, with silky edges. Semi-transparent. Form at great heights. First clouds to show color before sunrise and last to darken at sunset.
		Cirrocumulus (Cc)	Lumpy, fibrous small bands. Often called "mackerel sky." Rippled to look like sand on the beach. Wave-like appearance.
		Cirrostratus (Cs)	Thin milky veil with whitish haze. Does not obscure but often produces halo around sun or moon. Sometimes called "mare's tail" clouds.
Middle Clouds	(6,500 to 16,500 ft.)	Altocumulus (Ac)	Patches or layers of fluffy roll-like clouds. Usually arranged in rows. One form is "sheep's back," which looks like a layer of cotton balls. Another form appears as long bands or rolls of cotton crowded together.
		Altostratus (As)	Heavy gray sheet or gray film, lightly striped. Almost obscures the sun or moon like viewing through a heavy, frosted glass. Causes a corona or soft luminous circle on the edge of the sun or moon.
		Nimbostratus (Ns)	Form beneath altostratus. Have a wet look. Low formless dark clouds of bad weather. Ragged rain clouds.
Low Clouds	(0 to 6,500 ft.)	Stratocumulus (Sc)	Series of gray patches of roll-like clouds. Has shadow effect. Fluffy and wavy surface. Long, flattened puffs.
		Stratus (St)	Lowest of clouds. Shapeless, smooth layer with fog-like appearance. Often form heavy leaden sky. If broken into shreds are called fractostratus.
Towering Clouds *(range from low to highest levels caused by strong vertical wind currents)*		Cumulus (Cli)	Puffy, billowy, changeable, thick clouds. Usually scattered over a fair weather sky.
		Cumulonimbus (Cb)	Typical "thunderhead." Often with flat horizontal bases and tops that are flat anvil-like. Pile to great heights. Strong light shadows.

when these clouds change from patches into layers and blankets; if their movement is from the south or southwest with surface wind prevailing from the east; if a "corona" or soft luminous circle forms on the edge of the sun or moon. The weather will later change to warmer temperatures and it will be partly cloudy with winds from the southwest.

If the clouds remain apart and open blue sky can be seen between the cloud patches, or if the clouds are moving in the same general direction as the surface wind is blowing, there will be little or no change in the weather and it will remain fair.

If the cloud patches are swiftly moving from the west or from the northwest, or if surface winds are from the south or southwest, there

is a possibility of quick showers, hard but of short duration. The wind will shift to come from the northwest and it will be clear with cooler temperatures.

If the cloud patches are noticeable about midmorning during the humid part of summer or if the clouds have high-peaked humps coming from a broad base there will be gusty winds soon with a good possibility of thunderstorms.

When the sun becomes hazy, surface winds are from the east or southeast, and the altostratus layers become lower and darken, especially in the south or southwest, be prepared for continuous and steady rain in a short while. This will be followed by warm southwest winds.

Low Clouds

If stratocumulus clouds come together creating an overcast with much gray coloring, there is a very good chance of rain.

When stratocumulus clouds appear puffed with open blue sky showing between the patches and the clouds move in the same general direction as the surface wind there will be no change in the weather for twenty-four to forty-eight hours.

If there is a heavy, thick stratocumulus covering that continues to rise higher and crumbles and breaks in places when the wind is from the west, you can expect cooler temperatures and clearing.

When a stratocumulus cloud bank that is rolled and very long shows in the west or northwest with strong surface winds prevailing from the south or southwest, there is a good possibility of short, sudden, hard rain storms. These will be followed by clear weather with lower temperatures.

When there are higher stratus clouds in the morning and surface winds are light, these clouds will soon break and the sky will become clear.

Low, heavy stratus clouds forming a heavy, leaden sky frequently cause only drizzle, especially in valleys and along coastlines.

When dark nimbostratus clouds form from low altostratus clouds with movement from the south or southwest while surface winds prevail from the southeast, there is almost a 100 percent probability of

steady rain. This will be followed by warmer weather when the clouds break up and the wind will then prevail from the south or southwest.

Towering Clouds

When cumulus clouds float alone in a blue sky, especially in the afternoon, you can expect fair weather and a break-up of the clouds by sunset.

When cumulus clouds form about midmorning or a little later, especially on a humid day, and continue to build rapidly by mid-afternoon, there will be thundershowers, usually in the late afternoon or evening.

When cumulonimbus clouds build in separate masses and drift in from the south or southwest, there will be sharp winds from the south and southwest. There should be thunderstorms in the later afternoon and evening, and there might also be hail and short, hard gusting winds.

Watch for heavy cumulus or cumulonimbus clouds forming in solid banks in the west, northwest, and north. Surface winds will be strong from the south or southwest, and there are strong possibilities of severe thunderstorms, with squall lines moving through the area and wind prevailing from the west or north:

- "When the wind veers against the sun, Trust it not, for back 'twill run."
- "Mackerel sky and mare's tails, Make lofty ships carry low sails."
- "If clouds look as if scratched by a hen, Get ready to reef your topsails then."
- "When the wind is in the South The rain is in it's mouth, When the wind is in the East, It's neither good for man nor beast, The wind in the West, Suits everyone best."

Foul-Weather Signs

- A red morning sky signifies a day of bad weather.
- Cirro-cumulus clouds appearing in winter mean warm, wet weather.
- The sight of threadlike cirrus clouds brushed back from the west is an indication of rain and wind.
- The formation of cirrus clouds in good weather, with the barometer falling, means rain is certain.
- Cirrus clouds are forerunners of the east wind. If the cloud wisps streak upward, rain is indicated.
- Clouds that sail contrary to the wind foretoken rain.
- When a heavy cloud builds up in the west and then appears to settle back, be on the watch for a storm.

- Clouds moving in opposite directions at differing rates and heights foretell heavy rains.
- Masses of thick clouds of a greenish hue gathering in the southeast and remaining for a few hours indicate a series of heavy rains and gales.
- If cumulus clouds continue to increase in an evening sky, rain can be expected.
- Clouds over hills, when descending, portend rain; clouds that are rising over hills do not cause rain.

Fair-Weather Signs

- The approach of clear weather is heralded by the appearance in the northwest of a patch of blue sky big enough to tailor a Scotsman's jacket.
- When cirrus clouds disappear, fine weather can be expected.
- When clouds that are driven by the wind at the same height slowly thin and descend, good weather can be anticipated.
- Upper clouds coming out of the northwest in the morning ensure a day of fair weather.
- When cumulus clouds begin to diminish at sunset, fine weather can be expected.

Dry-Weather Signs

- When wisps of cirrus clouds streak downward, expect dry weather with wind.
- The longer the duration of dry weather, the less is the likelihood that cirrus clouds will be followed by rain.

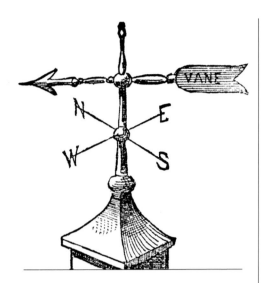

Signs of Wind

Sayings of the past concerning winds are in general borne out by today's findings. Winds are prognosticators of the weather. As Bacon put it, "Every wind has its weather."

East winds proverbially bring rain; west winds herald fair or clearing conditions. Winds from the northeast forewarn of violent storms of wind and moisture. Winds blowing from the southeast indicate storms of less severity. Both northwesterly and southwesterly winds are harbingers of fair weather, the chief difference between them being that those from the northwest are cold and those from the southwest, warm.

Three hundred years ago, Izaak Walton put his observations of wind behavior into rhyme:

When the wind is in the north,
The skillful fisher goes not forth;
When the wind is in the east,
'Tis good for neither man nor beast;
When the wind is in the south,
It blows the flies in the fish's mouth;
When the wind is in the west,
There it is the very best.

Winds are created by variations in the temperature of the atmosphere over land masses and water surfaces. The following sayings are concerned with various types of weather generated by specific winds:
• People in the Southwest foretell relief from drought when there is a sudden, strong shift of wind.
• When a lively wind from the south and southwest blows for a day or more, folks prepare for a "norther."
• In most parts of the country, a strong, steady southeast wind means rainfall within thirty-six hours.
• When winds come from a northeasterly direction, look out for severe cold and heavy snow.
• When the wind is centered between north and west, and the temperature descends to 40 degrees or less, expect frost.
• A sudden wind shift in the midst of a storm is a sign that foul weather will soon turn to fair.

Signs of Rain

• Leaves turn over and show their bottom sides before a rain.
• Red sunrise with clouds lowering later in the morning tells of rain.
• A south wind brings rain.
• Winds from the east bring wet weather.
• Watch for rain when distant sounds are loud and sharp.
• Rain with an east wind is of long duration.

Estimating Wind Speeds by the Beaufort Scale

In 1805, Admiral Beaufort of the British Navy composed a scale that estimated wind speeds from their effects on ships sails. His scale is changed here for use on land.

Beaufort Number	Miles Per Hour	Knots	Description	Visible Sign
0	0–1	0–1	Calm	Smoke rises skyward
1	1–3	1–3	Light air	Smoke slowly drifts
2	4–7	4–6	Light breeze	Tree leaves rustle
3	8–12	7–10	Gentle breeze	Tree leaves and twigs move
4	13–18	11–16	Moderate breeze	Small branches of trees move
5	19–24	17–21	Fresh breeze	Small trees sway
6	25–31	22–27	Strong breeze	Large tree branches sway
7	32–38	28–33	Moderate gale	Whole trees sway
8	39–46	34–40	Fresh gale	Twigs break from trees
9	47–54	41–47	Strong gale	Tree branches break
10	55–63	48–55	Full gale	Whole trees snap or blow down
11	64–72	56–63	Storm	Violent storm—much damage
12	73–82	64–71	Hurricane	Severe destruction

- When smoke is sluggish in rising be prepared for wet weather.
- Rain can come when the quarter moon is tipping downward.
- Sudden rain is of short duration. Slow rain lasts a long time.
- High clouds won't bring rain.
- A strip of seaweed in the house stays dry and dusty-like in fine weather; with rains on the way it gets damp and sticky.
- Night cloudiness in patches foretells rain.
- "When the stars begin to huddle, the earth will soon become a puddle."
- Big rains usually begin about midmorning.
- If there is a thunderstorm before noon on any day in September you can expect much rain and snow through the winter.
- If the sun comes out while it is raining, it will rain the next day.
- A gray sunset with lowering clouds or one in which the sky is green or yellowish-green indicates rain.

- A morning rainbow is a sign of rain.
- "Rain before seven, quits before eleven."
- Rain on Sunday means some rain during the next week.
- "The moon with a circle brings water in her back."
- "If the moon shows a silver shield, Be not afraid to reap your field, But if she rises haloed round, Soon we'll tread on deluged ground."
- "Rain long foretold, long last, Short notice, soon past."
- "When grass is dry in morning light, Look for rain before the night, When dew is on the grass, Rain will never come to pass."
- "When ye see a cloud rise out of the west, straightway cometh the rain; and so it is."—Luke 12 :54
- "Mackerel sky, mackerel sky, Not long wet, nor yet long dry."
- "If the sun goes pale to bed, 'Twill rain tomorrow, it is said."
- "An evening gray and morning red, Will send the shepherd wet to bed."

How Much Rain Fell?

To have an idea of the amount of rain water that falls on an acre of ground, the following should be of interest:

0.01 inch of rain equals	62,726 cubic inches or	11 tons
0.05	13,632	5.6
0.10	627,264	11.3
1.00	6,272,640	113.0
2.00	12,545,280	226.0
5.00	31,363,200	565.0

The number of inches of snow that corresponds to 1 inch of water is not constant due to variations in the texture of snow. It can vary from 6 inches to 25, but a good average is about 10 inches of snow equals 1 inch of water.

Signs of Storm

- When the atmosphere is telescopic, and distant objects (the stars at night, for instance) stand out unusually clear and sharp, a storm could be near. So, too, for sounds: "Sound traveling far and wide, a stormy day will betide."
- Broad, deep, and angry redness in the east in the early morning means storm.
- Clouds are sometimes not so indicative of a storm as the total absence of clouds when other signs prevail.
- An obscured sunset after a bright day foretells a storm.
- A growing whiteness in the sky tells of an approaching storm.
- Red sky in the morning is usually a storm warning.

- When the needles of pine trees turn west there will be heavy snow.
- Halos or sun dogs are large circles, or parts of circles, around the sun or moon. When they occur after fine weather it indicates stormy weather will follow.
- Storms, rain, and snow may come when the barometer falls steadily.
- Storms come often when the south wind increases in speed with clouds moving from the west.
- A dark, threatening western sky indicates storm.
- A wind shift in a counterclockwise direction, as from north to west, indicates a storm or rain, especially when it starts as a north wind.
- "Evening red and morning gray Sends the traveler on his way, Evening gray and morning red Brings rain down on his head."
- "Rainbow at night, shepherd's delight Rainbow in morning, shepherd's warning."

How to Judge the Distance of a Thunderstorm

Light travels at about 186,000 miles per second. Sound travels at roughly 1,100 feet per second. This means that sound travels about 1 mile in five seconds. To judge how far a thunderstorm is from you, you must time how long it takes the sound of thunder to reach you after you see the lightning flash. By counting " 1,001, 1,002, 1,003, 1,004, 1,005," at normal speed you can count seconds. Using this system, if you can count from 1,001 to 1,010 at normal speed from the time you see the lightning until you hear the thunder, you know the thunderstorm is about two miles away.

A thunderstorm usually announces its appearance by a sudden blast of cold air that flows over the ground ahead of the rain and storm. This cold blast usually precedes the storm by about three miles.

Signs of Fair Weather

- If just before sunrise the undersides of the eastern clouds turn to pink or rose and eventually the whole sky flushes, fair weather will always follow.
- A clear sunset is a sign of good weather.
- A rainbow in the evening says fair weather will follow.
- Soft, fluffy clouds mean fine weather to come.

- Wind from the west brings fine weather.
- Good weather comes with high clouds.
- A steady or rising barometer means fair weather.
- The weather will remain fair when fluffy cumulus clouds dot the afternoon summer sky.
- When morning fog "burns off" or disappears by noon, expect a fair weather day.
- "Red sky in the morning is the sailor's sure warning, Red sky at night is the sailor's delight."
- "Rainbow to windward, foul falls the day; Rainbow to leeward, rain runs away."
- "Do business with men when the wind is from the northwest." (There is often a link between weather and human behavior. In this case, when the weather is most likely to be fair, people tend to be in better spirits and easier to deal with.)

Signs of Dry Weather

- Heavy dew in the early mornings means that dry weather will follow.
- A north wind brings dry air.

- A dry summer will follow a winter with few storms and blizzards.

Signs of Temperature Change

- Temperature will fall when the wind blows from the north or northwest or shifts to the north or northwest.
- Temperature will fall when the night sky is clear and the wind is light.
- Temperature will fall in the winter when the barometer rises steadily.
- Temperature will rise when the wind is from the south, especially with a cloud cover at night or clear sky during the day.

Signs of Spring and Summer

- When trees split their bark in the winter, it will be a dry, hot spring.
- Thunderstorms that come before seven in the morning in April and May foretell a wet summer.
- When snowdrifts face to the north, spring will arrive early.
- When the hay in the fields leans to the northeast, summer will be long and hot.

Signs of Fall and Winter

- When tree leaves drop early, the fall will be short and winter will be mild.
- When the tree leaves fall late, winter will be severe.
- A late frost means a long, hard winter.
- Two frosts mean winter will soon appear.
- The longer and hotter the summer, the longer and colder the winter. Extremes breed extremes.
- If the moss on the north side of a tree dries up in the fall it is to be a mild winter.
- If the husks of corn and nuts grow thick and tight, the winter will be hard.
- Rolling thunder in the fall means a hard winter.
- The first frost will occur six months after the first thunder of spring.
- Sun dogs in the winter means cold weather ahead.
- "Clear moon, frost soon." (Moonlight nights bring the heaviest frosts.)
- "If Candlemas Day be bright and clear, We'll have two winters in the year."
- "If on the trees the leaves still hold, the coming winter will be cold."

A Barometer for General Forecasting

The barometer measures the pressure of the atmosphere, which is useful in determining future weather. A low barometer is associated with stormy conditions and a high barometer with fair weather or clearing. The indications of the barometer precede wind shifts. Rapid alterations in barometric readings are indicative of pronounced changes in weather.

We deal mostly with natural signs from nature without the use of equipment or instruments. A barometer, however, is a good mechanical device for helping you be more accurate in your weather forecasting from signs. A dependable, inexpensive barometer can be purchased from most hardware stores. Before using your new instrument you must calibrate it to sea-level pressures. This can be done free of charge by checking with your nearest weather station or airport.

Use the following chart to determine your general forecast. It is wise to keep a record of your forecasts determined from this chart and of actual local weather changes. This way you can soon learn how your local weather fits with this chart and make allowances accordingly.

Wind Direction	Barometric or Atmospheric Pressure	General Forecast Indicated
SW to NW	30.10 to 30.20 barometer steady	Fair, little temperature change for 24 to 48 hours.
SW to NW	30.10 to 30.20 rising rapidly	Fair, warmer weather; rain possible within 48 hours.
SW to NW	30.20 or above barometer steady	Continued fair; little change in temperature
SW to NW	30.20 or above falling slowly	Fair, slowly rising temperatures for about 48 hours.
S to SE	30.10 to 30.20 falling slowly	Increasing wind; rain possible within 24 hours.
S to SE	30.10 to 30.20 falling rapidly	Rain within 12 to 24 hours. Rising wind.
SE to NE	30.10 to 30.20 falling slowly	Rain within 12 to 18 hours. Rising wind.
SE to NE	30.10 to 30.20 falling rapidly	Rain within 12 hours. Rising wind.
SE to NE	30.00 or below falling slowly	Rain to continue for 24 hours or more.
SE to NE	30.00 or below falling rapidly	High wind and rain in a few hours. Clearing in 36 hours—colder in winter.
E to NE	30.10 or above falling slowly	In summer, with light winds there will be rain in 2 to 4 days. In winter, rain or snow in 24 hours.
E to NE	30.10 or above falling rapidly	In summer, rain possible in 12 to 24 hours. In winter, rain or snow in 12 hours.
S to SW	30.00 or below rising slowly	Clearing in a few hours. Fair for several days.
S to E	29.80 or below falling rapidly	Severe storm in a few hours, clearing in 24 hours. Colder in winter.
E to N	29.80 or below falling rapidly	Severe storm in a few hours. Heavy rains or snowstorm. Winter cold wave.
Turning to W	29.80 or below rising rapidly	End of storm. Colder and clear.

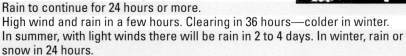

Barometric Weather Signs

• Winds frequently are strongest just as the barometer, immediately after having been very low, starts to rise.

• If the barometer remains low although the sky is clear, more precipitation can be expected within twenty-four hours.

• If the barometer slowly falls for a few days while the weather is fair, much rain will probably fall. If the barometer continues to rise during wet weather, fair weather will follow within several days and last for some time.

• If the barometer and the thermometer both rise together, it is a very sure sign of coming fine weather.

• If the barometer does not rise again after a storm in summer, expect several days of unstable weather.

• A summer storm that fails to depress the barometer will be local and not very severe.

• When weather is unchanged despite a falling barometer, a storm is raging at some distance.

• In winter, descending atmospheric pressure coupled with rising temperature foretokens heavy rain.

• Stormy winds depress a barometer more than heavy rains.

• When the glass falls low, Prepare for a blow; When it rises high, Let all your kites fly.

Unseasonable Weather

Unseasonable weather accompanies abnormal atmospheric pressure. Summers of unusually low temperature are associated with below-normal barometric pressure and an excess of rainfall. Summers of extraordinarily high temperature are associated with above-normal barometric pressure and a marked lack of rain. Extremely cold winters are associated with above-normal barometric readings and scarce or no precipitation. Unusually high winter temperatures are associated with barometric pressure below the norm and with rain or snow.

Warm and Cold Fronts

The following tables show the usual succession of weather conditions before, during, and after a warm front and a cold front. The more rapidly the front travels, the faster such weather conditions form and dissipate. The changes and their duration also depend upon the hour of the day or night, the season, and the general weather picture. The following sequences of weather variations attending the movement of a warm front and a cold front are, therefore, generalized ones.

WARM FRONT	Prior to the Warm Front	At the Time of Arrival	After the Warm Front
Wind	Increases in velocity; direction frequently easterly	Alters direction to southeast	Changes direction to southwest
Barometer	Descends; the more rapid the fall, the faster the arrival of the front	Falls to its lowest reading	Frequently rises but slightly
Temperature	Minimal rise	Gradual rise	Rise; amount depending on discrepancy of temperature between cold air prior to front and warm air after it
Humidity	Augments slowly	Increases rapidly to almost 100 percent	Possible minimal increase
Visibility	Steadily worsening	Poor, sometimes fog or mist	Slight betterment possible
Clouds	Cirrus overhead, followed by cirrostratus, then stratus or nimbostratus	Nimbostratus or sometimes	Usually significant clearing of bad weather with scattered nimbostratus, stratus, or stratocumulus
Weather	Light rain from altostratus, followed by heavy rain or snow from nimbostratus	Drizzle, rain showers, or snow	Possibility of occasional rain or snow, but usually clear or clearing conditions

COLD FRONT	Prior to the Cold Front	At the Time of Arrival	After the Cold Front
Wind	Velocity increases; direction frequently easterly	Quick change of direction to the west, with gusting	Strong and steady from the west to northwest
Barometer	Rapid, steady falling; the quicker the fall, the earlier the front arrives	Descends to lowest reading	Fast rise
Temperature	Constant rise	Slight change	Abrupt fall, amount depending on difference of temperature between warm air prior to front and cold air after it
Humidity	Constant	Decreases	Marked fall, except during rain
Visibility	Poor, possibly fog or mist (low wind velocity)	Poor to good, according to intensity of precipitation	Fine
Clouds	Altocumulus or altostratus, followed by stratus, stratocumulus and cumulonimbus or (sometimes) nimbostratus	Cumulonimbus with low stratus; sometimes nimbostratus	Altocumulus and cumulus or stratocumulus; speedy decline in amount of clouds; pronounced increase in the height of their bases
Weather	Fog, rain, snow, or thundershowers developing in strength	Heavy rain or snow	Sometimes intermittent showers; in general, clearing conditions

Comparison of Fahrenheit and Celsius (Centigrade) Scales

Freezing:
32 degrees Fahrenheit (F.)
0 degrees Celsius (C.)

Boiling:
212 degrees F.
100 degrees C.

To change F. to C.,
subtract 32 and multiply by $\frac{5}{9}$

Thus 212 degrees F. =
$(212 - 32) \times \frac{5}{9}$ = 100 degrees C.

176 degrees F. =
$(176 - 32) \times \frac{5}{9}$ = 80 degrees C.

To change C. to F.,
multiply by $\frac{9}{5}$ and add 32.

Thus 0 degrees C. =
$(0 \times \frac{9}{5})$ + 32 = 32 degrees F

80 degrees C. =
$(80 \times \frac{9}{5})$ + 32 = 176 degrees F.

What Dew, Frost, and Dew Point Tell Us

The amount of dew depends on the coolness of the weather and on the type of surface upon which it collects. Some objects such as cotton, fur, silk, vegetables, and wool, collect dew more readily than others. Sand, gravel, rocks, and cement do not collect much dew. It seems that Mother Nature allows dew to collect upon the things that can benefit most from its refreshing influence. Dew seldom, if ever, collects during cloudy nights.

The "dew point" as indicated by a hygrometer (which can be purchased from most hardware stores) can be used in the evening to foretell the lowest temperature of the coming night. By determining the dew point, an approaching low temperature or frost can be forecast and proper precautions for vegetation and livestock can be taken. When the dew point appears below freezing level, frost will form instead of dew.

A heavy dew in the morning is a sure sign of fine weather for that day. As dew is not formed during heavy cloudiness and wind it is almost proof positive of fair weather ahead.

Hoar frost (a silver-white deposit of ice needles usually perpendicular to the objects on which they occur) is a sure sign of changeable weather.

Effects of Weather on Living Things

Atmospheric Pressure

Atmospheric pressure exercises a definite influence on living creatures and their bodily functions. This is not difficult to imagine when we consider that the normal weight of the atmosphere is approximately 1 ton to each square foot of surface at sea level, and a variation of 1 inch in the barometer means a change in pressure of about 70 pounds to each square foot of surface. A

barometric change of 1 inch in twenty-four hours is not unusual. Such a change is related to a change of one-half ton in the atmosphere's weight sustained by the human body. Instinctively man has come to associate sensations felt under various atmospheric pressures with the types of weather that they evidence.

Those in delicate health and many animals are especially susceptible to atmospheric variations. During the period of rapidly decreasing atmospheric pressure that precedes and accompanies storms, these effects are manifested by nervousness, aches, and pains in humans and by restlessness among animals, birds, and insects. The flight of birds is higher when the barometer is high and low when the barometer is low. A high barometer signifies heavier, denser air with more sustaining power. Consequently, birds are able to fly high with less exertion than is needed at those periods when the barometer is low and the air less concentrated.

- A coming storm your shooting corns presage, And aches will throb, your hollow tooth will rage.
- When rooks wing low, expect rain.
- When a storm is nigh, bees will not swarm.
- When bees make but short trips from the hive or stay within, rain is due.
- Prior to rainfall, smoke descends to the ground.
- Wild geese fly high in fair weather and low in foul weather.
- The sound of the cuckoo in low lands signifies rain; when it is heard on high ground, the weather will be pleasant.
- Swallows flying high in the evening sky are a sign that fair weather follows. When they swoop low, rain will ensue.
- A favorable time for business transactions exists when the wind blows from the west, for then the barometer is high, and man experiences a greater feeling of well-being.

Temperature

During the warm months the temperature usually rises prior to rain, with the barometer falling. After rain starts to fall, the temperature drops, with a rising barometer. In cold months the temperature rises before and during rain or snow, remaining above normal until the rain or snow ceases, at which time it falls, with the barometer rising. Rainy periods in summer are unseasonably cool; periods of precipitation or snow in winter are unseasonably warm.

In the hinterland, high temperature is identified with south and southwest winds and low temperature with west and northwest winds. On coastlines, however, summer's warmth and winter's chill are affected by water temperature when onshore winds blow.

Variations in temperature before, during, and after storms also exert an influence on plant and animal life. Many weather adages stem from observation of these influences. Since temperature changes result from wind directions, proverbs concerning temperature are generally linked with those dealing with winds:

- The south wind's warmth is debilitating.
- The cold of the north wind is invigorating.
- The east wind's chill leads to aches and pains.
- In summer, when the sun burns excessively, thunderstorms can be expected.
- When the temperature rises between 9 p.m. and midnight and the sky is cloud free, watch out for rain.
- If, during an extended period of low temperature in winter, the temperature rises between midnight and dawn, a thaw is indicated.
- At some time in the past, people dwelling in the country observed a relationship between the number of calls of tree crickets and prevailing temperature. The chirps of the snowy tree cricket, for example, are so closely allied to air temperature that it has been called the "temperature cricket." Listen closely to the insect, and by counting the number of its chirps in fifteen seconds and adding forty, you can calculate the current temperature fairly accurately.

Humidity

The air's humidity and temperature increase before a rain. As the temperature rises, the air's moisture-holding capacity rises proportionately. Increase in humidity is not always a forerunner of rain. In coastal areas, it may be due to fog or wind temporarily blowing off the water. Generally, however, a rise in atmospheric moisture foreshadows rain by twelve to twenty-four hours.

The air's moisture probably shares with atmospheric pressure and temperature a role in affecting

animals and plants for good or ill. A falling and low barometer is attended by warm, moist air which causes physical and mental lethargy. A rising and high barometer with attendant cool, dry winds is felt to be invigorating.

These sayings developed from observations of the effects of humidity preceding rain:

- Prior to rain, tobacco becomes moist.
- The stone in quarries exudes moisture before a coming rain.
- The sweating of dishes and metal plates foretells foul weather.
- Salt increases in weight preceding rain.
- When humidity is high, doors and windows are difficult to close.
- A bunch of hemp that becomes damp forewarns of rain.
- Flies sting and are more annoying than is customary when humidity rises before rain.
- Rain is due when walls are unusually damp.
- Indians used to say rain was likely when the hair in the scalp house became damp.
- An increase of moisture in the atmosphere causes ropes to shorten. When ropes are difficult to straighten out, rain is due.
- Sailors are on the lookout for rain when the ship's rope-work tightens.
- When horses sweat in their stables, rain can be expected.
- With an increase of humidity, some plants contract their blossoms and leaves.

- If wounds, sores, and corns are more than ordinarily uncomfortable, there is the likelihood of rain.
- Three foggy mornings in succession foretell rain.
- When the scent of flowers is unusually noticeable, rain is in the offing.
- When pain of rheumatism is worse than usual, rain will probably fall.
- Hoarfrost is a sign of impending rain.
- Dry weather is indicated when floor matting shrinks, but when it expands, wet weather can be expected.
- Country wives say that when their cheese salt is soft, rain will come; when it tends to dry, they predict fair weather.
- The bigger the moon's halo, the closer the rain clouds, and the sooner rain will fall.
- Moss that is cushiony and moist indicates rain; dry and brittle moss means fair weather.
- When sunflowers raise their heads, expect rain.
- A lifting fog means fair weather; a settling fog, foul weather.
- When the aroma of a tobacco pipe is stronger and lasts longer, a storm can be predicted.
- Prior to rain, guitar strings tighten.
- A morning rainbow signifies that a shower to westward will soon approach; an evening rainbow signifies that rain is falling to the east and will pass away.

- Oiled floor boards turn damp immediately before rain.
- When rain is imminent, snakes come forth.
- Candles burn faintly and lamp wicks crackle prior to rainfall.
- Halos around sun and moon and the abnormal elevation of distant images through refraction, especially when inverted, are foretellers of foul weather.
- Hair tends to curl when a storm is imminent.
- The odor of ditches, drains, and dung heaps becomes more offensive previous to rain.
- When dry creeks and springs show moisture, approaching rain is indicated.

Nature and the Weather

Mother Nature has instilled animals, birds, and insects with an unknown sense of approaching weather changes long before we humans are aware of them. By this means they are able to take precautions against coming adversity. Being sensitive to minute atmospheric changes, they become unusually restless,

return to their lodgings, or eat with greater voracity than normally. Cats and dogs, in particular, have long been considered wise in the ways of weather. Folklore is replete with sayings regarding animals and their characteristic behavior when sensing subtle atmospheric changes prior to approaching weather.

Animals

- Good weather is in the offing when a cat cleans herself. If she licks her fur contrary to the grain, washes her face over her ears, or settles down with her tail to the hearth, bad weather is due.
- If dogs shun meat, eat grass in the morning, and dig holes, rain can be expected.
- Rain will soon fall when hogs run uneasily about with hay in their mouths.
- When cattle out at pasture recline early in the day, rain is indicated.
- Shepherds have observed that sheep gambol about before a storm.
- When cattle extend their necks and sniff the air, rain will come.
- Bats seen flying late at night signify good weather. When they

cry while flying, expect rain on the morrow.
- When cattle congregate at one end of a field, their tails toward the wind, rain or stronger wind can be expected.
- When cattle and horses stay in close groups, a storm is coming.
- When a cow bellers three times without stopping, a storm is coming.
- A sure sign of dry weather is horses and mules rolling in the dirt and shaking it off.
- When pack rats build nests with much height to them in the summer be prepared for a severe winter.
- Chattering squirrels tell of a mild winter. When squirrels do not chatter, and gather many nuts early in the fall, often green ones, expect a long, cold winter.
- Extra fluffy squirrel's tails, and nests built low in trees, tell of a cold winter.
- Dogs sniffing the air frequently indicates a change in weather.
- Dogs bury more food and bones in the fall before a bad winter.
- Heavy coats of hair on dogs in the fall is a good sign of a long, hard winter.
- If in the fall dogs curl up in a ball by the fireplace to sleep it will be a bad winter.
- When the beaver adds more wood to the north side of his home, the winter will be long.
- Heavy fur on the bottom of the feet of rabbits foretell a cold winter.

- When horses sniff the air and gather in fence corners, it usually means a summer shower if there was no early morning dew.

Birds

- When bird song ceases, listen for thunder.
- Birds and fowl oil their plumage before a rain.
- If crows are noisy and agitated, rain is on the way.
- Chimney swallows that fly in circles, calling on the wing, tell of rain.
- A solitary crow in flight signifies bad weather; a pair of flying crows means good weather.
- If the cock goes crowing to bed, He'll certainly rise with a watery head.
- When birds that are accustomed to flying long distances stay near home, a storm is nigh.
- A noisy crane means rain.
- Wild geese honking south over water mean that the weather will turn colder. Geese flying north mean the weather will grow warmer.
- When birds take dust baths, rain is close.
- When grouse are heard to drum,

in the night, a heavy snowfall can be predicted.

- A whistling parrot foretells rain.
- Gulls circling aloft and crying shrilly mean a storm is approaching.
- When chickens pick up pebbles and are unusually noisy, rain is coming.
- If roosters crow early and late, flapping their wings now and then, rain is due.
- Rain is expected when herons appear indecisive about a place to roost.
- Pigeons return home earlier than is customary when rain is close.
- When the peacock loudly bawls, Soon we'll have both rain and squalls.
- Robins alight high in treetops and sing loudly and long before a rain.
- Sea birds seeking shelter on shore or in marshes mean a storm will ensue.
- When blackbirds sing more than usually of a morning, rain will come.
- A flock of stormy petrels assembling in a ship's wake is an omen of impending storm.
- When birds ruffle their feathers and huddle together watch for rain.
- When swallows are seen flying high it is an indication of good weather. The insects upon which they feed venture high only in the best weather.
- When chickens stay out in the rain, the rain will last all day.

- Birds eat more just before a storm.
- When geese can walk on top of the snow in March, there will be a muddy spring.
- When birds fly low, there will be much snow (or rain).
- When birds stop singing, and trees start swinging, a storm is on its way.
- When it is hard to scare crows out of the com field it will be a hard winter.
- When the rooster crows at noon, rain will come soon.

Fish

- Fish swimming close to the surface and biting avidly mean rain.
- Rain or wind is close when pike lie motionless in stream beds.
- When black fish congregate in schools, expect a gale.
- Trout leap and herring form schools more quickly preceding rain.
- Bubbles appearing over clam beds are a sign of rain.
- Trout swimming in circles in the stream signifies a mild winter.

Insects

- Swarming flies foretell rain.
- If spiders are inactive, rain will soon fall. When they are busy during rain, it will not last long.
- Stormy weather will come when ants move in columns; when they disperse, the weather will turn fair.
- Flies assemble in the house just before precipitation begins.
- When bees to distance wing their flight, Days are warm and skies are bright; But when their flight ends near at home, Stormy weather is sure to come.
- Crickets become energetic before a rain.
- When the ground is spread with spider webs sprinkled with dew, yet no dew is on the ground, rain will come before nightfall.
- Flies collect on horses immediately before a rain.
- Spiders hiding and breaking webs warn of a coming storm.
- Flies bite hard before a storm.

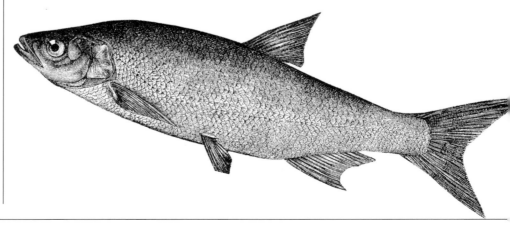

- The darker the color of caterpillars in the fall, the harder the winter will be.
- Bees are not good weather prophets as they will continue to leave the hive when a storm is imminent.
- When fireflies are about in numbers, the weather will be fair for the next three days.
- Earthworms leave their holes in the ground and roam about when rains are coming.
- A very reliable weather sign is given by ants. They often bring their eggs up out of their underground retreats and expose them to the warmth of the sun to be hatched. When they are seen carrying them in again in great haste, beware of a coming storm.
- When ants build small hills, it will be a hot, dry summer.
- Crickets singing in the house tell of a long, cold winter.
- When hornet and wasp nests are low and fat, winter will be hard.
- When butterflies migrate in the early fall, winter will come early.

Plants

Plants talk to us about the various needs they have while they are growing. They also give us a few things to consider about the weather, especially concerning the type of fall and winter we can expect.

- Mose Spooner of Colquitt, Georgia, always said that when the berry bushes bloomed heavily and produced their crop earlier than usual you better watch out for a rough winter. He was nearly always right. Some prophets of winter weather say they go only by the nut crop. Acorn, hickory, and pecan nuts grow thick, tight husks around an extra heavy shell when a bad winter is on the way.
- You need to watch for fruit trees and other bearing plants that seem to produce their harvest earlier than usual. In most cases they will have a larger than usual crop too. This forewarns. of early severe winter weather.
- Root crops such as carrots, onions, and turnips grow deeper before a severe winter. Onions have more layers and other root plants, such as potatoes, have tougher skins.

- Always watch the trees. Before a bad winter their bark is thicker than usual, especially on the north side, and the leaves stay on until very late in the fall.
- In West Texas the threat of a killing frost is never past until the mesquite tree puts out its leaves. Sometimes even it gets caught but not often. It's the best sign that spring is really here for us. There is a tree in your part of the country that is just as reliable—you need to ask one of the old-timers which one it is.
- The scent of flowers is more perceptible prior to a shower, the air being damp.
- Corn fodder is extremely sensitive to variations of moisture in the atmosphere. When dry and crisp, it indicates fine weather; when damp and limp, it indicates rain.
- Mushrooms and toadstools are abundant before rain.
- Clover tells us that rain is coming by turning up its leaves, showing their light undersurface.
- If milkweed closes at night, rain will follow.
- Before precipitation the leaves of the linden, plane, poplar, and sycamore trees expose more of their undersides when fluttering in the wind.
- Rain can be expected when the pink-eyed pimpernel closes during the day.
- Before a storm, trees turn dark.
- When the sugar maple turns its leaves upside down, watch for rain.
- Expect rain when tree leaves curl in a south wind.

If the new moon, first quarter, full moon, or last quarter, occurs:

Time of Day	In Summer	In Winter
Between midnight and 2 a.m.	Fair	Frost, unless wind southwest
2 and 4 a.m.	Cold and showers	Snow and stormy
4 and 6 a.m.	Rain	Rain
6 and 8 a.m.	Wind and rain	Stormy
8 and 10 a.m.	Changeable	Cold rain if wind from the west, snow if from the east
10 and 12 a.m.	Frequent showers	Cold and high wind
12 and 2 p.m.	Very rainy	Snow or rain
2 and 4 p.m.	Changeable	Fair and mild
4 and 6 p.m.	Fair	Fair
6 and 8 p.m.	Fair if wind northwest	Fair and frosty if wind north or northeast
8 and 10 p.m.	Rainy if south or southwest wind	Rain or snow if south or southwest wind
10 p.m. and midnight	Fair	Fair and frosty

Heavenly Bodies and the Weather

The sun, moon, and stars are indicators of future weather only as their appearance is altered by prevailing atmospheric conditions.

Sun

• When the sun sets bright and clear, An easterly wind you need not fear.

• If the sun draws water in the morning, rain will fall before evening.

• When the sun goes down after a pleasant day behind a bank of clouds, with the barometer falling, rain or snow is indicated (depending upon the season) either that night or the following morning.

• When the sun is a dazzling white before setting, its light diffuse, a storm will ensue.

• If the sun goes down amid heavy dark clouds, rain will fall on the morrow.

• When the sun sets in a purple-tinted sky, the zenith being vivid blue, fair weather can be expected.

• A halo around the sun means bad weather.

• When it is evening, ye say, It will be fair weather: for the sky is red. And in the morning, It will be foul weather today: for the sky is red and lowering. —Matthew XVI: 2, 3

• Red evening skies are followed by fair tomorrows.

• Haziness about the sun is a sign of storm.

• When a burning morning sun breaks through clouds, expect thunderstorms in the afternoon.

• Evening red and morning gray, Two sure signs of one fine day.

Moon

• "This table (above) and the accompanying remarks are the results of many years of actual observation, the whole being constructed on a due consideration of the attraction

of the Sun and Moon, in their several positions respecting the Earth, and will, by simple inspection, show the observer what kind of weather will most probably follow the entrance of the Moon into any of its quarters, and that so near the truth, as to be seldom or never found to fail." —*Francis H. Buzzacott, The Complete American and Canadian Sportsman's Encyclopedia of Valuable Instruction, 1913*

• When the full moon is pale on rising, expect rain.

• A large lunar halo with low clouds means rain within twenty-four hours.

• It is a sign of rain when the moon is darkest close to the horizon.

- A small ring around the moon with high clouds means rain in a few days.
- When a large red moon rises, accompanied by clouds, rain will fall in twelve hours.
- A full moon rising clear indicates good weather.
- A halo about the moon is a sign of rain; the bigger the halo, the sooner will rain fall.

Stars

- When the stars appear to twinkle excessively, heavy dews, rain, snow, or storms can be anticipated in the near future.
- If stars seem to flicker in a dark sky, rain or snow is due.
- When the North Star seems nearer than usual and flickers oddly, look out for rain.
- A sky studded with very large, dull stars means rain is in the offing.
- When the sky appears crowded with stars, be prepared for rain, or frost in winter.

Long-Range Weather Prediction

Centuries ago onions were used for long-range weather forecasting. Six onions were sliced in half, each half being heavily salted and designated as a particular month of the year. On the following day the wetness of future months could be determined from the condition of the salt on each half.

In very early times people were receptive to the pronouncements

of those held to be wise men and sages. Much stock was put in their predictions of future events and of future weather as well.

The following are sayings embodying long-range forecasts.

Sun

Sun spots were thought to exert an influence on the earth's weather:

- When sun spots are most numerous, rainfall will be greatest.
- Solar changes are related to excessive heat waves, prolonged droughts, and great floods.

Moon

The belief that the moon has a controlling influence on the weather has been handed down through centuries of time in the form of sayings or proverbs:

- If three days old her face be bright and clear, No rain or stormy gale the sailors fear; But if she rise with bright and blushing cheek,

The blustering winds the bending mast will shake. — J. Lamb's "Aratus"

- If a dry moon appears, a crescent with tips pointing upward, a dry month will ensue; if the tips are turned down, it is a wet moon and the month will have rain.
- The Indian reasoned that if he could hang his powder horn on the crescent, the woods would be too dry for still-hunting. If he could not hang it on the crescent, he prepared to hunt, carrying his powder horn with him, knowing this was a sign that the woods would be wet for silent stalking of prey.
- The Welsh, too, say, "It is sure to be a dry moon if it lies on its back, so that you can hang your hat on its horns." Sailors, however, often believed the opposite concerning the crescent moon.
- It has been said that the moon's rays cause specific chemical effects, spoiling fish and certain kinds of meat. This is probably the source of the belief that hogs should be slaughtered in the dark of the moon.

Though this cannot be classified as a weather saying, it does show a correlation between weather and activity, a dark-of-the-moon time or a cloudy and rainy night being favorable to certain pursuits.

Stars

Long before the calendar was devised, putting in order the time periods for the months and seasons, country people depended upon the rising and setting of constellations to plan their farming operations, including the breeding of animals. A Greek poet once wrote that the harvest begins when the Pleiades, that group of stars representing the seven daughters of Atlas, rise. Sayings of this nature often came to be interpreted as pointing out either a beneficent or a harmful influence of stars, whereas originally such weather lore had only signified a need of the observer to note an approaching season and its attendant weather.

Animals, Birds, Etc.

A persistent belief among rural people of the past was that animals are endowed with an ability to determine in advance weather conditions for an entire season. In fact, such a faculty is limited to an instinctive interpretation of prevailing atmospheric conditions which indicate weather changes in the near future, from one to twelve hours away. Migrating birds commence their southern migration when autumn first chills the air and return north

at the first hint of temperature modification in their wintering grounds. Oftentimes their flights are premature. The physical state of animals—for example, the thickness of their coats—depends upon past weather and its effect on their food supply and health in general, instead of upon future weather. This thinking applies also to plants that are the subject of sayings predicting the weather of a coming season.

The following are old weather sayings concerning the habits of birds and animals and the appearance of plants as signs of long-range weather conditions:

- When bears store food in autumn, a cold winter will follow.
- The chattering of flying squirrels in midwinter indicates an early spring.
- When the winter is expected to be early and long, beavers ready their lodges and stock their larders sooner than before mild, late winters.
- You can anticipate the direction of future storms and winds by observing which of its two holes the hedgehog plugs up.
- When the ground squirrel frisks about in winter, it means that snow is almost over.
- Severe weather can be expected when migrating birds wing south early.
- If the first snowfall is patterned with bear tracks, a mild winter is ahead.
- If the cat basks in a February sun, it will warm itself by the stove in March.
- The mole stores his food supply of worms in abundance in a winter that is expected to be severe. When less food is stocked, the coming winter will be mild.
- The early arrival of cranes in the fall signifies a cold winter.
- When squirrels are seldom seen in the fall, a cold winter can be anticipated.
- When summer birds fly away, summer goes too.
- An early arrival of the woodcock means a hard winter is due.
- When woodpeckers depart, expect a severe winter. When they peck low on tree trunks, it is a sign of future warm weather.
- The swan makes its nest low when the coming season will not be rainy; the nest is built high when a season of rain and high water is expected.
- Intense cold can be predicted when field larks are seen to assemble in flocks.
- If crows wing south, a cold winter will follow; if they fly north, the opposite is true.

- The first robins betoken the coming of spring.
- When wrens are about in winter, snow can be expected.
- The whiteness of a goose's breastbone is believed to show the amount of snow that will fall during the coming winter: If the breastbone has red spots, a cold, stormy winter will ensue; if but few spots are evident, a mild winter is due.
- After martins appear there will be no killing frost.

Days, Months, Seasons, and Years

Rural folk paid special attention to weather during winter and spring because of its effects on the seasons of planting and harvesting. Saints' days were believed to have particular influence on the weather.

Days

- If St. Vincent's (January 22) has sunshine, one hopes much rye and wine.

  If St. Paul's (January 25) is bright and clear, one does hope a good year.

  Candlemas Day (February 2)! Candlemas Day! Half our fire and half our hay.

  (The last line means that we are halfway through winter and should have half our fuel and hay supply remaining.)
- If Candlemas Day be fair and bright, winter will have another flight. But if Candlemas

Day bring clouds and rain, winter is gone and won't come again.
- Badger, bear, and woodchuck come forth at noon on Candlemas Day to look for their shadow. If they fail to see it, they remain out. If their shadow is visible, they return to their dens for another six weeks, and cold weather will last for six weeks more.
- If the ground hog is seen basking in the sun on February 2, he will go back to his winter lodging for four to six weeks.
- If February 2 is a stormy day, spring is close at hand; if the day is fair, spring will arrive late.
- The warm side of a stone turns up on St. Patrick's Day (March 17), and the broadback goose begins to lay.

- Is't on St. Joseph's Day (March 19) clear, So follows a fertile year.
- Is't on St. Mary's (March 25) bright and clear, Fertile is said to be the year.
- If it thunders on All Fools' Day (April 1), It brings good crops of corn and hay.
- Hoarfrost on May 1 means a good harvest.
- Rainfall on St. Barnabas' Day (June 11) is favorable to grapes.
- We pray for rain before St. John's Day (June 24); After that it comes anyway.
- A rainy St. John's Day means harm to the nut harvest.
- However dog days (July 3 to August 11) begin, in such a way do they end.
- Dog days bright and clear Indicate a good year; But when

accompanied by rain, We hope for better times in vain.

- In this month is St. Swithin's Day (July 15), on which, if that it rain, they say full forty days after it will, or more or less, some rain distill. —*Poor Robin's Almanack, 1697*
- St. Barthelemy's (August 24) mantle wipes dry, all the tears that St. Swithin can cry. If the 24th of August be fair and clear, then hope for a prosperous autumn that year.
- September 15 is said to be fair six years in seven.
- If acorns are abundant on St. Michael's Day (September 29), the fields will be white with snow at Christmas.
- On the 1st of November (All Saints' Day), if the weather hold clear, an end of wheat sowing do make for the year.
- If the beechnut is dry on All Saints' Day, winter will be severe; if the nut is wet, a wet winter will follow.
- If All Saints' Day brings out the winter, St. Martin's Day (November 11) will bring Indian Summer.
- If Martinmas is fair and cold, winter's cold will not long endure.
- If tree and grapevine leaves do not fall before St. Martin's Day, a cold winter is due.
- A green Christmas means a heavy harvest.
- If on Friday it rain, 'twill on Sunday again; if Friday be clear, have for Sunday no fear.
- When the first Sunday in the month is stormy, every Sunday of that month will be stormy.

Months

- The month that starts with fair weather will end with foul.
- If no snow falls before January, more will fall in March and April.
- A favorable January means a good year.
- A thaw can always be expected in January.
- A mild January, a chilly May.
- If February gives much snow, a fine summer it doth foreshow.
- The rain of February is good only for filling ditches.
- Thunder in February or March indicates a poor maple-sugar year.
- A dusty March means foliage and grass.
- Snow in March harms fruit tree and grapevine.
- March flowers make no summer bowers.
- March damp and warm will do the farmer much harm.
- When March has April weather, April will have March weather.
- However much rain falls in March, the same amount will fall in June.
- March comes in like a lion and goes out like a lamb. March comes in like a lamb and goes out like a lion.
- March winds and April showers Bring forth May flowers.
- The winds of March and rains of April make for a bounteous May.
- Rainy April, fair June.
- A damp, cool May fills the barns and wine barrels.
- Rainy May, Dry July.
- Calm weather in June sets corn in tune.

- A damp, warm June does not impoverish the farmer.
- When June is cold and wet, the rest of the year will be unpleasant.
- July, God send thee calm and fayre, That happy harvest we may see.
- As is July, so will next January be.
- Don't trust the sky in the month of July.
- Whatever July and August do boil, September can not fry.
- As is August, so will the following February be.
- August's rain is honey and wine.
- Dry August and warm Doth harvest no harm.
- As September is, so will the next March be.
- Heavy rainfall in September brings drought.
- Much rain in October, much wind in December.
- Warm October, cold February.

- Heavy frost and winds in October mean that January and February will be mild.
- Whatever the weather in October, the same will occur in March.
- As the weather is in November, so will it be the next March.
- A cold, snowy December is favorable to rye.

Seasons
- Early thunder means early spring.
- A great blessing is a late spring.
- Better late spring and bear than early blossom and blast.
- A late spring never misleads.
- A late spring is favorable to corn but unfavorable to cattle.
- When spring is dry, a rainy summer follows.
- If wet and chilly the spring, then cold and dry will be the fall.
- Rain in midsummer spoils grain, stock, and wine.
- A wet fall with a mild winter means a cold, dry spring that retards plant growth.
- A mild winter means a poor wheat crop.
- A mild winter and a cold summer mean a poor harvest.
- After a wet winter comes a fruitful spring.

Years
- A cold year follows a rainy one.
- Rainy and dry years come in threes.
- Wet year, fruit dear.
- Snow year, good year. Frost year, good year.
- Years of radishes, years of health.

False Weather Signs

There are signs that are thought to be reliable that often are not, because the area of coverage is too great. Some farmers look upon the Milky Way as a weather vane, and will tell you that the way it points at night indicates the direction of the wind the next day. So, also, every new moon is either a dry moon or a wet moon. Dry if a hat would hang on the lower point, wet if it would not. They forget the fact that, as a rule, when it is dry in one part of the continent it is wet in some other part, and vice versa.

When the farmer kills his hogs in the fall, if the pork is hard and solid he predicts a severe winter; if soft and loose he predicts the opposite. Overlooked is the fact that the type of feed the hog has eaten and the temperature of the fall makes the pork hard or soft. So, too, with a hundred other signs, all the result of hasty or incomplete observations.

John Burroughs, in his book entitled *Signs and Seasons*, said:

"One season, the last day of December was very warm. The bees were out of the hive, and there was no frost in the air or on the ground. I was walking in the woods, and as I paused in the shade of a hemlock tree I heard a sound from beneath the wet leaves on the ground but a few feet from me that suggested a frog. Following it cautiously, I at last determined the exact spot from whence the sound issued; lifting up the thick layer of leaves, there sat a frog–the wood frog, one of the first to appear in the marshes in spring, and which I have called the 'ducking frog'–in a little excavation in the surface of the ground. This, then, was its hibernaculum; here it was prepared to pass the winter, with only a coverlid of wet matted leaves between it and zero weather.

"Forthwith I became a prophet of warm weather, and among other things predicted a failure of the ice crop on the river; which, indeed, others who had not heard frogs croak on the 31st of December had also begun to predict. Surely, I thought, this frog knows what it is about; here is the wisdom of nature; it would have gone deeper into the ground than that if a severe winter was approaching; so I was not anxious about my coal bin, nor disturbed by longings for Florida. But what a winter followed! The winter of 1885, when the Hudson became coated with ice nearly two feet thick, and when March was as cold as January! I thought of my frog under the hemlock and wondered how it was faring. So one day the latter part of March, when the snow was gone, and there was a feeling of spring in the air, I turned aside in my walk to investigate it. The matted leaves were still frozen hard, but I succeeded in lifting them up and exposing the frog. There it sat as fresh and unscathed as in the fall. The ground beneath and all about it was still frozen like a rock, but apparently it had some means of its own of resisting the frost. It winked and bowed its head when I touched it, but did not seem inclined to leave its retreat. Some days later, after the frost was nearly all out of the ground, I passed that way, and found my frog had come out of its seclusion and was resting amid the dry leaves. There was not much jump in it yet, but its color was growing lighter. A few more warm days, and its fellows, and doubtless itself too, were croaking and gamboling in the marshes.

"This incident convinced me of two things; namely, that frogs know no more about the coming weather than we do, and that they do not retreat as deep into the ground to pass the winter as has been supposed. I used to think the muskrats could foretell an early and severe winter and have so written. But I am now convinced they cannot; they know as little about it as I do. Sometimes on an early and severe frost they seem to get alarmed and go to building their houses, but usually they seem to build early or late, high or low, just as the whim takes them.

"In most of the operations of nature there is at least one unknown quantity; to find the exact value of this unknown factor is not so easy. The fur of the animals, the feathers of the fowls, the husks of the maize, why are they thicker some seasons than others; what is the value of the unknown quantity here? Does it indicate a severe winter approaching? Only observations extending over a series of years can determine the point. How much patient observation it takes to settle many of the facts in the lives of the birds, animals, and insects!"

Special Weather Signs

There are a few points in reading the weather signs of nature that must be kept in mind at all times. These general rules were closely observed and followed by the most accurate early-day weather prognosticators. To improve your own forecasting skill always keep these in mind:

- In forecasting weather the critical moments of the day are sunrise and sunset.
- All weather signs fail in a drought. The same theory is true during a wet spell. At these times nature is caught in a rut and reverses itself slowly.
- On most occasions the weather is very sure to declare itself by or before eleven o'clock in the morning. If the morning is unsettled wait until about eleven and you will know what the remainder of the day will be like. Other old-timers have said: "You can tell between eleven and two what the weather will do."
- Midday clouds and afternoon clouds, except in the season of thunderstorms, are usually harmless idlers and vagabonds. Pay little attention to them.

2 | MOON LORE

A few people laugh when you mention doing anything by the "signs." They consider it to be the "old way," and surely couldn't be the "best way." Oft times the old way has been tried, tested, and proved by many people over long periods of time. The new way sometimes looks and sounds good but has not been put to the test of time. We cannot say that all the information about moon signs in this book is absolutely correct and one hundred per cent foolproof. Some of it is fact and some of it is folklore and superstition, but it makes interesting reading and many of the old bits of wisdom found here have stood the test of time. They might be worth another try today.

Everything within the patterns of nature operates in cycles.

The study of these cycles has nothing to do with fortunetelling, soothsaying, or mysticism. There is a harmony in nature. There is a harmony between the sun, moon, stars, and the earth. This information is derived from comparisons, investigations, and studies made by men for centuries concerning the relationship of things on this earth to the heavenly bodies above and about the earth. As we have just seen with the weather, when one thing happens in nature it foretells of other things that are about to happen. Proper study of certain events and what happens after they occur can help us in many of our day-to-day activities. There is a "best time" to do everything.

Folks who use the moon as their guide in farming and gardening believe that rhythm and timing are important in these activities. To be really successful with your farm, garden, or other enterprises using moon phases and signs, you must learn to set your pace with Mother Nature.

The time to break sod, to plant seed, to set out plants, to cultivate, to eradicate weeds and pests, to eliminate noxious growths, the time to harvest, the time to store the harvest, all come in due season with the timing and rhythm of the moon phases and the moon zodiac signs. Students of moon sign agricultural procedures believe there is a precise and special time for every chore to be done within the lunar year. This timing and rhythm exist on the broad scale of each month within the year. The same rhythm is found in the daily moon signs. By using the daily sign with the broad general signs that are in effect at a given time, proper timing and rhythm can be achieved in farming, gardening, and other activities.

There are many signs in nature that are quite obvious to us.

We know that summer will follow spring, we know that winter will follow fall. By knowing this we will not plant crops that require heat in the wintertime. In this respect we understand nature and co-operate with her. She gives us many other signs that we should follow, many not as obvious as the signs of the seasons. If we will come into harmony with nature by knowing, studying, and reading her many signs we will live a better life, live easier, and enjoy life more.

Phases of the Moon

The phases of the moon are caused by the varying angle at which its lighted surface is visible from the earth.

There are four moon phases. The new moon and the full moon are the most familiar and easiest to recognize. There are only two moon phases known as "quarters"; the "first quarter" and the "third

33

MOON'S PHASES

New Moon   Full Moon

First Quar.   Last Quar.

(or last) quarter." They are both actually seen in the sky as half-moons. Numerous publications picture them as one quarter of a full moon and call them quarters but this is incorrect. The correct profile of each quarter is that of one half of the full moon. The term quarter refers not to the shape of the moon as it appears in the sky but to time elapsed between each twenty-eight-day "month."

On this basis the new moon is the start of the first half and the full moon is the start of the last half of the lunar month. Each of the four segments or phases has an approximate length of seven days. New moon to new moon is the full cycle of twenty-eight days. Knowing these moon phases *correctly* is the first step in learning moon lore and working with moon signs.

Moonrise

The new moon always rises with the sunrise in the east to start a new lunar month. The sun blots out the visibility of the new moon as it comes up but it can be seen as a thin crescent setting in the west at sunset a day or two after its rise.

The first quarter (waxing) moon always rises about noon in the east seven days after the new moon and appears as a pale half-moon.

The full moon always rises in the east at sunset seven days after the first quarter moon and will shed its light through the night.

The third or last quarter (waning) moon always rises about midnight in the eastern sky seven days after the full moon and appears as a half-moon.

The waxing or increasing moon is known and easily remembered as the "right-hand moon." The curve of the right-hand index finger and thumb follows the curve of the increasing crescent. In a similar fashion the waning or decreasing moon can be remembered as the "left-hand moon."

To establish the time of moonrise for each day of the month you add fifty minutes for each day after the beginning of a phase or subtract that amount for each day prior to the beginning of a new phase.

Luck and Weather

- Clear moon, frost soon.
- To sweep the house in the dark of the moon will rid it of both moths and spiders.
- If Christmas comes during a waxing moon we will have a very good year. The nearer Christmas comes to the new moon the better the next year will be.

- If Christmas comes during a waning moon we will have a hard year and the nearer the end of the waning moon so much worse the next year will be.
- When the new moon falls on Saturday the following twenty-one days will be wet and windy in nine times out of ten.
- When the new moon falls on Monday or "moon-day" it is thought everywhere to be a sign of good luck and good weather.
- Two full moons in one calendar month brings good luck.

- If the moon changes on Sunday there will be a flood before the month is over.
- The nearer the moon's phase change is to midnight the fairer the weather will be for the next seven days. The nearer the moon's change is to noontime the more changeable the weather will be for the following seven days.
- A wish on a new moon is a wish come true, if you do not tell your wish and if you kiss the person nearest you.
- Thunder coming at the moon's change in the spring often means that the weather will be mild and moist and good crops will follow.

- It has been predicted that if the full moon and equinox meet, violent storms will occur followed by a dry spring.
- To point to the new moon brings bad luck.
- A halo around the moon means rain. If there are stars in the halo it will rain as many days as there are stars, or rain will come after that many days. Five stars or more in the ring means cold weather; fewer stars means warm weather.
- Medicines and tonics are more effective when given at the full moon.
- The new moon is the most powerful phase of the waxing or increasing moon as it has full growth ahead.

Marriage and Babies

- Marriage should be performed on a growing moon and the full moon is best.
- Children and animals that are born in the full moon are larger and stronger than those born in the wane of the moon.
- When a boy baby is born in the wane of the moon the next child will be a girl and vice versa.
- When a birth takes place on the growing or waxing moon the next child will be of the same sex.
- Wean boy babies on the waxing or growing moon, but wean girl babies on the waning or decreasing moon. This will make sturdy boys and slim, delicate girls.

Moon Months

From folklore we have received these names:

January	Winter Moon
February	Trapper's Moon
March	Fish Moon or Fisherman's Moon
April	Easter Moon or Planter's Moon
May	Mother's Moon or Spring Moon
June	Stockman's Moon or Mid-Year Moon
July	Summer Moon
August	Dog Days' Moon or Woodcutter's Moon
September	Fall Moon
October	Harvest Moon
November	Hunter's Moon
December	Christ's Moon or Christmas Moon

Planting by the Moon

Neither sowing, planting, or grafting should ever be undertaken without scrupulous attention to the increase or waning of the moon.
—*Sir Edward Tylor in* **Primitive Culture,** *1871*

When the moon is in the phases and signs called "fruitful" it has been established and proven by many that seeds planted at this time germinate in a higher percentage, grow more, thrive better, and produce with more abundance and quality than seeds planted in the "barren" phases and signs.

The old rule used for years was to plant in the new moon period and in a fruitful zodiac sign anything that grows *above* the ground, and in an old moon period with a fruitful zodiac sign anything that produces *underground*. We should, however, be more specific in our planting to properly follow the rhythm and harmony of nature. We should plant in the proper season with the moon's signs and the moon's phases in mind.

As an example: When it is the proper season of the year to plant and we are in a "watery and fruitful" sign such as Cancer and when the moon is in the phase of the first or second quarter, it would be an excellent time to plant any vegetation that is of a juicy, moist, and watery type.

Occasionally it is good to prove the influence of the moon signs. This is best done by planting a portion of your seed in a fruitful sign such as Cancer (June 1 to July 23), and plant more of your seed in Leo (July 23 to August 23),

which is the most barren sign. You can do this with only a day or two between plantings as these are adjoining signs. Watch and record the results of plant growth and yield. You may be impressed by the better germination of the seed, growth of the plants, and the amount of yield under these two different signs but also you probably will notice a significant difference in the quality and flavor of the produce.

Planting in the proper season, sign, and phase must of course be accompanied by good agricultural practices. Fertility, soil, moisture, insect control, and other contributing factors must always be considered. Patience, practice, and perseverance in using nature's rules will payoff in better crops and better yields.

The Signs of the Zodiac

The twelve signs of the zodiac each have certain characteristics, elements, and tendencies that have a specific influence on all growing things. The zodiac signs through which the moon passes are used as a guide to planting, harvesting, breeding livestock, butchering, and practically all other chores.

The moon makes a complete circle of the earth in about twenty-nine and a half days. The path the moon follows in this monthly voyage is divided into twelve equal parts of 30 degrees each. The separate divisions of this path are called the "Twelve Signs of the Zodiac." Each sign received its name from the constellation of stars contained in it. With the exception of Libra, all the constellations were named after living creatures; "zodiac" means "circle of animals."

The twelve signs are: Aries the ram, Taurus the bull, Gemini the twins, Cancer the crab, Leo the lion, Virgo the virgin, Libra the balance,

These are the twelve basic signs of the zodiac covering the cycle of one calendar year:

Sign	Dates	Nature and Character	Governs Body Zones	Planetary Rules
Aquarius	Jan. 20 to Feb. 18	Fixed, airy, barren, dry, masculine	Ankles, legs, body fluids	Uranus
Pisces	Feb. 18 to March 21	Flexible, fruitful, watery, feminine	Feet	Neptune
Aries	Mar. 21 to April 20	Movable, fiery, barren, dry, masculine	Head, face	Mars
Taurus	April 20 to May 21	Fixed, semi-fruitful, productive, earthy, moist, feminine	Throat, neck	Venus
Gemini	May 21 to June 21	Flexible, fiery, barren, dry, masculine	Hands, arms, lungs, chest, shoulders, nervous system	Mercury
Cancer	June 21 to July 23	Movable, most fruitful, watery, feminine	Breast, stomach	Moon
Leo	July 23 to Aug. 23	Fixed, fiery, most barren, dry, masculine	Heart, sides, upper back	Sun
Virgo	Aug. 23 to Sept. 22	Flexible, earthy, barren, moist, feminine	Bowels, solar-plexus	Mercury
Libra	Sept. 22 to Oct. 23	Movable, semi-fruitful, airy, moist, masculine	Kidneys, loins, lower back, ovaries	Venus
Scorpio	Oct. 23 to Nov. 22	Fixed, very fruitful, water, feminine	Sex organs, bladder	Pluto
Sagittarius	Nov. 22 to Dec. 22	Flexible, fiery, barren, dry, masculine	Hips, thighs, liver, blood	Jupiter
Capricorn	Dec. 22 to Jan. 20	Movable, productive, earthy, moist, feminine	Knees	Saturn

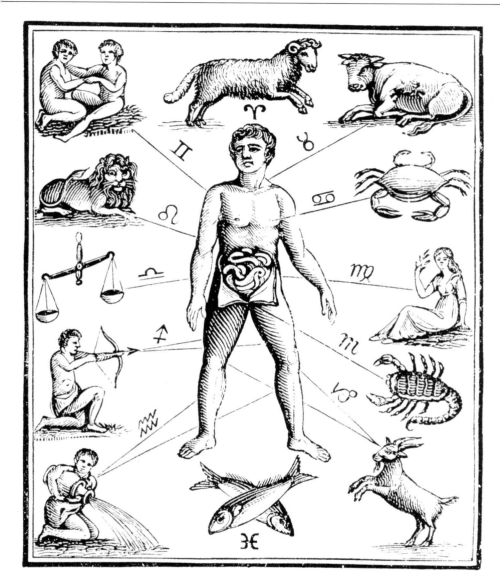

The calendar year is also divided into the twelve zodiac signs.

Moon sign followers use this broad area for determining when to do certain general chores.

When they are pinpointing times to do specific activities such as planting, fishing, or hunting, they want to know the moon sign for that particular day. For this they must know the "moon's place."

Most almanacs carry a column called "moon's place." This specifies the zodiac sign that influences each specific day of the month. Every two or three days the moon's place is considered to be ruled by a different zodiac sign. Many farmers heed this daily position of the moon. For example, if the moon's place on a specific day is in a fruitful sign even though the general monthly period is in a dry and barren sign, then the barren period may be overruled on that particular day by the strength of the moon's place daily sign.

Daily Moon Signs

The zodiac signs not only change on the cycle of twelve changes each calendar year but there are also intraweek changes of the signs, called "daily moon signs." These are the signs we must consider in our day-to-day activities. The following is an example of how these weekly changes occur over a one-month period:

Scorpio the scorpion, Sagittarius the bowman, Capricorn the goat, Aquarius the waterman, and Pisces the fishes.

The symbols that represent these various signs are usually pictures of the objects they represent. The twelve signs are also identified with the various parts of the human body as early astronomers believed that there

was a definite relationship between the heavenly bodies and the earthly body.

The zodiac signs given in most good almanacs today relate to the moon's path around the earth. A few give the signs in relation to constellations of stars which is confusing. The proper zodiac for working with the signs is the moon zodiac.

Time and Date when Luna (The Moon) Enters Each Sign

Date	Sign	Time	Phase
1 Mon.	in Aquarius	all day	
2 Tues.	in Aquarius	all day, until	
3 Wed.	enters Pisces	at 11:12 A.M.	
4 Thurs.	in Pisces	all day	
5 Fri.	in Pisces	all day, until	
6 Sat.	enters Aries	at 0:12 A.M.	
(First quarter begins on 7th, at 1:18 P.M.)			Moon on Increase
7 Sun.	in Aries	all day, until	
8 Mon.	enters Taurus	at 0:40 P.M.	
9 Tues.	in Taurus	all day, until	
10 Wed.	enters Gemini	at 11:35 P.M.	
11 Thurs.	in Gemini	all day	
12 Fri.	in Gemini	all day, until	
13 Sat.	enters Cancer	at 8:18 A.M.	
14 Sun.	in Cancer	all day, until	
(Second quarter begins on 15th, at 5:40 A.M.)			Moon on Increase
15 Mon.	enters Leo	at 1:42 P.M.	
16 Tues.	in Leo	all day, until	
17 Wed.	enters Virgo	at 4:32 P.M.	
18 Thurs.	in Virgo	all day, until	
19 Fri.	enters Libra	at 5:32 P.M.	
20 Sat.	in Libra	all day, until	
(Third quarter) begins on 21st, at 8:38 P.M.)			Moon on Decrease
21 Sun.	enters Scorpio	at 5:38 P.M.	
22 Mon.	in Scorpio	all day, until	
23 Tues.	enters Sagittarius	at 6:50 P.M.	
24 Wed.	in Sagittarius	all day, until	
25 Thurs.	enters Capricorn	at 10:49 P.M.	
26 Fri.	in Capricorn	all day	
27 Sat.	in Capricorn	all day, until	
(Fourth quarter begins on 28th, at 11:47 P.M.)			Moon on Decrease
28 Sun.	enters Aquarius	at 6:48 A.M.	
29 Mon.	in Aquarius	all day, until	
30 Tues.	enters Pisces	at 5:55 P.M.	

The above is only an example and is not to be followed. Charts of this type which show exactly where the moon is every day of the year, its phase, and its time of entry into the next sign may be obtained from various almanacs.

General Guide to Planting by the Moon's Signs

When the moon is in:

Aquarius — A dry, barren sign. Not good for planting. Cultivate, turn sod, destroy pests and unwanted growths.

Pisces — Third in the line of most productive signs, exceeded only by Cancer and Scorpio. Fruitful and productive. A good time to plant when interested in exceptional root growth.

Aries — A dry, barren sign. Not good for general planting, but good for planting onions and garlic. Cultivate, turn sod, dig weeds, destroy noxious growths and pests.

Taurus — A semi-fruitful and fairly productive sign. Has an earthy nature. Excellent for planting potatoes and root crops for quick growth, good for leafy vegetables.

Gemini — A dry, barren sign. Not good for any planting or transplanting. Cultivate, turn sod, destroy pests, weeds, and noxious growths.

Cancer — The most fruitful of all signs. Best sign for planting, transplanting, grafting, budding. Any kind of reliable seed or plants should produce and yield well when started in this sign.

When the moon is in:

Leo	The most barren zodiac sign. Do no planting. Cultivate and destroy only.
Virgo	Moist but next to Leo in barrenness. Do not plant or transplant. Good for cultivating and destroying.
Libra	A semi-fruitful, moist sign. Very good for pulp and root growth. Plant flowers, root crops, vines, hay, lettuce, cabbage, and corn or hybrids for fodder.
Scorpio	Second in line of most productive signs, exceeded only by Cancer. Good for vine growth and strength. Excellent for any planting, transplanting, budding, etc.
Sagittarius	Has a barren trend. Good for cultivation and turning sod. Also considered good for seeding hay crops and planting onions.
Capricorn	Productive, earthy, and moist. Good for planting root crops, tubers, potatoes, etc. Similar in nature to Taurus but a little dryer.

Do you notice how the signs change from barren to fruitful and back again? Nothing stays the same in nature. Change is ever with us. Nothing is always good; nothing is always bad. We can work with these changes and they will work for us.

Nothing that is can pause or stay
The moon will wax the moon will
wane The mist and cloud will turn to
rain The rain to mist and cloud again,
Tomorrow be today. —Keramos

Planting by the Moon's Phases

In addition to the twelve signs of the zodiac, attention should also be given to the quarters or four phases of the moon. The moon's first and second quarters are called "increasing phases." At this time the moon is steadily growing in size. Plants that produce their fruits above the ground are planted during these two phases. The third quarter is called a "decreasing phase," sometimes referred to as the "dark of the moon." Crops that yield their fruits underground are planted during this quarter. The fourth quarter of the moon, also a decreasing phase,

is the best for turning sod, cultivating, and for ridding areas of weeds and noxious growths.

During the first and second quarters the moon is in *increasing* light. Always plant vegetation that yields its produce *above* the ground during this phase. This is particularly true in the case of "annuals," which are those plants that do not continue life from one growing season to the next but must be seeded each year.

First Quarter
(new moon, waxing, and increasing crescent)
Plant leafy annuals that yield above the ground and have visible outside seed.

Examples: asparagus, broccoli, Brussels sprouts, cabbage, cauliflower, cereals (corn, barley, oats, rye, wheat), celery, leek, lettuce, parsley, spinach.

Second Quarter
(half-moon, first quarter moon, waxing gibbous, and increasing light)
Plant leafy annuals that yield above the ground and usually

contain seed within their yield.

Examples: beans, cereals (corn, barley, oats, rye, wheat), cantaloupe, cucumbers, eggplant, muskmelon, peas, peppers, pumpkins, squash, tomatoes, and watermelons.

This is a very fruitful phase and is also good for planting flowers. Many plants do well planted in either of these quarters as they are both "growing phases" for vegetation. For best results plant when the moon is in the most fruitful zodiac day signs of Cancer, Scorpio, and Pisces. The semi-fruitful day signs of Taurus, Capricorn, and Libra can also be used as second best. Avoid planting any of the above type plants in the other six zodiac signs.

Third Quarter
(full moon, waning gibbous, and decreasing light)

Plant bulb and root crops, also biennials and perennials. Plant vegetation that produces its yield *in* the ground.

Example: beets, carrots, chicory, garlic, onions, parsnips, peanuts, potatoes, radishes, rhubarb, rutabagas, strawberries, turnips, winter wheat, also any tubers for seed crops. Plant berries, grapes, shrubs, and trees.

Fourth Quarter
(last quarter, old moon, dark of the moon, last half-moon, waning crescent, decreasing light)

No planting is recommended but if you must plant pick a fruitful

zodiac day sign. This is the best period to turn sod, cultivate, pull weeds, destroy noxious growths, and rid areas of pests. Do this especially when the moon is in the barren signs of Leo, Virgo, and Gemini and the barren trend signs of Aries, Aquarius, and Sagittarius.

Planting Time vs. Germination Time

When planting by the signs there is a question as to which time to count, from the time you plant the seed or the time the seed germinates or sprouts.

The time of germination with different bulbs and seeds often varies by several days. The type and nature of the plant, the moisture, the soil, and the temperature have a definite bearing on the time of germination. Beets require seven to ten days; carrots twelve to eighteen; celery ten to twenty; peppers nine to fifteen; radishes three to six; and turnips four to eight days. Since there is such a variation in germination times for different seeds and so many other factors to be considered, it would be very difficult and would require complicated charts to compute times from germination.

Thus remember, when planting by the signs, the time always starts when you put the seed into the earth.

Summary

Use logic and some "horse sense" when planting by the signs. Plant when the moisture, season, soil, temperature, weather, and any other influencing factors are right. The signs and phases are to be used along with and not in opposition to general conditions. The secret is to try to get as many of these things going for you at one time as you possibly can. The more you have in line, working for you, the better are your chances for outstanding results.

Through trial and error, many attempts, and much experimentation, most folks who "plant by the signs" or do any other activity by the signs, use both the moon's *phase* (quarter) and the moon's daily zodiac *sign* in determining when to act. Just as the moon is in a phase at all times, it is also in a specific zodiac sign every day of the year. If we plan our work by using only the *Phase* of moon we may be working during a barren zodiac *sign* and the results will not be good. The two must work hand-in-hand. Knowing where the moon is placed in both phase and sign on each day will help you determine what to do and when to do it—in harmony and rhythm with nature.

We would recommend the use of an accurate almanac in determining the moon's place and the signs of the zodiac for planting and for doing any other activity by the signs. Many almanacs express the daily position of the moon in relation to star constellations. This is incorrect for planting, working livestock, and other activities by about one day. Some people say they have tried planting by the moon signs and it didn't work. They probably missed the fruitful day sign and were in a barren period. Calculations must be made to show the moon's position in the earth's zodiac, not its position in the star constellations. The moon has to be in a fruitful sign of the earth's zodiac for complete success.

The Harvest

If the moon shows like a silver shield,
You need not be afraid to reap your field,
But if she rises haloed-round,
Soon we will tread on deluged ground.
—Traditional

The decay of the old customs of country living and farming are most noticeable in respect to the gathering of the increase. The completion of the growing of crops was a time of joy and celebration. Neighbors would flock together to perform the necessary chores, tables would be set for feasts of mammoth proportions, the air would be filled with laughter and song. Evenings were taken with dancing to the music of an old fiddle in the crisp autumn air under a harvest moon.

Lately, farming has become an industry. There no longer exists the real satisfaction and pleasure of harvest that folks knew in bygone years. With families moving from the farm, the loss of farm labor and the introduction of machinery to do such a large part of the harvesting, the social enjoyment of this part of rural life is past in most communities. Yet there is still a great sense of personal enjoyment and satisfaction when people produce their own crops and livestock and feel the pride of production and a job well done.

Harvesting by the Moon Signs

All harvesting should be done in a dry moon sign for both easier gathering and better preservation of the crop. The dry zodiac signs to use are Aquarius, Aries, Gemini, Leo, and Sagittarius.

The best moon phases to follow in harvesting are the decreasing moons of the third and fourth quarters.

Pick apples, peaches, pears, and other fruits when the moon is in decreasing light of the third and fourth quarters. If they are harvested in the increasing moon phases they bruise easily and these spots will rot.

Here are some of the best ways to have good fresh vegetables all through the winter months:

• Tomatoes—This is one of the few and perhaps the only vegetable that needs to be canned in order to have a good supply through the cold months. They should be canned for whole tomatoes and for juice.

• Carrots—These golden tubers can be stored right in the ground where they grow unless the season turns out to be a very wet one.

Cover the whole carrot patch with hay or leaves to prevent freezing. You can then harvest them as you have need. If you have a wet winter, just pull the whole crop and tuck them away in boxes of dry sand in a root cellar.

• Potatoes—Sweet potatoes will need to be harvested about the time of frost. Store them in a dry place that has a temperature of about 50–55° F. Irish potatoes can stay in the ground until just before the bone-rattlin' freeze. Then dig them and store in a dark spot at about 40° F. Pick a spot that has good air circulation as these white potatoes are sometimes a little hard to keep.

• Squash—The winter variety will keep a few months if you will gather just before the frost and leave a short length of stem on each squash. Store at about 40° F. in a dry place.

• Turnips and Rutabagas—These can be covered with hay or leaves as carrots and you can eat them through the early winter months. They will keep for a while in a dry, dark root cellar at about 40° F.

• Cabbage—Bury the heads upside down in dry sand, they will keep a month or two after the bad weather really begins.

• Onions—Harvest before the freeze. Store in a cool, dry, dark place and you will have good, sweet onions all winter.

• Endive and Kale—These can stand until the temperature gets to 15–20° F. right in the garden with a little protection from blasts of cold wind.

• Beans and Peas—Some folks like to can these when they are at the peak of freshness during the summer and fall months. They can be dried and stored in a cool, dry place.

• Broccoli, Brussels Sprouts, and Kohlrabi—All can take a lot of cold winter weather. Best to just leave them in the garden and eat them as long as they last.

• Parsnips—This can be your fresh winter vegetable when most others fail. You can pick them right out of the garden in January, February, and March.

• There are others that are special to your locality that offer good eating during the long, dreary winter days. You will need to talk to some of the old-timers in your neighborhood to find out which are best to plant, when to harvest, and how to store them.

TOMATO
EARLIEST OF ALL

PRICE
10¢

BURT'S SEED FOR QUALITY

Livestock and the Moon

The timing of livestock handling chores, according to numbers of zodiac-following ranchers and stockfarmers throughout the country, should be in harmony and rhythm with the moon and its phases.

Castration, Sterilization, and Surgery: Pecos Caldwell of New Mexico, who has had considerable experience in "marking" livestock, says these operations should be performed only when the moon is in the "feet." This is the Pisces zodiac sign during the decrease of the moon in the third and fourth quarters. Many old-time ranchmen would mark their stock only from February 19 to March 21 when the monthly zodiac sign of Pisces was in effect. Others believe you can operate anytime the *daily* moon sign is in Pisces, but never in Virgo, Libra, Scorpio, or Sagittarius as the animal will bleed too much, not heal properly, and might even die. Most agree that the best time to operate is no earlier than twenty-four hours after the full moon has passed, and some stockmen do this work within one week of the new moon, before or after.

Shearing: Sheep and goats should be sheared when the moon is increasing for better quality and more quantities of wool and mohair on the next clip.

Dehorning: Remove horns at the new moon or one week before or after. Avoid the daily moon signs of Aries and Taurus as the governing body zone is too near the horn area.

Butchering and Slaughtering: Roger Smith of Kansas has had many years experience in the butchering of large numbers of cattle, hogs, and sheep. He believes that meat "will keep better, have a fine flavor, and be 'fork cuttin' tender' if you slaughter the first three days after a full moon and don't do any killing during the Leo sign."

Grazing: If you have a pasture on which you want the grass to grow back quickly and with increased forage, have the livestock on it only during the first and second quarter phases of the moon. Always have the stock off it from the full moon through the third and fourth quarters. It would be well to time this procedure so that the grass can grow without stock on it during

one of the fruitful monthly signs of Pisces, Taurus, Cancer (the best), Scorpio, or Capricorn.

Breeding of Livestock

Set breeding dates so that the birth will occur during the *increasing* light of the moon. The new moon and first quarter are believed to be best.

Set the time of birth to occur in both a feminine and fruitful *daily* moon sign. Cancer, Scorpio, or Pisces are best as they are the most feminine, the most fruitful, and are also water signs. Taurus and Capricorn, the semi-fruitful signs, should be avoided as the date of birth.

Moon Signs for Farm and Home Activities

- Cement—Make and pour cement during the fixed signs of Aquarius, Taurus, Leo, or Scorpio and the cement will "set" better. Also observe the third and fourth quarter moon for this.
- Construction—Foundations should be dug on fixed signs of Aquarius, Taurus, Leo, and

Scorpio in the moon's third and fourth quarters.

• Cultivation and Sod Turning—Always do these tasks when the moon is in the barren signs of Aries, Gemini, Leo, Virgo, Sagittarius, or Aquarius. It is best if the moon is in a decreasing light phase such as the fourth quarter.

• Dehydrating or Drying—These chores should be done immediately following a full moon in a dry and fiery sign such as Aries, Leo, or Sagittarius.

• Fencing—Fence posts will not "heave out" of the ground if set on fixed signs of Aquarius, Taurus, Leo, or Scorpio, and the fourth moon quarter.

• Fertilizing—The moon should be in a fruitful sign as Taurus, Cancer, Libra, Scorpio, Capricorn, or Pisces. Moon in decreasing light phase, third or fourth quarter.

• Flowers—Plant in fruitful signs and with moon in increasing light phase, first quarter best. For abundant flowers plant in Cancer, Scorpio, or Pisces; for beautiful flowers and fragrance plant in Libra; for sturdy flowers plant in Scorpio; for hardy flowers plant in Taurus.

• Haircuts—For faster growth the moon should be in a daily zodiac sign of Pisces, Cancer, or Scorpio which are watery signs, and in an increasing moon phase. For slow hair growth, cut the hair in the daily zodiac sign of Leo, Virgo, or Gemini in the third or fourth moon quarter.

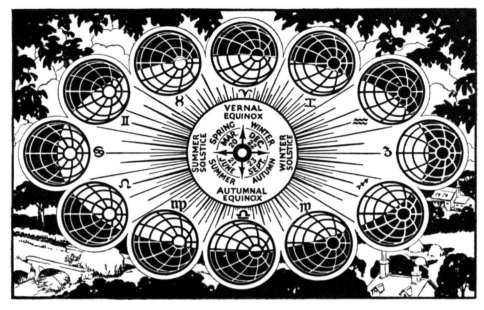

• Irrigation—For best advantage of water, irrigate when the moon is in a watery day sign, and in the increasing light of the first and second phase.

• Mowing—If you wish the grass to come back quickly with increased growth, mowing should be done in the moon's first and second quarter. To retard the growth, mow in the third and fourth quarter on a barren day sign.

• Painting—The best time for applying paint is in the decreasing light of the third and fourth quarters of the moon in the fixed signs of Aquarius, Taurus, Leo, and especially Scorpio. Edgar Delaney in Colorado says he will never paint during the watery sign of Cancer in late June. He says the paint will not dry properly, won't make a good finish, and has a tendency to peel.

• Pruning—Scorpio is by far the best sign for pruning to limit branch growth and to make better fruit. Should be done with moon in decreasing light phase, third and fourth quarters.

• Roofing and Shingling—The third and fourth quarters, or the decreasing moon, should be used in the fixed signs of Aquarius, Taurus, Leo, and Scorpio. Work of this type done during the first and second quarters is apt to cause the shingles to buckle and warp. Shingles laid in the waxing moon will swell as the moon grows.

• Spraying—Destroy unwanted growths and pests in a barren sign during the decreasing light phase of moon's fourth quarter.

• Transplanting—Same as planting; under fruitful signs with moon in increasing light phase of first or second quarter.

3 | WATER WITCHING

Dowsing

Anyone who has witnessed dowsing in action is already familiar with its procedure and fascination. For the uninitiated, the gift of dowsing is the ability of a person to locate underground sources of water or minerals while carrying in his hands a Y-shaped stick called a dowsing rod or divining rod. Other terms synonymous with dowsing are doodlebugging, striking, water witching, radiesthesia, and rhabdomancy.

Most dowsers, sometimes referred to as water witches, are men in their middle years and older. However, there are also women dowsers. And children up to the age of fifteen or sixteen are especially sensitive to the dowsing reaction. I have seen very young boys with the power, their wand forcefully turning down over water veins.

Because the ability to dowse sometimes runs in families, some persons believe that dowsing is a learned art, passed along from one family member or generation to another. Others contend that the familial pursuit of dowsing means it is an inherited gift. People seem to have this ability in varying degrees: in some the skill is immediately obvious; others achieve success only through patient practice.

Dowsing is practiced in England, continental Europe, Africa, North and South America, Australia, New Zealand, and parts of Asia. It is continental Europeans more than any other peoples who have used dowsing rods.

Over the ages the most popular rods have been made from peach or hazel trees, though maple, persimmon, willow, witch hazel, poison oak, and plum have also served. Divining rods have been fashioned from materials other than wood, such as oxhorn, ivory, gold, silver, and whalebone. Dowsers seem to have had equal success with bent coat hangers, watch springs, scissors, pliers, specially cast metal rods, and rods of wood with metal coils attached, with compass-like pointing devices, or with battery-powered lights.

The dowsing rod is generally a forked twig, one branch of which is held in each hand, the juncture usually pointing upward. The two most common holds are with the palms up and with the palms down. When the rod is carried over a spot where underground water or minerals lie hidden, the pointed end will be attracted downward; it has been known to whirl around. Straight twigs are sometimes used. The smaller end is held, while the opposite end bobs up and down when indicating water or ore, the number of bobs signifying the depth in some unit of measure.

Dowsers often experience one or more kinds of distress, to a greater or lesser degree, while working: convulsive pains, pounding heart, racing pulse, muscle spasms, a stinging sensation on the skin, and dizziness and nausea. Some develop a feeling of nausea immediately prior to the stick's downward thrust. All agree that their work is physically exhausting, leaving them with the feeling of being drained of energy. For this reason, finding three to four wells per day is the limit.

The original dowser could have been a magician, discovering his gift accidentally while using his wand. Early manifestations of dowsing were related to magic and sorcery. The ancients used it to predict future events, to warn of the presence of ghosts, and even to forecast the weather. Long ago, wizards accompanied their use of the forked rod with incantations. Righteous men, spurning incantations, nonetheless retained the practice of dowsing.

The birthplace of modern-day dowsing was in the Harz Mountains of Germany, where the most advanced mining practices were developed. Miners believed that metallic ores attracted certain trees, causing them to lean over the spot where the ore lay underground. A branch of such a tree would be cut so that it might be observed where else it drooped. Later, a branch was cut for each hand, their extremities being tied together. Finally, as a matter of convenience, a forked branch was cut, an end grasped in each hand with the palms upward.

A common practice in those times was to bury money for safekeeping. So the rod functioned as a detector of buried treasure as well as of metallic lodes.

The churches held that the power of dowsing meant an affiliation with the Devil. Those persons found engaged in mysterious practices risked being burned at the stake for sorcery. In Germany, dowsing was therefore enveloped with religious ceremonies and prayers as a shield against persecution. In an attempt to prove that both operator and rod were not under demoniac influence but were recipients of a divine gift, elaborate rituals were observed: 1. The dowser must purify himself through fasts, novenas, and sexual abstention. 2. Rods must be cut only on holy days. 3. The rod, wrapped in swaddling clothes, should be carried to church for baptism and laid in the bed of a newly baptized infant, by whose name it was thereafter to be addressed.

Early dowsing reflected the credence that the rod was the source of power; therefore, its manufacture, as to both ritual and material, was of utmost importance. Hazel twigs were considered most efficacious in searching for silver, ash twigs for copper, pitch pine for lead and especially tin, rods of iron and steel being best for finding gold.

German dowsers achieved excellent results in locating deposits of metals. The French tried to vie with them by training their own miners. The English, following the more expedient path, wisely imported German dowsers.

A favorite Cornish toast is "fish, tin, and copper," for Cornwall's wealth lies chiefly underground and in the surrounding seas, mining and fishing being her primary industries. The mining industry endured periods of depression, as it did shortly before Queen Elizabeth I came to power.

During her reign German miners were imported to revive the industry. Thus the dowsing rod was introduced to England. Tradition among Cornwall's miners has it that fairies, custodians of the earth's mineral treasure, guide the rod to ore deposits.

The dowsing rod was used in Europe as much in the quest for water as for metals. Water was an important factor in mining; if its taste was metallic, the dowser could be confident that metal deposits were nearby. Those lacking interest in mining but desirous of a water supply would ask the dowser to stop once water was found. Early water dowsers called themselves "water switchers," referring to their work as "switching for water." By this time dowsers were able to determine not only the location of water but its width and depth as well, estimation of its volume remaining yet unsolved.

Prior to the end of the seventeenth century, use of the rod spread throughout Europe and was transported to Asia, Africa, and the New World by colonists.

Early Spanish explorers employed dowsing instruments in mining operations in the Southwest and Mexico. During the days of colonization, there was an urgent need for water. Settlers developed numberless wells through the aid of dowsers, wells that continued to furnish water until at least the end of the last century. The Indians were ignorant of dowsing until it was introduced into North America by European settlers and their descendants.

By the late 1700's, dowsing power had become associated in America with witchcraft, which is why the practice became known here as water witching. The term is not used in any other English-speaking country.

Despite the preaching of churchmen that dowsing was anti-religious, people in every walk of life experimented with it. Innumerable theories were proposed to explain the operation of dowsing. In the fifteenth century the view was held that the failure of a twig to turn downward over a metal deposit indicated that some peculiarity in the user impeded the power of the vein to attract. Five conditions for successful dowsing were set forth: 1. The twig should be of proper size: the vein of ore is unable to turn too large a stick. 2. It should be of a forked shape. 3. The power of the vein to turn the stick must be present. 4. The stick must be properly held. 5. Impeding peculiarities in the operator must be absent.

Others concluded, in the 1600's, that because the rod did not work in all hands, its movement was due to some specific favorable quality within the dowser. Since the rod was only the instrument through which the dowser's gift worked, its shape and material were of less consequence than the power controlling it.

Some men explained the power of dowsing by the principle of attraction and repulsion, influenced, no doubt, by the evident phenomena of gravity and magnetism. They believed that the rod received magnetic vibrations from underground ore and water.

In the late 1700's the study of electricity was making great strides.

The theory was proposed that water witching was an electrical phenomenon, the explanation being that the rod depended on electrical currents transmitted from the ground through the body, forming a magnetic field between the rod and the ground.

At the beginning of the twentieth century, French dowsers called themselves practitioners of radiesthesia—believing that unseen currents emanating from the rod were affected by the presence of water or minerals, causing the rod to move. Currents of physical force, perhaps similar to electricity, were thought to travel from underground water up through both dowser and rod, moving spirally up one branch of the stick, through the man, and down the other fork, returning to the water's source in the earth, thus making a complete cycle. Some dowsers, wearing leather gloves and

rubber boots, were hampered by what they considered the insulating effect of these clothing articles; other dowsers, similarly attired, experienced no hindrance to their dowsing performance. Electrical and magnetic theories have been used in support of the radiesthesia reasoning.

In the late 1930's, German dowsers purported the existence of rays rising from the earth's center which continually pierce the earth's crust, traveling into space. Underground water, oil, or minerals soak up these rays so that the surface over them is lacking in rays. Such places are referred to as "shadow" areas. Devoid of rays, they act on the sympathetic nervous system of the dowser. This idea was widely entertained in Europe, even outside the circle of dowsers. Adolph Hitler, in an effort to locate a restful "shade" area, requested that his sleeping quarters be dowsed so that he might sleep undisturbed by rays. In Mexico the ray, not the shadow, is believed to affect the nervous system.

More recent theories are modifications of the principle of the radiesthesiasts. Some physical force, it is believed, is responsible for dowsing, but its effect is not so much on the rod as on the muscles of the operator's forearms, inciting the dowsing reflex—an imperceptible movement but made obvious by the action of the rod. One school of thought is that the rod senses currents of radiation from water molecules underground. Some people believe that a physical power from underground water acts directly on the nerves of the dowser's hands, stimulating unconscious muscle movement made manifest by the rod or other dowsing device.

There are those who look on dowsing as a natural gift. The water-witching talent is considered an enlargement of normal perception through which the dowser accepts information, subconsciously sending it to the rod by indiscernible muscular movement of fingers and palms. Telekinesis, the ability to move objects by mental power, has been suggested, as has the idea that dowsing is a seventh sense, physical rather than psychic. Long-distance dowsing by use of a rod over a map of the area in question borders on the parapsychological stand.

What dowsing has detected makes up a varied and fascinating list: water, petroleum, potash, diamonds, gold, graves, and buried treasure. Over the ages the dowsing rod has been used to ensure immunity against misfortune when preserved as a fetish; to analyze human character; to locate lost landmarks and redefine property boundaries; to determine the direction of the cardinal points, measure heights of trees, detect criminals, find archeological sites; to trace lost domestic animals, pinpoint malfunctions in

appliances, cure diseases, trace underground streams; to ascertain the amount and depth of water present at a specific underground spot; and to analyze ore and water. Dowsing has revealed that ancient stone monuments were invariably constructed over underground water sources. The military has used dowsing to detect buried land and underwater mines, underground

bunkers, and enemy caches of food, ammunition, and fuel. Some unusual experiments to which dowsing has been put are revealing human blood types, answering questions, tracing escaped prisoners, finding lost disaster victims by use of the rod over a map of the disaster area, and distinguishing the paintings of one artist from those of another.

Should you be prompted to try your hand at dowsing, make your initial step that of locating a good Y-shaped branch with a 45 to 60-degree angle between the forks. The stick should be no more than 2 feet in length. One from a young tree is most likely to have the required supple, resilient quality. The most common hold is with the branches in upturned palms, the fingers encircling the wood, thumbs held firmly against the ends. Some dowsers have the branch passing inside the little and third fingers, grasping the branch by the middle and index fingers and allowing it to protrude beyond the palms. Others prefer the rod to lie loosely in the palms with the ends extending beyond the hands. Dowsers believe that anyone can achieve success through patient practice, perseverance, and concentration. Concentration on the material sought is considered very important.

A good many dowsers, after much practice, have been able to dispose of the divining device, depending solely upon concentration and their bare hands, believing that the true dowsing instrument is the dowser's body. There are dowsers who feel that the rod can be unfavorably influenced by metallic objects on the operator's person—objects such as rings, coins, and eyeglasses. Some find that they have "active" and "inactive" fingers on each hand, those which are sensitive to the dowsing reaction and those which are not. Skillful dowsers are able to identify different underground metals and to distinguish water and petroleum from metal. Some dowsers are so sensitive as to detect the very grade of the ore deposit. I personally have never witnessed the use of the divining rod in locating metal deposits or buried treasure but have seen it used in finding water. Roy Baker of Tennyson, Texas, witched for water on our little farm and discovered a pretty good well in what was otherwise thought to be a dry area. While watching others successfully dowse for water, I've seen the rod turn downward with such power that the bark on the branch was skinned off or broken in the hands of the operator.

In the southern United States, a twig of the accepted shape is used, but one considerably longer and more flexible. In this area, branches from fruit trees are preferred. Elsewhere in the country, more complex man-made rods have become popular—the swing rod, the magnetic mineral rod, the gold-digging compass, the Spanish needle, and the pendulum fork, to name a few.

Those accepting dowsing as a mysterious but important potential for the future perceive it as one day functioning for the general good. Dowsers in Mexico find the rod sensitive to rock variations, such as faults. Should this prove consistently true, dowsing could be valuable for mapping possible earthquake areas. Claims have been made for its use in detecting certain organic diseases when it is passed over a person's photograph, just as land areas have been dowsed first by map. Further inquiry into this aspect could lead to diagnosis and healing. Opportunities for the employment of dowsing are limitless.

Dowsing has proved successful an outstanding number of times. To reject it solely because its secret defies scientific explanation would be to preclude us from a realm fraught with untold possibilities for the betterment of mankind.

Testing Water

In days gone by people devised simple methods of testing water which, though not completely scientific, were generally effective. Here are two methods that were used to determine the color, odor, taste, and purity of water.

- Fill a clear glass bottle with water. View some black object through the water to judge its clarity. The object's outline should appear well defined. Then empty half of the water, cork the bottle, and set it in a warm place to stand for several hours. Now shake the bottle, uncork it, and smell the air inside. If there is any odor, the water is not fit for domestic purposes. If there is no odor, see if one develops when the water is warmed. After it has been warmed, the water should be tasteless as well as odorless for home use.

- Put water in a gallon jug, and add a good amount of sugar. Let the jug stand for a week. If, at the end of that time, the sugar is not discolored, the water is safe for drinking. If it has become discolored, boiling the water will be necessary for safe consumption.

4 | TREE TALK

In olden times trees played an even more vital role in the lives of people than they do today. Perhaps because they provided so many of man's basic needs, people revered them and were more acutely aware of their individual beauty and characteristics.

Some trees were considered sacred, and to them many powers of good and evil were attributed. Delving into the past, we find fascinating legends about them that developed over the ages and were handed down from one generation to the next. Centuries ago people discovered which tree furnished wood most appropriate for a particular purpose.

Learning the ways that trees were used in the past, legends and superstitions concerning them, and their uses today can enhance our appreciation of these wonders of Nature, too often taken for granted.

Ash

The ash is unique in being the only tree in the world to produce black buds.

Through the centuries, supernatural powers have been attributed to it. Country people would split an ash sapling and then pass a sick infant through the opening to waiting hands on the opposite side. This procedure was repeated three times. The opening was then smeared with mud and bandaged. If the young tree healed, the baby would recover; if the wound failed to close, the child

would die. When cattle developed sore limbs, it was believed that a shrew had scampered over them. As a countermeasure a shrew was put into a cavity in an ash tree and the hole stopped up, the tree thereafter being called a shrew ash. The mere touch of a branch from a shrew ash was supposed to cure the animal suffering from painful legs. The tree was also said to have an adverse effect on snakes, and its leaves were considered a cure for their bites.

The ash was thought to have medicinal properties as well as supernatural powers. A tea made of the leaves was advocated in cases of gout and rheumatism and was prescribed for longevity.

White ash timber is valuable for its dual qualities of strength and elasticity. From the earliest ages it was used for weapons of war. It was favored for making wheels, shafts, and other articles that

are required to be light and springy. Today ash wood goes into staircases, kitchen furniture, and bedroom furniture, especially dressers. Because of its toughness and flexibility, baseball bats, polo mallets, hockey sticks, tennis-racket frames, shovel and hoe handles, oars, and swing seats are manufactured from it. Ash wood is also used for butter tubs, baskets, boxes, and crates. The roots of the tree, being beautifully veined and receptive to high polish, are prized by cabinet-makers.

From the bark of the blue ash, early settlers of North America extracted a pigment which was used to dye cloth blue.

Indians customarily used splints from the black ash to fashion pack baskets; hence the tree became known as the basket tree.

Beech

In literature of the past, one finds many references to the carving of letters on the beech tree's bark. Its extreme smoothness, which is maintained throughout the tree's life, seems to invite such action.

Pigs are as fond of beechnuts as they are of acorns. Indians valued them for their oil; it is slow to become rancid, and they favored it for cooking purposes. American pioneers fattened their Thanksgiving turkeys on the nuts. Some people claim that eating beechnuts can cause headaches.

Many years ago country folk picked small leaves from beech trees to use as mattress stuffing. They give off a pleasant aroma and do not become brittle and musty as fast as straw.

Because beechwood has no detectable odor or taste, barrels and other wooden containers for food are made from it. The beech tree provides the woodsman with the finest firewood. Its timber burns with a hot flame, eventually leaving a bed of long-lasting embers.

Birch

In the days of the country schoolhouse, the first thing to come to mind at mention of the birch tree might have been the birch rod. However, over the ages the birch has been put to many and varied uses other than the schoolmaster's disciplinary stick.

Birch bark is extremely durable—almost everlasting—and waterproof. The tree turns its sap into an aromatic oil, which it stores in the bark.

The sole tree to grow in Lapland is the birch. Being waterproof and long lasting, it was used as roofing material. After removing a large section of bark from a tree and cutting a hole in it big enough for their heads to go through, people wore it as a moisture-proof covering. From bark they fashioned waterproof shoes and boots, baskets, cords, and mats. Their torches, made from twisted bark strips, burned brightly because of the oil stored there. When food was scarce, the natives ground the bark's lining into flour for making bread.

In some areas the birch produces clumps of twigs among its branches, often referred to as witches' knots. Years ago people employed birch wood for making footwear and even their houses.

Being easily separated into delicate layers, birch bark was used in the past for papermaking. The bark and leaves of some types of birch are used as a remedy for skin diseases.

Country people tap birch trees for their sap, which they call "birch water" or "birch blood." Each spring they collect a supply to use medicinally for curing skin afflictions and rheumatism. The sweet sap is sometimes made into a wine similar to champagne.

One kind of birch, the paper birch, was put to good use by northern Indians. They used it as a covering for their shelters and in making lightweight canoes, utensils, and containers for food storage. Today it finds its way into shoe lasts, clothespins, spools, toothpicks, and pulpwood.

The hard, strong, straight-grained wood of the birch is used to advantage in flooring, interior finish, furniture, veneer, baskets, boxes, crates, and hoops for casks. Certain chemicals are derived from it through distillation. It makes excellent fuel, burning fiercely with a bright, clear flame. Because the oil of the birch makes it both waterproof and flammable, woodsmen seek it for their campfires, particularly when the forest is soaked with rain.

Black Gum

The pioneers tried in vain to split the wood of the black gum tree to make rail fences. The wood's twisted, interlocking grain defied their axes. So they sawed hollow trunks of the black gum into short sections and converted them into beehives. The tree became commonly known as the "bee gum."

Today black gum timber is used for egg crates, berry boxes, barrels, furniture, and gunstocks.

Black Walnut

Pioneers of the North American continent derived a dye from the hulls of black walnuts. With it they colored their homemade cloth brown.

Colonists used the hard but easily worked wood of the black walnut tree for furniture and staircases in both town and country homes. Recognizing the durability of the timber, they made fence rails and barn beams from it.

Since black walnut trees are scarce today, their wood is usually limited to furniture veneer. It is particularly sought for gunstocks, because it sustains shock without splintering and retains its beautiful finish through long use.

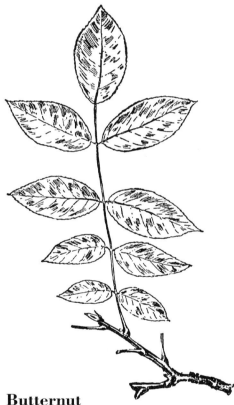

Butternut

Country dwellers almost everywhere are familiar with the white walnut, or butternut tree. Women gather the nuts while they are yet soft and pickle them with vinegar, sugar, and spices.

The Indians made sugar from the sap of the tree and from its nuts extracted oil. A gentle cathartic can be made from the roots' inner bark. Pioneer women used husks of the butternut and the bark lining to dye their homespun fabric brown or tan. During the Civil War days many a soldier's uniform owed its color to butternut dye.

Butternut wood is beautifully grained, and when polished takes on a satiny glow. The altars of some of America's old churches were made of it. Today it is used for furniture and paneling.

Cabbage Palmetto

A bud resembling a cabbage sprouts in the middle of the cabbage palmetto's crown. The Indians of Florida relished it, and Spanish explorers pronounced the large, tender bud palatable. Today's people have developed a taste for it, which proves detrimental to the tree: removal of the bud often causes its death.

In colonial times the trunks of the cabbage palmetto were valued for docks and wharf pilings because of their resistance to shipworms. A fort built of the wood was reported to withstand cannon balls. Florida's Seminole Indians build their houses of the trunks, thatching them with the tree's fan-shaped leaves.

Whisk brooms and brushes are manufactured from fibers of the leaf stalks; the leaves go into hats, mats, baskets, and other woven articles.

Flowers of the cabbage palmetto furnish bees with nectar, and the tree's sweet fruit is enjoyed by the Seminoles. Birds and raccoons share the Indians' fondness for it.

Cedar

Indians steeped small branches of the northern white cedar in boiling water, making a tea that cured scurvy. The sap of the tree has been found to contain vitamin C, which no doubt was responsible for the treatment's success. A fragrant oil from the leaves and branches of this cedar has been used in medicines.

The timber, being resistant to decay, is made into poles, posts, railroad ties, tanks, shingles, buckets, and boats. The lightweight wood makes good floats for the nets of fishermen.

Alaskan Indians use red cedars for carving their totem poles. From the trees' massive logs, they hollow out their canoes, known as dugouts.

Cottonwood

During pioneer days on the western expanses of prairies and plains, cottonwood trees were of exceptional importance, their presence determining the site for a homestead. They provided cooling shade in summer and in winter furnished firewood. Homes and stockades were constructed from their timber. Livestock was nourished with cottonwood leaves.

Today the soft, easily worked wood of the cottonwood is used for papermaking, excelsior, baskets, crates, and boxes.

Dogwood

The bitter bark of the dogwood tree was made into a tea by the Indians to treat fevers. The pioneers used it as a remedy for malaria. When the South was unable to get quinine during the Civil War, dogwood bark served as a substitute. The Indians made a dye from it, which they used to color their feathers scarlet. Sometimes the leaves and unripe fruit of the dogwood were used as tonics and astringents.

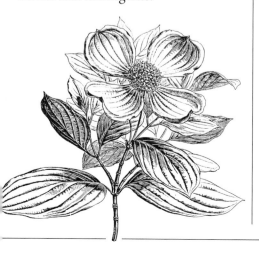

Today the tree's tough, close-grained wood is used for mallets, tool handles, jeweler's blocks, meat skewers, bobbins, and spools. It is especially suited for the shuttles of textile mills, because it retains its smoothness under constant use.

Elder

Young shoots of the elder tree were a source of fun for country boys generations ago. Their soft, pithy interior was easily removed with a pocketknife, resulting in a quickly made pop-gun. In earlier times, flutes were fashioned from these hollow stalks.

The elder was valued for its medicinal properties. At a time when country people concocted many home remedies, elder buds were brewed for a tea to reduce fevers; a skin ointment was also made from the flowers; and they were used to add flavor to vinegar. Sleep could be induced through the medicinal qualities of both flowers and leaves. A decoction of elder leaves was said to destroy insect pests on other vegetation. Farmers put garlands of ill-smelling elder leaves on their horses' heads to drive away annoying flies. A healing salve was prepared from elder bark to treat burns. Many a rural household made elderberry wine, regarded as a good cold remedy as well as a pleasing drink. Regular imbibing of this was believed to ensure a long, healthy life. Some folks even used the berries to dye their hair.

The timber of the elder has been employed in the making of boxes, toys, and shoemaker's pegs. Butchers prefer skewers of elder wood, claiming that they never taint the meat.

Elm

During lean times of the past, the inner lining of elm bark was ground into meal for making bread. Country people fed elm leaves to cattle, which seemed to prefer them to oats.

A certain variety of elm was thought to have magical properties. Dairymaids fastened a twig of it to their churns, believing that butter would form only in its presence.

Elm wood is excellent for articles subjected to moisture, such as keels of ships, water wheels, and troughs. Before iron piping came into use, water pipes were made of it. The hard, tough wood of the elm goes into coffins, boxes, barrels, baskets, crates,

some furniture, vehicle parts, the frames of saddles, and dairy, poultry, and apiary supplies. The inner bark is twisted to form a coarse rope.

Country boys on their ramblings often chew a twig or piece of inner bark from the slippery elm. It contains a slimy, palatable mucilage, which accounts for the tree's name. The sticky bark lining served as nourishment for the Indians, as an appeaser of thirst among the pioneers, and as a valued medicine of frontier days. Many rural households still use it for coughs and fevers and in poultices for boils and sores.

Eucalyptus

Because the eucalyptus tree soaks up tremendous quantities of water, it has been planted in marshy areas that were considered breeding places for fevers. Thus it became known as the "fever tree."

A tea made from its leaves has been used to treat fevers, colds, respiratory troubles, and various infections. The dried leaves, when smoked in cigarette form, are said to benefit asthma sufferers. Eucalyptus wine is considered an aid to digestion.

Over a century ago the eucalyptus tree was imported from Australia by railroad men, who planned to use the hard wood for track ties. However, the wood proved too difficult to cut for profit.

Since that time the wood has been put to many other uses.

Able to endure drought, eucalyptus trees serve as fine windbreaks in arid regions. A medicinal oil has been extracted from the bark. The tree also provides nectar for honey, tannin for leather-tanning, and good fuel for warmth. In some areas of our country, sweet-scented smoke curling from the chimney at a house probably means that slow-burning eucalyptus logs are flaming on the hearth.

Holly

Have you ever wondered what wood goes into black piano keys? They are usually made from the hard, easily dyed wood of the holly tree. The wood is also used in riding switches, whip handles, and furniture inlays. However, its chief use is in the making of musical and scientific instruments.

The holly tree contains a fragrant resin that has medicinal properties. A tea made from the leaves has served as a remedy for rheumatism and fevers.

Country dwellers used faggots of holly to sweep their chimneys. Many believed that holly branches would protect a home from lightning and its residents from witchcraft.

Hornbeam

The wood of the hornbeam is tougher than that of any other tree. In early times objects requiring strong, hard wood were made from it, such as rake teeth, cogs of mill wheels, and yokes for oxen. Because of its durability when in contact with soil, it is frequently used for fence posts. In addition, tool handles, levers, and mallets are manufactured from it.

Its bark is utilized in homeopathic medicine and, being rich in tannin, is used in tanneries.

Hornbeam timber provides good firewood. Torches made of it burn with a bright, candle-like flame.

For its qualities of solidity, toughness, and strength, the hornbeam has been referred to as the ironwood tree.

Horse Chestnut

The horse chestnut tree (which is not a true chestnut) originated in the mountains of Asia. Its nuts (which are not true nuts) are unpalatable to man, but deer

relish them, and when they are boiled poultry will eat them. In some areas they are fed to horses and are used to fatten sheep. The American Indians tossed ground horse chestnuts into the waters of their favorite fishing sites. Fish, intoxicated by the narcotic properties of the nuts, rose to the surface and were easily scooped up in nets.

Horse chestnuts are used in veterinary practice. The tree's bitter, astringent bark has been used in treating fevers.

Both nuts and roots contain a substance that can be worked into a lather as a substitute for soap. It serves as a bleach for linens. An adhesive paste and a very good starch are made from the seeds. Years ago, candles were made from horse chestnut flour and tallow. They burned longer than ordinary candles, but less brightly.

The soft, easily worked wood of the horse chestnut is used in the manufacture of small objects. Throughout the United States it is planted as a shade tree.

The state tree of Ohio is one of our native horse chestnuts, the buckeye. It is so named for its large, polished seed, which somewhat resembles the eye of a male deer. Superstitious people keep one in their pocket as a defense against rheumatism.

Country boys used to gather the shiny brown nuts to play the game of "conquerors." They tied horse chestnuts to both ends of a string, whirled them rapidly around, and let them fly to land on telegraph wires, where they hung indefinitely.

Linden
Honey made from the flowers of the linden tree is ranked by many as the most delicious of all varieties. Rural households steep the blossoms, using the resulting tea as a remedy for coughs, indigestion, and nervousness.

In ancient times the tough inner bark was used for writing tablets and its fibers for tying garlands. During the days of the old oaken bucket, well ropes were made of these fibers, as was a coarse cloth. Fishermen made nets from them, and gardeners used them for binding bouquets and for making mats to protect plants. In generations past, poor people fashioned footwear from the bark, using the outer part for soles and the bark lining for the tops. When a tree had been stripped of its bark, it was used for charcoal.

During winter, the tiny nuts and buds of the linden tree have often meant survival to a lost and starving trapper.

The soft white wood of the linden is used in papermaking, woodenware, paneling, and cabinetwork. The sounding boards of pianos are made of it, and its smooth grain renders it ideal for carving and wood engraver's blocks.

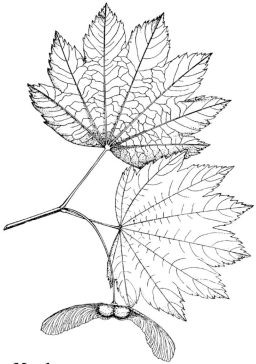

Maple
Early settlers of North America were amazed to find that the Indians made sugar from the maple tree's sap. The news was carried to Europe, where it was hailed as an outstanding scientific discovery. The colonists quickly adopted the practice, making both sugar and syrup.

The smooth yellow wood of the maple tree is hard, strong, and uniform in texture. When polished, it gleams like satin. From colonial times it has been considered one of the finest woods for furniture and flooring. Spools and bobbins, handles, boxes, crates, shoe lasts, and agricultural implements have been manufactured from it. In the past, before steel took the place of wood, ships' keels were made of it.

Bird's-eye maple is a favorite wood with cabinetmakers and is used for gunstocks and the backs of violins. Certain chemicals are distilled from it.

When used for fuel, maple burns with a steady, clear flame.

Oak

There are many species of oak trees varying greatly in appearance, but they have one thing in common: all of them produce acorns. Centuries ago, oak trees marched over half of England. Pigs were fattened on their acorns. Country people, when referring to the size of an oak forest, mentioned the number of swine it could sustain rather than the number of its trees or acres. When famine plagued the land, people ate acorns, too.

The acorns of America's white oak are relished by jays, wild turkeys, squirrels, deer, and other creatures. The Indians and many white settlers ground them into meal for bread making. You can roast them to make acorn coffee, which is not a stimulant and is reputed to benefit people with poor digestion.

Certain insects lay their eggs in the oak tree's bark. Each egg is surrounded by a drop of irritating liquid, causing the bark to swell and form a gall, resembling a miniature apple. The juicy contents of oak galls are used in dyes and medicines, in photographic work, and to make black ink.

The oak's bark is much in demand by tanners. It is rich in the tannin that transforms soft skins into leather. Long ago the bark's lining was soaked and then pounded to produce a thin material for ladies' garments. The padding of the bark provides cork for bottle stoppers,

life jackets, and buoys. Much of the furniture in country homes of the past was made of the oak's heavy, hard, firm wood. Of oak wood, too, are many of the beautiful old carvings in churches and mansions of bygone days. Generations ago rural people in America preferred it for well buckets, wash tubs, kegs, and barrels for containing liquids. Mindful of its strength and durability, early seagoing traders constructed their vessels of it, and Americans chose it for bridges, beams of barns, agricultural implements, wagons, fence posts, railroad ties, and mine props.

Even the sawdust of oak trees serves a purpose. Brown and yellow dyes are made from it. When combined with water and vinegar, it is excellent for cleaning bottles.

The oak is said to be struck by lightning more frequently than any other tree. Country folk, wise in the ways of Nature, never seek shelter from a storm under its branches.

Pecan

To the Indians the pecan tree represented the Great Spirit. They relished the nuts of wild pecan trees.

Hard, tough pecan wood goes into flooring, furniture, tool handles, and boxes and crates. It is used widely for smoking meat and provides a good fuel wood.

Persimmon Tree

Persimmons are a favorite food of wild creatures. They were enjoyed, either fresh or dried,

by southeastern Indians, who also ground them into meal for breadmaking. Not only a kind of beer but an indelible ink can be made from the fruit. Both bark and unripe fruit have been utilized in the treatment of fevers. The pioneers made a drink from persimmon seeds as a substitute for coffee. A very good tea can be made from the leaves, which have a high content of vitamin C.

The persimmon tree's hard wood is used in golf-club heads, rollers, and shuttles in textile mills.

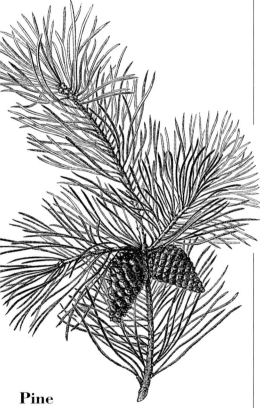

Pine

In the past the Scotch pine provided wood for strong ship masts. Its cones have been used to flavor wines.

Turpentine and its oil, yellow rosin, wood tar, and pitch are processed from the tree's juices.

During times of scarcity, country folks made a bread from the inner lining of the bark. The leaves of the tree, mixed with wool, became stuffing for mattresses.

The eastern white pine formerly served many purposes. Its even-textured, easily worked wood was used for covered bridges, barns, houses, furniture, coffins, and matches.

Indians were reported to have included the inner bark in their diet, and even today it is sometimes used in cough remedies.

The extensively used eastern white pine soon became scarce, and the western white pine took its place in building construction. It is used, too, in the manufacture of matches, crates, sashes, doors, frames, and foundry patterns.

Over the centuries, the seeds of the pinon pine were a staple food of southwestern Indians. The timber of the tree makes excellent fuel and charcoal. Its wood sometimes goes into mine timbers, poles, and posts.

The hard, resinous wood of the longleaf pine is widely used for boxes, crates, and poles. Its pulpwood is manufactured into cartons, bags, and wrapping paper. Turpentine and rosin are made from its sap.

The ponderosa pine's somewhat soft, even-grained wood is used chiefly for lumber but also for railroad ties, mine timbers, posts, poles, and veneer. Finer-quality ponderosa pine goes into cabinets, paneling, trim, doors, and sashes; inferior grades become boxes and crates.

Saplings of the lodge-pole pine provided the Indians with poles for their tepees or lodges-hence its name. Today its wood is used for railroad ties, mine timbers, poles and posts, pulpwood, and lumber.

Poplar

The down of black poplar seeds has been manufactured into cloth and paper, but neither has proved very satisfactory. Poplar bark is so light in weight that in water it is extremely buoyant. For that reason fishermen prefer strips of poplar bark to string for tying their nets. Because the wood does not ignite easily, it is chosen for flooring but shunned by campers as firewood.

When celebrating their independence from England, Americans planted poplars as symbols of freedom, calling them "liberty trees."

The white poplar acts as a sort of weather gauge. When the white undersides of its leaves are uplifted, a storm is in the offing. Its wood is used for toy-making, and at one time bakery ovens were heated with it because of its slow-burning quality.

The United States utilizes the soft wood of the balsam poplar as pulpwood for paper and to

make boxes and crates. From the fragrant resin of the tree's buds, an ointment and cough medicine are made. Indians pressed the aromatic wax from the buds and used it to waterproof the seams of their birch bark canoes.

Redbud

Legend has it that the Old World relative of the redbud was the tree from which Judas hanged himself after his betrayal of Jesus. The tree is said to have blushed with shame, and hence the pinkish-red hue of its flowers. The story was brought to America by colonists and applied to this country's species.

Some folks enjoy the young pods and flowers of the redbud tree as fritters. The acid flowers are used in pickles and salads.

The tree's inner bark furnishes an ingredient long used in cough medicine.

Redwood

Seeds of the mighty redwood are so delicate and minuscule that roughly eight thousand of them would not exceed an ounce in weight. The redwood tree was regarded as sacred by the Indians. It was called "sequoia" in honor of Sequoyah, the Cherokee Indian who developed an alphabet for his people.

The hard, strong timber of the sequoia is particularly resistant to both decay and harmful insects. It is useful for construction, siding,

doors, and sashes. The wood's long-lasting quality makes it ideal for outdoor furniture, silos, tanks, garden trellises, greenhouses, and fences. The bark is excellent for insulation purposes.

Rowan Tree

The rowan tree is often called the mountain ash, though it is no relation to the ash.

In olden times supernatural powers were associated with it.

If cattle were thought to be in danger of the evil eye, country people protected them by fastening rowan branches to cowsheds and stables. As an extra precaution, farmers drove their cows with a rowan stick. Crosses made from such wood were believed to ward off evil spirits.

A type of beer is made from the tree's astringent bright scarlet berries, and they are used for making jelly.

Long ago, slender branches of the rowan tree served as wood for archers' bows.

Saguaro

The saguaro is a giant tree cactus. Over the centuries, southwestern Indians have used the woody interior skeleton of this immense cactus as a framework for their homes.

Indian women dry the fruits of the saguaro and make preserves and syrups from it. The fruit is often eaten raw and is enjoyed by wild creatures as well as humans.

Birds excavate nesting places in the cactus. The exposed sap dries, forming a lacquer-like coating on the hole's interior. When the rest of the cactus falls to decay, this bowl-shaped vessel remains, to last for years. The Indians store the preserved fruit of the saguaro in it.

Today fences and rafters for ranch houses are often made from the woody skeleton of the saguaro.

Sassafras

Early colonists of North America had great faith in the healing powers of the sassafras tree. All parts of it have a spicy taste. A tea made from the roots' bark was used to reduce fever and treat dropsy and skin diseases.

The oil from sassafras roots is used for flavoring candies and medicines, for perfuming soap, and occasionally for making the glue on stamps.

Southerners thicken their soups with the dried and powdered sticky new leaves of the tree together with the pith from its smaller branches.

Many a country child, strolling home from school, has eaten sassafras buds or chewed on a bit of fragrant bark dug with a pocketknife from the tree's roots.

Rural folk find sassafras timber useful for their fence posts, because it does not rot easily in soil. In days gone by they made ox yokes and barrels from it.

Spruce

Eons ago gummy sap oozed from spruce trees and congealed into transparent stones which today we value as amber. Country people have brewed beer from tender sprouts of the spruce tree. Planks for flooring are made from its wood.

The easily worked, hard wood of the red spruce is used for papermaking, ladder rails, and general millwork. Parts of violins and the sounding boards of pianos are often made from it.

The black spruce brings cheer to many a home during the yuletide as a Christmas tree. Its wood goes into canoe paddles and oars, ladder rungs, boxes, and crates.

The white fibers of the wood require so little bleaching that they make excellent pulpwood.

North American Indians used the pliable roots of the white spruce to weave baskets and to lace their birch-bark canoes.

The state tree of Alaska is the Sitka spruce. Its timber goes into boats, ladders, doors, sashes, furniture, boxes, crates, and sounding boards for pianos. In our modern times, the chief wood used in aircraft construction has come from the Sitka spruce.

Sycamore

The sycamore is known as the button ball tree because of its fruit, which resembles small balls suspended on stems. The tree's life span is a long one, some sycamores reaching the age of five hundred years or more.

Their trunks are frequently hollow, providing havens for owls, dens for raccoons, and sometimes an abode for man. In the 1700s two men were reported to have lived in the wilderness for three years with the hollow trunk of an immense sycamore serving as their home.

The hard wood has an interlocking grain, making it difficult to split. It is excellent for butcher's blocks and is used for flooring, furniture, boxes, barrels, crates, and handles. Many a violin owes its existence to the wood of the sycamore. Berry boxes and baskets are made from its veneer.

Shagbark Hickory

The Indians made a sweet, milky liquor from the nuts of the shagbark hickory. The name "hickory" was derived from the Indian word for this drink.

In the old days, country folk gathered hickory nuts in the fall to put into candies and cakes. The bitter, astringent inner bark of the tree was used to treat indigestion and fevers. Its tough, strong wood went into the rims and spokes of wheels for buggies and wagons and was made into buggy shafts and whipple trees.

Today it is used for tool handles, ladder rungs, agricultural implements, furniture, and archer's bows. Hickory is considered the best wood for smoking meat.

Willow

Indians used the lining of willow bark to make fish nets and lines. In spring, pioneer farmers cut strong, supple willow stems to bind together fence rails; as they seasoned, the knotted willow wands hardened, lasting year after year.

In some parts of the world, the down from willow seeds was used to stuff mattresses and pillows. It was also made into paper.

One type of willow, the osier, has tough, flexible branches appropriate for basket-making. Centuries ago, boats were woven from slender osier branches and covered with animal skins. Warriors made light but sturdy shields in the same fashion. When firearms required black powder, the willow's high-grade charcoal was utilized.

The lightweight wood of the black willow goes into baskets, furniture, coffins, boxes, and crates. From its bitter bark medicines are made.

Yew

Because the leaves of the yew are poisonous, the tree is never planted in fields or along roadways where cattle might eat them.

Before the advent of the gun, bows were made from the yew tree. Today its strong, fine-grained wood is still used for archer's bows and for canoe paddles, posts, poles, cabinetwork, and inlaying.

State Trees

A good many of our states have adopted state trees. They are listed here:

- Balsam Poplar: Wyoming
- Blue Spruce: Colorado, Utah
- Cabbage Palmetto: South Carolina, Florida
- Douglas Fir: Oregon
- Eastern Hemlock: Pennsylvania
- Eastern Redbud: Oklahoma
- Eastern White Pine: Maine, Michigan, Wisconsin
- Elm: Massachusetts, North Dakota, Nebraska
- Flowering Dogwood: Missouri
- Live Oak: Georgia
- Longleaf Pine: Alabama
- Northern Red Oak: New Jersey
- Ohio Buckeye: Ohio
- Pecan: Texas
- Pinon Pine: New Mexico
- Ponderosa Pine: Montana
- Red Pine: Minnesota
- Shortleaf Pine: Arkansas
- Single-Leaf Pinon: Nevada
- Sitka Spruce: Alaska
- Southern Magnolia: Mississippi
- Sugar Maple: New York, Vermont, West Virginia
- Tulip Tree: Indiana, Kentucky, Tennessee
- Western White Pine: Idaho
- White Oak: Connecticut, Maryland

Tree Growth

In a period of ten years, trees grow approximately as follows:

Tree	Height (Feet)	Diameter
Birch	17	8 inches
Elm	17	8
Butternut	17	8
Black walnut	17	8
Chestnut	17	8
White ash	17	8
Larch	21	6½
Ash-leaf maple	17	5–6 feet
White maple	17	5–6
Yellow willow	29	1¼
White willow	33	1¼

Trees and the Signs

Farmers of a generation or two ago lived much closer to nature than we do and were aware, or more aware, of trees as indicators of the changing of the seasons. They gauged their planting activities by what the trees told them. Farmers trying to get an early crop of corn didn't want it to be ruined by a slight, late frost. Seth Mowery of Ohio says he planted his entire corn crop by what he read from the hickory buds. Hickory trees have a habit of developing buds slowly no matter how enticing the weather of early spring. They are not often fooled, according to Seth, when nature "runs a little dab of winter back on us." For generations the saying has been: "Plant your corn when the hickory buds are as big as a crow's beak." (Most farmers know about crows, and the size of a crow's beak, since they have chased enough of the pesky rascals out of their fields.) The farmers who have patiently waited for the hickory buds to reach about one inch in length, give or take a little, usually will be the ones with the best and earliest crop.

T. P. Clements used to say "it's corn plantin' time when oak leaves are the size of a nickel and the zodiac signs are in the feet, that makes the stalk take a firm grip in the ground."

Cutting Timber by the Moon

The phase of the moon, if waxing or waning, is considered to be of great importance in the felling of timber. This moon sign goes back to the days of Caesar. In those days the very best time to fell trees was when the moon was in conjunction with the sun. The name of this day is "interlinium," sometimes referred to as the "moon's silence."

Cato in *De Re Rustica* instructs on the cutting of timber as follows: "When you root up the elm, the pine, the nut tree, or indeed any other kind of tree, mind and do so when the moon is on the wane, after midday, and when there is no south wind blowing. The proper time for cutting a tree is when the seed is ripe, but be careful not to draw it away or plane it when the dew is falling. Never touch the timber except when the moon is on the change, or else at the end of the second quarter; at these periods you may either root up the tree or fell it as it stands. The next seven days after the full moon are the best of all for grubbing up a tree. Be particularly careful not to rough-hew timber, or indeed, to cut or touch it unless it is perfectly dry; and by no means while it is covered with frost or dew."

Many old-time woodsmen of this country have believed in cutting timber only during the waning of the moon. The belief is that as the moon waned the sap in the timber decreased or moved downward. The wood was then dryer and much easier to cut. They believe the moon has an effect on trees in much the same way as it affects the seas and oceans.

Early-day carpenters would not use wood that had been cut during the waxing moon, saying the wood was full of moisture and would warp, shrink, and was generally unsuitable for construction purposes. Across the country the

general rules for cutting timber or wood to give it the greatest durability are:

Cut chestnut, oak, and other hard woods in the month of August, before noon, after the full moon in the waning quarters.

Cut pine, maple, and white woods in August, before noon, between the new moon and the full moon phases, in the sign of Virgo.

Grafting and Pruning by the Signs

Claude Johnson of Arkansas grafted and budded trees to obtain better varieties of fruit. When he did this work he always used an increasing moon in a fruitful sign. He cut his grafts from good bearing, "never shy" trees during the time the trees were dormant, usually from December through February. The cuttings would be kept in a cool, dark place, preferably with some humidity. He did not want the cuttings to get too dry or too damp while waiting for the right time to make the graft. Grafting would be done just before the sap began to flow. It was always done while the moon was from new to full between the first and second quarters. He would choose, if possible, to do the full job during these increasing phases when the moon was in Cancer—the most fruitful, movable, watery, and feminine of signs. The next best signs were Scorpio, which was a highly rated second, Pisces, for its fruitfulness and good rooting

characteristics, and Capricorn, for its productive and earthy nature.

To produce better fruit he would carefully prune his trees. By controlling limb growth in this way he could divert the sap to the primary branches of the tree instead of allowing it to dissipate into greatly spreading and unnecessary branches. The time chosen for this farm chore was usually, but not always, during the trees' dormant months while the sap was down. His pruning was always done during *fruitful* signs in a *decreasing* moon phase, usually the fourth quarter.

Ways with Wood

Curing and Splitting Wood

To cure wood for planking, proceed in this way: Melt paraffin in a double boiler, and paint all the logs on their cut ends with the melted paraffin. Then stack them off the ground on skids. Cover the wood with a tarpaulin, and leave it to season for one year.

After curing, logs may be transported to a sawmill for cutting into planks. The boards must be stored in a dark, dry place. Stack them flat, with strips of wood between them to permit air circulation.

Splitting hardwoods for firewood is particularly difficult.

To make the task easier, cut logs to the desired length and stand them on end for five or six months. Then, when set on their opposite ends, they can be split readily, especially if you cut from the sides instead of in the center.

A precision-sharpened ax blade is a boon when cutting wood. One that has been too thinly sharpened may break; a too-thick blade tends to glance off the wood. Make an ax-bit gauge for keeping the original profile of a new blade. First, take a piece of sheet metal and place the ax head upright on it. Then draw around the cutting half of the head. Using sheet-metal scissors, cut along the inside of the outline. Work slowly and carefully to achieve an accurate gauge. With a file or sandpaper, smooth any rough edges.

Insert the blade in the slot. If it fits smoothly, neither loosely nor too snugly, your gauge is precise.

Label each ax and its gauge with a matching number.

When grinding or honing an ax blade, use the appropriate gauge to help you maintain its correct cutting profile.

Making a Lasting Fire

To build a fire of low blaze that burns with steady heat and does not require constant attention, start with a bed of ashes reaching several inches above the andiron legs. Place a good-sized log, about 10 inches in diameter, against the back wall of the fireplace. Balance a smaller log on top of it. Now place a log just behind and against the andirons. The front and rear logs must be sufficiently bedded down in ashes to keep draft and flames from getting under them. Only their tops and faces should burn. Put paper and dry kindling wood in the center of the fireplace and light them. Gradually the logs at front and back will burn through. Move them to the middle of the fire and substitute new logs, well-embedded in ashes.

A fire constructed in this manner will use a minimum of wood. They will also have red-hot coals that can be covered over with ashes from the sides of the fireplace and will last through the night, even well into the following day. Uncover them and the fire can be rekindled. In country homes of old, fire and heat were maintained day after day in this way.

Furniture
Lamp Table

Large cable reels can be converted into lamp tables with little effort or expense. Ask utilities companies for one of these empty spools; they come in different sizes and are cost-free.

Buy a cheap floor lamp at a rummage sale or secondhand store, find a round piece of plywood in a scrap pile at a construction site, and purchase some paint.

Disassemble the reel and put aside the hardware. Then sand the spool and paint or stain it to suit your taste, making the plywood and lamp parts the same color.

Reassemble the reel. Cut the center of the circular plywood to fit the circumference of the lamp shaft. Insert the lamp pole in the middle of the plywood top and the spool.

Utilize the bottom shelf as a circular bookcase.

Rustic Patio and Garden Furniture

For making rustic wooden furniture, select a hardwood. Oak is preferable, but any hardwood, such as beech or chestnut, will do. Thick branches about three inches in diameter are required for the main structure. Branches of this size, unwanted by orchardists, farmers, foresters, and lumber dealers, are generally consigned to the flames. So you may get your material simply for the asking or for a nominal fee. Inquire at orchards during spring pruning time. Consult the forest supervisor of a national forest. He is authorized to give away wood intended for private use. Or, if you live near a state forest, contact the state forester's office. Check in areas where land is being cleared for farming or building purposes.

In general, try to procure straight branches; however, irregularly shaped branches or roots can often be utilized interestingly in rustic furniture. Cut away all growths, twigs, and small branches from the main branch. Decide whether you want to retain or remove the bark on the poles. If you strip the bark, allow the timber to season for some weeks before staining and polishing it. Watch for areas of unusual grain in the wood, and plan a piece of furniture so as to set it off to advantage.

The easiest way to join the poles is by nailing them together with wrought-iron nails or flathead nails. While hammering, support the pieces from behind to facilitate nailing. A firm and attractive joining can be achieved by first shaping a smooth, concave area at the end of a horizontal pole to fit partially around the convex curve of the vertical pole to which it will be nailed. Use a wood chopper or ax to carve the concave curve. Always set nails deeply enough to avoid snagging your clothing.

When you connect sections of the furniture where stress will occur—for example, the seat support to the legs—use a stronger means of joining. Cut an opening in the vertical piece of timber, and insert, glue, and nail the end of the horizontal piece. A chair seat or table top can be constructed by lashing together the required number of poles (as in raft-making), which can be nailed together or to a back support.

For the most effective results, design your rustic furniture simply.

Making Pine Tar and Cough Remedies
Pine Tar: Wood Source and Extraction

Pine tar is contained in many cold remedies. Here is how to obtain this ingredient.

First, locate some yellow heart pine. Look for this greasy-looking, lemon-colored wood in damp places.

Cut it into slender, short pieces. Put them in a cast-iron pot, such as a Dutch oven. Wedge the wood splinters snugly into the pot so that they will remain in place when the vessel is inverted.

Take a flat board, larger than the iron pot, and scoop grooves in it with a knife. Make sure that the grooves are cut deeply enough to carry the flow of heavy tar. Lay one end of the board on a high enough pile of bricks or rocks to provide a slant after propping the other end with a container to catch the tar.

Invert the pot on the high end of the board, and cover it with a thick layer of clay. The clay will prevent the wood splinters from getting excessively hot and starting to burn. On the clay-covered pot, start a fire. In about ½ hour the wood should be hot enough to release tar. At first a watery, yellowish fluid will run along the grooves, but eventually it will become sticky and thick.

A Dutch oven packed with wood splinters should yield about three cups of pine tar. Scrape the thick syrup from the container and store it in jars.

Cough Remedies: Cough Syrup and Candy

- *Pine Tar Cough Syrup:* For a single dose of cough medicine, mix ½ teaspoon of pine tar with 3 teaspoons of honey. Blend thoroughly.
- *Red Clover Cough Medicine:* Cough medicine can be made from red clover, which grows almost everywhere. Gather 1 cup of red clover blossoms. Put them in an earthenware crock, and add 2 cups of boiling water. Cover the crock. Allow the contents to steep until cool. Strain. Mix 1 tablespoon of honey with the liquid. To check the cough of a cold, take 1 teaspoonful.

- *Pine Tar Cough Candy:* Add 3 cups of water to 5 pounds of sugar. Boil to the hard snap. Spread in another container. As it is cooling, add the following ingredients: 5 drops of pine tar (made by dissolving 1½ teaspoons of tar in 1 tablespoon of alcohol); 1½ teaspoons of oil of capsicum; and 1¾ teaspoons of oil of wintergreen. Work the mixture together with your hands until all substances are thoroughly blended. Keep the mass warm— near a fire—as you proceed. Roll the cough candy into round sticks, and continue rolling them until they are cold.

- *Horehound Candy:* Boil the downy, white leaves of the hoarhound plant in a small amount of water until juice is extracted. Strain it through cheesecloth. Depending upon the quantity of cough candy you desire, boil an amount of sugar in barely enough water to dissolve it. Blend in the juice. Using a spoon, work the sugar against the sides of the saucepan until it reaches a creamy, thick consistency. Pour into a buttered pan. When almost cool, it should be marked into squares and allowed to dry. (Or you can boil the sugar until candied, and then stir in dry, powdered hoarhound.) Put it in buttered tins to cool.

Sap Gathering and Sugar Making

Drown those golden pancakes in syrup of your own making.

Sap-gathering time ranges from mid-February to April (depending on where you live). It generally commences after the first good thaw. The most favorable days are sunny and warm, preceded by a frosty night. Preferred sap comes from sugar maples, but most maples produce sugar sap.

Fashioning a Spigot

Make a spigot for tapping trees from an elderberry stem. (Hollowed-out sticks of sumac and willow or stalks of bamboo and mullein can also be used as spouts.) Cut a piece about 5 or 6 inches in length. Push out the soft, pithy center with red-hot wire from a heated coat hanger. Sharpen one end of the stem to facilitate its insertion in the tree hole.

On the sunny side of a maple tree, bore a hole three feet from the ground using a brace and $^7/_{16}$-inch bit. The hole should be about 3 inches deep and slant upward. After inserting the spigot, hammer in a nail above the spout for hanging the bucket. Make covers for the sap pails from tin or wood to protect the contents from rain, snow, dust, twigs, and insects.

Tapping Trees

You will need about 20 gallons of sap to make ½ gallon of syrup. One tapping of a tree that is no less than 12 inches in diameter will produce roughly 20 gallons of sap. Bore no more than one tap hole in a 12-inch trunk. An 18-inch tree will yield enough sap for two tap holes, a 24-inch tree enough for three buckets, and so on.

Making Maple Syrup

Collect the sap as soon as several gallons have flowed into the pails, for the juice will spoil if

allowed to stand too long. To make syrup, boil down the sap. When white scum appears on the surface, scoop it out with a fine-meshed strainer. Although this step is not absolutely necessary, it will result in a cleaner product. Check continually to prevent the syrup's boiling over or scorching. If the foam starts to rise, add a little fresh sap and the contents will subside. Old-timers used to remedy the situation by tying a chunk of fat to one end of a stick and drawing it over the bubbles.

Watch for the liquid to attain the desired consistency. A candy thermometer will help you determine

this. At the moment the sap starts to boil, read the temperature; when it increases by 70, the proper sugar consistency has developed. The seething liquid generally becomes syrup at 219° F.

Fasten a double thickness of clean dishtoweling over the top of a bucket with clothespins. As you draw off the syrup, strain it through the cloth to remove impurities. You can also clarify it by letting it settle.

The syrup must be bottled or canned while hot to preserve its flavor. Store it in a cool place.

If you boil sap in the kitchen, be sure to have a fan above the stove to help eliminate the clouds of steam. You may find it more convenient to work outdoors with a large vessel—a big iron kettle or metal tub—set over a wood fire.

Making Maple Sugar

Making maple sugar entails further evaporation. If you allow the kettle's contents to reach 242° F, the result will be hard cake sugar. A temperature of 237° F will result in a softer sugar.

To test for the hard sugar stage, let the syrup drip from the ladle. When it forms a fine thread, take the syrup from the fire. Permit it to cool for several minutes, and then stir it. The stirring will insure sugar of a finer grain. The syrup will begin to crystallize suddenly. Pour the mass into lightly greased molds and let stand. Muffin tins can serve as molds, if need be.

Maple Syrup Pie

½ cup boiling water
1 cup maple syrup
3 tablespoons cornstarch
3 tablespoons cold water
1 tablespoon butter
chopped nuts

Put the water and maple syrup in a saucepan; boil for five minutes. Mix the cornstarch and cold water. Use it as thickening for the boiling syrup. Stir in the butter.

Pour the mixture into a pastry-lined pie plate. Sprinkle the chopped nuts over it. Cover with pastry. Bake in a 400° F oven for thirty minutes or until the crust is golden brown.

Maple Sugar Cough Remedy

Roast a lemon; be careful not to burn it. Slice it in two, and squeeze out the juice. Thoroughly blend in 3 tablespoons of powdered maple sugar. Take 1 teaspoonful to alleviate a cough due to a cold.

5 | FLOWERS, HERBS, AND SHRUBS

Flowering plants do more than brighten our world with their myriad hues and diversify the landscape with an infinite variety of silhouettes and textures. Through countless generations of experiments and accidental experiences, man has discovered the special properties of each plant and its specific value in his life. Plants have been used as food, drink, and flavoring, as perfume, cosmetics, and dyes, and in medicine, religion, and myths to account for earthly life. This relationship with plants that share our environment multiplies our appreciation of the interlocking associations among all of God's creations.

Hundreds of years ago herb gathering was an essential pursuit in life. Herbs were the chief source of dyes (chemical dyes were not developed until the mid-1800s), cosmetics, and medications. Medicinal herbs and the medicines obtained therefrom were called "simples," because each plant was believed to possess its individual virtue and so to embody a simple remedy. The herbalist who collected simples was known as a "simpler," or "simplist."

People of those times believed that effective medicine must have an offensive smell and bitter taste. Often medicinal plants were chosen at first because of their rank odor and found later actually to contain tonic properties—horehound being one such plant.

For the relief of headaches, aromatic flowers were held to temples and forehead. Some were applied to wounds to hasten their healing. Bay leaves in bath water were found to have a soothing effect on sore and aching bodies. Powdered leaves of alehoof, chamomile, peppermint, sneezewort, sweet flag, thyme, and woodruff were used as snuff to cure head colds and relieve depression. As

protection against disease, people fumigated their houses with many kinds of fragrant substances, such as aloes, rosemary, sage, angelica, cinnamon, and thyme. Rue was particularly popular because it repelled fleas, considered bearers of the plague. The powdered seeds of love-in-a-mist were sprinkled in the hair, their scent being loathsome to lice. Sufferers from insomnia slept on pillows stuffed with hops; besides exuding a pleasant scent, the hops exerted a gently narcotic influence, inducing sleep.

Strongly aromatic leaves and resins are said to possess antibiotic properties. Plants produce aromatic substances, known as essential oils, which are their waste products. As a general rule, oils taken from the leaves have stronger antiseptic powers than those extracted from the petals. So potent is the antiseptic quality of the oil from thyme leaves that in the past it was applied to soldiers' uniforms to protect them from vermin. Doctors customarily carried aromatics at the upper tips of their walking sticks, which they frequently raised to their noses as discreetly as possible when tending the sick.

The odor of herbs and flowers was used to combat odors of a less pleasant variety. Known as "strewing herbs," such plants as thyme, sage, chamomile, basil, lavender, and hyssop were scattered on the floors of churches and other places where people,

usually unbathed, congregated in large numbers. In courts of law, judges were presented with aromatic flowers to counteract the offensive odors of unwashed prisoners. Potpourris were an old-fashioned way of scenting musty houses. Mixtures of rose petals, lavender, rosemary, thyme, cloves, and dried, powdered orange peel were placed in potpourri jars of china or wood, holes in their lids releasing the aroma. A properly made potpourri was said to maintain its perfume for fifty years or more. Housewives used lavender and peppermint to freshen bedrooms with fragrance as well as to cool them in summer. Aromatic foliage is actually capable of lowering air temperature; as the essential oils in the leaves oxidize, an invisible haze forms that impedes heat rays.

The emotional response to floral fragrance influenced a good part of folk medicine, flower healing, and herbalism. Certain flower scents (for example, white jasmine) were alleged to produce sensual effects, some to evoke changes in temperament (sweet basil being used to incite feelings of good cheer), and others (for instance, withering strawberry leaves) to engender an exhilarating atmosphere conducive to creative work.

Early perfume consisted of the dried parts of aromatic plants, among them cinnamon, iris, sweet marjoram, myrrh, saffron, spikenard, sweet flag, carnation, narcissus, rose, lotus, lily, and dill. Perfumed powders were sprinkled in bedding to be absorbed by the skin during sleep. Saffron was spread on floors, the aroma being released as it was trodden upon. Dried crocus petals and the leaves of agrimony and woodruff provided fragrant stuffing for pillows and cushions.

The distillation of flowers and leaves for perfume began at the start of the seventeenth century. Sweet waters were concocted from balm, marigold, sage, tansy, lavender, and rosemary. They were used for personal cleanliness, medicine, and cooking.

The most fragrant flowers are white. In general, with the increase of pigment in the petals, perfume lessens. Experience taught that the most favorable time to gather flower petals was just before the morning sun rose to evaporate their oils.

The floral kingdom provides some four thousand aromatic substances for perfumery. To deter the too-rapid evaporation of the scent of perfume, a fixative assumes this role formerly fulfilled by the planes resin or wax. From earliest times animal secretions were considered the best fixatives. Castor from the beaver, musk from the musk deer, the civet of the civet cat, and ambergris from the intestines of a species of whale were valued as perfume fixatives. However, plant resins and sweet gums were used

too, such as the oils of sandalwood and cedarwood.

Early settlers of America were concerned with the basic necessities for sustaining life. Perfume was frowned upon as frivolous. Indeed, young women discovered using scent to entice a member of the opposite sex were liable to dunking, according to the law.

Colonists used the wax enclosing berries of the wax myrtle shrub to make their candles. By continually rubbing furniture with balm, the herb melissa, they gave it both scent and luster. To impart sheen and pleasant aroma to oaken floors, they polished them with the seeds of sweet fern. The calycanthus

shrub of the Carolinas was found to have flowers redolent of apple scent, bark with the odor of cinnamon, and roots that smelled like camphor. Colonists used the bark as a substitute for cinnamon and fumigated their houses by burning the dried roots.

The following are some of the flowers, herbs, and shrubs that have served man in a variety of ways through the centuries. You will notice that among them are plant names ending in 'wort, such as "sticklewort." Wort is a word from the Old English meaning "root," "herb," or "plant."

Agrimony (Sticklewort)

Because the fruits of agrimony possess tiny hooks which serve in seed dispersal as they catch in the fur of passing animals, the plant is known also as sticklewort.

Colonists brought it to North America for medicinal purposes. They used it to doctor snake bite. Lemonade containing its flowers was a standard remedy for colds.

Early country folk made a tea of agrimony leaves to treat sore throats, kidney and bladder trouble, and disorders of the liver. The wounds of humans and animals were ministered to with the leaves boiled in wine. The seeds were used in salves and balms and in wine as a cure for dysentery.

A yellow or gold dye can be made from the agrimony's yellow flowers.

Alkanet

Alkanet was brought to North America by some of the first settlers for use in medicine and as a dye.

Medicinally it was employed to treat rheumatism and kidney problems and to induce perspiring in cases of fever.

Sap from the roots of the plant yields a red coloring used to dye paper and cloth. Cosmetically it served as a rouge for the cheeks.

Balm (Melissa)

Balm is a favorite plant of bees.

In the past, a drink distilled from the flowers and leaves was used to alter human temperament in cases of depression, mania, and lethargy and to treat apoplexy and epilepsy. It was also regarded as an elixir of youth.

Barberry

A first fruit carried to the New World by early colonists was the barberry. They used it for medicine as well as food. It was a remedy for indigestion, dropsy, jaundice, and rheumatism. Fevers were reduced with a tea made from the red berries, which were also made into jelly.

All parts of the plant yield a yellow dye for coloring cloth and staining wood. It imparts a tawny gloss to leather when used as polish.

Basil

Basil originated in India, where it figures in religion. Long ago the plant was regarded as sacred, and offerings of flowers and rice were made to it. People believed it was a guardian spirit.

According to prevailing superstition, a pounded twig of basil placed under a stone would become a scorpion. Strangely enough, the herb was considered an antidote to the sting of a scorpion.

Early settlers, noting basil's tranquilizing properties, employed it as a cure for epilepsy, nervousness, insomnia, vertigo, migraine, and stomach disorders. Folk medicine advocates the putting of several drops of juice from the leaves into an inflamed ear.

Bilberry (Blueberry)

Bilberries are excellent for making brandy, jam, and pies.

Country people value them as a treatment for bladder inflammation, diarrhea, and skin diseases. They are also reputed to improve night vision.

Bilberries yield a dye which colors cloth in shades ranging from pink to purple.

Blackberry

The blackberry bush is sometimes referred to as the "mother of the oak" because new trees sprout best beneath its sheltering branches.

While gathering blackberries for jam and syrup, country people learned that the crushed leaves would quickly stop bleeding from thorn scratches. An excellent tea can be brewed from the dried leaves. Long ago blackberries were believed to be a cure for loose teeth and protruding eyes. Considered beneficial to mucous membranes, they are employed as a mouthwash and gargle for sore throats.

A dye for coloring fabric a pale gray can be extracted from the berries.

Black Currant

In the past, black currants were regarded as a veritable elixir of life. People supposed that frequent partaking of them would preserve youthfulness and ensure longevity. They were used as a remedy for dropsy, diarrhea, bladder and kidney ailments, inflammation of the stomach, and chronic fatigue.

Their juice dyes cloth in hues of deep lilac to purple.

Bloodroot

North American Indians extracted a dye from the orange-red juice of bloodroot to color porcupine quills. Finding it so quick to stain whatever it encounters, they employed it as war paint.

An old-fashioned country cure for children's head colds was a lump of sugar saturated with the juice of bloodroot.

Bouncing Bet (Soapwort)

Early settlers brought bouncing Bet from Europe as much for a domestic convenience as for a garden bloom. Its bruised leaves, stems, and roots make a lather for washing delicate fabrics and cleaning woolens just before dyeing. Because of these cleansing properties, it is known too as soapwort. Ladies particularly favored it for shampooing hair and for laundering dainty undergarments. For this reason it acquired the name "my lady's washbowl."

A decoction of the plant's leaves is said to be a good remedy for itch. Long ago it was prescribed for ulcers, leprosy, and venereal disease.

Broom (Genista)

As its name implies, the broom shrub provides material for broomsticks. In medieval times witches were reputed to ride such brooms. Paradoxically, the plant was believed to keep witches away. Its branches have furnished firewood for baker's ovens and potter's kilns and material for constructing huts. Yarn and strong rope can be made from the bark.

Medicinally it has been used as an antivenom, a heart tonic, and a diuretic and in the treatment of rheumatism and malarial fever. Country people drink wine containing ashes of the broom shrub to cure dropsy.

The plant gives a good yellow dye.

Buckthorn

The stems of the buckthorn, being flexible, are used to advantage in making wicker furniture.

During colonial times housewives brewed tea with its leaves, thus avoiding England's tea tax. A drink made from the plant is said to alleviate constipation and the berry juice, used in compresses, to ameliorate skin problems.

Burdock (Beggar's Buttons)

Burdock serves as both food and medicine. Its young, tender leaves are a tasty addition to salads; the roots are palatable when boiled and buttered; and the stalks, stripped of their skin, provide a food reminiscent of asparagus. Sometimes the nutritious stalks are candied.

The plant has been used medicinally to treat the following ills: skin afflictions, arthritis, colds, falling hair, measles, respiratory ailments, and rheumatism. It has been used as a diuretic and laxative.

Country children fashion baskets and chains out of the flowering burrs.

Calamus (Sweet Flag)

In times past calamus was regarded as a medicinal plant. Chewing its roots was a remedy for stomach disorders and a means of sweetening the breath.

Over the years country lads have enjoyed munching on the hot, sweet roots of calamus, or sweet flag.

Chamomile (Mayweed)

An aromatic but bitter tea brewed from chamomile flowers has been taken over the years as a blood purifier and tonic. Chamomile has been employed as a home remedy to treat skin infections, inflamed eyelids, rheumatic pains, fever, indigestion, and insomnia. Used as

a shampoo, it enhances blond hair with golden highlights.

The scent of chamomile flowers is said to discourage bees from stinging collectors of honey.

Centaury

Herbalists sought the centaury for its tonic properties. Internally it was used to fight contagious disease, cure jaundice, lower fevers, and kill worms. Externally it was employed to treat ulcers and wounds and to stop the falling of hair.

Chicory

Chicory came to North America from Europe. It makes excellent hay, said to be superior to alfalfa.

The dried roots often serve as a coffee substitute or an additive. Tender new plant shoots can be used in salads.

Medicinally chicory is said to purify the blood, stimulate the appetite, and cure anemia, indigestion, arthritis, dropsy, liver problems, and constipation. A massage with alcohol containing chicory root is advocated as a treatment to check the withering of paralyzed limbs.

Climbing Ivy

The climbing ivy was at one time considered a preventive against inebriation. With that thought in mind, craftsmen carved goblets of the ivy's wood from which to sip wine.

A drink of ivy berries steeped in wine was prescribed to ward off the plague. Country folk have used the berries as a purgative. Poultices of crushed ivy leaves were placed on sores and wounds to hasten healing. It was said that injured animals in the woodland rolled amid ivy to cure their wounds. Country mothers fashioned caps of ivy for babies whose heads were afflicted with impetigo. A tea made from the leaves was a remedy for inflamed mucous membranes, bronchitis, whooping cough, rheumatic pains, and neuralgia. Ivy juice rubbed on temples and forehead was recommended to relieve headaches.

Comfrey

For centuries comfrey has been employed as an aid in healing wounds and mending broken bones. In compress form it is used to relieve the pain of burns, sprains, gout, and phlebitis.

Crane's-Bill

Country people have used crane's-bill to treat a great many ills: tonsillitis, diabetes, gastric ulcers, diarrhea, cancer, and bone fractures. It was given to nursing mothers to help them retain milk. A compress of crane's-bill was applied to skin irritations and inflamed eyes. Country dwellers crush the leaves to drive away mosquitoes with their odor.

Daisy

In former times daisy leaves were cooked as a vegetable or served in salads. Rural folk make a tea from the whole daisy plant, including its flowers; taken every spring, it is considered a tonic for cleansing the blood of impurities accumulated during the winter months. A decoction of the leaves and flowers is used as a home remedy for pains of rheumatism, respiratory troubles, general stiffness, and skin ailments.

Dandelion

The dandelion provides both food and drink. Its leaves furnish palatable table greens, and wine can be made from the plant.

The white sap is used as a treatment for eye afflictions,

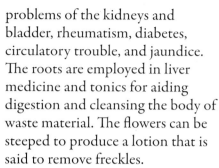

problems of the kidneys and bladder, rheumatism, diabetes, circulatory trouble, and jaundice. The roots are employed in liver medicine and tonics for aiding digestion and cleansing the body of waste material. The flowers can be steeped to produce a lotion that is said to remove freckles.

Long ago it was believed that if the white sap was rubbed on the entire body, all of one's desires would be granted. Country maids wistfully figure the number of years until their marriage by counting the breaths needed to blow away the dandelion down. Children puff on the fluffy balls to tell the time of day.

The vireo chooses the down of the dandelion to cushion the interior of its nest.

Elecampane

The mucilaginous roots of elecampane are sometimes made into sweetmeats and for centuries have been employed as horse medicine. The plant has been used as a home remedy to treat respiratory ailments, kidney and bladder problems, and indigestion. Elecampane wine was taken as a cough syrup, diuretic, and tonic.

Eyebright

The small herb eyebright blossoms but once, on a sunny day. Country people believed that the linnet used it to improve its eyesight.

As a rural remedy it was recommended for conjunctivitis,

watering eyes, and poor vision. It was also a treatment for head colds, coughs, and indigestion.

Fennel

Fennel has been used for centuries in preparing food. Wet nurses partook of it to maintain milk production. It was prescribed as an antidote for scorpion stings and snake bite and as a treatment for failing eyesight.

A great deal of superstition was associated with the herb. Hanging twigs of fennel from the rafters was supposed to force harmful spirits from the house; a few seeds placed in the keyhole would prevent ghosts from entering.

In rural areas fennel has been employed as a home remedy for the

following conditions: kidney and gall bladder disorders, anemia, weakness, bronchitis, poor appetite, headaches, indigestion, and eye problems.

Goldenrod

Medicinally, goldenrod has been used to treat skin diseases, arthritis, rheumatism, and dropsy and to stimulate the liver and kidneys.

A pigment extracted from the plant dyes cloth in shades of lemon yellow to warm gold.

Greater Celandine (Swallowwort)

According to an old legend, swallows brush the eyes of their young with a twig of greater celandine, or swallowwort, to protect them from blindness. The name celandine comes from the Greek word for "swallow," because the plant first appears when that bird arrives and fades when it departs.

The yellow-flowered herb was believed to have supernatural powers. Wearing a sprig in the shoes was supposed to cure yellow jaundice. Carrying celandine on the person, along with a mole's heart, would ensure a favorable outcome in lawsuits. People believed that the plant sang when an ailing man was on the verge of death; if he was destined to get well, it would weep. Various illnesses were treated with the plant: blindness, cancer, dropsy, and plague.

Ground Ivy

During long sea voyages of the past, leaves of the ground ivy were put in beer as a preservative.

When cockfighting was legal and popular, the owner of a bird with an eye injury would chew several ivy leaves and spit the juice into its eye to promote healing. The plant in lotion or compress form is used to treat sores and wounds. Sniffing ivy juice into the nostrils is said to relieve migraine and long-lasting headaches. Several drops of ivy oil in an aching ear are supposed to check pain.

Used as a dye, ground ivy produces colors of yellow-green or greenish gray.

Hawkweed

Long ago, people believed that birds of prey fed on hawkweed to make their eyesight keen; hence its name.

The plant is said to be an efficacious treatment for infectious abortions among cattle and for undulant fever in humans. It has been used as a remedy for various other ills: dropsy, jaundice, hardening of the arteries, fevers, gall bladder ailments, and kidney disorders.

Hollyhock

The hollyhock originated in China and the Mediterranean area and was introduced to Europe in the sixteenth century, thence to North America.

A drink made from the hollyhock was advocated as a remedy for bronchitis and coughs and as a mouthwash for ulcers of the mouth. A lotion concocted from the plant was prescribed for facial blotches and general redness. Wine was tinted with its dark purple flowers.

Honeysuckle

For hundreds of years honeysuckle was used in treating wounds. A tea made from the leaves is an old country cure for constipation, kidney stones, and coughs. A drink concocted from its bark and roots has been used as a tonic and remedy for liver disorders and gout.

Hop

In ancient times the yellow powder found on the female flowers of the hop vine was used in treating ulcers and tumors of the liver and spleen. It was also prescribed in cases of depression. Today it is used as a tonic, diuretic, sedative, and aid to digestion.

Brewers employ it to give aroma and flavor to beer. Because of the sedative properties of the female flowers' dried ripe cones, pillows stuffed with them benefit those suffering from insomnia and nervousness.

Horsetail (Mare's-Tail)

Horsetail is a plant of very ancient lineage. Over the eons it created deep layers of coal.

The ancients valued it as a general tonic. It has been prescribed for anemia, tuberculosis, kidney complaints, skin disorders, and weak fingernails. A tincture made from horsetail is said to remedy perspiring feet. Because a high percentage of silica and other minerals are stored in the plant, it is considered a strong remineralizing substance when taken internally.

The tender shoots of horsetail make good salad greens.

Country housewives scour vessels of wood, brass, and pewter with the plant. Furniture makers have used it for polishing wood.

Horsetail furnishes a yellow-greenish dye.

Knotgrass

An old superstition once prevailed that the juice of knotgrass would

stunt the growth of young farm animals and children.

For the ancients the plant was a cure for the spitting of blood. Rural folk have long used its stems as a home remedy for diarrhea. In veterinary medicine knotgrass has been similarly used to treat farm animals. A decoction of the plant is said to alleviate gout, skin diseases, varicose veins, and arthritis. It has also been employed as a tonic for those suffering from tuberculosis. The plant's juice, rich in tannin and silicic acid, is reported to stop nosebleed when squirted into the nostrils and to staunch the flow of blood from wounds.

A blue dye can be extracted from the knotgrass leaves.

Lady's Bedstraw (Cheese Rennet)

The scent of lady's bedstraw has been likened to that of honey or lime blossoms. In times past the plant afforded a pleasant stuffing for mattresses and so acquired its descriptive name. It is frequently called "cheese rennet" because its flowers were once used as a substitute for rennet to curdle milk during cheese making.

Formerly the plant was prescribed as a cure for epilepsy. It is used in treating dropsy, obesity, skin ailments, and illnesses of nervous origin. A lotion from the boiled stems is recommended for soothing sunburn and removing freckles.

A drink can be made from bedstraw seeds that is an excellent alternative to coffee. The plant has been used to fashion crude sieves for straining milk. At one time Scotsmen colored their tartans with the roots' red dye.

Lavender

For countless years lavender has been used as perfume, sedative, tonic, disinfectant, and healer of wounds.

Ladies of long ago scented their bath water with lavender, and closets and chests were perfumed with sachets of it.

A tea brewed from the plant's blue flowers had sedative properties and was taken in cases of migraine and indigestion. It was also used to treat asthma, bronchitis, whooping cough, and chills. A tincture of lavender applied as a lotion was said to strengthen hair. It was employed as a compress for bruises and as a massage for rheumatic pain.

Oil of lavender was smeared on bedsteads to discourage bedbugs and rubbed into children's hair to destroy lice and their nits.

It was utilized to further the healing of burns and wounds.

When hunting hounds became victims of snake bite, the punctures were quickly treated with crushed lavender leaves. Lavender oil is felt to be a strong antiseptic and neutralizing agent of poison.

Lesser Celandine (Figwort)

An irritating element contained in lesser celandine was once used by country people to poison rats. Beggars used the substance to intentionally create sores as a means of gaining sympathy and alms. In olden times doctors prescribed it for wens and hemorrhoids.

Lily of the Valley

From spring through summer the leaves of lily of the valley yield a yellow dye; in the fall when they turn yellow, the dye extracted is of a bronze-gold hue.

A tea made from the flowers was a standard country remedy for a weak heart. The dried flowers in powdered form, used like snuff, are supposed to ease a prolonged headache.

Madonna Lily

At one time an antiseptic was produced from petals of the madonna lily as an aid in healing burns and sores. The boiled bulb of the plant was made into poultices for chapped skin, abscesses, and carbuncles. The uncooked bulb, when mashed, is said to rid the feet of corns. Lily water is supposed to remove blotches from facial skin.

Marsh Mallow

The ancients esteemed the marsh mallow for its medicinal properties. Every part of this mucilaginous plant was used. The roots were made into a salve for softening the skin. In the days when people endured trial by red-hot iron, the sap combined with egg white and the seeds of the plantain was rubbed in the hands as a protective unguent, enabling the accused to better bear the pain and prove his innocence, because the burns would not be severe. Early-day Georgia swamp dwellers smeared oil from crushed marsh mallow seeds on their bodies as a defense against snakes.

Internally the marsh mallow has been used to treat bronchitis, laryngitis, head colds, gastritis, and constipation. As a gargle it is said to soothe sore throats and tonsillitis, and as a mouthwash to relieve gum inflammations and dental abscesses. It is made into healing compresses for boils and sores. Country mothers give teething babies a piece of marsh mallow root to suck on.

When the plant's petals have fallen, a ring of seeds is revealed at the flower's center, resembling a small flat cheese. Many a country boy has munched on such cheeses while they are yet soft and fresh.

Marsh Marigold (American Cowslip)

Because the marsh marigold had been dedicated to the Virgin Mary, it was used in church ceremonies throughout the Middle Ages.

Country people cook tender young marigold plants for table greens. The buds are added to sauces as a substitute for capers.

The plant is a source of yellow dye.

Meadowsweet

Meadowsweet has properties similar to those of aspirin. It is a natural remedy prescribed for kidney and bladder problems, dropsy, gout, fevers, and insomnia. A brew made of its leaves benefits ulcers and sores, the tannin content of the leaves causing them to dry up quickly.

The roots of meadowsweet are a source of black dye.

Mullein

The roots of mullein were used by colonists of North America to treat hoarseness and lung afflictions.

Marjoram

Marjoram has long been used as a flavorful herb in cooking and as a home remedy. It was considered soothing to liver and stomach pain and was used to treat asthma, catarrh, bronchitis, whooping cough, head colds, migraine, insomnia, and rheumatism. The leaves, dried and powdered, were taken like snuff to evoke sneezing and thus clear a stuffy nose.

The herb was also a remedy for gout and hemorrhoids. Long ago it was believed to be a cure for leprosy. A tea made from mullein produces a sedative effect. It is said that asthma sufferers experience relief by smoking the plant's dried leaves.

Mullein is sometimes called "candlewicks" because country people collected the quantities of hair from its leaves to make wicks for their candles. Hummingbirds also filch the minute hairs that cover the plant, using them to line their tiny nests. The lightweight but sturdy stalk provides an excellent walking cane, especially when the root has grown in a curved fashion to form a handle.

Rural maids massage their faces with the velvety leaves to impart a glow to their cheeks. Country boys delight in smoking them, for they resemble the tobacco used by grown men.

Nasturtium

In olden times the nasturtium was used more as table fare than as medicine. Tender new leaves and the flowers served as a substitute for water cress in salads. The buds and green seeds were often used like capers.

The plant was later recognized as having powerful antibiotic properties. It was believed to possess aphrodisiac and youth-restoring elements, too. The fruits were employed as a purgative. Because of the nasturtium's high content of sulfur, it is said to check hair loss, foster hair growth, and benefit the scalp.

Nettle

In some countries nettles are eaten as a cooked vegetable. Newly sprouted plants make flavorful salads. In the 1800s a popular drink was an herbal tea brewed from nettle leaves.

Formerly the leaves were put in the feed of swine and poultry, and they were employed as a scouring agent in cleaning dairy utensils. To induce hens to lay more eggs, nettle seeds were added to their mash. After being steeped, the stems furnished a strong yarn for the nets and ropes of fishermen.

The plant was thought to have magical powers. To overcome fear one had only to hold a sprig of nettle and yarrow in the hand. Country people believe that coating the skin with nettle and tarragon juice would render one capable of seizing fast-swimming fish with the bare hands. As a love potion the seeds were swallowed in wine.

The nettle was used as a tonic, an aid to digestion, and a rejuvenator of the blood. It was recommended for treating diabetes, rheumatism, and dropsy. The plant was a classic rural remedy for bed-wetting. Applied to the scalp in lotion form, it was said to combat dandruff and check hair loss.

A greenish-yellow dye can be extracted from the nettle.

Periwinkle

Because the periwinkle retains its green leaves throughout the year, it is identified with immortality.

Long ago this creeping plant was used in magic rituals. Casting it into a fire with other herbs would cause the ghosts of loved ones to arise in the smoke. To render a snake bite harmless, the wound was rubbed with the periwinkle while mysterious formulas were repeated. Women wore it about their thighs as a safeguard against miscarriage. It was also used as an ingredient in love potions.

From the herb's astringent property came the belief that it

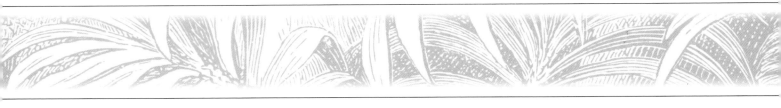

could check any kind of bleeding. Crushed leaves placed in the nostrils are said to arrest bleeding from the nose. The periwinkle has been used to treat fever, tiredness, tonsillitis, mouth ulcers, sores, and wounds. A rural remedy for pleurisy consists of a mixture of one-half glass of white wine and one-half glass of periwinkle juice.

Pokeweed

New leaves of pokeweed are sometimes boiled and served as table greens, especially in the southern United States.

The plant's dried fruit and roots possess a property used in diminishing the swelling and caking of cows' udders. Farmers blend it with wool oil and apply it to the afflicted udders.

In days gone by, country children made a red ink from pokeweed berries.

Red Rose

The red rose is thought to be the flower earliest cultivated by man. Many religions have used it symbolically.

People have long feasted on foods flavored with roses, such as rose cakes and rose jams. Wines have been infused with the flowers. Ladies scented themselves with rose powder and added luster to their eyelids by applying rose oil. They perfumed their breath with candies of myrrh and rose petals mashed in honey.

Medicinally the red rose was used to treat tuberculosis and other lung afflictions. Sore throats were soothed with rose honey. A lotion made from the plant's dried leaves was a remedy for eye inflammations.

Rosemary

Rosemary has been used for centuries in cooking as a seasoning for meat and sauces.

In olden times it was an ingredient in salves to heal wounds and assuage pains. The herb was used in treating loss of memory, vertigo, general weakness, and jaundice. It was recommended that it be eaten with salt the first thing upon rising for strengthening eyesight. Its candied blossoms were considered a good defense against plague. Rosemary wine was said to aid digestion and benefit the kidneys. An infusion of the plant was employed in compresses to ease the pain of contusions and rheumatism.

It was a cherished belief in those early days that homes scented with rosemary would be safeguarded against harm.

Sage

Through the centuries sage was valued as a healer of all ills. People believed that it helped to create life and protect it; so the herb was prescribed for those wanting to conceive and for those already with child.

Chewing a sage leaf before dining has been recommended to

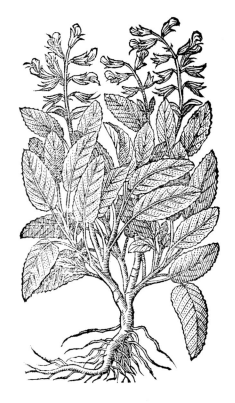

avoid indigestion. As a seasoning it not only flavors food but is said to prevent spoilage. In tonic form sage is felt to increase circulation and aid in convalescence. Sage tea is used to treat bronchitis and vertigo. A decoction of the herb is advocated for sore throats, inflamed gums, and dental abscesses. Added to rum and applied to the scalp, it is used to cure dandruff and check hair loss. Sage salve is employed for relieving the discomfort of muscular pains, rheumatism, sciatica, and gout. Asthma victims claim to find relief by smoking the plant's dried leaves. Sage leaves allowed to smoke on hot coals in the fireplace or boiled in an open vessel have been employed as a disinfectant for sick rooms.

Tansy

Tansy was so highly regarded as a heal-all in Europe that early colonists felt obliged to bring it to the New World. Tansy tea was used as a remedy for indigestion, head colds, and intestinal worms. The leaves, fresh or dried, discourage the presence of bedbugs and fleas; country folk scattered them amid the bedding and sprinkled them in the straw of dog kennels. Country lasses steeped the leaves in buttermilk for more than a week and used the wash to improve their complexions.

In the past tansy was used in cookery. Its leaves were an ingredient in cakes known as tansies. Tansy pudding was traditionally served at the end of Lent.

The plant's flower heads give a yellow dye.

Thyme

The Egyptians and Etruscans employed thyme in embalming procedures. Greeks burned it for incense when worshiping their gods. Both Greeks and Romans used the herb in the preparation of food. For Roman women it was a beauty aid.

Over the centuries thyme has been used to improve circulatory, digestive, and respiratory functions and to relieve insomnia, exhaustion, coughs, chills, and anemia. As a scalp tonic it is recommended for preventing and stopping hair loss. The plant's dried and powdered leaves, when used like snuff, are said to act as a decongestant for the respiratory tract and to check nosebleed.

Valerian

Only the roots of valerian are used medicinally. They constitute one of the earliest treatments for nervous conditions. Formerly the plant was used in treating epilepsy. Today it is used as a calmative for nervousness, breathlessness, palpitations, hysteria, convulsions, insomnia, migraine, and dizziness.

Valerian has a powerful effect upon cats, sending them into paroxysms of delight.

Vervain

For centuries superstition and religion have been associated with vervain. Hung over a doorway, along with dill and a horseshoe, it was a standard safeguard against witchcraft. Because of its brush-like structure, it was used in churches to sprinkle holy water.

Perhaps as a result of vervain's religious use, people developed faith in its healing properties. They employed it in treating pleurisy, bronchitis, and bladder troubles. The bruised leaves are reputed to relieve the pain of earache, headache, and rheumatism. The plant is used externally in hot compresses on bruises, sprains, and wounds.

Vervain also found its way into cooking. The minced leaves were included in soups and in stuffing for roasted meats.

Being mostly stems, the plant provides excellent swatters with which country boys do battle with bees while pilfering their honey. Through the ages both Indian and white boys have used the tough slender stalks of vervain as arrows for their bows.

Wild Rose

A honey found on the fluff surrounding seeds of the wild rose has been used to combat intestinal worms in humans as well as animals. Country people dry and powder the seeds as a home cure for kidney stones. From the hips enclosing the seeds, they make a tonic to purify the blood in springtime. The hips possess a goodly amount of vitamin C and are considered an aid to resisting infection and a remedy for diarrhea and bleeding gums.

Wild Touch-Me-Not

The stems of wild touch-me-not are engorged with juice. This juice is a boon to poison ivy sufferers, for when applied to affected areas it affords almost instantaneous relief. A complete cure is said to take place in a period of twenty-four hours.

Wood Betony (Lousewort)

At one time country dwellers believed that sheep which fed on wood betony risked developing a skin disease caused by a louse, and so the plant is sometimes called "lousewort."

It is claimed that betony's aromatic scent often makes its collectors dizzy. Rural folk gather the leaves and flowers for a tea brewed as a remedy for inflammation and congestion of the respiratory tract. The leaves, dried and steeped, are used in compresses to aid the healing of ulcers and wounds. In powdered form they act as a decongestant in cases of head colds by provoking sneezing and are also used to stop hiccups. Wood betony has also served as a treatment for stomach, kidney, and liver discomfort, brain disorders, rheumatism, sciatica, gout, and shortness of breath.

The ancients prescribed it as a medicine for women in prolonged labor. According to prevailing superstition, the plant would protect journeyers by night from all harm, even witchcraft.

Yellow Dock

Yellow dock has nutritive and medicinal value. Its leaves are often used as edible greens.

For generations country families have made yellow dock into salves, tonics, and laxatives. The roots, being high in iron content, have been prescribed for weakness, anemia, rheumatism, and skin disorders. When dried and powdered, the roots are said to provide an acceptable dentifrice.

Yellow Gentian

The life of the yellow gentian sometimes spans more than fifty years.

During earlier times the plant's roots, collected in the fall and steeped in water, were used as a cure-all for disorders of the bowels, liver, stomach, and heart. It was believed that the gentian's particular medicinal properties could prolong life and render poisons ineffectual. Vinegar made from the plant was a remedy for fevers and a safeguard against communicable diseases.

Today it finds its way into alcoholic beverages—aperitifs and liqueur—and is used to treat stomach problems, general weakness, and nervous conditions.

Armadillo: Living Xerox Machine

Long of snout, with naked, mule-like ears, the armadillo ambles about on stubby legs covered with hardened scales. Its body is encased in an armor of bony plates (mottled brown to yellowish white in color), interspersed with flexible transverse bands. A flat plate covers the head from nose tip to crown; the tail is safeguarded by a series of hard rings. This mail-clad, pig-like animal is about 30 inches long, 7 inches in height, and weighs from 12 to 17 pounds.

Picture, if you can, a creature similar in all respects, but having the proportions of a modern-day rhinoceros. This was the ancestor of the armadillo that roved the plains of South America eons ago. A smaller version of the original armadillo is now found from Patagonia to Texas and Louisiana. It is the nine-banded armadillo, one of the larger members of the present-day family and the only species living in the United States.

The front of its mouth is devoid of teeth. The existing molars are rootless pegs, lacking in enamel, which continue to grow as they are worn down. A relative of sloths and anteaters, it too is equipped with a long, sticky tongue for capturing its favorite food, insects. Ants, including fire ants, and their eggs; roaches; cane borers; termites; scarab beetles and their larvae; wireworms; centipedes;

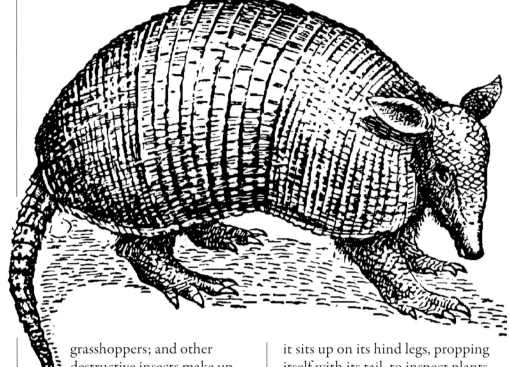

grasshoppers; and other destructive insects make up 90 percent of its diet. The armadillo's hunger for ants, which assail freshly hatched chicks, has been to the advantage of quail and other bird populations. Scorpions, tarantulas, snake eggs, and occasionally an unwary salamander add variety to its nutritional intake. Fungi (especially puffballs), blackberries, mulberries, and wild plums are also part of the armadillo's fare. In searching for insects it moves erratically, sometimes walking, sometimes trotting, pushing its long, pointed snout into loose soil and plowing a furrow about 4 inches deep. After locating an insect beneath the soil through its sense of smell, it quickly digs a hole with its front feet, grunting softly as it labors. At times

it sits up on its hind legs, propping itself with its tail, to inspect plants for insects and berries. It also assumes this position when sniffing the air for danger.

Despite its armor, the armadillo is a good swimmer. Should it estimate that the width of a waterway is not sufficient to warrant the effort of swimming, it will nonchalantly stroll across the bottom to the farther side. If it finds that one deep breath is not providing enough oxygen for the crossing, it feverishly paddles its short legs until, reaching the surface, it can gulp in air. When it has taken in enough, the buoyed body relaxes, and the armadillo swims vigorously toward its destination.

As far as land locomotion is concerned, the armadillo can most times outrun a man by weaving

through underbrush. And fortunate this is, for the nine-banded armadillo, when threatened, is not sufficiently armored to find protection by rolling up tightly, as can its South American cousins. The armadillo is not adequately forewarned of menace through the senses of hearing and eyesight, for both are poor. Therefore, speed is its only recourse. Once in the safe refuge of tangled brush, it digs frantically, the two large middle claws on its front feet gouging the earth. Upon disappearing into this emergency tunnel, the armadillo arches its body, and the plates become embedded in the soil. So tenaciously does it maintain a hold that extricating the animal is almost impossible. If the creature is cornered, with no opportunity for rapid digging, lacerating claws and offensive odor from a pair of anal glands are its only means of defense.

Though the armadillo favors the protection of tall grasses and thickets, it appreciates limestone formations where ready-made burrows have been created by seeping water. If such a prefabricated dwelling is not handy, the armadillo sets to work excavating one himself. The earth is first loosened with its pointed snout and forefeet. After a small heap of soil has accumulated under its belly, it balances on its forefeet and tail and, with arched back, brings its hind feet over the pile and with a quick backward kick scatters the

dirt to a distance of several feet. Digging a few more inches at a time, it continues the same routine. The completed tunnel is about 8 inches in diameter and can be as long as 25 feet, though it is usually shorter. At the enlarged end, roughly 1½ feet in diameter, the nest is made. The armadillo gathers nest material—grass, mesquite leaves, or weeds—composing it into small bundles with its forefeet. Pushing these back into the area between the raised body and hind legs, it lowers its shell, clamping the material securely. Slowly working its way backward into the tunnel, picking up any fallen litter with mouth and forefeet, it deposits the bedding at the nest site. The nest is actually no more than a heap into which the armadillo wriggles.

With few exceptions, a mother armadillo consistently bears four babies. The offspring are all of the same sex, identical down to the smallest detail—the size, shape, and number of scales, the number of hairs sprinkled on their tiny bellies, etc. Armadillo young

enter the world with wide-open eyes and are otherwise well developed, though their shell is as pliable at first as soft leather. Since they do not change their shells periodically through life, as do lobsters or crabs, the armor does not harden completely until they are fully grown. Within several hours after birth, these miniature replicas of their parents are able to toddle after the mother to explore for insects. Equipped with exactly the appropriate number of breasts, four, the mother nurses her "quadruplicates" for the first two months.

The armadillo usually has several dens, sometimes as many as ten. Those with very shallow tunnels are used to lure insects, whereas the larger ones serve as emergency refuges. The armadillo is gregarious and generous of nature and often shares its home with other animals—opossums, rabbits, and rats. Abandoned armadillo tunnels provide shelter for skunks, rabbits, burrowing owls, opossums, and minks.

Prolonged periods of severe cold can prove fatal to the armadillo. It does not hibernate and must seek sustenance. Those armadillos which do not freeze to death in their dens find digging in frozen soil for food a futile effort: most of the surface-dwelling insects that would suffice as nourishment have perished from the cold. Therefore, the armadillo either starves to death or expires from defenselessness against the elements. It is better able to tolerate extreme heat by remaining in underground shelter and confining its search for food to the cooler hours of evening. Its eyes are well suited for nocturnal hunting.

The armadillo is a sociable animal. When captured, it is easily tamed and makes an unusual, interesting, and clean pet, uncommonly exempt from parasites, such as fleas, lice, or ticks.

After the Civil War, armadillos were not a familiar sight in Texas outside of the Rio Grande Valley. With the spread of civilization, however, and resulting decrease in their natural enemies, the animals ranged farther and farther northeast. Shortly before the turn of the century they had reached the Brazos River, and by the first quarter of the twentieth century they had entered Oklahoma, Louisiana, and Arkansas. Even prior to the construction of bridges spanning the Mississippi River, they began to appear on the east bank. The animal has been gradually increasing its range and is now found as far east as Florida.

All armadillos look and act alike; at maturity their size and weight are the same. So to see one armadillo is truly to have seen them all. Though their physical selves and habits seem to be Xeroxed copies of one another, perhaps each individual's personality is unique— at least to its mate!

The shells of armadillos have long been turned into ornamental baskets by craftsmen. The value of their meat also should not be overlooked. It is a favorite food with dogs, coyotes, peccaries, and other carnivores. Country folk often find its pork-like flavor delicious. One old-timer in Texas insists that the only way to serve the white, tender meat of the armadillo is to barbecue it over an open campfire and then flavor each juicy morsel with hot chili sauce.

Badger: Grave Robber?

When you see dirt flying through the air for yards, propelled by the short legs of a flattened-appearing animal with retrousse nose, you are witnessing the now-you-see-me, now-you-don't vanishing act of the badger. This large, grayish animal is ideally adapted to digging, using all four feet and its mouth to burrow beneath the ground in a matter of seconds. When completely buried, it clogs up the hole behind a disappearing tail. If cornered, it slashes with long, powerful claws and knife-like teeth set in strong jaws. Because of this ferocity and the ability to disappear into the earth almost in the wink of an eye, few animals willingly assault it. However, in England dogs were deliberately set against badgers, the sport being known as badger-baiting, or badger-drawing. By the mid-1800s this unfortunate pastime was prohibited. From it

comes the expression "to badger," meaning to tease or worry a weaker opponent. An attacker has difficulty in grasping the badger firmly with its teeth, because of the heavy fur and loose skin. Thick neck and shoulder muscles on the sturdy, low-slung body protect nerves and arteries. When angered the badger hisses a warning to the world.

A body 30 inches long and weighing 15 pounds, supported on bowed legs with pigeon-toed feet, does not exactly evoke the picture of a fastidious dandy. Nonetheless, when it comes to nails, the badger is fastidious indeed. It gives itself frequent manicures and pedicures, leaving not a trace of dirt beneath the nails or between the toes. The blackish face is distinguished by a white stripe over the forehead and a white crescent behind and encircling each eyes. These facial markings led our ancestors to call the animal "bageard," meaning one who wears a badge.

The badger's long claws are used not only for defense but as a means of securing food. By digging faster than its prey, underground inhabitants such as marmots and moles, it overtakes and devours them. In the northern and eastern parts of the United States, the badger feeds on ground squirrels, field mice, deer mice, rabbits, insects, and ground-nesting birds and their eggs; in the Southwest, prairie dogs, pocket gophers, kangaroo rats, wood rats, mice, insects, and lizards make up the diet. In the open country of the West, horn sheaths shed by the antelope and made soft by rain or snow find favor with hungry badgers.

During the mating season, in autumn or early winter, the male badger—in skunk-like fashion—raises his short tail and discharges an odoriferous secretion when courting the object of his affection. One litter per year is produced, averaging three in number. At four to six weeks of age, the babies' eyes open in their nest of dried grasses in a chamber 2 to 6 feet beneath the ground, located at the end of a long tunnel. When half grown they are weaned, after which the mother supplies solid food until they are two-thirds grown. From then on they are capable of accompanying her on foraging trips. Since the father undertakes no responsibility for the young, the mother must, perforce, be an even fiercer, more competent fighter. By the following autumn, young badgers are almost fully grown and can hunt for themselves. The family then breaks up. Their substantial appetites require a more extensive food range for them to survive.

The badger goes into winter well padded with fat. Actually it does not hibernate but retires underground below the frost line, shoving dirt back up the tunnel to prevent drafts. Nature helps the animal to survive the winter by curtailing the desire for food and keeping it drowsy. From time to time, nudged from napping by appetite, the badger emerges for food. If fortunate enough to find an abundance, it buries the surplus, digging some up when necessary. A rather unsocial creature, the badger leaves its burrow after sundown, a lonely hunter in the night.

Not only is the badger a facile swimmer, but on land it can travel backward almost as swiftly and easily as forward.

It is an affectionate pet when caught while small. Perhaps because it is relieved of self-responsibility, in captivity it is carefree to the point of prancing and skipping about.

Among some country folk the badger has been indicted as a grave robber. The animal favors sandy hillocks, where digging is less difficult and rodents tend to abide. Coincidentally, sites of this sort were chosen by early American settlers for burial places. During the badger's energetic excavating for food, skulls and bones would often fly about with the loosened dirt. However, I feel sure that satisfying its hunger, not robbing graves, was the badger's sole aim.

Because badger hairs maintain a fine point, they are used for shaving brushes, for good-quality artist's brushes, and for pointing up lower grades of fox fur. Besides serving man with its usable hair, the badger is influential in reducing the rodent population that consumes grain and other crops. It is one of Nature's best natural exterminators.

Beaver: Environmentalist

Eons ago a gigantic rodent, 8 feet in height and weighing 700 pounds, lumbered over the earth. The sole descendant of this immense creature is our present-day beaver.

Indians regarded the animal with profound respect. Cherokee legend has it that the Great Spirit enlisted the help of giant beavers to create the world.

The beaver is North America's largest, cleanest, cleverest rodent. It can grow to 4 feet in length, the tail being one-third of this dimension, and weigh as much as 60 pounds. In captivity a beaver survives approximately nineteen years; in the wild it seldom exceeds twelve years of age. An oddity in the world of mammals, the beaver, like reptiles, continues to grow until death.

The heavy body, supported on short legs, is covered with fur composed of two types of hair: one, silky, gray, and close set, the guard hairs; the other, coarser, longer, and reddish brown in color, the woolly undercoat.

For years old-time woodsmen and trappers said that the teeth of beavers were orange. Folks who fancied themselves knowledgeable about such matters labeled this a myth. However, improbable as it sounds, the beaver's teeth are orange; the four front incisors are covered with bright-orange enamel, their backs being of softer dentine. Since the dentine wears away faster than the enameled sides, constant gnawing hones the incisors to chisel-like sharpness. The lower incisors, grinding against the upper teeth, also help to keep them keen edged. With such admirable equipment the beaver is capable of felling a tree 10 feet in circumference. Because the teeth grow continuously, they are never eroded away. Between the four incisors in front and the remainder of the teeth lies a considerable gap. Enough space is afforded so that two folds of skin can converge behind the incisors, sealing off the rest of the mouth. For this reason the beaver can gnaw down a tree without risking a mouthful of splinters and can chew under water without danger of drowning. Early pioneers believed that powdered beavers' teeth served in soup would cure almost any ailment.

Both nose and ears are valvular, closing as the beaver submerges. By being positioned on the sides of the nose, the nostrils are spared direct water pressure when the animal dives. The transparent lids of the eyes furnish the beaver with a pair of underwater goggles.

The other end of the animal is as functionally designed as are the

eyes, ears, and teeth. The broad, flat, scaly tail, 12 inches long, 6 inches wide, and almost an inch thick, serves three main purposes: when the beaver is swimming, it is used as a rudder and, sometimes, a diving plane; it provides a convenient prop to lean back on when the beaver is gnawing a tree; in times of danger it works as an alarm signal, being slapped loudly against the water's surface.

The back feet have five fully webbed toes. The claw of the second hind toe is split and serves as a comb. Upon emerging from the water, the beaver preens his fur with this double nail, using oil from its castor glands as a grooming aid.

This oil, castoreum, is a creamy, bitter orange-brown substance. It is a secretion of many uses, for both beaver and man.

In addition to being used for grooming, castoreum helps the animal to communicate with other beavers by sign heaps. These are small mud patties which the beaver forms and places in strategic spots in the shallows or along the shore, moistening them with castoreum. They mark the boundaries of beaver territory or announce the beaver's presence to the opposite sex. This musky substance also plays an important role in mating. The beavers' love-making takes place in an intoxicating cloud of musk.

Beaver musk, so stimulating during coupling, possesses such tantalizing properties that for

generations trappers have employed it as a bait to catch a variety of animals, for almost all animals are attracted to its scent. Early American settlers used castoreum as a remedy for a long list of afflictions, including hiccups, apoplexy, deafness, poor eyesight, colic, and sciatica. Man has long used castoreum as a base for expensive perfume. It possesses the quality of retaining a fragrance until warmth of the body releases it.

The industrious and gregarious beaver is one of the few animals able to alter their environment. To make a pond a suitable habitat, the beaver constructs a dam in the stream feeding it, both upstream and down. The dam may be crooked or straight, from several to 100 yards long, and from 1 to 12 feet high. Its purpose is to maintain a

constant water level in the pool and prevent its freezing to the bottom. The beaver is then assured of reaching its underwater larder of wood and bark throughout the winter months.

To start the dam, the beaver cuts willow and alder limbs, transporting them to the stream's bottom and arranging them with the stub ends pointing upstream. To this are added mud, gravel, and stones, followed by another layer of saplings plus more mud and stones, until the desired height is reached. The beaver sometimes constructs canals to float its cuttings to the pond. These canals are more common in the western part of the country than in the East; they may be as long as 750 feet, having two or three water levels. When it comes to

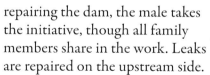

repairing the dam, the male takes the initiative, though all family members share in the work. Leaks are repaired on the upstream side.

The beaver's lodge is built of the same materials as the dam, and both are constructed in the autumn. The animal seems to prefer working at night. Before starting its noisy labor of felling trees, the beaver—according to the Indians—posts a sentinel. When a menace nears, the heavy tail is slapped loudly on the water as a warning, and the beavers dive to safety. To fell a tree, the beaver first notches the trunk and then removes a piece of wood about three inches below the notch. Saplings are cut through from one side; larger trees, from two sides; very large trees are brought down by cutting around the entire circumference of the trunk. Louis Viccinelli of Mississippi says that, contrary to popular belief, the beaver is not able to control the direction of the tree's fall and must scurry to safety at the final gnaw.

Limbs are chewed from the trunks and stacked in mounds under water. These reach from 6 to 7 feet in height and more than 30 feet in diameter. The one large room within is lined with grass; the outside is plastered with mud, which freezes as hard as stone, protecting the inhabitants from enemies, such as wolves. The spacious room is left both floorless and roofless until the dam is

completed, raising the water level. The lodge is built to accommodate the beaver couple and its last two litters. At the age of two, being on the brink of maturity, the young are driven from the family to prevent overpopulation. Passageways leading to the lodge are dug downward through a bank into the water. Not all beavers dwell in lodges; some, at least temporarily, may inhabit burrows that open under water, which they dig in the banks of streams.

When lodge and dam are completed, the beaver sets to work building up his winter food supply. In the pond's muddy bottom near the lodge, it infixes branches and tree trunks of poplar, aspen, cottonwood, and willow, using the bark as food through the long, cold months. They are submerged deeply enough to prevent their being frozen in ice. Each beaver requires from 20 to 30 ounces of bark per day for food.

The beaver's extra-large lungs and liver permit it to stay under water for periods of fifteen minutes or to swim submerged to a distance of one-half mile or more. Upon returning to the surface for air, the animal renews 75 percent of its lungs' content, in contrast to the renewal of the 15 to 20 percent in man's lungs. During swimming, nine-tenths of the body is beneath water. The front legs, unused for locomotion in water, are folded back under the chest. The hind legs alone, moving simultaneously, drive

the animal forward. By employing only its tail, it can paddle along at slow speed.

When the ice thaws, beavers leave their lodge for a rambling existence, feeding on berries and aquatic plants. Roots of water lilies are real gourmet fare to the beaver. The father beaver usually stays away from his family in summer, rejoining it in autumn.

European hatters, long before America's pelts were available, used the fur of beavers on their own continent, finding that it was easily incorporated with felt because of its infinitesimal barbs. In England all hats had to be fashioned from beaver fur by royal decree. The pelts were much sought after and highly valued by European noblemen.

The widespread demand for this product in Europe made it imperative that new sources be found. Because beavers were far more plentiful in North America than abroad, much of the exploration of this continent was due to the search for their pelts. Thus the beaver played a major role in opening up the North American continent.

The French, seeking pelts, explored along the St. Lawrence and westward through Canada. The Dutch combed the Hudson River Valley. The English chartered the Hudson's Bay Company, whose men scoured the Far West for beavers long before gold was discovered there. The beaver pelt soon became a unit of barter: one pelt equaled one pound of tobacco, two axes, or a kettle; six pelts equaled a fancy lace coat; twelve pelts, a long rifle. The Hudson's Bay Company became famed not only for its success in trapping beavers, but also for its manufacture of fine blankets. Black bars woven into their edges represented the number of pelts at which each was valued.

Until the early 1800s, beavers were trapped by deadfalls and snares. Then the steel trap was invented, increasing catches. The quest for beavers continued for three centuries until beaver hats were no longer fashionable. By this time the beaver population was heavily depleted. In 1900 protective measures were advocated by conservationists, and since that time the population has increased.

The beaver was not valued for its fur alone. Many found its flesh very palatable. The front part of this semi-aquatic animal was considered meat; the nether parts, usually submerged, were looked upon as fish and, therefore, could be eaten on fast days as Lenten food. Beaver meat is said to have a pork-like flavor.

North American Indians too enjoyed the beaver's flesh, especially its large, flat tail. The Indians held that the manner in which one treated the dead animal's bones would determine later success or failure in hunting it. The souls of defunct beavers visited the men who had killed them to ascertain the fate of their bones. If they discovered dogs chewing on them, the offense was indignantly reported to other beavers. They would then make themselves less available to their hunters in the future. It was the consensus among Indians that the beaver was satisfied to have his bones thrown into either fire or a river.

The Indians utilized beaver pelts for warm clothing, stitching the skins together for robes. Traders soon discovered that used Indian beaver robes were superior to new skins, because they were saturated with the oils which the red men rubbed on their bodies. Indians were much amused by the exorbitant prices willingly paid for their used clothing.

The beaver has donated more to the world than its pelt. Its dams, by stopping the outflow of silt, create areas of richly fertile, arable land. For this reason such silted areas were highly valued by North America's pioneers, who termed them "beaver meadows." The beaver acts as a conscientious environmentalist by reclaiming land along streams in wasteland areas. Had the beaver been properly protected during the past three hundred years, the value

of its flood-control work would have outweighed the total worth of all pelts seized.

Fox Facts

A group of foxes is known as a skulk. In North America there are the red fox, the gray, the Arctic fox, and the kit fox—cross foxes, black foxes, and silver being color phases of the red fox.

Have you ever wondered whether foxes climb trees? Red do not, but gray foxes are able to climb as easily as a cat and can go up a perfectly straight tree trunk.

Fox fare consists of field mice, wood rats, rabbits, wild grapes, various berries, some game birds, insects, frogs, and shellfish.

If someone labels you foxy, accept it as a compliment! The fox is a clever creature who has learned to outwit man on numerous occasions. When being pursued by hunters and hounds he has devised many cunning means to break the line of scent left on the soil by his paws, even to jumping upon the backs of sheep.

Pet owners might well wish that their dogs would adopt the following custom developed by the fox to rid himself of fleas. Holding a tuft of fur or piece of wood between his teeth, he will slowly submerge himself in a pond, tail first, gradually driving the frantic fleas to seek refuge on the only thing remaining above water— the wool or wood. The fox then allows the parasite-ridden object to float away from him and, well groomed, swims to the nearest bank.

In Pennsylvania, Matt Sikes says folks have a sure-fire scheme for foiling a fox. Across a field plow a furrow. Set No. 2 traps along it, and cover them with soil. He'll trot into one of them every time, as he can't pass up the opportunity to walk on newly plowed ground. Since foxes don't hibernate, they are as active in the winter months as in summer. So you can trap one at any season—if you can outwit him!

The Prancing Porcupine

If some morning you wake up to find your axe, hoe, or shovel missing its handle, there's no need for assistance from the sheriff to solve the mystery: the culprit is probably the porcupine. Its strong desire for salt drives it to consume anything bearing a trace of it, even a trace so slight as that left by human perspiration. With its powerful incisor teeth, the porcupine will devour sweat-stained saddles and harness or barrels in which salted meat had once been stored, though but a hint of salt be found there.

The porcupine is a squat, heavy-bodied animal with stiff quills scattered through its fur. The quills are actually hairs modified into sharp spines; like hair, they can be replaced when lost. Erect only in fear or anger, the quills normally lie passively along the back and sides, protected by coarse guard hairs. They are loosely fastened to the skin by a slender base. When threatened, the porcupine thrashes its tail wildly, sending loosened quills flying. From this action developed the myth that the porcupine could truly eject, or "shoot," its quills at will.

Under attack it assumes this typical defensive posture: drawing its feet together, it hunches down close to the ground and, by a contraction of the skin, erects all of its 25,000 to 30,000 quills, thus appearing twice its size. As the porcupine flails its tail, ever moving backward into its attacker, the quills become embedded in the assailant's flesh. The structure of the quill is such that it can move by itself into the victim's body. From ½ to 5 inches in length, the quills are equipped with thousands of diamond-shaped scales on their black tips which induce them to progress deeper into the flesh, furthered by the victim's muscle movement. Many a large animal has been found dead with internal organs punctured by porcupine quills.

One old-timer vows that you can safely pick up a disturbed porcupine, in spite of its quills, if you proceed in the right way.

When the tail has stopped moving, grasp the long hairs that extend past the tail quills and tug hard. This action, according to Paul English of Texas, causes the animal to try to pull out of your grip, neither backing nor biting. Because the possibility exists that the porcupine may not be aware of the behavior expected of him, I don't really recommend that you try this method of capture. A porcupine's powerful incisor teeth can nip off a finger at one bite.

To the nearsighted porcupine, anything more than 6 feet away appears as a shadow. But the animal does not rely on eyes alone to encounter the fairer sex. Using its nose, it snuffs along the ground and up tree trunks for that very particular porcupine odor—much like that of a fruit salad, with the aroma of pineapple predominating.

Porcupine babies are referred to as porcupettes. While they are yet in the womb, their quills, overlaid with silky hairs, are soft and moist. At birth, when helped from the fetal sac by the mother, the porcupette erects its quills several times to encourage drying. They become dry and harden after a period of fifteen minutes in the air. The baby porcupine makes its appearance in the world in a very well-developed state, weighing more than a pound. Within two days it is able to make its way up tree trunks and feast on leaves and tender shoots. A porcupette is easily tamed and soon learns to respond to its owner.

What the porcupine lacks in eyesight is compensated for by its acute hearing. In spite of other sounds in its vicinity, it can detect a whisper at 30 feet.

Slow and awkward, the porcupine ambles along at a sluggish rate, its jauntiest pace only equaling a human's leisurely sauntering. When under attack, a porcupine tucks in its nose as much as possible, for the nose is so sensitive that its being struck by a stick could cause the death of the animal. These two characteristics of the porcupine, slowness of movement and sensitivity of nose, are a boon to a lost camper or hiker, ill from hunger. The porcupine is easily overtaken, and a blow on the nose from stick or stone will quickly dispatch it.

In winter should you come upon trees with trunks bare of bark to

a great height, you may be in the feeding areas of porcupines. During that season their diet consists solely of the inner bark of hardwoods and evergreens. In spring they favor the sap-filled cambium (a soft layer of formative tissue under the bark) of maples, especially of the sugar maple. Tree-dwelling porcupines almost never descend to the ground to quench their thirst; they obtain moisture from dew and the juice of leaves.

Few animals care to contend with the porcupine, with the exception of the fisher, a large marten known also as the North American sable, or black fox. It is about 20 inches in length and weighs approximately 20 pounds. The fisher successfully flips the porcupine over on its back and attacks the soft belly. Any quills it may swallow somehow pass through its digestive tract without piercing the stomach lining. Quills that become embedded in its hide do not penetrate far, because an underlying layer of skin and muscle forces them to work their way back out.

The fisher's name is misleading, since the animal rarely fishes. If, however, you enjoy fishing frequently, a porcupine can be responsible for increasing your catch. For still-fishing, the very lightest bobber available should be used; a porcupine's quill, being hollow, has the required buoyancy. To the back tip, the pointed end of the quill, fasten a loop of fine

wire—either copper or brass. Turn the loop, using an inch of the wire to fasten it securely to the quill. Run the line through the loop. Blacky Adams says that the quill bobber responds so sensitively to the most delicate touch that at least fifty percent more fish are caught by its use.

The porcupine has an odd, rather appealing custom rarely witnessed by humans. An adult animal, despite its bulky 10 to 25 pounds of weight, stands on hind legs and tail, rhythmically swaying from side to side, while lifting and stamping the hind feet. In an attempt to explain this baffling behavior, naturalists conjectured that it is done to burn up excess energy. Some country folks who have witnessed this prancing think that the porcupine is simply dancing to music that humans can't hear.

Possum: Unintelligent and Unique

When the word *marsupial* is mentioned, people tend to think of a female animal with a pouch. Features that characterize all members of this order are particular bones—marsupial bones—attached to the female's pelvis, a lower jaw that curves inward at the posterior end, and a very primitive brain.

For hundreds and millions of years marsupials inhabited all land areas. Today they exist in only a few places, among them

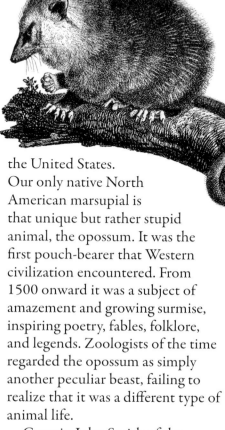

the United States. Our only native North American marsupial is that unique but rather stupid animal, the opossum. It was the first pouch-bearer that Western civilization encountered. From 1500 onward it was a subject of amazement and growing surmise, inspiring poetry, fables, folklore, and legends. Zoologists of the time regarded the opossum as simply another peculiar beast, failing to realize that it was a different type of animal life.

Captain John Smith of the Jamestown colony in Virginia was responsible for the name by which it is known. Opossum is a rendering of the Algonquian Indian word apasum, meaning "white animal," for the opossum has a pointed face covered with soft, short white hair. In most parts of the country it is commonly known as the possum.

In striking contrast to the white face are the prominent jet-black shiny eyeballs surrounded by a dusky area. Because the iris is visible only in very bright light, which the opossum avoids, the eye is all pupil, suited to the animal's

twilight and nocturnal habits. It does not have good eyesight and is thought to be lacking in color vision.

Well-developed whiskers help animals to avoid bumping into objects. The opossum has two groups of long, stiff whiskers located on either side of the face, one group sprouting on the cheeks, the other near the snout. At the base of these bristles is a highly sensitive nerve complex; the slightest touch triggers a defensive reaction.

The long, sharp-pointed snout is provided with an adequate sense of smell. It is of major importance in foraging for food.

The thin black ears, rounded and hairless, have been likened to those of a bat and are sometimes, as in the Virginia opossum, banded on the tips with white. The outer ear serves not only for hearing but also for shutting the ear canal against the intrusion of insects while the animal slumbers.

A coat of gray to yellowish white covers the thick, rounded body, 2½ to 3 feet in length and weighing from 8 to 15 pounds. Oiliness renders the soft, dense underfur impermeable to rain, so that the skin beneath remains moisture free. Protective overhairs, long and coarse, reduce wearing of this underfur, which keeps the opossum both warm and dry.

Though clumsy when walking—waddling along in a ponderous, shuffling gait on short legs—the opossum is adept at climbing, because of its well-developed dark paws and gripping tail. The five toes of the front feet are provided with white claws as sharp as those of a squirrel. The big toe on the hind feet, nailless and flexible, serves as a thumb, enabling the opossum to grasp branches firmly. This opposable first digit is a feature the opossum shares with man and apes. Except for the hairy base, the tail is covered with small scales—the first half being black, the remainder, white. Loosely wrapped around a bough, the tail is of great value when the animal is traversing a tree limb. Should the branch be shaken and the opossum slip, the tail immediately tightens, safely anchoring the animal. Young possums, weighing little, suspend themselves more easily than do adults.

The tail is borne in a downward, curled-under position.

People find the tail a convenience when picking up the animal, using it as a handle. When being transported by it, the opossum is perfectly capable of climbing up its own tail and will bite the hand holding it. One should carry the animal by the tail with one hand and firmly seize the nape of the neck with the other.

To satisfy its chief needs—water, food, and shelter—the opossum chooses to live along wooded stream beds where hunting and fishing are good. In seeking a den for safe drowsing during daylight hours, it selects a cavity in a hollow tree, a secluded nook under a wood pile, a rock crevice, or a vacated squirrel nest. If these are not available, it may move in underground with an armadillo or skunk or take over an abandoned den, not being itself a dexterous digger.

The possum always lines its lodgings with grass and dead leaves. In the Deep South where trees bearded with Spanish moss abound, it filches these festoons for its nest. The bedding material is transported in a unique manner. After gathering mouthfuls of dry grass and leaves, the opossum shoves them under its body, where the prehensile tail is readied in a loop to receive them. Roughly seven mouthfuls make a good loopful. The possum then makes its way home, dragging the load of bedding along behind in the curled tail. Among country people of the South, a legend has survived concerning the nest material of this unusual little animal. It is said that the female possum, shortly before giving birth, gathers suitable bedding with her mate. She then lies upon her back while the male piles the grass and leaves between her paws. He drags her home by the tail, her body serving as a sort of sled.

Pregnancy for the possum is a scant twelve days and eighteen hours. The babies, extremely premature at birth, urgently seek the haven of the mother's pouch, which acts as a kind of incubator while they are continuing to develop.

Prior to giving birth (January or February in the South, later in the North) the mother becomes restless, and sitting on her haunches, the tail extending forward between her legs, she commences to ready her pouch for the young. From time to time, inserting her muzzle, she cleans it with her tongue. The babies do not travel the length of the two vaginal canals but take a short cut directly down the middle, a new birth passage being forced through the tissue connecting them. Each baby makes its appearance capsulated in a membrane filled with fluid, from which it is freed by the mother's tongue. The female opossum does not actively aid her young in their 3-inch-long journey to the pouch, but by moistening the furry route over which they struggle, she facilitates their progress. The babies are extremely underdeveloped—so tiny that the entire litter can nest in a teaspoon, and their transparent bodies weigh a total of about one-fifteenth of an ounce. The internal organs are visible through the skin, and eyes and ears are not yet completely formed. Though blind, they instinctively work their way upward toward the pouch, depending totally on their well-developed front legs, armed with strong claws, for locomotion. The immature hind legs are still nothing more than stubs.

The pouch is small, with a strong muscle at the rim, enabling the mother to close it at will. Within are thirteen teats no bigger than the heads of straight pins. Since the usual litter consists of eighteen to twenty young, some are destined to perish from starvation. Once safely in the confines of the pouch, the young explore for a nipple, and the luckier ones quickly attach themselves to it with the aid of their powerful tongues. Sucking starts immediately, and within an hour the nipple's length is doubled. Little by little it becomes elongated, acting not only as a conduit for nourishment but also as a tether for wider mobility. For weeks the baby possums cling constantly to the teats. At this stage they have no functioning mechanism to control their body temperature, so they must depend upon their mother's body heat for warmth. The sharp deciduous claws, so essential for the hazardous climb to the pouch, are now unneeded and drop off. At one month the babies peep from the pouch, their first view being the grass-lined interior of their den. By two months they are approximately the size of mice.

During hunting trips the mother closes her pouch to prevent the babies from toppling out. She searches the treetops for birds and their eggs. Possums are good swimmers, and should the mother navigate a watercourse, the young will be safe and dry in their watertight compartment, the closed pouch. Before long the babes are mature enough to leave the sheltering pouch and view the world from their mother's back, clinging to her coarse fur. During the days following weaning, they

are most vulnerable as prey for meat-eaters: hawks, owls, coyotes, bobcats, foxes, and wolves. At three months the little possums are capable of fending for themselves.

Opossums passively accept the intrusion of others of their kind on their home territory or hunting range. Though meat is preferred, they eat a varied menu of insects, small mammals (such as moles and mice), snakes, lizards, frogs, crayfish, snails, fish, birds and their eggs, mushrooms, berries, grapes, apples, persimmons, pawpaws, greenbrier, field corn, and even carrion.

When cornered, the opossum bares its many teeth, set in powerful jaws. While confronting an antagonist, it coils and uncoils its tail, which serves as a sort of defense mechanism because of its resemblance to a snake. The customary means of protection is feigning death, or "playing possum." The opossum falls on its side, inert, pulse and heartbeat lowered. Closed eyes and lolling tongue complete the deceptive picture of death. When the enemy leaves the scene, the opossum returns to its normal state. This action has sometimes been attributed to cleverness and cunning on the part of the opossum. Jack Denton Scott of Connecticut, however, believes that "the possum isn't playing," it is out cold with fright.

The animal does not truly hibernate but roams about during the cooler months until a cold

spell strikes. Then, insulated by its considerable fat, it rolls up in leaves in some hole and there remains torpid for a few weeks.

Because possums have spurred the imagination of man over a period of four centuries, a great deal of folklore exists concerning this common yet extraordinary little animal. The forked penis of the possum is doubtless responsible for the long-held belief that copulation took place through the female's nostrils, those openings being the only obviously visible dual orifices. Since the mother was frequently seen pushing her snout into the pouch shortly before delivery, country people believed she was blowing the babies out of her nose into it. This belief was strengthened when soon thereafter babies were discovered in the pouch. The American Indian supposed that the young were not only bred in the pouch but conceived there, and not inside the female's body. Early American settlers and explorers, perplexed by the external pouch, presumed that young were born in it, somehow growing from the female's nipples and then breaking off.

Generations ago, medicinal properties were ascribed to the possum's tail. A woman suffering unduly prolonged labor was given a broth of the tail to bring about immediate delivery. The broth was also considered a remedy for constipation, a severe cough,

and distress of the kidneys. For the easy removal of a thorn, a piece of the possum's tail was thoroughly chewed and then held on the spot where the spine was embedded.

The possum's white flesh has long been considered palatable but fat by country people. As a first step in preparing the possum for cooking, they recommend the removal of all the fat around the kidneys, which is presumed to be the source of the animal's offensive odor.

Lacking intelligence, possums are easily caught in traps.

Those caught this way are not nearly as savory as the ones hauled down from a tree. The trauma of injury produces changes in the body which influence the flavor of the meat. Anyone who cooks possum seems to have his own idea as to how this should be done, but all cooks agree that sweet potatoes are essential to a possum feast.

The possum is not an animal one would recommend as a pet.

Being nocturnal, it is sluggish and unresponsive by day. The animal is dirty in its personal habits and has a repellent odor. In spite of not indulging in self-grooming, it is surprisingly free of ticks and fleas. Because of its small brain, the opossum exhibits a rather dull personality.

Despite the animal's defense of "playing possum" and its remarkable ability to recover from injury, its life expectancy is short. Yet the breed has continued to expand its range, possibly because it eats anything—animal or vegetable—and reproduces prolifically.

Raccoon or Screech Owl?

The raccoon, better known most places as coon, exists nowhere in the world but in North America. Though it is found through the northern United States and Canada, it is not a cold-climate creature; it is most widely spread throughout the southern states and more temperate parts of the West Coast.

Since much of the raccoon's diet comes from the water, it generally makes its nest in forest areas less than a mile from a stream or lake. It prefers to reside high in a hollow tree. Though a nocturnal meanderer and hunter, by day it enjoys draping itself in the crotch of a tree to sunbathe.

Sure-footed in trees, it uses them not only as lodgings but as a haven when threatened.

An excellent tree-climber, the raccoon is not a swift runner.

When hunted, it relies upon clever tactics invented spontaneously to fit the circumstances, intelligence compensating for its lack of speed. An old, wise coon has been known to draw a pursuing dog into water, climb on its head, and drown it. Often as cunning as a fox, the raccoon may destroy its trail by wading along the edge of a stream or crossing fallen logs. It will even, as a last recourse, dive into water. When cornered, it defends itself by cutting and slashing at its attacker.

If a hollow tree is not available for living quarters, the raccoon uses the abandoned dens of other animals. Trees being scarce on the plains of Central Texas, here the coon lives in large rock crevices or the burrows of skunks and badgers. In New Mexico and Arizona it finds water and shelter in canyon cliffs.

A relative of the giant panda, the raccoon is a bushy-haired animal some 30 to 36 inches long, weighing from 10 to 25 pounds. Its pointed face is marked with a black band across the cheeks and eyes and a streak running from forehead to nose. The black mask serves as protective coloration, making the black eyes more difficult to detect in a fight. The fur coloring ranges

from gray to brown and blackish. Six or seven black bands ring the yellow-gray tail.

The raccoon tends toward gluttony but is redeemed from uncouthness by its dainty manner of eating, facilitated by delicate front paws equipped with long, marvelously dexterous fingers. Its diet varies from fresh-water foods to nuts and fruits, vegetables, and birds and their eggs. Full-sized mussels usually prove too great a challenge to the raccoon, which finds smaller mollusks easier to crush and eat. It customarily washes muddy frogs, turtles, crayfish, and clams prior to consuming them. Science has given the coon the Latin name of *lotor*, meaning "the washer," and its name in German is *Waschbär*. Several theories to explain the habit have been put forth. Some naturalists believe that the raccoon is not so much washing its food as dipping it for the sensory satisfaction of feeling the food under water with its sensitive fingers. Another, and perhaps more valid theory, is offered by John Brazier of California. He believes that the raccoon softens and dampens its food whenever possible to help swallowing. It is reported, however, that where water wasn't available, raccoons have been observed "washing" their food in dust.

In April the raccoon's undercoat becomes less heavy and the outer guard hairs thinner. The first signs of the developing winter coat become evident in late August.

Since food is scarce in northern winters, several coon families, for both warmth and sociability, will snuggle down to sleep in a den. From time to time, during less severe spells, they are stirred from slumber by quickening appetites and venture forth to catch mice, rabbits, and other prey.

The urge to mate also rouses the raccoon from slumber.

Mating takes place in December in the South, during February in the North. Nine weeks later, four to five blind young are born, complete with masks and furry coats. At three weeks their eyes are open, and at two months they are able to sally forth on short hunting trips with their mother.

At sunset mother and young, with flat-footed gait, make their way to the margin of a stream to explore shallow pools for their favorite food, crayfish. Their tapering, agile fingers flip over rocks to reveal insects, mussels, and snails. Coon babies are instructed in the delicate art of catching frogs and slower-swimming fish. Slippery earthworms that emerge after a summer shower are easily picked up with their long black fingers. Crumbling rotten logs are

investigated for grubs; crickets are pounced upon in the grass; fragile-shelled turtle eggs are dug from nests; and the eggs of ground-nesting birds are discovered. Periodically a raccoon family will raid cornfields. Pokeweed berries, cherries, blackberries, raspberries, grapes, plums, persimmons, and pecans are all relished by these animals. In short, they will consume anything edible and when favorite foods are not available, will adapt to whatever circumstances provide.

The mother keeps the cubs by her side for nearly a year, and it is not unheard of for her to adopt an orphan. They travel long distances while foraging for food, the mother continually guiding and instructing them. At night they wander considerable distances from the den, from one-half mile to a mile, sometimes covering as much as five miles. Footprints left by the roving raccoons resemble those of little children. When danger strikes, the mother will lead her young up a tree and then dash away, luring the dogs after her. The polygamous father assumes no responsibility for his offspring and lives alone.

When sensing trouble, the raccoon makes a noise somewhere between a hiss and a snort. It can also purr like a cat, though its usual talk is a churring birdlike sound. Some dark night when your ears are assailed by the eerie call of a screech owl, coming not from a tree but

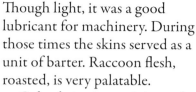

from the ground, its source may not be an owl. The raccoon makes a sound strongly resembling the fluttering reiterations of the screech owl's tremolo.

Trappers have discovered that coons are attracted by bright, shiny objects. They take advantage of this trait by affixing tin foil to their traps. The pelts of northern raccoons are considerably heavier than those of the South.

Country people value raccoon oil as an aid to keeping leather in prime condition. Pioneers used it in both farm and home.

Though light, it was a good lubricant for machinery. During those times the skins served as a unit of barter. Raccoon flesh, roasted, is very palatable.

Cubs thrive in captivity and quickly adapt to human ways.

They make affectionate and intelligent pets, although decidedly mischievous ones. With age, coons tend to become surly.

It is true that raccoons have been known to invade chicken coops to dine on poultry; however, they are mainly beneficial because of their great consumption of harmful insects.

The Short-Lived Shrew

When on a walk in the country, should you spy a tiny mouse-like creature scampering over the surface of a pond or stream, your eyes are not deceiving you. What you are watching is the shrew, not only adept at swimming, diving, and walking along the bottom of a stream, but actually able to run on the water itself. The long hairs on its delicate feet prevent it from submerging.

The shrew, smallest of all mammals, weighs when fully grown approximately one-fourteenth of an ounce—less than the weight of a dime. At quick glance it resembles a mouse, but its long, narrow muzzle, extending far beyond the lower lip, betrays its relation to the mole. Minute bright eyes, always on the alert for food, peer from a densely furry face topped by wide ears with

deep folds inside, which are used to close off the openings when necessary. Its soft, thick fur is brown above and gray below. The tail, in section, is four sided.

The tiny shrew possesses courage and savagery considerably out of proportion to its size. Ferocious and bloodthirsty, it will attack and eat quarry of twice its own dimensions, even cannibalizing on another shrew if no other food is at hand. The animal lives at a frenzied pace, necessitating a large food intake. Every twenty-four hours it eats the equivalent of its own body weight. Even a few hours without sustenance can result in its death. Chiefly an insect-eater, the shrew feeds on tent caterpillars, cutworms, moths, slugs, grasshoppers, crickets, flies, bees, and centipedes and their larvae. In its incessant search for food, it will invade a nest of rats, slaughtering and devouring the young. Snails also form part of the shrew's diet, and in an emergency it will eat vegetation. When food abounds, the shrew burrows in soft soil and buries the surplus, caching reserves of pieces of small animals, large beetles, and mollusks.

Primarily nocturnal, the shrew is frequently about by day as well. It sleeps for periods of one to two hours, alternating them with periods of activity of the same length.

When pursuing a female with amorous intent, the male makes a series of unmelodious clicking sounds. Though shrews generally

live in damp moss and earth, for raising a family the female fashions a nest of dry grass and leaves in a stump hole or under a rock. Two to ten fast-growing young are born. When the mother shrew and her offspring move about, they travel in caravan formation: the mother leads, with the first baby grasping her skin near the base of the tail with its teeth and the rest following in single file, each holding to the one in front in the same manner. They are so strongly linked that when the mother is picked up, the whole family is lifted.

So tense and delicately balanced is the nervous system of this little animal that when caught in the human hand, it often dies instantly from shock. Nervous and high strung, it can die from hearing a loud noise, such as a clap of thunder. In a state of fear, its heart beats 1,200 times per minute, and it breathes 800 times in the same period. A shrew's life span seldom exceeds one year; should it survive longer, at sixteen months it dies of old age.

For generations country people, trappers, and woodsmen asserted that the bite of the

shrew was venomous. Learned men dismissed the claim as a piece of traditional superstition. Investigation has since proved that the shrew does indeed have a toxic bite. Its saliva is poisonous, and the venom, drop for drop, is as potent as the cobra's. A small amount is sufficient to kill mice and other prey, but not enough to harm humans. That the shrew's bite is venomous is no longer considered a myth; folklore has been vindicated and the claim incorporated in our store of animal knowledge.

Life Spans	Years
Bat	3–5
Mouse	3–5
Snail	8
Fox	10
Rabbit	8–10
Squirrel	8–10
Wolf	10–15
Beaver	12
Dog	15
Cat	15–20
Goat	15–20
Deer	18–25
Pig	20
Bear	20–30
Horse	20–35
Newt and lizard	25
Large snake, toad	25
Crocodile	30–50 plus

7 | ABOUT BIRDS

The first written record we have concerning winged creatures and signs comes from the Bible. Many an old-time country preacher has taken his text for a brush arbor meeting from the story in Genesis about Noah, the ark, and the birds:

"And it came to pass at the end of forty days, that Noah opened the window of the ark which he had made: And he sent forth a raven, which went forth to and fro, until the waters were dried up from off the earth. Also he sent forth a dove from him, to see if the waters were abated from the face of the ground; But the dove found no rest for the sole of her foot, and she returned unto him into the ark, for the waters were on the face of the whole earth: then he put forth his hand, and took her, and pulled her in unto him into the ark. And he stayed yet other seven days; and again he sent forth the dove out of the ark; And the dove came in to him in the evening; and, lo, in her mouth was an olive leaf pluckt off: so Noah knew that the waters were abated from the earth. And he stayed yet other seven days; and sent forth the dove; which returned not again unto him any more." (Genesis 8:6–12)

Since Noah first used the dove for a sign of dry land, country people have long worked the land by using the signs given by birds.

Birds and the Seasons

In early rural America birds were often depended upon to forecast weather for a whole season. Some country folks believed, and some still do, that "a dry summer will follow when birds build their nests in exposed places," or "if birds in autumn grow tame, the winter will be cold for game." Many feel that an unusually early arrival of birds which migrate from the north indicates a severely cold winter will follow. This is backed by the beliefs of some northwestern residents, and Helmer Harper of Minnesota who tells us that when birds leave Lake Superior earlier than usual, fly south fast with few delays en route, and do not linger at their usual resting places, a hard winter is on its way.

Birds and Wind

Folks who live in coastal regions say that birds always announce the approach of windy weather. Magpies do their loudest chattering just before a strong wind. Swallows go toward trees, pigeons race after one another with a fierce beating of their wings, sea birds fly inland in groups, and sea gulls gather on land as a sign of an approaching hurricane or bad weather.

If there is any breeze on the beach, gulls and terns can be relied upon to give the direction of the wind. They always rest facing the oncoming wind. This allows them to have unruffled feathers and prepares them for immediate take-off.

Bird Migration

Migration, the movement of birds between their summer and winter homes, has attracted attention and speculation over the ages. Mention of it is made in the Bible and other writings of long ago.

The phenomenon of bird migration was graphically evident to early colonists because of the sheer multitudes of birds at that time. So numerous were passenger pigeons, for example, that when they roosted for the night their combined weight broke the limbs from trees. Shooting them was a needless effort;

because of their dense swarming, catching them in nets was easier.

As an aid to understanding migration, isolated attempts were made over the years to mark individual birds by various means for later identification. John James Audubon, by banding several phoebes with silver thread tied around the leg, discovered that these birds return year after year to the identical nesting site. Not until 1899, however, was the banding method (metal bands took the place of Audubon's thread) used scientifically in Denmark, whence it spread to Europe and the United States.

In addition to bird banding, other studies have revealed many interesting facts about bird migration. The ruby-throated hummingbird, though less than 3 inches in length and weighing only slightly more than one-tenth of an ounce, defies 500 miles of open water when crossing the Gulf of Mexico on its migratory journey.

A means to observe bird migration, used by men since the days of Galileo, can be practiced by anyone having a telescope. Simply point it at the moon, preferably between 8 p.m. and 12 midnight, to note the passage of birds silhouetted against its illumination and estimate their number on a given night. Though the bulk of birds fly during those hours, from 4 to 6 a.m. is also a favorite period.

Smaller birds, such as mixed warblers, flycatchers, orioles, and small perching birds, generally fly by night. Being accustomed to the shelter of wooded areas, they seem to prefer the protective cover of darkness for their flight. Then, too, they are less conspicuous as prey for destructive enemies during the dark hours. Feeding is probably the most important factor governing the choice of nocturnal flight among the smaller birds. It enables them to arrive by day to find food according to their diurnal habits. Some birds, such as swallows, swifts, and nighthawks, feed on the wing. Night navigation is thought to be guided by an innate sense of direction and

superior eyesight, with the visual orientation of moon and stars as a compass bearing.

Because of certain distinct characteristics peculiar to their families, some birds fly segregated from other groups; for example, nighthawks, by reason of their erratic flight, do not fly in mixed company. Other migrating flocks are composed of a variety of birds drawn together by similarity of size, form, and methods of searching for food.

Flight patterns, too, differ. Some birds—blackbirds, wax-wings, snow buntings, shore birds—move in close formation; others, such as vultures, blue jays, warblers, larks, and bluebirds, fly in loose order. Still others travel separately—owls, wrens, shrikes, grebes, kingfishers—flocking occasionally where food is abundant along the way.

In certain species males migrate first, reaching their breeding grounds to stake out territory a week or more before the arrival of the females. Robins, rose-breasted grosbeaks, sparrows, and black-capped vireos are some birds of this practice. Among others, such as shore birds, male and female arrive

simultaneously. Large birds of some species, such as the Canada goose, mate for life.

The urge to migrate, even in the absence of whatever original motives, has become hereditary. Birds don't wait until their food supply is depleted and cold weather sets in before commencing migration. Exemplifying the hereditary urge are young birds which find their way to the specific winter quarters of their species, despite their parents' having migrated earlier, and cowbirds which, though reared by a different species, still reach their appropriate wintering grounds.

The four chief factors prompting the start of migration are day length, temperature, amount of available food, and changes within the bird's body.

Increasing light of lengthening days stimulates activity in birds' reproductive organs. (An interesting fact to note is that almost every species has but one functioning ovary, the left, which is active only during breeding season.) In addition, there is a fat accumulation—flight fuel—equaling one-third of the body weight. These changes trigger urges to return north to breeding grounds. At this period birds experience *Zugunruhe*, or nocturnal restlessness, most migrations taking place at night.

The benefit of migration is that it permits birds to live in each area when it is at its most favorable

season. Both summer and winter quarters provide a milder climate and more abundant food supply; northern summers afford extra-long days for hunting food for nestlings.

The bobolinks travel farther than any other members of their family—5,000 miles from their wintering grounds in Brazil and northern Argentina to their summer quarters in the northern United States and southern Canada. New Englanders in colonial times found them nesting in coastal marshes and grassy river valleys. Over the years bobolinks gradually followed the spread of grain fields westward and now breed as far as California. Bobolinks that have nested in the West, prompted by their original hereditary instinct, return east to follow ancestral migratory routes. They head south along a flyway that in the nineteenth century took them over the extensive rice fields of South Carolina.

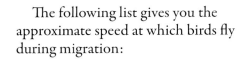

The following list gives you the approximate speed at which birds fly during migration:

small perching birds (larks, pipits, buntings)	20 to 37 mph
members of the crow family (jays, magpies, ravens)	31 to 45 mph
starlings	38 to 49 mph
falcons (A peregrine falcon, diving after its prey, speeds at the rate of 180 miles per hour!)	40 to 48 mph
geese	42 to 55 mph
grouse	43 to 47 mph
ducks	44 to 59 mph
swifts	70 mph

In their daily search for food, songbirds fly at an altitude of less than 150 feet. Hawks and vultures, scanning vast distances for food, may fly as high as a mile. When migrating, birds usually fly below 3,000 feet, although ducks and occasionally smaller birds have been observed above 20,000 feet.

Below is a list of migratory birds, the months of their migrations, and their summer and winter quarters:

Bird	Arrives in Summer Quarters	Departs for Winter Quarters
Purple martin	Jan. North America	Sept. South America

Some southern Indian tribes stationed old squaws near newly planted fields outside the village to protect crops from hungry birds. Being isolated, the women often lost their lives and scalps to hostile Indians of other tribes. The Choctaws and Chickasaws capitalized on their knowledge of the purple martin's preference for breeding in colonies, thus sparing the scalps of their old women. They lured martins to appropriate spots by hanging up groups of hollowed-out gourds for nesting. The martins fearlessly drove away marauding crows and hawks from both crops and poultry.

Bird	Arrives in Summer Quarters	Departs for Winter Quarters
Purple grackle	late Feb. and March east of Rockies to Texas and Florida	Oct. southern states, South America

Bird	Arrives in Summer Quarters	Departs for Winter Quarters
Belted kingfisher	March North America	Dec. southern states, South America

At the end of a tunnel, sometimes 15 feet long, the belted kingfisher lays its eggs on a pile of regurgitated fish bones. Since the female is too short-legged to stand over the hatchlings, the newborn naked babies are obliged to cling together in a mass for warmth.

Bird	Arrives in Summer Quarters	Departs for Winter Quarters
Yellow-shafted flicker	March North America, east of Rockies	Oct. southern Texas, Gulf Coast, Arizona, California

Alabama adopted the yellow-shafted flicker as its state bird, dubbing it the "yellowhammer." Civil War soldiers went off to battle with "yellowhammer" feathers decorating their hats.

Bird	Arrives in Summer Quarters	Departs for Winter Quarters
Eastern phoebe	March North America, east of Rockies	Oct. south of Carolinas to Gulf states, southern Mexico
Scissor-tailed flycatcher	March central and southwestern states	Oct. southern Mexico, Panama

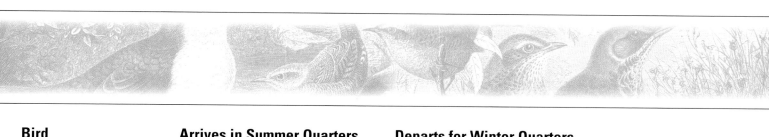

Bird	Arrives in Summer Quarters	Departs for Winter Quarters
Robin	March North America	Oct., Nov. south as far as Guatemala (some remain north in winter)

Have you ever wondered why the robin is obliged to tug repeatedly to free a worm from the earth? Each body segment of the worm, except for the first and last, is equipped with hooklike bristles with which it grips the soil around it. A robin nestling requires at least 14 feet of earthworms each day!

Bird	Arrives in Summer Quarters	Departs for Winter Quarters
Wood thrush	March eastern United States	Oct. Mexico, Central America
Bluebird	March North America	Oct. middle states to Bermuda, West Indies (some remain north in winter)
Field sparrow	March eastern United States	Oct. Missouri and New Jersey to Gulf Coast (some remain north in winter)
Red-winged blackbird	March North America east of the Plains	Oct. southern United States
Purple finch	March northern United States	Nov. south of Pennsylvania to southern Arizona, Texas, Florida
Cowbird	March throughout North America	Nov. southern states, Mexico

The cowbird is well named: it alights on the backs of cattle, where it picks off ticks. In the 1860's the cowbird was known as the buffalo bird when it performed the same service for herds of buffalo.

Bird	Arrives in Summer Quarters	Departs for Winter Quarters
Eastern meadowlark	March, April North America, westward to the Plains	Oct. southward, to South America (some remain north in winter)
Canada goose	March, April northern United States, Canada	Nov., Dec. southward to Mexico

Canada geese fly in V formation because this flight pattern maintains each bird in a position to see ahead and at the same time avoid air disturbances from the wing beats of birds in front. The leader may fly in any position in the wedge, guiding the flight by calling to the rest.

Bird	Arrives in Summer Quarters	Departs for Winter Quarters
White-breasted nuthatch	April eastern United States	Oct. southward
Brown creeper	April northern United States	Oct. Gulf Coast
House wren	April northern United States	Oct. below the Carolinas

Indians, hearing prodigious bird song and noting its small brown source, gave the wren a long Indian name meaning "a big noise for its small size."

Bird	Arrives in Summer Quarters	Departs for Winter Quarters
Ruby-crowned kinglet	April northern United States	Oct. southern United States, Mexico, Central America
Red-eyed vireo	April northern United States, west to Rockies	Oct. South America
Black-and-white warbler	April eastern United States, west to the Plains	late Sept. Baja California; central Florida, northern South America
Summer tanager	April southern and eastern states	Oct. Central Mexico to Bolivia

The summer tanager breaks the stingers from wasps in order to feed undisturbed on their larvae.

Bird	Arrives in Summer Quarters	Departs for Winter Quarters
Rufous-sided towhee	April northern United States	Sept. southern United States, Central America

Bird	Arrives in Summer Quarters	Departs for Winter Quarters
Vesper sparrow	April northern United States	Oct. Baja California, Gulf Coast
Junco	April northern United States	Sept. south to Gulf (some remain north in winter)
Rusty blackbird	April northern United States	Nov. Gulf Coast, Colorado
Short-eared owl	April northern United States	Nov. southern United States
Rail	April Atlantic Coast salt marshes	Oct. south of New Jersey
Spotted sandpiper	April northern United States to Gulf	Sept. southern states to Brazil
Chimney swift	April east of Plains from Canada to Gulf	Sept. Central and South America
Barn swallow	late April throughout United States	Sept. Central and South America
Barn thrasher	late April northern states east of Rockies	Oct. south of Virginia
Bobolink	early May northern United States west to the prairies	July to Oct. Central and South America
Rose-breasted grosbeak	early May southern Canada south to Kansas, Georgia	Sept. southern Mexico to Ecuador
Baltimore oriole	early May United States east of Rockies	Sept. southern Mexico to Central America
Indigo bunting	middle May Canada to Gulf	Sept. Mexico, Central America
Ruby-throated hummingbird	May eastern North America to Gulf	Oct. Central America

The hummingbird was first observed in Canada and New England about 1600. Jesuit fathers, unable to detect the act of feeding, believed it lived solely upon the fragrance of flowers.

Bird	Arrives in Summer Quarters	Departs for Winter Quarters
Catbird	May northern United States Rockies, south to Arizona, Georgia	Nov. southern states, Central to America, Cuba
Logger-head shrike	May eastern United States west to the Plains	Oct. southern states
Scarlet tanager	May Canada south to Oklahoma, South Carolina	Oct. northern South America
Goldfinch	May northern United States	Oct. Gulf Coast, Mexico (some remain north in winter)

The goldfinch's nest is so tightly woven that it holds water, and hatchlings left unprotected by their parents have been known to drown during a rain.

Bird	Arrives in Summer Quarters	Departs for Winter Quarters
Bittern	May north of Virginia	Oct. Virginia, southward

Were we to witness the arrival of migrating birds at their wintering grounds, birds so familiar to us in the North might prove difficult of identification. At the close of the nesting season, most birds begin to molt, a few feathers being lost at a time while others grow in. The resulting plumage differs in color from that of spring. Some birds change color without molting: feather tips break off, exposing already existent plumage of a different hue beneath.

Indian legends sometimes offered explanations for plumage of various colors. The Alaskan Indians, to account for the yellow crown patch of the northern three-toed woodpecker, claimed that famine forced this bird to consume its mate. After eating, he cleaned his claws on top of his head, and the fat he wiped there left a yellow mark.

There is vertical as well as horizontal migration. Some birds travel hundreds of miles to reach summer or winter quarters; others accomplish this by moving altitudinally up or down the sides of mountains. A few hundred feet of altitude are the equivalent of hundreds of miles of latitude. Birds that nest in the higher zones of mountains winter at their base.

Some birds are year-round northern residents. Those which, in spite of cold and lack of flying insects, can find food, such as weed seeds, dry berries, and hibernating insects and their eggs or can feed on other winter residents, as does the snowy owl, risk less by remaining in a severe climate than by hazarding migration. However, even among resident birds, like the blue jays, woodpeckers, nuthatches, and chickadees, there is migratory movement, though on a smaller scale. They often wander widely in flocks according to the degree of food shortage or overcrowding.

A list of year-round resident birds follows:

Bird	Range
Red-headed woodpecker	eastern United States, except New England

The red-headed woodpecker pecks out his home in trees and utility poles. Its ability to endure the shock of such drilling is due to these factors: the bones of the skull are unusually thick and extremely hard; the bony roots of the tongue, in most birds attached to the bottom of the skull, in woodpeckers are wrapped around the cranium and fastened at the base of the bill so that part of its tongue is actually on top of its head!

Blue jay	Canada to Gulf states, east of Rockies

The blue jay and his mate gather twigs, dragging them along with them until a proper nesting site is discovered. Southerners say that the jaybird is carrying sticks to the Devil.

Black-billed magpie	northern United States, south to California, New Mexico, Kansas

The black-billed magpie, besides being scavenger and mimic, is a thief. Magpies were reported to have rushed into tents of the Lewis and Clark expedition, seizing food from the dishes.

Common crow	throughout North America to Gulf

Tufted titmouse	Nebraska to Connecticut, south to Texas and Florida

A fearless pilferer, the tufted titmouse has been known to take hair for nesting purposes from living animals—including humans!

Mockingbird	California to South Dakota, southeastern States

A great mimic, the mockingbird was called "four hundred tongues" by the Indians.

Cedar waxwing	Canada to Kansas and North Carolina

The tips of wings, and sometimes tail feathers, of the cedar waxwing bear red splotches resembling sealing-wax drippings, hence its name.

Starling	throughout the United States

Cardinal	Connecticut to South Dakota, from Florida to Gulf Coast

The arrival and departure of birds have long been thought of as heralding seasonal changes. When the call of the phoebe bird is heard, one can expect to see the first traces of green across the land in early spring. In spite of the fact that swallows don't appear in their northern breeding grounds until late April, people are accustomed to dubbing them "harbingers of spring." New England folks are on the lookout for the gold of tasseled pussy willows and the red glow of swamp maple blooms at the first song burst from the brown thrasher. Naturalist John Burroughs noted that sap rises in the sugar maple simultaneously with the arrival of the bluebird. Residents of northern states have no need to consult their calendars to know that the first week in May has come when they hear the notes of the ovenbird. It appears on the same date every year at given points along its flyways.

Besides being thought of as vanguards of the seasons, birds have often been considered omens. The magpie, in English folklore, is such a bird. The appearance of one means sorrow; three magpies mean a wedding is in the offing. Over the centuries the raven has been viewed as a foretoken of evil. If its shadow crossed in front of a bird, she was doomed to disaster. Supernatural powers have been attributed to ravens. They have been kept for centuries, one wing clipped, at the Tower of London; Charles II firmly believed that if they departed, England would collapse.

Among the Indians of colonial America, fascinating superstitions about certain birds were many. Cherokee Indians thought of the wren as an eavesdropper who reported everyone's business. A wren brought the news of a

newborn baby. If it was a boy, the birds appeared downcast, knowing the papoose would one day hunt them; if a girl, they were joyful, for she would do them no harm.

Early settlers of the North American continent believed the woodcock responsible for malaria, because where woodcocks were prevalent, so was malaria. Woodcocks favor swampy areas, where mosquitoes breed. The supposition was based on the wrong connection.

There were superstitions not only about the birds themselves, but about their migratory habits as well. In olden times people thought that small birds hitchhiked on the backs of larger birds. The view was even expressed that migratory birds wintered on the moon! Centuries ago certain birds were alleged to hibernate as an explanation for their disappearance during the cold months. They were believed to remain in a torpid state hidden in recesses or embedded in the mud of ponds and marshes. Such claims were made concerning swallows, kites, storks, ouzels, turtledoves, larks, and others.

Actually, some birds become torpid by slowing down their bodily processes to adapt to adverse circumstances, such as food shortage. When European swifts are unable to procure food for their brood, the nestlings become temporarily dormant, remaining motionless for days, their temperature below normal.

With resumption of food intake, they revive immediately. Such torpor is the equivalent of small-scale hibernation. Though the theory that birds hibernate had long been considered superstition, recent observations have proved that whippoorwills do indeed

sometimes hibernate, lying torpid in some sheltered retreat with respiration and temperature well below normal. Interestingly enough, the Indians named the whippoorwill "sleeper."

The movements of nomadic peoples have been governed by the migration of birds. Perhaps one of the most propitious effects of bird migration on the human race occurred in October, the month of mass migration. Mariners on three small ships bobbing in the Atlantic, despairing of ever sighting land, felt their hearts burst with excitement at the spectacle of feathered multitudes winging south. Where there are birds, land must be! Columbus changed his direction in pursuit, eventually finding safe harbor in San Salvador. Thus migrating birds determined the course of Columbus and of history as well.

Life Spans of Birds

Birds	Years	Birds	Years
Wren	3	Nightingale	18
Thrush	10	Linnet	23
Blackbird	10	Crane	24
Robin	10	Crow	25–30
Pheasant	15	Skylark	30
Partridge	15	Sparrow hawk	15
Goldfinch		Pelican	50
Blackcap	15	Canada goose	70
Lark	18	Heron	80

Poultry Proverbs

There are many old weather proverbs that speak of "signs" given us by the various unusual actions of poultry. Crowing at unusual times, violent and sudden clapping of wings, nervousness in the flock, rolling in the dirt, a crowding together, frantic scratching in search of food, and any other unusual activities and movements are all good indicators. Barnyard fowls and wild birds become nervous and very noisy before there is a drastic and unfavorable change in the weather. Country weather forecasters would say: "When the peacock loudly bawls, we'll soon have both rain and squalls."

We cannot ignore the warnings that poultry and birds tell us about weather and its changes. Their instinct

is quite often ahead of any of man's instruments for recording weather changes. Perhaps they can feel the electrical change in the atmosphere that precedes a storm. Though we do not yet know what devices they have as alarms to change, we do know they have them.

Using the Signs with Birds and Poultry

Robert Swenson of Minnesota always tries to set eggs so the hatch will come under the sign of Cancer (June 21 to July 22). This is a fruitful sign and he believes the pullets will mature much more rapidly than those hatched under other signs and will be better layers. If at all possible he tries to have them hatch under the first quarter moon, early in the sign of Cancer.

To follow the signs in hatching birds and poultry you should observe the following:

Select good quality, healthy birds for breeding; know the incubation period of the type birds you are hatching; use the incubation table to select a *day of hatch* when the moon is increasing and in a fruitful sign. The sign of Cancer is best, followed by Scorpio or Pisces. Chicks hatched under the proper sign will be rapid in their maturity, thrifty, and make excellent layers. Birds and chicks hatched during the

decreasing moon phases and in a barren sign will not be nearly as good. This has been proven by many good poultrymen. Sid Greenway of Rhode Island says, "Chicks hatched under the right signs are twice as good and worth twice the money as those not incubated with the signs in mind."

Instruct your hatcheryman to have *your* eggs set so they will hatch off on an increasing moon and on a fruitful day. Use this incubation table and a good almanac and you can tell him the exact day to set the eggs for you.

Domestic Fowls	Incubation Days
Canary	13–14
Chicken	19–24 (average 21)
Duck	28
Duck (Muscovy)	33–35
Goose	27–33
Guinea	28
Ostrich	42
Pea Hen	28–30
Pheasant	22–24
Pigeon	16–20
Turkey	26–30

Raising Birds for Song and Beauty

The sign of Taurus rules the throat and many bird breeders believe that having birds hatched under this sign produces good singers. Some breeders strive to have birds hatch under the sign of Libra as this sign is noted for beauty, color, form, and grace. Richard Schuman, at one time a highly recognized birdman in Missouri, says, "Use good breeders, choose a fruitful sign with good aspects for mating, and you can considerably improve bird quality."

Nature's Warnings about Birds and Poultry

Nature does a fine job of warning keepers of birds and poultry of coming problems. Observation can prevent serious losses. Always notice the appearance of the birds, as a sick bird will look sick and act sick, most times early enough for you to correct the problem. Any sick bird will lose eye brightness and will have a listless, pale appearance.

Keep your ears open to strange sounds when you are near your birds. Coughs, sneezes, and wheezing are indicators that action must be taken to prevent serious losses. Drop in feed consumption, weight loss, and any change in appearance and action can be an early warning to health problems.

Birds and Superstition

Birds are sometimes regarded as being supernaturally wise and there are many country omens about them, here are but a few.

Old southern plantation workers believed that doves knew before cotton planting time whether the crops would be good or bad. They thought that before the new ground was broken or the "middles were busted out" the dove knew what the crop yield would be for that season. If the dove flew on the right-hand side of the man as he first started plowing there would be a good crop that year. If it flew on the left hand, the crop would be a failure. They also thought that the dove was particularly accurate in predicting the yield of corn, following the same signs.

These same farm workers believed that the direction from which the cry of the first mourning dove of the season came was important. If the sound of the dove came from above the worker, he would prosper.

Another warning that nature gives, which is rather interesting but of a less serious character, is that birds tell us when they are receiving insufficient protein in their feed. Protein requirements vary with various strains of birds and poultry, but from 14 to 18 percent is usually adequate. When protein drops below the necessary amounts the hen will immediately tell the poultryman by laying smaller eggs. Increased protein in the feed will immediately increase egg size.

Yolks of eggs tell a lot about what chickens have been eating. A bright orange yolk (it's loaded with vitamin A) shows the birds have been allowed to range and feed on grass. Light-colored yolks show they have been caged or confined.

If it came from any other direction, things would probably not go very well that season.

In the New England states it is still considered unlucky if you see two crows flying together on your left.

In the South it is thought that if two quails fly up in front of you when you are on your way to a business transaction it would be well to postpone the business until another day.

If you break up a killdeer's nest, you will soon break an arm or a leg.

In many parts of the country it is considered bad luck for a bird to flutter against a closed window when you are near that window.

If a rooster crows into the open door of a house it foretells that visitors are on the way.

Of all birds in folklore and mythology, the cuckoo is rated as the highest for its possession of great wisdom. The cuckoo's wisdom is thought to surpass that of other birds in that it knows not only present events but also things that are to come.

This is a carryover from the myths of the ancient Hindu and the early Greeks who thought that cuckoos had these supernatural qualities. Many country folks we have talked with still think the cuckoo has them. Daniel Eaton of Pennsylvania says the old-time farmers of his area would do corn planting only when the song of the brown thrasher or cuckoo was first heard in the spring. To farmers, especially in the old country, the cuckoo has been a reliable omen for weather and crop planting for many centuries.

Merry Thought

If someone asked you, with regard to a bird, what a merry thought was, would you reply that it was probably what prompted his outburst of song?

The merry thought is the furcula—that forked bone between the neck and breast of a bird commonly called the wishbone. The name "merry thought" has reference to the long-time custom of two people's pulling a fowl's furcula to see who holds the longer piece when it breaks, the idea being that the one with the longer piece will be married first or be granted whatever happy wish was made at the moment. This expressive word was coined in England about 1600.

If the clavicles forming the merry thought are broken, the bird is unable to fly. In running birds they are absent or rudimentary, and in certain birds that do not fly much, such as some parrots, they are small.

This Thanksgiving, share a merry thought with a friend!

Cicada: Denizen of Two Worlds

Perhaps there is no more typical sound of the summer countryside than that made by the cicada. As soon as the sun heats the earth, the insect rasps the air incessantly with a harsh whir that rises in a crescendo and slowly tapers off. Only the male produces this unmelodious sound, thought to be a sexual call to attract a mate. Ironically, the female lacks auditory organs as well as those for generating noise. A more appropriate arrangement might have been for the female to possess a hearing faculty in order to appreciate her suitor's overtures, and for the male to lack hearing in order to be spared his own din! When cicadas emit their call in concert, they can be heard more than one-quarter mile distant.

With her spear-like egg-laying tube, the female penetrates twigs, depositing eggs, which often cause the death of the wood. Little more than a week later they hatch, and the ant-like nymphs drop to the ground, where they bury themselves. Life is sustained by their sucking juices from tree roots. With the passage of time, they burrow ever deeper into the earth, as much as 6 feet below the surface, remaining close to their food source, the roots. After more than a decade and a half in the dark, silent underground, Nature prompts them to move upward toward the surface. By now their brown bodies are a bit more than 1 inch long and equipped with enlarged, spined front legs, well adapted for digging.

During the dark of night, the cicada makes its debut into the upper world and clumsily inches its way up a tree trunk. Here it patiently awaits the final change to adulthood. A split begins down the back, ever widening until the mature cicada is revealed. At first nothing more than fluid-filled sacs, the two pairs of wings, large and membranous, gradually expand. Now, after its long internment beneath the earth, the insect is free to fly. One of the heaviest bodies of the insect world to be supported in air is that of the cicada.

On hot summer days innumerable cicadas can be found clinging to trees, their folded wings resembling peaked roofs. The cicada is a lover of heat and sunshine, perhaps as a result of having spent more than 95 percent of its life as an underground lodger in darkness. During the daylight hours of its short adult life, it endlessly repeats its shrill call, reminding us that summers too are short.

Cicada-Killer Wasp

One of North America's largest wasps, exceeding an inch in length, is the cicada killer, belonging to a group called digger wasps. Endowed

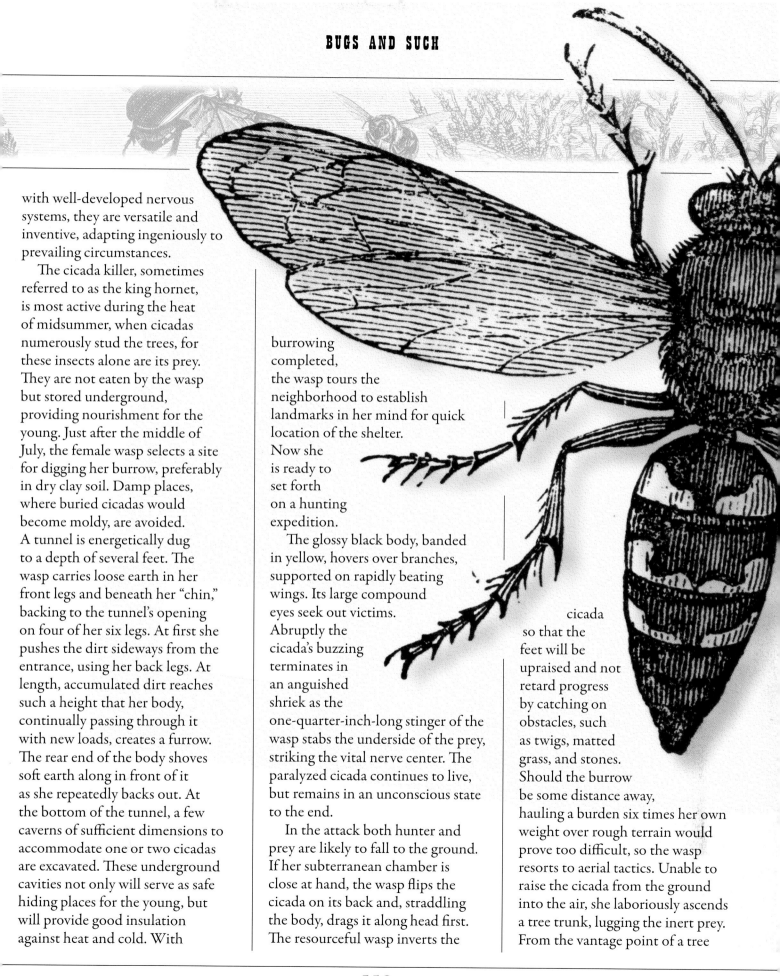

with well-developed nervous systems, they are versatile and inventive, adapting ingeniously to prevailing circumstances.

The cicada killer, sometimes referred to as the king hornet, is most active during the heat of midsummer, when cicadas numerously stud the trees, for these insects alone are its prey. They are not eaten by the wasp but stored underground, providing nourishment for the young. Just after the middle of July, the female wasp selects a site for digging her burrow, preferably in dry clay soil. Damp places, where buried cicadas would become moldy, are avoided. A tunnel is energetically dug to a depth of several feet. The wasp carries loose earth in her front legs and beneath her "chin," backing to the tunnel's opening on four of her six legs. At first she pushes the dirt sideways from the entrance, using her back legs. At length, accumulated dirt reaches such a height that her body, continually passing through it with new loads, creates a furrow. The rear end of the body shoves soft earth along in front of it as she repeatedly backs out. At the bottom of the tunnel, a few caverns of sufficient dimensions to accommodate one or two cicadas are excavated. These underground cavities not only will serve as safe hiding places for the young, but will provide good insulation against heat and cold. With

burrowing completed, the wasp tours the neighborhood to establish landmarks in her mind for quick location of the shelter. Now she is ready to set forth on a hunting expedition.

The glossy black body, banded in yellow, hovers over branches, supported on rapidly beating wings. Its large compound eyes seek out victims. Abruptly the cicada's buzzing terminates in an anguished shriek as the one-quarter-inch-long stinger of the wasp stabs the underside of the prey, striking the vital nerve center. The paralyzed cicada continues to live, but remains in an unconscious state to the end.

In the attack both hunter and prey are likely to fall to the ground. If her subterranean chamber is close at hand, the wasp flips the cicada on its back and, straddling the body, drags it along head first. The resourceful wasp inverts the cicada so that the feet will be upraised and not retard progress by catching on obstacles, such as twigs, matted grass, and stones. Should the burrow be some distance away, hauling a burden six times her own weight over rough terrain would prove too difficult, so the wasp resorts to aerial tactics. Unable to raise the cicada from the ground into the air, she laboriously ascends a tree trunk, lugging the inert prey. From the vantage point of a tree

limb, grasping her heavy cargo, she projects herself into the air, wings throbbing rapidly. Sometimes she is able to reach her destination with but one such launching. If the victim is particularly weighty, she may have to repeat the maneuver several times, for the wings are able to support the cicada's body only on a descending flight course.

The immobilized cicada is dragged down the tunnel and placed in the circular cavern at the bottom. Occasionally another cicada is deposited, but no more than one egg is laid in each tiny chamber. The single egg is fastened to the underside of the cicada, close to the front legs. Two to three days later, the larva hatches from the egg and immediately takes sustenance from the paralyzed insect. The fluid injected by the wasp's sting not only insensitizes and immobilizes the cicada without killing it so that the food supply remains fresh, but acts as a preservative should the insect die. After a week or so of continual feeding, the larva has devoured most of the food and attains full growth as an immature wasp. For the next two days, it busies itself in forming a cocoon of silk and soil. In this snug capsule it lies dormant through the chill of autumn and winter, changing into a pupa with the advent of spring.

When the earth is softened by summer showers and warmed by the sun's rays, the would-be wasp frees itself from the pupal shell and chews through the encasing cocoon. Now it must scratch its way upward through several feet of earth to freedom in the open air, emerging a fully developed wasp.

Though the female's short life is one of feverish activity, the male's existence is leisurely. With the exception of his one duty, to fertilize the female's eggs, he is free to explore whatever arouses his curiosity.

Only the larva of the cicada killer is carnivorous. Both male and female adults feed on nectar, varying this diet with sap. Trailing the flight of sapsuckers, they cluster at the holes made by these birds to sip the tree's oozing juice. They are especially fond of fermented sap and have been known to become inebriated from overindulgence.

With the first autumnal frost, wasps' tissues freeze, and death overtakes them. Beneath the cold soil, the next generation, silent in its cocoons, awaits the prod of summer's warmth to begin the cycle once more.

Cricket: Gladiator and Musician

Along about dusk in country homes, a reassuring chirping sounds from the vicinity of the hearth. The source is the brownish house cricket, which, being fond of warmth, seeks fireplaces. Its music is a symbol of peace and contentment to rural folk.

Throughout the world there are 22,500 species of crickets; the most common of these is the black field cricket. This ubiquitous little musician, when heard in English homes, was said to bring good luck. In both China and Japan, valued for its music, it was often kept as a pet in cages. During the years of the Chinese Empire, crickets were carefully tended in the royal palace. Their cages were veritable works of art, many being preserved in today's museums. They were made of porcelain or ivory with covers of carved jade. In humbler abodes crickets were confined in delicate bamboo cages or coconut shells. Even today they are sometimes kept as pets in Japan, Italy, Spain, and Portugal.

Cricket is a word formed in imitation of the creature's call.

The insect should be termed an instrumentalist, not a singer, for it produces its sound by rubbing parts of its body together, not by forcing air between vocal cords. The wings of the two sexes differ in that the male's alone are characterized by the file and scraper for sound-making. A heavy vein at the front of each forewing has a rasplike surface of numerous ridges on the underside; a smooth rib on the upper side of the wings serves as a scraper. The cricket raises its forewings to a 45-degree angle and moves one across the other, like a bow and fiddle, to make music. The taut wing membranes act as a

sounding board so that the chirping can be heard at surprising distances.

There is a direct relationship between temperature and call rate. During cool weather it is slower; when the mercury rises the tempo increases. Though most of the cricket's sounds are for communication, to announce its dominion or to attract a mate, some are thought to be for the sheer joy of living. The sounds are of varying quality: with the approach of a rival, the chirping is shriller, more defiant; when the cricket is attracting and courting a female, it is more musical.

Sometimes two crickets will engage in combat over a female. Their kicking and biting can be so fierce as to terminate in the death of one of the males. After attracting a female with his melodious serenade, the suitor caresses her with his antennae. Just prior to the first frost of autumn, the female deposits eggs in the ground for protection against the cold to come. With a needlelike appendage, sometimes as long as her body, she inserts tiny cream-colored eggs, as many as three hundred, under the soil. The eggs resemble diminutive peeled bananas, no more than one-twelfth of an inch in length. They remain underground through the winter, dormancy and cold being essential for successful hatching.

When the sun's rays sufficiently warm the soil in late May or early June, the eggs hatch, and cricket babies, lacking wings and egg-laying apparatus, make their way to the surface. Omnivorous like their parents, they eat dead insects and plants. Each day brings conspicuous growth until at last their horny garb no longer fits. The skin splits down the back, and out they crawl in new attire. This will be the first molt of many before they reach adulthood. With each molt their size increases. Wing pads appear at the next-to-last molt. Roughly twelve weeks after birth, the cricket reaches maturity, sporting fully developed wings at the final molt.

Some crickets carry the right wing higher; others, the left.

During the first hour following the last molt, the wings are yet soft. However the cricket has lapped its wings, once they have hardened the arrangement is maintained for life. If the natural position is forcibly changed, the uncomfortable insect moves about until the wings are restored to their original placement.

The cricket seldom flies, but projects itself through the air in great leaps by the aid of its powerfully muscled hind legs. They are equipped with spikes that dig into the ground for traction, enabling it to jump remarkable distances for its size. Other spikes on the legs, pointing backward, help the cricket to maintain a firm hold as it climbs and runs about amid grass blades and leafy plants. The little creature is as capable of propelling itself through water as it is of leaping about on land.

The front legs hold the food while the strong jaws are at work. There is great variety in a cricket menu—vegetables, seeds, grain, meat, rubber, and clothing, particularly when stained with food or perspiration. Meat is an essential in the diet, and if it is unavailable the cricket will not hesitate to cannibalize.

The body of the adult cricket is about 1 inch in length. The antennae are half again as long as the body. Though only the male has the file-and-scraper feature on its wings, both male and female have dual spines projecting from the rear. Minute hairs on them detect vibrations on land and in the air. They act as auxiliary hearing aids, the major auditory organs being small elongated apertures on the front legs. So the insect truly listens with its legs!

The cricket often sits at the entrance of its home, a small, cavelike hole scooped out beneath a stone or dirt clod. When possible it chooses a homesite where the sun's rays are sure to strike the doorway. Here the little instrumentalist grooms itself, passing the many-jointed antennae through its jaws, thoroughly washing them. By bringing the wings forward, it is able to clean them. The body's personal hygiene the insect attends to by rubbing it on the ground. To complete its toilet, the cricket puts its foot in its mouth to nip off any bits of dirt.

An interesting species of cricket is the ant-loving cricket that dwells underground in ant nests. It is tolerated as a kind of house pet by the ants, corresponding in height to a point about midway on an ant's leg. This tiny cricket survives by licking oily secretions from the bodies and legs of its ant hosts.

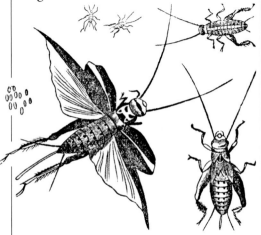

The carnivorous leaf-rolling cricket hunts aphids by night.

Its long, responsive antennae, twice the length of its body, are typical of nocturnal insects. During the day it must have safe lodging, so it creates its own by constructing a tent from a leaf. Using its jaws, it makes slits along the leaf's edge. Then, positioning itself on the leaf, it gathers the severed portions around it with its feet. As the margins begin to meet, the cricket commences attaching them together with fine silk thread from its mouth. This creature's capability of producing silk is unique among crickets. The head moves back and forth, fastening silk on one side and then the other. Gradually the thread hardens, contracting and drawing the leaf edges closer and closer together. In this leaf-tube shelter the cricket settles down to pass the daylight hours in safety, the long antennae wrapped lengthwise about its body. Each evening a new structure is built.

Crickets have long been esteemed for more than just their music. As early as the latter half of the tenth century, the cricket was valued in China for its fighting abilities. Cricket combat became a national diversion. Records of individual accomplishments were preserved much as records of athletes are kept today. A fighting cricket was given a special diet consisting of rice and boiled chestnuts. It was believed that female mosquitoes should be included in its nutrition to augment the cricket's fighting skills, but only those which had fed on the trainer's blood. The combatants were meticulously weighed on tiny scales for proper classification as to heavyweight, middleweight, or lightweight. Before the contest the crickets were stirred to belligerency by being antagonized and tickled with small brushes of rabbit or rat whiskers. The struggle ended only with the death of the defeated. Considerable sums of money were wagered on the outcome.

The life span of a cricket is short, stretching from early summer to the first heavy frost-giving us not many months in which to enjoy the music of this energetic little instrumentalist!

Doodlebug

In sandy areas of the country, miniature craters with occasional spuns of soil flying from them are not an unusual sight. Though children very often play with their small architects, few intimate facts are generally known about them.

The excavator of these funnel-shaped pits is an insect commonly dubbed the "doodlebug." Actually, it is the larval form of the ant lion.

The ant lion does not go abroad in active search and capture of food. It combines stratagem and patience to accomplish this end. Crawling repeatedly backward from a central point and constantly moving in a circle, the ant lion tosses loose sand out of the way with its jaws. A pit is gradually formed with steeply graded sides, measuring an inch or more in diameter and 1 inch in depth. The ant lion conceals itself under loose sand at the bottom, with only its sickle-like jaws protruding. Here it resolutely awaits the approach of an unwary or curious ant. This is the moment when dirt flies! The ant lion flings up the sand, causing small-scale avalanches on the sloping walls. Caught in the din slides, the ant is swept to the bottom, where it is seized by the ambusher's jaws. Long and curved, they act as hypodermic needles to inject the body of the prey with potent venom, reducing its interior to liquid, which is then sucked up through the hollow jaws. In order to dine in leisurely fashion, the ant lion feeds, undisturbed, beneath the sand. When the victim's body has been siphoned dry, it is cast from the pit, and the ant lion resumes its silent, expectant waiting.

When the ant lion first emerges from the egg its mother has laid in the sandy dust, its tiny dimensions dictate that it restrict itself to the capture of equally tiny prey. In keeping with its constantly increasing size, it constructs bigger craters and traps larger insects.

Eventually, the fully grown larva is ready for the pupal stage. Skillfully a cocoon of sand and silk is fashioned while the little creature is under the sandy soil. Several months later the pupa breaks from confinement and heads for the world above. Along the back a rent in the skin appears, and the mature ant lion crawls forth. Once its wings spread and harden in the air, it is somewhat similar to the dragonfly in appearance. Unlike the dragonfly, however, it is not a strong flyer. The adult ant lion never eats. Whatever it consumed during its youth in the pitfalls must suffice it now and for the rest of its days.

Ant lion pits can usually be found in places somewhat protected from rainfall, such as close to barns or under rock outcroppings. Country children enjoy watching the unusual behavior of these insects. Sometimes they keep them as temporary pets in jars of sugar or salt to observe close at hand their excavating technique.

Dragonfly: Colorful Aerialist

Many a fisherman out on a lake or along the bank of a stream has been pleasantly surprised at the sight of a dragonfly alighting on his rod, its long jewel-toned body and glassy wings glinting in the sun. Though a common insect, it is, nonetheless, remarkably unique.

The dragonfly begins life as a drab mud-colored nymph, denizen of an underwater world. The squat body creeps along the muddy bottom on six spindly legs or climbs amid small-scale jungles of aquatic plants. The bloodthirsty dragonfly nymph is stalking prey. The means for capture is singular in Nature. A jointed underlip, half the length of the insect's body, shoots out, impaling the living food with two sharp inward-curving claws at the tip. Just as quickly does it drag the victim back to the waiting mouth, equipped with powerful teeth. When not in use, the jointed lip folds conveniently beneath the body, the turned-up end fitting over the lower face like a mask. The nymph's food ranges from invisible one-celled animals to small minnows and tadpoles. However, the insect is cannibal as well as carnivore, devouring its own kind at the first opportunity.

When frightened, the nymph escapes by lifting its legs from the silty bottom and flashing forward in quick bursts of speed, using the legs as oars. It achieves such swift forward locomotion by rapidly sucking in water and expelling it from the rectum, combining breathing with jet propulsion. If captured, a nymph will play possum, simulating death. When an appendage becomes tangled in vegetation or is caught by an enemy, it is shed, enabling the insect to make its escape. Protective coloration is another form of defense; the brown body is inconspicuous in the muddy stream bed. The nymph is capable of making a shrill sound by rubbing its hind legs over a serrated area on either side of the body. The noise is generated when the insect is alarmed and is, perhaps, a defense mechanism.

Dragonflies of some species complete their aquatic life in one year; others need two years for fulfillment; and some remain in their watery realm for five years.

Gradually the nymph's form and size are altered by repeated molts.

At last, when darkness settles over the water, the nymph creeps out and ascends a plant, hanging on with hooked feet. Gradually a split lengthens down its back, and eventually the insect, no longer water-breathing, partially emerges from its former sheath. Motionless, it waits until the legs become firm before freeing them. The wings begin to expand and harden; often several hours pass before they are fit for flight. During this time the dragonfly's dazzling hues are heightened. Depending upon the species, it may be copper brown, vivid green, azure blue, lavender, ultramarine, scarlet, lilac, or ivory.

A strong, swift flyer, the dragonfly has no aerial equal in speed or grace. Its well-designed

wings permit it to shoot forward or upward, to dive, and even to fly backward. They are so timed that as the front wings move upward, the back wings beat downward. Thus each pair of wings encounters undisturbed air, making for efficiency of flight. With wings throbbing at a rate of 1,600 times per minute, the dragonfly speeds through the summer air to capture insects. It sometimes catches them with its jaws but more often uses its legs. The spiny legs are bunched forward, forming a sort of net for scooping up insects, whence they are transferred to the mouth. Of insatiable hunger, the dragonfly consumes quantities of horseflies, bees, moths, butterflies, and mosquitoes. Because of its voracious appetite for the last, it is sometimes called the mosquito hawk.

The large, mobile head, capable of pivoting, is set with great compound eyes that can see in all directions simultaneously. The upper part of the eyes serves for long-distance vision; the lower part is suited for close viewing. With such acute sight the dragonfly is able to detect moving insects several hundred feet away.

When dragonflies are seen darting over trees and fields, they are on a hunting trip. Their presence over streams and ponds means that mating time has arrived. Male dragonflies fix territorial boundaries, remaining ever vigilant to intruders, who are forcefully driven off.

During mating the insects often stay linked for some time, flitting about in tandem.

Female dragonflies of those species which produce elongated eggs slip beneath the water after mating, their closed wings entrapping an air bubble to sustain breathing during submergence. The eggs are inserted into slits in the stalks of aquatic plants. Those which lay rounded eggs drop them on the water's surface; dragonflies of still other types fasten their eggs to plants above water. In certain dragonfly species the females deposit their eggs while yet attached to the male.

So responsive are these insects to sunshine that a small cloud temporarily darkening the sun will cause them to alight on the nearest perch. At twilight dragonflies seek cover amid rank growth. Few species are about at dusk's end.

Strong wing muscles enable the dragonfly to cover amazing distances at high speed. In the fall, larger specimens migrate considerable distances to the south. Mass migrations of dragonflies were recorded as early as the end of the fifteenth century. Winds and storms take their toll, as do living enemies: swifts and swallows, bats, frogs, fish, and water snakes. Sharp vision and

swift wings are the dragonfly's only defense.

The dragonfly can boast of ancient ancestry, for it is one of the oldest and largest insects of the world. Scientists tell us that skies were punctuated by its darting flight before the advent of dinosaurs. The gigantic ancestors flashed over ageless forests on wings spanning 2½ feet. Today the wingspread varies from 1 inch to 7½ inches.

Among country folk the dragonfly has been known by various names due to prevailing superstitions. Some called it the horse stinger, despite the fact that it is incapable of stinging. Perhaps its most common nickname is the Devil's darning needle. People believed that the insect could sew up children's ears. Another superstition held that the insect doctored and fed snakes; hence it was often referred to as the snake doctor.

Although the dragonfly occasionally feasts on honeybees, it benefits man by its consumption of vast numbers of gnats, flies, and mosquitoes. Even as a nymph it devoured mosquito larvae, and it was itself an important fish food.

As the days begin to cool, the dragonfly's activity diminishes. The first frost brings death.

Ladybug: Friend to Man

Rare is the child, playing in the summer countryside, who hasn't delighted at the sight of a ladybug. Somehow he senses, whether because of the insect's inoffensive appearance or through knowledge passed along by grandparents or parents, that it will do no harm. Indeed, this tiny domed beetle, lacquered scarlet with black polka dots, is an invaluable friend to man.

In spring, farmers justifiably predict a good crop upon the arrival of ladybugs. During their larval and adult stages, they wage unrelenting war against scale insects, aphids, and other plant-eating lice. Not long after the Civil War, scale insects ravaged citrus groves. In the late 1800s a particular species of ladybug with a ravening appetite for such destructive pests was imported from Australia, with favorable results. This was an early example of the biological control of harmful insects.

Ladybugs, in both immature and adult form, relish the eggs of other insects. Where farmers specialize in potato-growing, they serve them by devouring innumerable eggs of the potato beetle.

However, farmers did not always appreciate the efforts of ladybugs. Spotting them continually among plant lice, they wrongly concluded that ladybugs were the parents of the destructive insects. So ladybugs and lice were eradicated simultaneously. Their true offspring, also found amid insect pests, met the same fate.

The ladybug picks out a protected site—the underside of a leaf or a crevice in bark—for depositing her eggs. When the young emerge from the eggs, they look like miniature alligators. Their insatiable appetites immediately spur them to hunt and consume plant lice. They suck the vital fluids from aphids and gobble up the hollow bodies. A tiny ladybug larva is not hard put to devour some forty aphids within an hour. Such an intake of food means rapid growth, and the lizard-like larva is busy changing its skin to keep pace. Upon attaining full size, it suspends itself by the tail from a leaf and becomes a chrysalis. When the days as a pupa are fulfilled, the shell splits, and into the world comes the winged beetle. After the polka-dotted wing covers are moved forward, the folded rear wings are exposed. Fanning the air approximately ninety times per

second, they launch the ladybug on its first flight.

The adult, having reached full size, eats somewhat less than the gluttonous larva, but still has an immense appetite for insect eggs and plant lice. As ladybugs and their young assault a cluster of aphids, however, they are often driven away by ants. Aphids have no form of self-protection and would be easy prey except for these defenders. When ants are collecting honeydew, a sweet substance secreted by aphids, they are most anxious to protect its source against any threat.

Late in autumn, ladybug beetles begin their unusual hibernating practices. They tend to be social, massing together on rocks. Sometimes so many converge on a boulder that their closely packed bodies color it scarlet. For hibernation they select almost any spot that affords shelter: beneath bark, under shingles, in haystacks, or in woodland mold. During winter thaws they sometimes creep out to enjoy the temporary warmth. The common two-spotted variety often seeks the interior of farmhouses for overwintering.

The most dramatic massing of these colorful beetles occurs in the West. On late autumnal days millions of ladybugs fly up from the valleys into the mountains, where they pass the winter months in rock crevices. Their habit of mass hibernation gave rise to a new and unusual occupation, that of ladybug prospecting. After searching out great conglomerations of the insects, prospectors shovel them into sacks and refrigerate them for the remainder of winter. With the arrival of spring, they are marketed. Farmers and orchardists are guided in their purchasing by the standard recipe for successful insect control: 2 ounces of ladybugs for 1 acre of ground. (Approximately 1,500 ladybugs equal 1 ounce.)

Should you chance upon the empty shell of this little beetle, it will mean that the assassin bug has been abroad. Through a vulnerable spot, between body and head, in the ladybug's armor, the bloodthirsty insect forces its beak to suck out the juices until nothing but the brightly polished shell remains.

Two stratagems are employed by the ladybug to foil most enemies. By contracting its body, it so forcefully constricts its blood that the skin breaks at weak points. The drops discharged are repellent as to both taste and smell, discouraging presumptuous assailants. When confronted by too disproportionate an enemy, such as man, the tiny insect reasons to playing possum. Falling over as though dead, it lies motionless.

From generations past, many names for the ladybug have come down to us: ladybird, ladycow, ladyfly. They evolved from the fact that the ladybug was consecrated to Our Lady, The Virgin Mary. Superstition as well as religion is associated with the insect. Country girls catch a ladybug, place it on their palms, and expectantly wait for it to cross. Its reaching the other side before winging away is believed to make marriage a certainty before the year is out. During pioneer days a ladybug discovered passing the winter in the homestead was an omen of good luck. Farmers claim that ladybugs bring good weather and that the sight of them, come spring, means abundant crops. The ladybug was believed to possess medicinal properties as well. Rural folk recommended reducing the seven-spotted variety to pulp and placing it in the cavity of a tooth to relieve the ache.

Strange as it may seem, the infamous boll weevil is kin to the invaluable ladybug.

Ingestion of Insects

Eating insects for survival, a thought that might make one's flesh crawl when one is comfortably at home, could prove the only way to preserve that flesh were one lost in the wilderness, without knowledge of safe, edible plants or means to hunt and fish. Bees, beetles, caterpillars, cicadas, leeches, locust, maggots, termites, and many other insects and their eggs are excellent nutritional sources.

the sweetest food in the western Indians' diet. Now they, along with black bears, rapidly developed a zeal for honey. Black bears stole honey from the bees; the Indians robbed the men collecting it.

Even if bees produced no honey, they would perform a valuable service in their role as pollinators. In addition to pollinating flowers, bees fertilize many of our most important agricultural crops—among them alfalfa, cucumbers, melons, and almonds.

Most persons associate bees with pollination and honey-making; few regard the bee itself as a food. However, some primitive people consider roasted bees (and wasps) a delectable dish.

Bees

Not native to the Americas, bees were brought to our continent in early colonial days by Spanish and British settlers. Black bees, obtained from a bee colony owned by Pilgrims in Holland, were the first to be introduced. They were brought to Massachusetts in the 1600s and soon escaped to the forests. In William Penn's time, bee trees were numerous in the woods of eastern Pennsylvania. Until about 1750 bees had not yet traveled beyond the Susquehanna River.

During the 1800s they swarmed across the Mississippi as far as the Rockies, always maintaining a 100-mile lead over the ever-westering frontier. The Indians

noted the advance of bees with apprehension, recognizing that the "white man's fly" was a precursor of the invader's intrusion into new territories. The bees progressed over the countryside at a rate of about 10 miles per year, lured westward by flower-blanketed prairies and hollow cottonwood trees.

By the early 1800s, bee trees extended some 600 miles up the Missouri River. Gathering honey soon became a trade, some trees containing 8 to 10 gallons each. Colonial settlers and frontiersmen were not alone in collecting honey; black bears quickly became adept at pilfering it from bee trees. Previously, cornstalks had been

Beetles

In Mexico people are fond of eating a particular beetle, the jumil. It is high in iodine content.

Leeches

The word *leech*, from the Old English *laece*, originally meant "one who practices healing; a physician." As the application of aquatic blood-sucking worms by leeches, or physicians, became widespread in Europe late in the eighteenth century, the name *leech* was gradually transferred from the doctor to the worm itself. By the mid-1800s, France was importing over fifty million leeches a year, and leech farming was a very profitable business.

Though seldom used for bloodletting in modern times, leeches still render valuable services. Their saliva contains a blood coagulant, hirudin, used to treat humans. An unusual purpose for leeches is their function as a barometer. Country folk keep them in a bowl of water with dirt in the bottom. Weather is predicted by the degree of their elevation in the water.

A fact unrecognized by the general public is that leeches can provide life-sustaining nourishment in times of dire need. They afford high-quality protein; in order to preserve this protein, leeches should be eaten raw. Walleyes, imbued with the instinctive selection of a nutritious diet, prefer leeches to worms or

minnows and thrive on them. Should circumstances dictate, humans could survive on them.

Locusts

Locusts, rich in protein, are an important edible insect in certain desert areas. We read in the Bible that John the Baptist, while sojourning in the wilderness, fed on locusts and honey.

Shore Flies

Adult shore flies abound near tide pools and are often seen walking on the water's surface. Their larvae are marine insects living in sea water and brackish pools. Those shore flies which breed in western salt lakes are called "brine flies." They are so numerous there that great clouds of them hover over the lakes. Indians were familiar with brine flies. They gathered large numbers of them in their immature form to use as food.

Termites

Little-known vitamin T is an important factor in good health; it maintains stamina and increases resistance to stress and shock. A source of vitamin T for human consumption is sesame seed and its oil. Emergency rations for soldiers of former times consisted of cakes made from sesame seed and honey. It was found that a man could march farther on a given amount of

that food than on any other. In areas where sesame-seed products have always been part of the national diet, the stamina of the people is exceptional. The fact that so many of them survive to a

ripe old age has been attributed to the effect of sesame seed with its vitamin T content.

It is because this substance was first discovered in termites that it was designated vitamin T. There are many tribes of people that dine on termites, preferring them in a pickled state. These insects contain more protein than fish.

Water Boatmen

Water boatmen are common aquatic bugs resembling miniature submarines, propelled by oar-like legs. They fasten their eggs to water plants; some kinds glue them to crayfish. So plentiful are the eggs of water boatmen in Mexico that, it is said, people gather them for a nutritious food.

Wood Borers

The body fluid of wood borers contains carbon compounds and a good many minerals. As the days of autumn chill, the fluid thickens. A sweet alcohol, called glycerol, starts to form, acting as a kind of antifreeze against the increasing cold. The flavor of wood borers has been likened to that of vanilla ice cream. Professor Roscoe Hawley of Indiana says that they are particularly delicious by November, when the accumulation of the syrupy-sweet glycerol is greatest.

Both animals and primitive peoples have found wood borers to be nutritious and tasty fare. Bears and skunks especially relish them.

So it is readily seen that in addition to whatever other functions insects may perform in the world, whether harmful or beneficial to man, they can serve him as survival food. The thought that these small creatures can be lifesaving—just in case—is comforting.

9 | HUNTER'S BAG

Hunting by Signs and Weather

Libra is the hunter's zodiac sign. Many old-time market hunters, those who would hunt game for sale to others, would only go to the fields and woods when the day sign was in Libra. Rudolph Tierce of Michigan market hunted for over forty years and told me that from records he kept over this long period he could prove that the days the signs were in the loins were the best nine times out of ten.

Roy Howell of Florida goes by moon position. He swears that the best hunting occurs when the moon is "the hour on either side of when the moon is overhead, day or night, and when it is calculated to be directly under us on the other side of the earth over China." He thinks this is the time for activity and feeding for most animals if the weather is right.

Ray Humphries of Oklahoma goes by the moon when he hunts deer. He follows the moonlight more than he follows the signs. Ray says that when deer are not disturbed they will feed almost as much in the daytime when the moon is up as they do at night. If the moon shines all night they will feed at night and rest during the day. If the moon is up all day they will feed during those hours and lie quietly at night. During the moon's last quarter, when it has been down and out of sight all day, the deer become very hungry and will range out and feed all night. For still-hunting in the daytime he tries to go when the moon is up or is rising whether it is the morning or afternoon.

Roy Alley of Texas watches the barometer for hunting signs. He says a rising barometer brings game to feeding areas. A falling glass is indicated in the field by upturned tree leaves, showing their light-colored undersides, and often there is possibility of approaching storm. At this time upland birds and most game will desert feeding grounds and go to cover. When the barometer glass begins to fall, Roy turns from deer to ducks. Ducks are most restless at this time and make the best hunting.

Most hunters agree that the wind should be in your face and the sun at your back to have three advantages over the game's wisdom. "They can't smell you,

they can't hear as good, and the light favors the hunter instead of the hunted." For the most part, early morning and late evening are considered the best times for all hunting. A good many old and successful hunters still prefer to hunt during the last quarter of the moon, during cold, cloudy weather when the sun is partly hidden.

Hunting Wisdom

Here are some helpful hints for better hunting that I've gleaned over the years from various parts of the country.

Sam Odin of New York State suggests that you start to grow a beard before hunting season. He claims that a beard cuts down the glare from your skin and you'll bag more game.

Break in your hunting boots with rubbing alcohol instead of water. It penetrates the leather faster, dries more quickly, and will make them fit your feet better.

If you plan to wear heavy woolen socks, your hunting boots should be two sizes larger than your normal shoe size; for light socks, boots should be one size longer and wider.

Old-timers say that excellent bootlaces can be made from the inner tube of an automobile tire. Cut narrow strips of the same thickness and length as leather laces from a tube that has not become dry and brittle. Thread them through the eyelets of your boots. You'll

find them nonslip and comfortable. Being flexible, they'll give with the movement of your feet.

If the noise of gunshot makes your horse bolt, tie 20 feet of stout rope to its halter with a large steel hook on the other end. Before

shooting, throw the anchor into the brush.

Because rifle-cleaning rods are too bulky in your pocket, carry a stiff leather lace. You can easily push it through the bore, pulling a patch fastened to it.

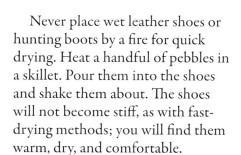

Never place wet leather shoes or hunting boots by a fire for quick drying. Heat a handful of pebbles in a skillet. Pour them into the shoes and shake them about. The shoes will not become stiff, as with fast-drying methods; you will find them warm, dry, and comfortable.

If you're hunting with a shotgun and become separated from companions, you can use it for sounding a distress call. Remove all the shells from your gun, leaving the breech open. Put the muzzle to your lips and blow hard. The first note will be high, gradually tapering to a lower note as your pressure declines. The sound will carry a surprising distance. Don't forget to clean the moisture from the gun's bore afterward. This was a method used long ago to call coon or fox hounds when the hunter lacked a proper horn.

You might enjoy the satisfaction of fabricating your own hunting horn. One can be made from cow horns or steer horns. A short cow horn emits a high sharp note; a long steer horn gives a deep sound.

Saw off the first two inches of the pointed end. Heat a piece of strong wire until red hot, and bore through the horn. Carve a mouthpiece at the blowing end similar to that of a bugle. To make the sound carry farther, carefully scrape it down with a piece of glass. You can give your horn a high polish by rubbing it with oil and pumice.

Cloudy, windless days are best for hunting, although a wet day is sometimes good. Early morning or late afternoon proves the most favorable time for hunting every kind of game. Try to avoid periods of temperature extremes. Check the direction of the wind; make sure it is blowing from the quarry toward the hunter.

When the wind is high and the leaves are dry it is a poor time for hunting. Most good hunters agree that a period of steady, light breezes after some rain is the best hunting weather.

There is a secret to hanging birds and game. Hang birds by the head; hang game by the legs.

When picking up birds from the water, lift them out by their heads, shake them off and they will be dry. Lifting them by the leg or wing brings water with them and they will be wet and heavy.

Folks who like to bird hunt, says Milton Beerman of New York, would do well to plant wild rice around ponds and streams in the fall of the year. Ducks and other birds will linger near areas of good feed.

Soak small game for about twenty-four hours in salt water with a little vinegar added. This both tenderizes the meat and removes the wild taste.

If it has rained for several days and looks like it will never let up,

watch for woodchucks. They follow the sun and will tell you that it will soon clear up enough to bring game out.

Any animal you hunt is most alert on windy days. Small game burrow up and big game go to heavy ground cover when it is windy. The wise hunter will use wind to his advantage to creep upwind to these hiding places but he must be quiet and remain out of sight as the game will instinctively bed down where they have the best visibility.

Paul Kline of New Jersey has studied ducks and duck hunting for about twenty years. He feels that the best times for shooting are just before daylight and just before dark. Paul would wear a red bandanna handkerchief during duck season, and tie it on a stick and keep himself out of sight while waving it over his head. Ducks have an inquisitive nature and will swim close to investigate unless they are real wild. Paul favors October and November for his duck hunting, on moonlit nights. He works smooth sheltered

water when the wind is up and fully believes a good duck hunter should spend more time looking for the favorite feeding and resting spots than in waiting for them to come to you at a blind or to decoys.

Of other birds he says:

Grouse or partridge hunting is best in the early morning during stormy or cold weather. The best places are around berry bushes or where there is plenty of feed. Learn their roosting places to find them toward night.

Quail are best found at midday when weather is sunny during October and November. The places are the middles of fields, around brush and stubble, and the edges of woods. A good pointer dog is invaluable.

Woodcock are best hunted in the late evening and at dawn.

The best places to hunt are moist lowlands and swamps and the north or wet sides of hills.

Wild geese are very regular in going to and from their feeding grounds. Learn their timetable and get the goose.

Game Birds

The ideal country for locating all species of game birds is well-watered land that affords a variety of terrain: hills, level ground, woods, meadows, and marshes.

When birds rise on the wing, they fly against the wind. Shoot at the moment when the bird is turning or steadying itself in the air. As birds are descending to alight on the ground, your aim should be underneath. Allow a bird that is flying head on in your direction to pass by without firing at it; otherwise, you will be shooting against the dense breast feathers instead of under the feathers.

Bay Snipe

In summer and fall, bay snipe are most effectively taken when a southwest wind is blowing steadily. Birds traveling out of the north and against the wind fly low, winging along the edges of bars and meadows. They spot decoys more clearly than when they are flying with the wind in the clouds. Wet summers are especially favorable for bay snipe shooting, for then the meadows furnish an abundance of feed.

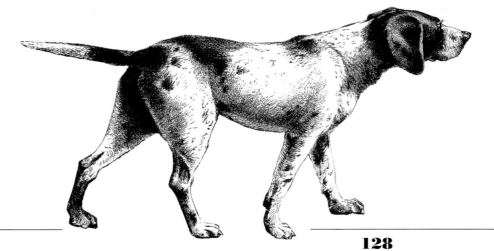

Pheasants

The pheasant is a wily bird. If a brook is in the vicinity, the bird will hop back and forth across it to confuse the trail. You'll need a sense of humor when hunting pheasants!

Doves

Though not waterfowl, doves must have water and won't stay in an area where water is not within easy flight. The best spot for successful dove shooting is over a water hole, where such holes are at some distance from one another. You can surprise the birds in pea patches, wheat stubble, or standing cornstalks.

Ducks

On windy days ducks will fly low, close to the water. Without the aid of the wind, ducks fly at the rate of about 90 miles an hour. When heading against the wind, they wing low in dense formation.

Don't shoot ducks when they are traveling "dead on"; the shot will be kept from entering their bodies by the thick breast feathers. Shoot when they have passed by or are on a line with you. Since all waterfowl have an acute sense of smell, approach ducks on the water against the wind.

Loons

Loons habitually plunge forward into water. So when hunting these birds, aim in front of them.

Prairie Chickens

Look for prairie chickens, or pinnated grouse, in fields of stubble during the morning and evening; at midday expect to find them in cornfields or near bottom-land creeks.

Quail

Early in the morning quail are running about in pea or wheat fields in search of food, providing poor targets. By the time the dew has evaporated, they will have finished eating and be resting in some sheltered spot in their feeding grounds or close by. They are not nearly so prone to take wing at this time, but if they do, their flight will be short and sluggish.

Ruffed Grouse

To tree a ruffed grouse, you should be familiar with its habitat and habits.

Exclusively a bird of the woods, the ruffed grouse is skilled at flying through brush and timber without slowing its speed. It can slip through any cover.

The favorite haunts of the ruffed grouse are hillsides dense with cedar, hemlock, and an undergrowth of laurel. In flat territory it seeks patches of scrub oak and swampy areas with briery, tangled coverts.

When disturbed, the ruffed grouse squats close to the ground or alights in a tree, concealing itself under branches close to the trunk. If flushed on a hillside, it will usually fly uphill and can be discovered just over the crest. When flushed on flat ground, the ruffed grouse will fly low and once again land on the ground. If it ascends gradually and suddenly shoots upward, the bird can probably be seen on the evergreen closest to the one where you last spotted it. When it rises

immediately to a treetop and then darts off, it will fly some distance. If the grouse flies up a steep incline, it will alight on the ground. Should it fly from a hill down toward a level area, the bird will alight in a tall spruce or hemlock and remain completely still on a limb close to the body of the tree. If it wings from one hill over a ravine to another rise, it will land on the ground. The shorter the ruffed grouse's flight, the more quickly it again takes to the air.

Snipe

Snipe can be found in low willow bottoms and marshy thickets. To hunt them to advantage, set out on a warm, sunny day with gentle winds. Make sure the wind is behind you, for snipe rise in a zigzag pattern against the wind.

Wild Turkeys

The hearing of turkeys is considerably better than that of deer, and their eyesight is as good as that of antelope and sheep. By nature they are as wary as all other game combined. Remember that one suspicious sight or sound is sufficient to cause their disappearance.

In the northern area of the wild turkey's range, hunting is frequently successful shortly after the first snowfall. You can judge the freshness of the turkeys' tracks and be alert while following them. In most of the range, however, careful preliminary planning is

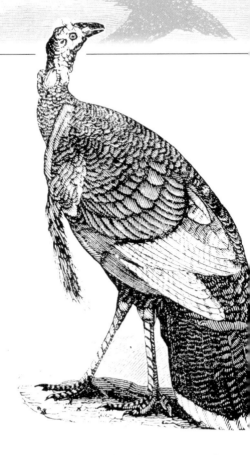

required. It's vital to learn where the turkeys run, what they're feeding on, the size of the bands, and, most important, where they are watering.

To find out where birds are running, look for shed feathers, for tracks, for spots where birds have scratched in search of bugs, or for acorns and pine nuts. Try to discover their preference in food; what they're eating will determine where to look for them. When autumn remains mild, plenty of insects are still available. With the early arrival of frost and snow, turkeys seek acorns and tiny pine seeds.

Try to locate their watering place. Turkeys are creatures of habit: unless disturbed, they will go to the same spring or the same spot

on a stream bank and at about the same time each day. Look for or build a natural-looking blind close by.

Keep an eye out for flocks in sunny spots during the morning; watch for them in shady places by afternoon.

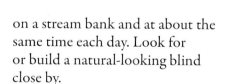

Calls

Old-timers didn't set out to hunt equipped with fancy "store-bought" bird calls; they generally made their own. Practice and experience in using them brought favorable results.

Duck Call

A squawker, or duck call, was made from a tube of wood, preferably bamboo, about 8 inches long and ¾ inch in diameter inside. To one end fit a 3-inch-long plug. Split it in two, and groove one half to within ¼ inch of its smaller end. The groove should be ¼ inch wide and deep. Pound a thin piece of metal about 2½ inches long and ½ inch wide to use as the tongue. One end should be thinner than the other, with rounded corners. Place this over the grooved half, the rounded end almost covering the groove. Shorten the other half of the plug 1½ inches from its smaller end. Place it on the grooved half. Holding the metal tongue in

place, push both pieces of the plug into the tube. Blowing into the opposite end of the tube will produce the duck call. You can vary it by moving the shortened end of the plug in or out.

Snipe Call

Use a curlew's leg to make a snipe whistle. Thoroughly dry it. With a red-hot knitting needle, push out the marrow. Plug up one end, and start practicing.

Turkey Calls

Maple or dogwood makes the best turkey calls. Take a piece some 6 inches long and 1½ inches in diameter, and bore a hole through it lengthwise with a small-sized bit. With a tapering bit ream out the interior to 1¼ inches. Insert a piece of wood or cane at the opposite end to serve as a mouthpiece. The size of the mouthpiece will control the tone of the call.

Some hunters put the caller in the middle of their mouth; others call from the side of the mouth. You'll want to vary the sound according to the game you're pursuing. If you're after an old hen, the note should imitate a young turkey; if a young one is your prey, mimic the hen.

Run a cedar stick (roughly the size of a pencil) through a corncob that is only a little longer than half the length of the stick. The cob is the handle, with the centered stick protruding from either end.

Take a piece of slate, three inches square, and round the edges. With the slate held in one hand, scratch it with the tip of the cedar stick, holding the cob loosely.

Some old-timers prefer the wing bone of a turkey, sucking on it to make the appropriate noise.

Calling can be overdone. One false note will cause a bird to vanish. Limit your calls to four.

Fowler's Terms

a *badelynge* of ducks
a *bevy* or *ovey* of grouse
a *bevy* of quail
a *brood* of hens
a *building* of rooks
a *charm* of goldfinches
a *colony* of gulls
a *congregation* of plovers
a *covert* of coots
a *covey* of partridge
a *depping* of sheldrakes
an *exultation* of larks
a *fall* of woodcocks
a *flight* of swallows
a *gaggle* of geese
a *herd* of swans, cranes, or curlews
a *host* of sparrows
a *murmuration* of starlings
a *muster* of peacocks
a *sege* of herons or bitterns
a *spring* of teals
a *sword* or *suten* of mallards
a *walk* of snipe
a *watch* of nightingales

Bird Flight

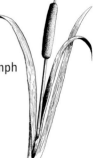

duck	80 to 100 mph
pheasant	25 mph
quail	50 mph
ruffed grouse	40 mph
woodcock	30 mph

Preserving Dead Birds

The following methods of preserving dead game birds were used by hunters in the past and are just as effective today:

- Draw the birds and stuff them with green grass. Cover the bottom of a box with coffee grounds that are absolutely dry. Place a layer of birds on top. Alternate layers of grounds and birds until all are packed in the box.
- Draw the birds. Suspend them by the head to allow them to drip thoroughly. When their natural body heat has dissipated, stuff them with fresh leaves. Put the birds head first into paper bags. Tie the bags tightly closed to keep out air. Place them in a shady cool spot until they are to be moved. Birds preserved in this way are said to keep for more than forty-eight hours and to be fresh and palatable when eaten.

Small Game Animals

Rabbits

After a night of meandering, cottontails will bed down by day, sleeping or sunning themselves in a small round nest in some sheltered spot. Look for them in bramble patches, cornfields with nearby cover, small copses, marshes, overgrown fields, and scrub pasture land.

In early autumn on a warm sunshiny day, cottontails can be found over the entire countryside. By midwinter with snow on the ground, rabbits seek shelter from the open country in the woods. Tracks in the snow will indicate the areas that rabbits are frequenting and how good the hunting will be. The dark gray fur of the rabbit will be a more obvious target against the snow, which also makes tracking a wounded animal easier.

A midwinter day just after a cold spell that ended in a sudden thaw is advantageous to the rabbit hunter. Rabbits will emerge to frisk in the mild air. You can make quiet progress toward your target in the soft snow. If it disappears into its hole, persevere. Rabbit holes are not very deep. Close to the entrance there is a crook, after which the passageway continues at an angle for a short way. A hunter can usually work his hand in to grasp the ears or hind legs of the fugitive. Failing this, cut a fairly long, supple stick with a strong fork at the end. Work it around the crook in the tunnel, inserting it as far as it will go. If you find bits of rabbit fur on the fork, push the stick in again, twisting it. You can twist the fur up so tightly that the rabbit can't move, and you can pull the animal from the hole as if he were part of the stick. If you can't reach the cottontail with the twister, and the den has more than one entrance, tie a piece of weasel fur to the stick. The sound of the switch working down the passageway, plus the scent of the weasel, will usually send your quarry into the open.

Squirrels

The best time to still-hunt squirrels is at break of day, when they frisk about, chattering noisily. At other hours they are silent.

In bygone days veteran hunters used to say that the only palatable squirrel was one shot squarely in the left eye. The most skilled of huntsmen didn't shoot squirrels

at all. They favored "barking them off," which required a great degree of accuracy. The target wasn't the squirrel but the bark immediately beneath its feet. The resulting concussion, not the bullet, killed the animal.

These are the requirements for a good squirrel call: a sharp knife; a piece of stiff paper; a forked stick roughly ⅜ inch in diameter and 5 inches in length. First peel the bark from the twig. Carefully split the twig down the middle with your knife; the fork will prevent the cut from splitting the twig completely. Insert the paper in the split. Holding the end tightly, trim the paper as close to the twig as possible. Blow against the paper, slightly squeezing the end opposite the fork to adjust tension. With a little practice you'll soon have an inquisitive squirrel peeking around a tree trunk to satisfy its curiosity.

Deer

Learn where deer are feeding and bedding, what trails they're using, and where these trails intersect. The presence of deer is revealed by their hoofprints and droppings, by saplings with bark rubbed away when bucks polish their antlers, and by the nipped-off tips of plants which form their diet.

In autumn, deer head for the woods to feast on acorns. When scouting for feeding grounds, check woods where oak trees are plentiful. In descending order of preference in the deer's diet are corn, buckbrush, sumac (including poison ivy!), grasses, and sedges.

In northern forest regions, whitetails favor white cedar, yew, apple, mountain maple, striped maple, dogwood, and red maple. If these are unavailable, they browse on elderberry, high-bush cranberry, hemlock, mountain ash, arbutus, honeysuckle, blueberry, and willow. During the hunting season mule deer prefer mountain mahogany, sagebrush, oaks, and evergreens, such as bearberry and myrtle. Blacktails feed on willow buds, evergreens, ferns, manzanitas, and acorns.

Deer in secluded areas will browse almost as much by day, when the moon is up, as by night. If the moon has shone throughout the night, they will bed down all the following day. If the moon has been up during the day, they will bed down for the night.

Dress the deer carcass as quickly as possible with a very sharp knife, emptying the body cavity. Remaining blood will drain out. Wipe the cavity with a cloth, except in blowfly country; there, allow dried blood to glaze the meat, forming a hard crust which flies won't be able to penetrate for laying eggs. You can also protect your freshly killed game from insects by sprinkling the carcass with pepper and covering it with cheesecloth. Another effective way to keep insects from game is to rub the meat, after hanging it, with cooking oil. Make a smoldering fire in a place where the smoke will reach the game. The meat will be kept moist by the oil, and the smoke imparts a delicate smokehouse flavor.

Trapping

Charlie Frazier of Alaska says that for trapping bear the very best bait he has ever found is fresh fish smeared with honey or burnt honey comb.

Good trappers say that traps should never be handled with bare hands. Cover your hands with rags or use buckskin gloves. Never spit near where traps are set.

One of the best places to place a trap is between two logs with a passageway that animals are apt to pass through.

Drag a piece of fresh raw meat or leave pieces along the ground between your run of traps to lead animals into them.

Never place bait on the trap pan. Always place it above the trap on a stick or hanging from a branch so the animal must step on the trap.

Andy Cefelo of California almost always uses the scent used by many old-time trappers. It is a fish oil scent and he says it works better than any other. He takes trout or fat fish of any kind, cuts them in small pieces and puts them in bottles. Leave these in the hot sun until they become oily and have a putrid smell. Smear this scent on the bait.

Animals are suspicious of a rusty trap. Rustproof them by dipping in a solution of melted beeswax and rosin.

Skunks are the first animals to get prime fur in the late fall and early winter. Water animals are last, bears and badgers have prime fur only in midwinter to early spring.

The best times to trap are the first stormy night of the winter and before any winter storm. The

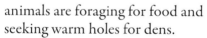

animals are foraging for food and seeking warm holes for dens.

Always sink traps to ground level.

After a catch, leave your trap where it is and reset it. This often pays off again, especially in dens. When sprung traps are found try a new place nearby. If the bait is gone and the trap is unsprung reset it in the same spot, but bait the other side of the trap.

Never dry skins by a fire, as it will spoil them.

I've never tried this one. V. L. Johansen of Utah says old trappers put their hands in skunk holes and pull them out by the tail, hitting them with a club as soon as their head appears. According to the old-timers they will not bite and will not throw their scent at this time.

According to J. E. Westbrook in Colorado, when you find a den or hole that is being used, insert your trap well inside, scent the bait well, and cover with leaves. If left outside near the hole, the animal will be suspicious and not usually take the bait.

Place the bait in a steel trap in such a way that when the animal sniffs the food its foot will be on the pan. Try suspending the bait from a stick over the trap, or put it in an enclosure, causing the animal to step over the trap in order to get it. After game has been caught, traps should be smoked or cleaned.

Bow Hunting

Long ago the bows of Indians in the Ozark wilderness area were noted

for their durability and strength. They were far superior to those of other tribes and of the French explorers, who recognized that these qualities were due to the wood of which they were made. They called this wood *bois d'arc*, meaning "wood of the bow." The name was corrupted into "bodock" by English settlers.

The bodock tree is easily identified by its large, inedible fruit which resembles an orange, so that the tree is also called Osage orange. For generations country people have made their fence posts from bodock wood, many being serviceable for more than fifty years.

Bodock trees were so highly valued by the Indians that wars were often fought for possession of land where they grew in abundance, for the bodock bows were held in high regard by the Indians themselves, as well as by explorers and traders.

Such a bow was a chief item of barter; a fair young squaw wasn't considered too high a price for a well-balanced bow.

Look for the bodock tree with its fruit the size, shape, and color of oranges. It sends up several stems rather than one trunk. You'll find making your own bow a genuine challenge and satisfying accomplishment. Make your arrow shafts from the straight branches of older bushes of the wild rose or from wild currant wood.

Small-Game Blunts

Small-game blunts are used for hunting rabbits, gophers, etc. You can make them easily by tipping ordinary arrows with old-fashioned erasers that slip over the end of pencils. These rubber tips won't stick in tree trunks or bury themselves in the ground as deeply as regular arrows.

Falconry

Falconry is more an art than a sport, requiring long hours not only for the initial training period but for daily practice to keep yourself and your bird in top form.

The choice of bird depends upon the area available for hunting. If the country is limited, broken by small fields and woods, choose a short-winged bird, like the sparrow hawk or goshawk. In open country, a long-winged falcon, such as the peregrine or

merlin, is best. To capture their hawks, the Plains Indians would conceal themselves in the carcass of a large animal and pounce upon the bird as it devoured the carrion.

The bells carried by the hawk on its legs are an interesting feature of falconry. One bell should be a half tone higher than the other. The resulting discord carries for very long distances.

Acquire a handbook on falconry to guide you in its intricacies. In order for your bird to attain and maintain peak physical condition and skill, she (the female in the hawk family is larger and more powerful than the male) must be flown every possible day throughout the season.

Blackfly Remedy
Hunters are often plagued by biting blackflies. Old-timers had an effective remedy: Combine equal parts of rubbing alcohol and household ammonia. Apply the mixture to the bites on a piece of cotton. It will reduce both itching and swelling.

Witch Hazel
While hunting, you may spot a shrub with yellow flowers, somewhat resembling forsythia. It is witch hazel, a shrub that blooms in late fall and winter. Note its location. In spring gather its leaves, soak them in water, and add alcohol, one part alcohol to five parts of the witch hazel infusion. You'll have an excellent liniment for tired, aching muscles after a long day of hunting.

Firewood
In gathering wood for a fire, pass up any that is on the ground. It is usually beginning to rot and may be damp or even water-logged. Choose deadwood that is standing or hanging in bushes or low trees.

For kindling select the bark of white birches. It ignites quickly and is easily removed from trees. Dead twigs from the tops of small evergreens also make good kindling.

Select hardwoods for a long-burning fire. Hickory is excellent because it burns well whether seasoned or green. Oak makes good firewood, particularly white oak. White ash and yellow birch burn better when green. White birch and northern alder burn well when somewhat green.

Softwoods, when dry, serve only as kindling or for quick-cooking fires.

To maintain a campfire, occasionally add resin-filled pine and balsam knots.

To start a campfire quickly when the woods are damp, cut an inch off

a candle. Place it next to a good-sized stone. Lean twigs against the stone above the wick. Light the candle. In no time it will dry the wood enough for it to ignite.

Camp Cookery

Bannock
    4 cups flour
    6 tablespoons sugar
    4 teaspoons baking soda
    1 teaspoon salt
    ⅓ cup cold bacon fat
    milk or water

Combine the dry ingredients. Cut in the fat with a fork, gradually adding a little water or milk until the dough becomes a ball without dry places. Press this into a 1-inch-thick pancake, dusting top and bottom with flour. Heat a heavy cast-iron pan. Grease it. Brown the bannock on both sides. Cook it for approximately 15 minutes or until done.

Cooking Small Birds
Dress the birds. Remove the head and legs. Bake each in a hollowed-out potato.

Woodcock Recipe

Cook the woodcock over burning coals for about 10 minutes. Meanwhile make a sauce of the following:

- 1 tablespoon prepared mustard
- 3 tablespoons red wine
- ½ cup currant jelly
- 1 tablespoon butter

Melt the jelly; stir it to prevent scorching. Add butter and mustard. Allow the mixture to boil for 1 minute. Stir in the wine. When the skin is brown with the flesh pink and juicy, remove the bird from the fire and serve with sauce.

Squirrel with Rice

If the squirrels you've bagged are too tough for frying, try preparing them this way:

Cut 2 squirrels into serving pieces. Rub them with salt and pepper and brown in a deep kettle with a chunk of salt pork. Add 2 quarts of water and simmer until tender, adding water when necessary. Put in 1 cup of rice, ¼ cup of ketchup, ½ sliced onion, and 1 teaspoonful of salt. Cook until the rice is done.

Broiled Venison Steak

Cut steaks approximately ½ inches thick. Carefully wipe them with a damp cloth to ensure removal of any stray hairs. Rub the steaks on both sides with cooking oil. Place them on a grill over the coals of your campfire. For the first 2 minutes turn them every 30 seconds. After that, turn them every 2 minutes until done to your liking: 10 minutes for rare steaks; longer if you prefer them well done.

Combine the following for an excellent venison-steak sauce:

- ¼ cup melted butter
- 2 tablespoons lemon juice
- 1 tablespoon finely chopped parsley
- ½ teaspoon salt

Pan-Cooked Venison

Cut venison into 1-inch-square pieces. Wrap bacon around each piece, securing it with a toothpick. Put them in a cast-iron skillet. Add the following:

- 2 cups water
- ½ cup Worcestershire sauce
- salt
- black pepper

Boil rapidly until most of the water has evaporated. When the fire dies down somewhat, cover the pan and continue cooking until the meat is brown.

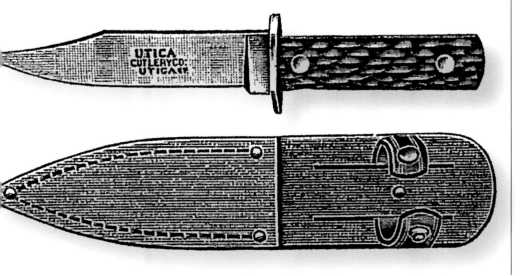

The successful country fisherman becomes familiar with the ways of fish. He studies and observes the various habits, traits, and haunts of the types of fish he wants to catch. He becomes an expert on their sense of sight, smell, and hearing. He learns their means of existence, their likes and dislikes, their foods and any other things that will help him to better understand their ways.

The good fisherman must be able to take advantage of their weakness, avoid their keen perception, and outsmart their cunning. Knowing as many things as possible about a certain species of fish helps to locate them. Once located he can then proceed to deceive or tempt them to take his bait.

Last Things First

Instead of waiting until the end of this chapter to give you a summary of country fishing wisdom let's take a look at the most important points right now.

Here are the highlights of how to catch fish, collected from anglers from every part of the country who have spent years studying nature, and fish in particular.

In the summer months the best times to fish are from sunset to one hour after. In the cooler months fishing is best from noon to three in the afternoon. The best day to fish, weatherwise, is

a warm, close, cloudy day that follows a bright moonlight night. The most favorable winds are from the south, southwest, and west. East winds are unfavorable.

"When the wind is in the north,
the skillful fisher goes not forth;
When the wind is in the south, it
blows the bait in the fishes mouth;
When the wind is in the east, 'tis
neither good for man or beast;
When the wind is in the west,
then fishing's at its very best."

Use an active lure. With live bait, attach the hook so the bait will have natural movements. With artificial lures, jig or pop the bait and vary the pace of the retrieve.

Present the lure to the water in a manner that will be interesting to the fish both in location and in action. Fish the shady sides of logs and rocks, the down-current sides of boulders and large stumps, and the windless side of ledges and cliffs. Let the bait sink and keep some action going all the time.

Know the fish. Know their patterns of life. What food are they eating right now? When do they feed, and for how long? How do they react when they strike? Polish your techniques to fit the fish.

Fish have a keen sense of sight. Stay out of their range of vision.

Fish have a keen sense of smell. Oil, gasoline, tobacco, onion, and certain other aromas are offensive to fish. Have clean hands, baits, and lures.

Fish have a keen sense of hearing by detecting vibrations.

Be as quiet in your movements as possible.

Keep two complete fishing outfits with you at all times. If your line should hang while the fish are biting you can keep catching them without losing any time. Nor will you scare that big one away while trying to release the hung line.

Fish are usually on three levels of most lakes, ponds, and streams. Some are near the surface, some mid-water, and some on the bottom. Work the various levels to find the area of biting fish.

Troll when you can. You can cover large areas to locate fish. You can fish otherwise inaccessible spots. You learn more about the water you are working.

Go with the weather. Sudden barometer changes, fronts, and rising waters often cause fish to start hitting any bait that comes close to them.

Position yourself to fish with your back to the wind, and don't allow your shadow to be on the water. In moving water, cast upstream and allow your bait to drift down with the flow.

Don't be in a hurry. Give the fish a chance to bite before moving to another spot.

Don't quit, keep fishing. Perseverance pays.

Fish Facts

Fish are greedy by nature and will swallow the largest bait they can safely handle. They have a sense as to the size object they can swallow and will go for larger baits up to their maximum swallowing capacity.

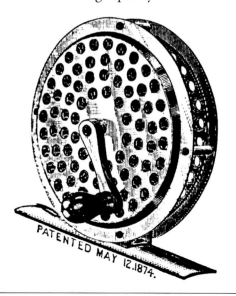

PATENTED MAY 12.1874.

Fish don't always bite because they are hungry. Sometimes the bait is attractive to them or they bite out of curiosity, greed, or viciousness.

Fish need time to turn the bait before they swallow it.

Minnows and other bait fish are always swallowed head first.

Fish feed on a fairly regular time schedule. If they feed in the early morning they will usually feed again in the late afternoon and then again early the next morning. This will be their regular feeding procedure day after day. Night feeders are equally regular.

Brown trout and rainbow trout seem to eat a greater portion of other fish, such as shiners, as they grow larger while smaller trout lean more toward an insect diet.

It is important to know what fish are eating. Often they will feed on only one insect or food for prolonged periods. During these times it is nearly impossible to catch them with any other bait.

Fish have a keen olfactory system. It allows them to have a knowledge of distant things by smell, which is helpful for their feeding and protection.

Fish can taste-test their food before taking it in their mouth by use of sensors on the barbels and fins as well as taste buds in the mouth.

Before and after spawning season fish will eagerly take a variety of baits. Brook trout and many other species will absolutely refuse food during spawning.

Most fish adjust their eyesight to the rhythms of the natural night and day cycle. Any sudden light thrown on them will cause them to leave the area rapidly.

The eyes of fish are placed in such a way that makes it impossible for them to see objects on their level or directly under them. They can, however, see plainly all that is happening above and around them for distances of fifty or more feet.

Shallow water game fish seem to have the best color sense.

Most fish species have a good sense of color perception.

The appearance of a bait seems to be more important than the smell or sound of it.

A very sensitive system of temperature sensation makes

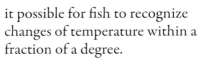

it possible for fish to recognize changes of temperature within a fraction of a degree.

A highly developed sense of "touch" helps fish to reject objects that they cannot eat.

The larger the size of a fish the faster it can swim. A general rule is that fish can swim about eight miles per hour for each foot of body length. A fish striking a bait or making any other sudden move can accelerate to about 50 per cent more than its usual cruising speed.

Fish can hear low-frequency sounds from all directions by means of an "ear" inside the head.

When to Fish

There are many theories, some of them conflicting, as to the most favorable times for fishing. The following are recommendations of rural folk from different parts of the country.

The best time to fish is:
- when the barometer is high or rising
- when a storm is imminent
- after a brief storm at any time of the year
- during a steady light rain
- when rain has just stopped
- when the wind is from the south or west, or while any offshore breeze is blowing (A slight breeze breaks up the surface of calm water, hindering the fish from spotting you.)

- when the moon is between the new and the full
- when water is clear
- when water is murky
- on an overcast day
- when water is rising
- when a lake starts to drop
- when oak leaves are the size of squirrel ears
- when the dogwood blossoms
- when ants build high mounds
- when spider webs are taut

- when cattle are up and grazing (Old-timers say that if they're resting, you can bet that's what the fish are doing.)
- when the water temperature is between 55 and 74° F (A good fishing thermometer should be used.)
- at the crack of dawn during hot, dry months (Large fish, in particular, are active during darkness and into the dawn.)
- one hour before and after high tide; one hour before and after low tide
- on a calm evening for bass and trout
- on stormy days, especially during warm months, for pike, pickerel, and walleyes
- after the first thunderstorm of spring for catfish (Since catfish usually don't bite until the weather is warm enough for a thunderstorm, this claim has some validity.)

Where to Fish

In ponds and lakes, fish frequent places where bottom springs or streams supply cold water to the larger body of water.

Fish prefer those spots in brooks where the water current carries the surface food. You'll find that the bigger fish dwell in such select areas.

Fish downstream when bait-fishing. When fly-fishing, fish either up or downstream, just so the sun is in front of you.

What to Wear

When wading and fly-fishing, wear clothes of brown, green, or gray. They will be least discernible to the fish's keen eye, for these colors of low intensity blend in with the background along stream banks. For fishing from a boat, clothing of light color is less visible against the sky and clouds.

Fishing by the Moon Signs

There seem to be as many theories concerning fishing by the moon signs as there are fishermen. However, from our talks with many anglers we've found most agree to these:

The best signs occur when the moon changes quarters, or when the moon goes into a watery sign (Pisces, Cancer, and Scorpio) or a moist sign (Taurus, Virgo, Libra, and Capricorn). The fish are most active and most likely to bite.

The best period for fishing falls in the period from three days before to three days after a full moon; the day after the full moon is outstanding.

Primo Martinez, a Texas fishing guide for several decades, says "The best time to catch fish is when the moon is directly overhead and the two hours before and two hours after. The next best time is the hour before and the hour after the moon is straight down on the other side of the earth." He says these periods work every time.

The best days of the month, according to information handed down to Louis Viccinelli of

Mississippi by old-time fishermen along the Delta, are the two days on either side of the date of the new moon. The first and last quarter phases are also good.

The Weather and Seasons

After heavy rains fish often won't bite because plenty of food has washed into the lake.

Fish are hard to catch when fresh snow water is in a stream.

July is generally the worst month for fishing, and June is usually the best fishing month.

Many folks believe that fish possess an instinct which makes it possible for them to feel a coming change in weather. Thomas J. Wheelis, who for many years fished off the rocky coasts of Maine, says, "Three days before dirty weather moves in fish will take the bait almost as soon as it is cast, but on the day of the change of weather they never even come near the lures." He also says that when large fish are swimming near the surface it is a sure sign of coming winds. On the sea he has noted that dolphins and

porpoises nearly always announce an approaching storm. They roll, jump, and appear to be "in their happiest hours" just before a great storm. He has also seen whales jump high out of the water in front of wind and storm. Crabs burying themselves deep into the sand is a sure sign of rain and windy weather.

The period immediately following a storm is sometimes the very best of fishing times. The winds stir the water and boil up food from the bottom. This brings in the small fish and behind them come the big fish to get the little ones. Work the shallow waters and be ready for a good catch.

When the air is warm in the spring catfish will swallow almost any bait, alive or dead. On cold days live bait is best. Always allow catfish plenty of time to swallow the hook.

During the summer months black bass go in pairs. If you catch one, try for the mate.

When fishing for black bass it is almost a waste of time to cast on perfectly smooth water.

"Fishing at night is fishing right,
Fishing midday hardly pays,
Dark days are best, they say."

The Lake Turned Over

When I was just a boy the old-timers would say "the fishing's no good now, the lake just turned over." This seasonal overturn occurs with the coming of spring and with the coming of autumn.

It is interesting to know how this happens. Let's take the fall of the year as an example. Water becomes denser and contracts when it begins to get cool. When the sun drifts toward the south a little each day and the nights show a slight chill in the air, the top layer of water in lakes and ponds begin to cool and become heavy.

The chilled water begins to sink, and the lower layers of warm water start to rise to the top. These layers then become cool and also sink toward the bottom. Thus the water is in a constant state of movement and this churning effect causes the whole body of water to turn completely over. The water becomes muddy and murky as this turning and mixing takes place.

It would make one wonder why the colder water doesn't go straight to the bottom and remain there as a body of cold water. While it is true that as water cools it becomes heavier and denser, this only occurs until it drops to a temperature of 39.20 F. Below 39 degrees, it tends to become lighter in weight.

As it approaches freezing it is so light in weight it starts its journey to the top. In the winter the top water is sometimes frozen into ice and remains in that state until the warmth of spring brings it back to 39 degrees and it again sinks.

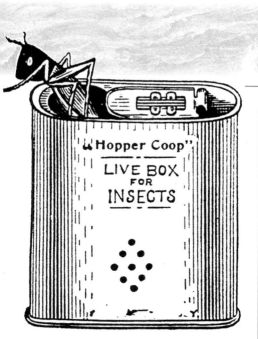

Bait and Equipment

Live Bait Wisdom

Grub worms are a good general purpose live bait. Small mice make a fine bait for large bass and trout.

A live chub or a hellgrammite found under a rock near the river make a good live bass bait.

A fine bait in the spring is raw hogs' liver.

Carp like white maggots smeared with honey. Also try stale doughy sweet bread, white potatoes, or a mix of flour, water, and honey rolled into a tight ball. Carp are slow biters so wait until they swim away with the bait before you set the hook.

Bass like live bait such as young carp, small green frogs, and live grasshoppers.

When using frogs for live bait, use small ones and pass the hook through both lips. Keep a bait frog moving by using very small jerks on the line.

When fishing with minnows keep them well under water except in rapid waters when the current will keep the minnow near the surface, which is the right spot for live bait in fast-moving water.

A spoonful of salt or a few drops of iodine in the water bucket will revive sluggish minnows.

An ordinary minnow pail can be aerated to keep minnows alive by using a rubber tube with air bulb attached. Fill the bulb with air and force the air through the water when the minnows appear to get sluggish. This will supply them with the much-needed oxygen to keep them alive for long periods of time.

Bass have a tendency to switch back and forth from insects to fish in their diets but the largest bass will almost exclusively eat fish such as minnows and perch if they are available in quantities to them. Crayfish are a delicacy to bass and if they can be found always give them a try. Don't overlook an eel for bass at night.

Earthworms are one of nature's greatest natural fishing baits.

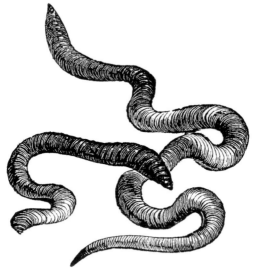

Don't keep them in a tin can, but in an earthen pot (flower pot) or plastic container. Fill it with peat moss or damp green moss, not mud or dirt. Feed them with the white of hard-boiled eggs, a teaspoonful of pure cream, bruised celery, cornmeal, or unmedicated poultry laying mash. They will also eat the powder of finely crushed brick, and although this has no food value a little mixed with their food will give them a healthy red appearance that is attractive to fish. Do not overfeed or overcrowd them.

Use white fat meat shaped like a minnow or frog as a bait for bank fishing.

A fine bait is live maggots taken from fly-blown meat.

Some southern fishermen leave fresh meat outdoors for this purpose. Keep the maggots in a small container and feed them cornmeal. Try them on one fishing trip and you'll be convinced.

Keep bait shrimp in wet grass, moss, seaweed, or sawdust.

Check the stomach of fish to know exactly what they are eating at the time you are fishing. They may switch from one form of food to another as it is available, and you can tell by the layers of food in the stomach as to what is in demand. Fish with that bait or something as close to it in size and appearance as possible.

A 2-inch strip of brightly colored knitting yarn placed on your hook along with the worm or other live bait sometimes does a good job of attracting fish.

Bring earthworms out of the ground by pouring a mixture of detergent and water over a likely area. Within an hour or so earthworms, garden worms, and nightcrawlers will appear. Any device that will vibrate the ground will also bring them to the surface.

The effectiveness of live bait drops quickly when the bait dies. Place all live baits on your hook with care. Minnows should be hooked through the small part of their body near the tail to miss vital organs. The same is true of worms, hook them as near the tapered end of the tail as possible, or better still, hook them through the tough egg sack band near their head. Hook small frogs through both lips. By following these rules you will have live and active bait much longer.

In spring and summer, suspend a light over a pond to attract insects for the fish. Hang it close to the water so that the bedazzled insects will hit the surface. You'll need to use this light lure for only the first few hours of evening.

Wherever cattails grow, frogs and minnows seek shelter. They make excellent bait for catching bass and pike.

Small creatures, like caddis worms, water beetles, and hellgrammites, make fine fresh-water bait. You can collect them by holding a piece of screening downstream while rocks are overturned upstream. The bait will be carried into the screen wire by the stream's current.

Crickets are good bait for catching panfish. Here's an easy way to capture them: Slice a loaf of bread in two. Remove the soft inside. Make a hole in one end about the size of a fifty-cent piece. Using rubber bands, fasten the two halves together again. Place the loaf in tall grass where crickets are most numerous. The following morning, put the end with the hole over a quart jar and shake out the crickets.

To maintain lively crickets for bait fishing, keep them in a clean garbage can. Polish and wax it inside for the first 10 inches down from the top; this will prevent the crickets from climbing out. Put about 5 inches of fine, moist sand in the bottom. Place a glass-jar drinking fountain (the kind used for chicks) on the sand. So that the crickets won't tumble in and drown, put cotton in the dish; they'll take needed moisture from the cotton. Give them a small container of poultry mash for food. The can will accommodate fifteen males and an equal number of females. Keep it in a spot where the temperature can be maintained at roughly 80 degrees. You'll be able to raise about four hundred crickets per month.

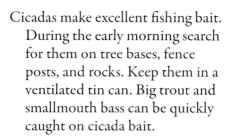

Cicadas make excellent fishing bait. During the early morning search for them on tree bases, fence posts, and rocks. Keep them in a ventilated tin can. Big trout and smallmouth bass can be quickly caught on cicada bait.

When you go fishing in the spring, take along a butterfly net to catch some dragonflies. They make excellent fly-fishing bait. Any surplus can be sprayed with plastic and preserved until the next fishing trip.

Salmon eggs for trout fishing can be kept unspoiled with sugar or salt. Spread out the roe to let it dry slightly. Put it into a container that can be closed tight, alternating layers of salmon eggs with the salt or sugar. Sugar, which is more generally used, will form a syrup, keeping the eggs for considerable time, provided that the jar is well sealed against air. With salt, the roe is preserved in brine.

Search for sand worms beside the sea at low tide. Look under large rocks for a red, fringed worm some 14 inches long. Beware of its pinching beak! To preserve sandworms for days, keep them in a box with a small quantity of sand. Place a little seaweed over them. A whole worm is needed for striped bass; a half portion is sufficient for other fish.

Wherever you see a large round hole in the sand at ebb tide, dig there for a soft-shelled clam. Toss the shells and soft portions of the clams overboard to lure fish. Use the firm parts for bait. Snapping mackerel and blackfish are particularly partial to soft-shelled clams, and other kinds of fish that do not frequent the bottom will feed on them.

Look for the best bait for salt-water fishing, the soft-shelled crab, among rocks or half-submerged logs at the margins of low water. Under its shell you'll find a thin but strong skin. Put the hook into it in such a way as to expose as much as possible of the white flesh. One crab should provide about five baits, including the claws. Blackfish, bluefish, eels, flounders, porgies, and weakfish accept it readily.

Pack soft-shelled crabs, claws up, close together in a box. Place fresh grass or seaweed over them; keep them cool.

All salt-water fishes favor shrimp. You can catch them in still-water areas of salt-water creeks or rivers by using a hand net among the reeds close to shore. Keep them in a box of moist sawdust or in a container of salt water to preserve them all day. Impale them on the end of the hook for lively mobility, or run the hook through from end to end, tail first, concealing the hook.

To keep minnows fresh, add 1 tablespoon of common salt to each 3 gallons of water. In chilly weather, several hundred minnows can be transported

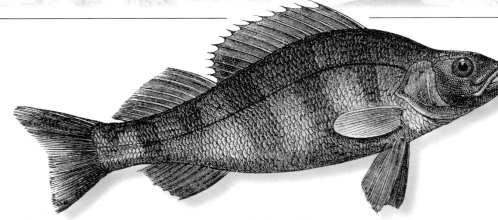

long distances in a 3-gallon container with a tight cover. Fill the container two-thirds with water and one-third with handfuls of clean wheat straw or rye. Some fishermen say that you can keep two minnows alive for more than a week by sealing them in an airtight jar two-thirds full of water.

Pack crayfish and frogs in wet moss to keep them alive for some days.

Bait Recipes

These days most folks are turning to natural foods for wholesome nutrition; fish, too, favor a variety of natural foods. To stir the fish's appetite, you might first chum the water (where it's legal) with diced pieces of the following tempting morsels, in addition to using them for bait:

Bass

pork chunks (what country people call "sow-belly"); small eels

Black Bass

live black chub minnows; small carp, not more than 4 inches in length (It makes a lively, long-lasting bait.)

Carp

Recipe I
   1 cup boiling water
   1 cup oats
   1 teaspoon vanilla
   ⅓ cup cottonseed meal
   ⅓ cup flour

Cook 1 cup of oats in 1 cup of boiling water. Add the other ingredients, working them into the oatmeal one at a time. Form small balls of this doughy mixture to bait your hook for carp.

————————

Recipe II
Make a dough ball of equal parts of corn meal and white flour by mixing in a bit of molasses or honey and enough water to make the mixture adhere. Heat the dough over a low fire for 5 minutes. Remove it from the heat, and knead it for 10 minutes or until it is a good-sized, firm ball. Use chunks about the size of a walnut as bait for carp.

Catfish

muskrat liver, chicken liver; striped frogs; pieces of unscented soap; fish or meat scraps in a burlap sack weighted down with stones; cooked macaroni (It is delicate when impaled on the hook, so cast with care.)

————————

Recipe I
Mix 2 parts of beef brains and 1 part Limburger cheese with a small amount of water. Put the mixture in a jug and bury it in the ground for 2 weeks. Then keep it refrigerated until needed for fishing. Dip small pieces of sponge into this odoriferous mess as bait for luring catfish from afar.

————————

Recipe II
Mix 1 pound of Limburger cheese with a 1-pound can of wallpaper cleaner. Add 1 tablespoon of vanilla. Blend the mixture thoroughly by kneading it. Keep it in a tightly sealed container.

Flounder

clam bait (Put clam bait in a jar, adding sufficient water to cover it. Add enough red or yellow food dye

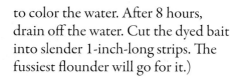

to color the water. After 8 hours, drain off the water. Cut the dyed bait into slender 1-inch-long strips. The fussiest flounder will go for it.)

Sunfish
cockroaches

Trout
crayfish; worms; salmon eggs; cicadas; dry fish meal; minnows (To restore vitality to listless minnows, add six drops of iodine to their water.)

Walleyes
leeches (Try to catch leeches in a screen trap, attracting them with a bait such as raw liver, which contains a lot of blood.)

Baiting Holes and Attracting Fish
Fresh meat or cut fish scattered in an area the day before you fish will sometimes bring in the big ones.

A fine fish decoy can be made by placing several big, bright minnows in a clear glass or plastic bottle with a small hole in the top. Suspend the bottle in the water in a likely spot by using a clear monofilament line. The moving, imprisoned minnows will attract fish from a considerable distance.

To attract minnows throw fresh meat scraps and bones in shallow waters and they will hover in the area.

A piece of fresh meat suspended over a fishing hole soon becomes fly blown and drops maggots continually into the water drawing fish.

A bag of grain or meal, a bale of hay, or a can of dog food with holes punched in the sides makes very good material to bait a fishing hole.

A drop of anise oil or sweet cicely on your bait can attract fish to it.

Build a big campfire that reflects upon the water and it will bring fish in at night.

More Bait Lore
Country people will tell you that bait is quickly seized when mixed with the juice of lovage. Several drops of rhodium oil also bring good results.

Catfish, carp, buffalo, and suckers (especially catfish) like cheese baits. Swiss cheese and cream cheese are very effective.

Don't use a sinker with a grasshopper bait; allow it to float on the water's surface. Use it for catching trout in very still areas of streams. Before worms can be dug in the spring, raw beef makes good trout bait.

Earthworms can be used to catch any kind of fresh-water fish. In salt water, eels and white perch are attracted to them. Place the worms in moss overnight to clean them. They will keep fresh and active for several days if you wrap them in earth inside a strong cloth.

One old-time fisherman recommends a piece of mackerel

as a trolling bait for pike. Cut a piece 1½ inches long and ¼ inch wide, tapering it at one end. Insert the hook as close to the edge of the broad end as possible.

When using bait for bottom fish, fasten the sinker loosely above the hook. Run the line through the hole in the sinker, and tie something (a small stick or button) between hook and sinker to keep them apart. In this way the fish can carry the bait without the sinker and will more likely mouth the hook.

Fly Facts

When you're fabricating artificial flies, make some that imitate the insects most frequently seen in the area to be fished.

On sunny days and in clear or shallow water, use small, plain-colored flies. On gray days, in the evenings, and in deep or murky waters, use large, brightly colored flies.

In areas where the soil doesn't get too dry, you can find the bright yellow flowers of the wild plant celandine. The orange-colored juice coloring fur and feathers for jig flies and streamers. This shade is unusually attractive to trout.

Learn to recognize bedstraw, a trailing weed that is easily uprooted. It can be identified by six to eight leaves sprouting in a whorl around the square stem. You can use the roots to dye streamer flies red.

Fish Poles

Before fishing rods were made of steel or fiber glass, traditional materials were Osage orange, hickory, straight-grained white ash, and split bamboo.

If you'd like to try your hand at making your own rod, Osage orange (the bodock tree) is the best when you can find straight-grained billets. Hickory has great strength, but its tendency to be slow in action makes it less than desirable for a casting rod. However, it's excellent as a big-game trolling rod, having greater shock resistance than other woods. White ash can be used for an acceptable rod, but since it is a softer wood, a larger diameter—especially in the tip—is required, which makes it rather clumsy.

Bamboo is actually a kind of grass. It's never perfect enough to

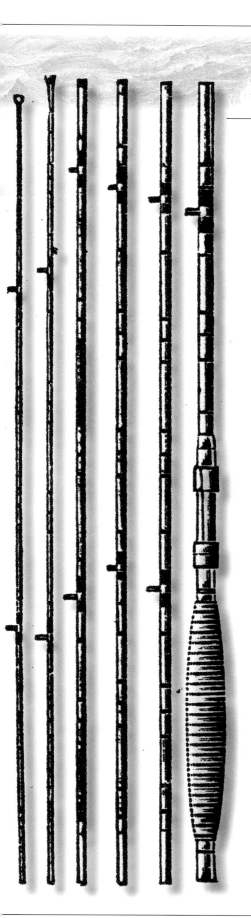

furnish a top-notch fishing pole. In order to make a proper rod, it must be seasoned, split, and then glued. It will last indefinitely if kept well sealed by a coat of varnish to prevent moisture from seeping in, rotting the wood, and softening the glue.

The notion of splitting bamboo into strips and then gluing them together to eliminate the hollow center, thus obtaining the complete strength of the cane, probably originated in China. The technique was used in that country almost three thousand years ago. The first split-bamboo rods were made in America in the 1860's.

For your fishhook, try using the hooked thorn of barrel cactus. You'll catch many a fish with it.

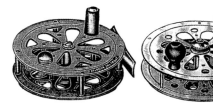

Water Temperature

Remember, it always has been and always will be that water temperature is by far the most important single bit of fishing wisdom you need to locate fish. This is a schedule of water temperatures most preferred by various species of fish. Fish will move in and out of these temperature ranges but will spend most of their time in these general zones and 10° F on either side of them.

Bass (largemouth)	67–70° F
Bass (rock)	60–70° F
Bass (smallmouth)	65–70° F
Bass (spotted)	73–76° F
Bass (striped)	55–60° F
Bass (white)	60–70° F
Bass (yellow)	64–70° F
Carp-bottom feeders but prefer	60–75° F
Catfish-bottom feeders but prefer	62–75° F
Muskellunge	60–70° F
Panfish	65–75° F
Perch (sun and yellow)	60–72° F
Pickerel	60–65° F
Pike (northern)	50–70° F
Salmon (Atlantic)	58–62° F
Salmon (coho)	52–58° F
Salmon (landlocked)	43–48° F
Salmon (Pacific)	52–55° F
Trout (brook)	55–58° F
Trout (lake)	45–50° F
Trout (brown and rainbow)	60–63° F
Walleye	62–72° F

Remember, most fish are found in the thermocline temperature area of 60° to 75° F. The 70° to 72° F level usually has the heaviest concentrations.

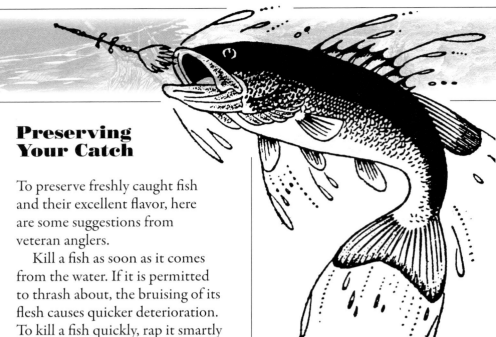

Preserving Your Catch

To preserve freshly caught fish and their excellent flavor, here are some suggestions from veteran anglers.

Kill a fish as soon as it comes from the water. If it is permitted to thrash about, the bruising of its flesh causes quicker deterioration. To kill a fish quickly, rap it smartly on the back just behind the head, using a knife handle or stick; or you can insert your thumb in the gill and break the neck. When killed as soon as caught, fish will keep for a longer period of time and the flesh will be better.

As soon as it's feasible, clean the fish, washing the body cavity thoroughly.

To preserve trout, clean them and wipe them dry. Sprinkle the insides with corn meal. Pack the fish in meal in a snug box.

Trout can be kept fresh and sweet for several days, without salt or ice, in the following way: Dress the fish and wrap them in the long white moss often found in marshy areas near trout streams. Keep them in a cool, shady place, such as a hole in the ground covered with at least a foot of earth.

Pack the body cavity of bass or trout with the large, broad leaves of the plantain, a common weed growing in fields or sunny spots in woods. This will keep the body from drying out and in addition lend a delicious flavor to the meat.

Cool your catch by evaporation: keep it in a wet burlap sack. Don't pack fish snugly; layer them, placing them on pine boughs or grass. Keep the bag moist and away from direct sunlight. If the sack is exposed to a breeze, evaporation will be increased and the temperature lowered even more. Following these pointers, you should be able to cool your catch some 30° F below air temperature with good results.

On fishing trips, stuff cleaned fish with mint. It helps to repel flies and serves as a deodorizer for the fishy smell. Place mint in the bottom of your creel, too.

Fish-Fin Wounds

There is a quick and simple remedy for the sting of a catfish barb. Mose Barlow of Missouri says that rubbing the sore place against the fish's belly will bring immediate relief.

Make a paste of the white of an egg and a spoonful each of common salt and gunpowder. Apply it to a fish-fin wound, and bandage it. Use a fresh application as the mixture dries. To keep the paste moist, cover it with a damp cloth.

When finned or cut by a fish, clean the wound with clean water and put vinegar on it or put a chew of tobacco on the cut and bind it on for a while.

Protection While Fishing

To prevent pesky insects from spoiling your fishing trip, here are some old-time remedies that have proved successful over the years.

Mix 3 ounces of sweet oil and 1 ounce of carbolic acid. Apply the mixture to all exposed parts, being careful to avoid the eyes. Use it every half hour when flies are irksome or for the first two or three days. From then on it will be needed only occasionally, as the skin will be filled with it.

A good preparation for repelling insects consists of 1 part creosote, 1 part pennyroyal, and 6 parts sweet oil.

Simmer 3 ounces of pine tar, 2 ounces of castor oil, and 1 ounce of pennyroyal over a low flame. Bottle it for use.

To make a mosquito smudge, evaporate a piece of gum camphor (about one-third the size of a hen's egg) in a tin vessel over a flame.

Cut 6-foot strips of bark from a dry fallen cedar log to make a bundle a bit larger than two hands can

encompass. Using strips of the white inner bark of a live cedar, bind the dead bark together at intervals of about 9 inches. Put it in your tent, and light one end. It will smudge in the tent with fragrant, pleasing smoke. Mosquitoes will leave, and none will return if you leave the smudge at the tent opening through the night.

When attacked by a squadron of mosquitoes, you may find that Nature has afforded you an antidote in the very vicinity of your fishing. Learn to recognize the wild geranium. You'll find it from April through summer in woods and thickets and along shady roadsides. Crush its leaves between your fingers; its unpleasant odor, similar to that of a he-goat, repels mosquitoes. (You may find yourself followed by a line of bleating nanny goats, but mosquitoes—never!)

Swimming Speeds of Fish	
Swordfish	70 mph
Blue marlin	50 mph
Bluefin tuna	45 mph
Tarpon	35 mph
Blue shark	35 mph
Atlantic salmon	25 mph
Brown trout	25 mph
Pike	20 mph
Striped bass	15 mph
Pacific salmon	10 mph
Perch	10 mph
Mullet	10 mph
Carp	8 mph
Eel	8 mph

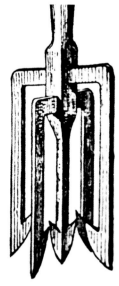

Kinds of Fishing

Over the ages men have devised many means of catching fish. Where waters teemed with big southern catfish, Indians would dive in holding anything red for bait. While the fish were trying to swallow the bright object, they were seized and lugged ashore.

Spear Fishing
Fish were often speared with cane, which wasn't sturdy enough to pull a fish out at first stab. Once the cane was driven in, the fish was permitted to run. Each time the spear reappeared on the surface, it was thrust in anew. Finally the fish tired and could be taken easily.

Bow Fishing
The Indians shot fish in the water with arrows. Though not as popular as pole fishing, this means is sometimes used today. Fishermen with bow and arrow

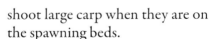

shoot large carp when they are on the spawning beds.

The biggest difficulty in getting your fish by this method is the distortion in distance caused by seeing an object from one medium, air, in another, water. Because of this problem of refraction, the target is really closer than it seems, except from a vertical angle. So aim low to be on target. The deeper the water, the lower should be your aim.

Ice Fishing

During the bitter winters of early North America, the Indians maintained their supply of fish by ice fishing. They built huts over holes in the ice, enabling them to see to a depth of some 50 feet, because they were peering from darkness into water which at that time was transparent. They could spear large muskellunge, bass, lake trout, pike, and pickerel with 40-foot poles.

If you enjoy ice fishing, you may find helpful these tips, contributed by experienced ice anglers.

The best line for ice fishing is one of your old, stiff fly-casting lines. It will run freely and won't freeze, tangle, or collect snow out of water.

To prevent your fishing hole from freezing up, pour glycerine or cooking oil into the hole. This will create a thin film, keeping ice from forming for some time.

A small, lightweight rod is best for ice fishing. The fish, being more sluggish in winter, bite more delicately. A light rod responds more easily to this gentle nibbling, so that you can quickly detect a potential catch.

Use a small hook and small bait in winter.

Ice-Fishing Bait

The following are baits for ice fishing, guaranteed to win you a winter feast of fish:

Meal worms: They are brownish beetle larvae an inch in length. You'll find them in stored grain that has become damp.

Mud daubers: Collect the larvae from the nests of mud dauber wasps.

June bugs: Look for the white larvae of the June bug in piles of decaying sawdust.

Goldenrod galls: Goldenrod galls are the knobs found on dry stalks, actually being a type of cocoon. Choose one without holes; cut it open, and you'll find tempting white grubs for fish.

Corn borers: These are small white worms that can be found in cornstalks left in fields during the winter.

Other Water Creatures

Dig clams at the entrance of the wet sign of Libra. Its first week, September 23 to 30, is thought by many moon sign followers to be the best clam digging time. Jewell Honeycutt in Massachusetts watches the weather, the tides, and marks special spots that look good for digging. She then uses this Libra week for harvesting the clams. They are at their best and most plentiful at the time of the full moon.

When frogging at night use a very bright light, locate the frog, and turn the light into his eyes. He will not jump away and you can pick him up and put him in the bag.

To catch frogs in the water use a hook and line with a small piece of red rag on the hook. Keep the little frogs for fish bait and fry and eat the frog legs from the big ones.

Keep frogs in a box with plenty of air holes and some moist moss or grass. Store in a cool place and drench them with water once or twice a day. They will not need food or drink for two or three days.

Lots of Louisiana folks think the best time to go crabbing is when the moon is full. They use a chicken neck for bait and the crabs bite quickly. The meat will be full and

juicy during the full of the moon but at other times the crabs are mostly shell.

You'll find turtles in almost all waters, including streams and man-made lakes. Use a sturdy fishing rod and raw meat for bait to capture them. Cautiously walk along the water's margin until you spot a turtle floating or sunning itself. Flip the bait just in front of the turtle, and leave it undisturbed for a while before another try.

For extra-good eating, try to catch soft-shelled fresh-water turtles or snapping turtles. Be on your guard when handling all turtles, but especially the snappers.

Camp Cookery

Use clean, dry hemlock bark to kindle your cooking fire. When the flame is bright and steady, keep it so with sweet woods, such as black birch, hickory, sugar maple, yellow birch, and red beech. Split wood is best. Sticks should be short and not over 2 inches in diameter.

Be sure to take salt along on your fishing trip. You'll find it has uses other than seasoning.

- Put a dash of salt in your coffee pot; it will enhance the flavor of the coffee.
- You can remove the odor of fish from your hands by washing them in salt water.
- Sprinkle a little salt in the frying pan before frying fish, and they won't stick to the bottom.

Brook Trout Recipe

2 pounds small trout, dressed;
2 tablespoons lemon juice;
1 pound sliced bacon

Clean the trout as if for frying. Brush them inside with lemon juice and sprinkle with salt, pepper, and preferred seasonings. Wrap each fish in slices of bacon. In a large skillet cook them for five minutes or until crisp. Turn them over, and crisp the other side.

Fiddlehead Fern Soup

The perfect appetizer before a trout dinner is fiddlehead fern soup:

Pick a bunch of these ferns, equaling about 1 quart. Boil them for 15 minutes, drain, and reserve the liquid. Chop the ferns fine. Add 1 cup of evaporated milk, ½ cup of regular milk, and 2 chicken bouillon cubes, dissolved. Add 2 tablespoons of butter, a pinch of basil, and salt and pepper. Mix with the liquid and simmer.

Pot-Baked Fish

Put a slice of bacon or salt pork in a heavy pot. Place 4 pounds of cleaned fish, cut into pieces of serving size, on top. Sprinkle with salt. Cook about 20 minutes over a low fire. Meanwhile, fry sliced onions, adding tomato paste, pepper, and 6 tablespoons of vinegar. Serve the fish with this sauce.

Planked Fish

Heat a slab of wood (avoid pine) until very hot. Clean the fish. Split it to open flat, and tack it to the wood, skin side down. Prop the slab vertically before the fire, periodically turning it end for end to ensure even cooking. Every half minute baste it with a chunk of salt pork dipped in vinegar.

Catfish Soup

2 or 3 pounds catfish
2 quarts cold water
1 onion, sliced
1 celery stalk, chopped
salt and pepper
bay leaf, parsley, thyme
1 cup milk
2 tablespoons butter

Cut the fish. Put all the ingredients in a pot over a low fire. Stir now and then. When the fish flakes easily, the soup is ready to serve.

Turtle Soup

    1 cup peas, tomatoes, or
        other vegetables
    salt and pepper
    2 cups water
    2 cups turtle meat, cut into bite-
        sized pieces
    onion, diced
    carrot, diced
    1 large potato, diced

Combine all ingredients and simmer until tender. Thicken with flour.

Chicken-Fried Frog Legs

Salt and pepper the legs to taste. Beat 2 eggs with ¼ cup of milk. Dip the legs into this mixture, then coat them with corn meal or dry bread crumbs. Fry in a skillet of hot vegetable oil, rolling them to ensure even browning, for no longer than five minutes.

Nature's Larder

If you discover you've forgotten to pack the seasonings, Nature will provide substitutes:

- **Wild onions:** They can be used fresh, cooked, or dried and in salads or soups.
- **Cow parsnip**: Burn its dried leaves and the lower part of the stalks. Use the ashes as a salt substitute. The lower stalks, after being dried, can be chopped and added to other foods for salt flavoring.
- **Coltsfoot:** The dried, burned leaves provide a good replacement for salt.
- **Yarrow:** This plant is often called "old man's pepper." Chop the fresh or dried leaves fine and use them as an alternative to pepper.

Watercress

Watercress, a member of the mustard family, can be found along stream beds. Some old-time anglers gather this nutritious plant, pour hot grease over it, and sprinkle it with salt. They also use it to keep their catch cool and fresh.

Anglers' Adages

- The harder you fish, the luckier you get.
- A boat is a hole in the water into which you throw money.
- The two best days in a fisherman's life are the day he buys a boat and the day he sells it.

11 | OUTDOOR GEAR

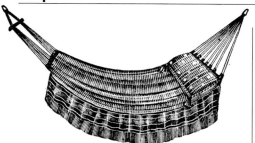

Hammock

You will need these materials to make an inexpensive hammock:

    25 feet of strong rope, cut in
        2 equal lengths
    1 10-foot piece of lumber,
        1 by 3 inches
    12 1½-inch wood screws
    1 piece of canvas, 2½ by
        7 feet

Cut the wood into four 2½-foot sections. Place each canvas end between two of the boards. To secure the canvas, insert six screws in each set of boards. Drill holes through the wood 3 inches in from the ends to accommodate the rope. Run the equal lengths of rope through the holes at either end, and knot them on the underside of the fastened boards.

Walking Cane

The first step in making a walking cane should be taken in the woods. Explore the ground for a fallen branch that approximates the diameter of cane you have in mind.

Make the next stop a junkyard. Buy a rod of lightweight steel to reinforce your walking stick.

Saw the chosen branch into cross sections about 1½ inches in thickness. Bore out their centers, and string them on the steel rod. Glue each addition to the one before.

When it comes to the cane head, let your imagination take over. Almost anything that strikes your fancy (the more unique the better) will serve, provided it fits comfortably in your grip.

Golf Tees

Purchase a polyethylene rod, 3⁄16 inch in diameter. Cut it in 2-inch segments. While holding one end of a segment with pliers, immerse the opposite end in boiling water. After a few seconds it will be soft. Press the softened end on a golf ball. It will expand slightly and become molded to the ball's curve. Keep it against the ball for several seconds until cooling and hardening take place. Sharpen the other end in a pencil sharpener.

Truckwagon

Cut four wheels by sawing 2-inch-thick cross sections of logs. The wheels may be of any desired size as long as all four diameters are similar; a suggested satisfactory diameter is 12 inches. In the center of each wheel, bore a 2-inch hole to accommodate the axle hub. Make the axle from a hardwood pole, 30 inches long and 3 inches in diameter. If desired, the rear axle may be longer than the front axle. Carefully trim the ends of the hubs, and fit them in their holes so that they extend about 1 inch beyond the wheels. Bore a hole close to the end of each axle; insert a peg to keep the wheel on the hub.

Connect the axles with a narrow coupling board that runs from the center of the rear axle to the middle of the one in front. Bore a hole through the coupling board and front axle for a metal bolt, which will enable the front wheels and axle

to rotate at almost 180 degrees. Bolt the rear axle in similar fashion, but do not allow it to rotate. Run short boards, as braces, at an angle from a position near the wheels on the rear axle to the coupling board. Secure the braces with bolts or pegs.

If your truckwagon is intended for the fun of racing down a hillside, fasten a board seat to the back axle and braces. Control direction by foot pressure on either side of the front axle or by pulling pressure exerted on wires that have been attached to the axle close to the wheels. If hauling is your truckwagon's purpose, build a wagon bed at the rear instead of a seat, or nail on a good-sized wooden box.

Bow Saw

If you have an old bicycle-tire rim from a 26-inch wheel, a few scraps of wood, some nuts and bolts, and a metal rod on hand, you are well equipped for making a bow saw. The only expense involved-and that a small one-will be the purchase of a 24-inch steel saw blade.

Make two handles from wooden dowels of a circumference to fit within the tire rim's groove. One handle should be 16 inches long; the other, 22 inches in length. Fasten the saw blade, its cutting edge lowermost, at one end of the 16-inch handle with a nut and bolt; the free end of the dowel should project downward. Fasten the opposite blade end approximately at the 16-inch point on the other handle so that the lower ends of the dowels are on an even plane. Six inches of the longer handle should project above the back of the blade.

Cut the wheel rim in half. Using one of the pieces, fit its groove around the inner side of the dowels, close to the blade's cutting edge; the arch of the bow should face downward.

Run a metal rod along the groove of the arch and through holes bored in the handles. Secure the rod with nuts. It will create tension in the rim and pull the blade taut.

When preparing stove or fireplace wood with your bow saw, grip the extension of the 22-inch handle. The bowed rim will act like a pendulum weight, keeping the saw blade vertical. If you need to cut a log that is too large to fit within the saw's frame, the blade can easily be reversed.

Backpack

Make a roomy, serviceable backpack from an old pair of bib overalls. Simply knot each lower leg securely, and the pack is ready to be filled. Slip the suspenders over your shoulders.

Old-Fashioned Lantern

An old-fashioned lantern can be completed in no time with a few discarded materials. Begin with a 1-pound can, preferably the old-style, squat variety of coffee can. If one is not at hand, almost any tin with a diameter of about 5 inches will serve as well—a 1-pound

the middle of the slits until it protrudes about 2 inches inside the container. The sharp metal points in the center of the slits will be forced inward and will secure the candle in place. As the wax is consumed in use, the candle can be shoved in further.

When the candle is lit, the can acts as a shield against wind, rain, or snow and as a reflector, spreading illumination over a wide area.

To store your candle lantern, hang it by the handle.

Snowshoes

If you need snowshoes, make a pair from string and saplings. They won't have much eye appeal, but they will serve their purpose well.

Cut four fairly straight saplings having a circumference approximating that of a man's thumb. Trim each to a length of 4 feet if the shoes are intended for a person of average height; for a taller person, make them 5 feet long. These sticks should be sufficiently supple to bend a little without breaking. They will serve as the frame of the snowshoes. Slice one side of their ends at an angle so that the resulting flat surfaces of each pair of sticks will fit together, forming a point. Bind together the ends of each pair in the following

way: Tie string (heavy cotton string or nylon fishnet twine) around one of the sticks at a point several inches before the two saplings join. Next, encircle both sticks with the string, spiraling toward the pointed end and stopping a few inches short of the tip. Now reverse your direction. Wind backward and finish by

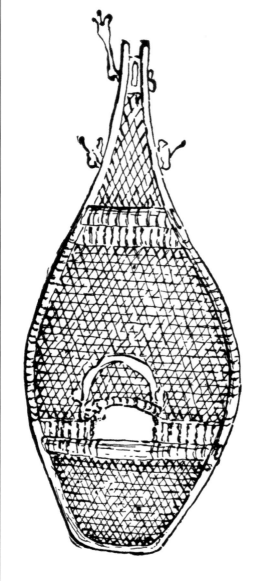

lard can, a large tobacco tin, etc. From the bail of a paint can, a piece of coat hanger, or any stiff wire, fashion a handle shape. Lay the can sideways, and punch one hole in the front edge and two more holes straight across at the rear edge. Hook the handle ends into these holes.

Through the side directly opposite the handle, cut a crisscross midway between the front and back of the can. Use a strong, sharply pointed knife to make each crosscut, which should be from 1½ to 2 inches in length. Gently push a utility candle, one that is thick and slow-burning, through

securing the string on the other stick, opposite the starting point on the first one. While working, keep the string taut.

Make cross supports for the frame by cutting four 1- by 2-inch bars roughly 8 to 10 inches in length. Using your knife, carve a concave opening in the ends of these crossbars so that they will fit snugly around the contour of the long saplings. Insert each cross support between the vertical sticks of the frame at the point where they are no longer parallel but begin to taper toward the pointed ends.

Bind the frame and crossbars together with a webbing of string. Tie strings securely near the ends of the long vertical sticks, and crisscross them rather closely for the length of the frame. Now run strings vertically, weaving them in and out of the horizontal cords to minimize slippage. By keeping the string taut as you weave, the tension will be evenly distributed throughout the snowshoes.

Make a rope bridle across each snowshoe to fit around the toes of your boots. Bind the bridle in place just in front of the snowshoe's center of balance. The toe of the snowshoe will then be raised each time you lift your foot and move forward. Fasten on your new footgear by running a loop of rope around your ankle and hooking it into the bridle rope with a bent nail or some other workable contrivance.

Add extra strength to the areas where your boots will be resting; use a piece of rawhide, a sturdy fabric, or rope for reinforcement purposes. Binding short sticks on the inner sides of the long saplings, from one cross support to the other, will strengthen the main part of the frame, especially the boot area. Your homemade snowshoes are now ready to be strapped on for a long trek over the snow.

Ice Chopper

An ax may be used to chip holes in ice, but take the precaution of first warming the blade near a fire or, at least, of blowing on it. A cold blade, being very brittle, can easily break.

Avoid the risk of damaging ax blades by making an ice chopper for winter fishing. Assemble these materials:

a chisel having a very wide blade (the kind used on brick or wood)a section of iron water pipe, 4 feet in length
1 bicycle handlebar grip
15 feet of rope

Drive the chisel into the pipe. In doing so, you may dull the cutting edge. Grind or file it sharp when your ice chopper is completed. Push the bicycle handlebar grip on the other end of the pipe to provide a comfortable handle. Tie the length of rope to the ice chopper so that you can retrieve it should the tool slip into the water.

Neckerchief Hood

Make a protective hood from a plain, 36-inch-square neckerchief. Spread it flat. Fold the two upper corners down to form contiguous right triangles. Now roll up the bottom of the neckerchief until the upper corners are included in the roll. Put your head in the gap between the two triangles. The ends of the roll can be

carried forward to be knotted beneath the chin.

Since the hood covers the back of the neck, you have only to pull your coat collar close against it to keep out chill air and wind. It also protects the back of the neck from sunburn on hikes and fishing trips.

Cowpokes of the old days originated these useful hoods.

Hobnailed Brogans

Hobnailed wading brogans are a boon to the sportsman fishing in streams where slippery, moss-covered rocks abound. Those on the market are expensive.

It is a simple matter to make your own hobnails from ordinary work shoes that have leather soles. Depending on the soles' thickness, you will need wood screws about ½ to ¾ inches in length. Although brass screws don't rust, they wear down more quickly than steel ones. Don't drive in too many screws or place them too near each other, or else they will fail to make proper contact. Be careful not to insert them too deeply. Screw them into the heels and soles, and leave ½ inch to function as hobs. You'll discover that the sharp screw edges do a better gripping job on slimy rocks than rounded hobnails

Fishing Flies and Lures

You will need the following tools and materials for tying flies:

Required Tools and Materials

Vise: You must have a steel vise with a clamp for fastening it securely to the work surface. The height should be adjustable for ease in working; the jaws should be adjustable to accommodate small and large hooks.

Rubber Bumper: A bumper can be purchased at a hardware store. Attach this rubber button by its screw center to the edge of your work table some 8 inches on the right side of the vise. It will serve to grip the tying thread, maintaining the necessary tension on it. Drive

a small nail into the work surface, several inches to the right of the button, as a spindle for the spool of thread.

Scissors: You will need a pair of steel scissors, no more than 4 inches in overall length, with strong, straight blades that taper to a sharp point.

Stylet: The stylet is used for many small jobs, such as the removal of hardened lacquer from the eyes of hooks. Make this handy tool by embedding a needle in a dowel of wood. A hat pin is a good substitute.

Hook Hone: Have a 4-inch hone at hand to keep sharp points on the hooks.

Thread: You will need a spool of white nylon thread.

Wax: Wax for the tying thread can be made as follows:

Fill a wide-mouthed jar (about 2½ to 20¾ inches wide and 3 or 4 inches high) with powdered rosin to a 1-inch depth. Add only enough turpentine to permeate the rosin. Put the open jar in hot water over low heat. When the contents become syrupy in consistency and clear amber in color, remove the jar from the stove, cover, and let cool. The cooled wax will be semi-firm and will harden when used to bond materials. It will not dissolve in water.

Wax Pad: A 2-inch square of oilcloth will serve to hold wax, making it accessible when you need to wax the tying thread. Simply pull the thread slowly through the wax.

Lacquer: Coat the fly head and other areas wound in thread with waterproof varnish. Colorless nail polish is inexpensive and convenient to use. For ease of application, sharpen the small brush.

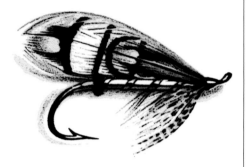

Attaching Thread to the Hook

The curve of the hook must be firmly clamped in the vise, with the barb below. Wax the thread by folding the wax pad over it and pulling it through the wax. Wax 6 inches at one time. The thread binds all parts of the fly to the hook in one continuous piece.

Slip the thread over the hook shank a short distance from the eye end. This spot will be designated as the wing site. Always keep the thread taut in your hands as you work. Bring the thread in your right hand down under the hook shank, up over the thread in your left hand, and over the shank. Follow this procedure three times. There should now be a spiral winding of thread, with the thread of the left hand bound firmly against the hook shank. Press the middle finger of your left hand against the wound thread to keep it from loosening.

Slide your right hand down the thread, and wedge it behind the rubber button to hold it taut. With your free right hand, cut the thread's short end close to the hook.

Making Fly Bodies

Two simple fly bodies that can be fashioned successfully with little practice are made of flat tinsel and chenille.

Flat Tinsel Body: After attaching the tying thread at the wing site, cut diagonally a 1-foot length of medium-width flat tinsel. Holding the strip between the left forefinger and thumb, press the thread

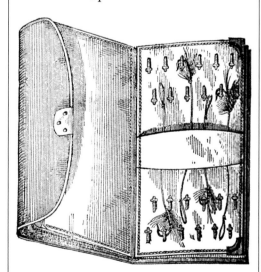

windings against the hook shank with the middle finger. Free the thread from the button with your right hand. Lay the diagonally cut end of tinsel against the hook's side at the wing site. Carry the thread up and over the tinsel. Bring the thread down under the hook shank, up, and across the tinsel again. The

second turn of the tying thread should be on the right side of the preliminary one. As the thread is brought down behind the shank the last time, slide your thumb and forefinger down the thread; catch it in back of the rubber button. Using the right thumbnail, bend the tinsel point back over the windings of thread. Holding the thread windings in place with the left hand's middle finger, free the thread with your right hand. Wind a fourth turn of thread over the folded tinsel and secure it. Fasten the thread behind the button. Keeping it flat, carry the tinsel forward and beneath the hook. Hold it slanted in the direction of winding — in this case toward the hook's curve. Bring it over the hook shank and down behind. Take it with the left hand as the right is on the point of meeting the thread. Make each turn of tinsel contiguous to the preceding strip but not overlapping. Always keep the tinsel taut between the hands and the hook, changing hands when required. Continue wrapping the tinsel around the hook shank until it reaches a point parallel to the barb. Be careful not to snag the tinsel on the tip of the hook as you near the curve. The point on the shank parallel to the barb marks the end of the body of your fly. It is the tail site. At this point, reverse the direction in which the tinsel is held. Holding it taut and slanting forward, wrap it over itself toward the eye of the hook.

Wind as previously described, with each turn flat and each edge touching the preceding one. Guard against overlapping. When the spot where the tinsel was tied to the hook is covered, press a left-hand finger on the tying thread, and free the thread from the button with your right hand. Wrap two turns of thread about the tinsel, winding in the direction of the hook eye. This will secure the tinsel. Catch the thread behind the button. Diagonally clip off the excess tinsel. Bend the tip of the tinsel over the thread with the left hand. After releasing the thread with your right hand, bind the folded tinsel with one turn of thread. The body is now finished.

Chenille Body: Clamp the curved end of the hook in the vise with the barb down. Wax about 6 inches of tying thread in the manner already described.

Fasten the thread at the tail site. Hold the short end in the left hand, and with the right hand, place the thread against the hook at the spot above and parallel to the hook's point. Bring the thread

down and in back of the hook shank and then up in front, crossing over the piece held in the left hand. Repeat this procedure four times, spiraling toward the curve of the hook and ending the windings just in front of the spot above the barb. Catch the thread behind the button. Cut off the short end of the thread.

Pull fuzz from one end of a chenille strand, and expose ½ inch of the thread's core. Place the core of thread directly over the spot above the barb. Have its end face in the direction of the hook eye. With the right hand, remove the thread from the rubber button and, spiraling toward the hook eye, wind it around the core. Continue winding an open spiral of thread; stop at the wing site. Catch the thread behind the button.

Now begin wrapping the chenille around the shank of

the hook. Make close spirals to completely cover the hook and the tying thread. Release the thread from the button. Carry it over the end of the chenille body at the wing site, and bind it twice to the hook shank. Secure the thread at the button. Clip off excess chenille. Bind down any fibers of chenille or core visible in front of the windings of thread. The chenille body is finished.

Making Tails and Wings

The tail hair of a deer is good material for tails and wings of fishing flies, particularly when the hair is slightly wavy. Such hair undulates in water currents and attracts fish better than straight hair.

Buckhair Tail: Put the hook in the vise; fasten on thread at the tail site.

Cut a small hair tuft from a buck's tail. Try to avoid trimming the edges to give a uniform appearance; take advantage of the naturally tapering hair ends. In order to even the tips, remove all short and long hairs. Longer hairs may sometimes be replaced lower in the wisp. Eliminate those with broken ends. The length of the tail should equal the length of the hook shank.

Grasp the hair tuft in the left hand just short of the middle and put a dab of nail polish on its center where the thread will cross over it. Hold the tuft on the hook shank at the tail site. Free

the thread with the right hand. Carrying it up and over the hook, slide it between the tuft and thumb and then between the tuft and forefinger on the farther side. Maintain the tuft on the top side of the shank, slightly in front of the spot above the barb. Bind it once more with thread. Raise the tuft, and bring the thread under and behind it to the other side. Encircle the tail's base with a complete turn of tying thread. Next, make two thread windings around both hair and hook shank. Have them spiral forward. The tail is now securely bound to the shank. Catch the thread at the rubber button. Clip away the hair projecting toward the hook eye at the spot just after the

thread windings. Cut at an angle so that the ends will taper.

Buckhair Wing: Fasten thread on the hook at the wing site. Cut a slender tuft of hair from a buck's tail. Make the ends uniform as you did for the fly tail. The wing length should extend just beyond the curve of the hook. Put a dab of nail polish on the tuft where the thread will cross over it. Make two complete windings of thread around the hair and hook shank to anchor the tuft. Now lift the wing; bring the thread around in back of it. Carry it forward on the farther side and above the hook. Repeat this procedure. Holding the hair close to the shank, make a turn of thread over

the spot where the encircling thread meets on the top side of the hook. This will keep the wing down in the correct position. Wind the thread twice more around the hook and hair; again, it should spiral forward. Catch the thread at the button. Cut off the forward shaft of hair, tapering it at an angle. Wind one more turn of tying thread around the cut ends. The wing should recline along the hook shank.

Practice

Practice tying each part separately until you develop skill and speed. When you have thoroughly mastered these steps, make a fly from start to finish with one continuous thread, beginning with the tail and ending at the head—formed by the final knot— known as the wrap knot. As you add each material, it must conceal the thread already in place and the snipped ends of materials already used. Cover the tail stub with the body material, hide the snipped end of the body with the wing, and cover the ends of wing material with the head, composed of the wrap knot.

Making the Fly Head

Attach the tying thread at the wing site. The thread should enter the right hand beneath the fourth finger, across the underside of the fingertips, and should be held by the thumb and index finger. With the left hand, seize the thread coming

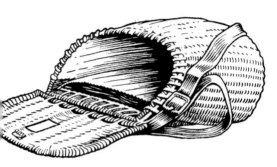

from the right hand, and hold it against and in front of the hook shank by extending the middle and fourth fingers and catching the tying thread between them. It should be parallel with the hook shank and on the side nearer you. The thread now forms a large loop from hook to fingers. In your right hand, tautly grasp the thread descending from the hook. Carry it up and then across the parallel thread that is in front of the shank. With the taut thread holding the parallel thread against the hook shank, the left hand is free to aid in wrapping it about the hook, thus binding the parallel thread to the shank. Going up, over, and around the hook shank and parallel thread four times, wind the taut thread spiraling closely in the direction of the hook eye.

While gripping the taut thread in the right hand, begin pulling the long end of the parallel thread with the left hand. The loop of thread will start to diminish in size. As it grows smaller, press it from in back against the thread windings on the hook with your right middle finger. The loop will

constantly diminish as you pull. Release your right hand's hold on the thread, but continue pressing on the threads with the middle finger until the loop completely disappears. Cut off the long end of the thread. The tying thread is now securely bound on the hook by the wrap knot, terminating your fishing fly. Several applications of nail polish or lacquer will completely cover the separate thread windings and give a finished appearance.

Fly Varieties

There are many types of flies and a variety of materials from which to create them. Fly bodies can be fashioned from rayon, silk, or synthetic floss, chenille, tinsel, wool, fur, and feathers. As much as possible, try to use recycled materials: scraps of fur that you can obtain free from furriers; local reed fibers; and discarded tinfoil. Let your dog donate a snip of hair!

After conquering the preliminaries, you may want to use a wider range of materials and progress to more complicated flies. You may also want to increase your supply of tools by adding fly-tying pliers with strongly gripping jaws and a hackle gauge to determine the correct hackle size for the different hook sizes.

Rubber Band Fly: Here is a fly requiring no skill and only a few seconds to make. Take a handful of rubber bands, preferably green or white, and push them through the

eye of a short-shanked hook. When they are centered in the eye, cut off the looped edges with scissors. Now encircle the rubber bands just below the eye with several windings of thread, and tie them to the shank. The rubber bands will quiver temptingly as they move through the water. For extra weight a small spinner may be added above the fly.

Nail Lure

An excellent and inexpensive homemade lure requires nothing more than a twenty-penny nail, two split rings, and a treble hook. Using a saw and file, remove both ends of the nail so that a 3½-inch length remains. Near each end drill a hole,

and on either side of it file a bevel. Insert a ring in each hole. Fasten your fishing line to one ring; attach a treble hook to the other.

A nail lure can be cast to a surprising distance right on target. You will find it especially effective where fish are schooling.

Spinner-Blades and Spoons

From the shallows and shores of lake and stream, gather freshwater mussel shells. You may find some quickly and in one spot, thanks to

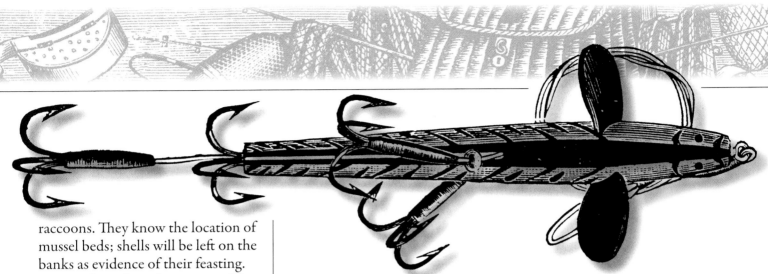

raccoons. They know the location of mussel beds; shells will be left on the banks as evidence of their feasting. The mother-of-pearl interiors of the mollusks, shining with iridescence like darting, brightly scaled minnows, make fine lures.

Shape shell pieces into spinner-blades and spoons with a coarse hand file. Drill a hole at each end to accommodate split ring, swivel, and treble hook.

Make small pearl spoons for trout lures; fashion bigger ones to attract large pike and bass.

Collapsible Fish Landing Net

Make the handle for your landing net from a sturdy broomstick. A length of 18 inches is generally satisfactory, but this dimension may be adjusted to suit your preference. From an electrical supply shop, acquire a ¾-inch piece of brass tubing. Turn the cut end of the handle on a lathe or use a wood rasp to diminish its circumference so that the tubing will slip on to a depth of 3¼ inches.

Fashion the hoop for the net from a piece of telegraph wire with a ³⁄₁₆-inch diameter. To shape it

smoothly and evenly, wrap it about a large crock or anything round of the proper circumference. Just short of closing the circle, bend the remaining two ends of wire (which should measure about 2½ inches) straight out from the hoop. Keep them parallel. The space between the parallel wires should be sufficient to accommodate the narrow end of the handle. Then

bend the tips of the wires inward, forming small right angles, by holding them in a vise or the jaws of a monkey wrench and hammering them down. Bore a ³⁄₁₆-inch hole on either side of the handle for inserting the right angle hooks. From these holes, gouge a groove along the handle for the wire to fit in flush with the wood. If you lack a gouge, use a piece of red-hot wire to burn in the groove.

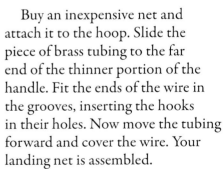

Buy an inexpensive net and attach it to the hoop. Slide the piece of brass tubing to the far end of the thinner portion of the handle. Fit the ends of the wire in the grooves, inserting the hooks in their holes. Now move the tubing forward and cover the wire. Your landing net is assembled.

Wind a good length of the handle with some old fish line to make it easy to grip. Putting a screw eye "g" in the end of the handle will enable you to hang the net from a hook in your belt.

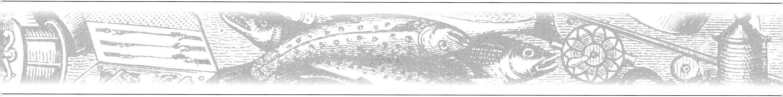

For storage or carrying, slip the tubing back and fold the net back over the handle.

Creel

An excellent creel can be fashioned from the simplest of materials. Use shingles, preferably of cedar, for the sides and ends. Make the top and bottom of ¼- or ½-inch boards. These boards should be cut curved to fit the shingle sides of the creel, which will bend accommodatingly without splitting. Use small nails to tack the shingles to the top and bottom boards. Before nailing on the front, saw a generous notch in it for the insertion of fish. Make a cover for the opening, attaching it to the creel by a strap or a small pair of hinges. Tack a shoulder strap onto the back. The creel can be made in whatever size suits you.

A box of this kind will maintain your catch in a firm, fresh condition, especially if you layer leaves, moss, or green clover between the fish.

Fish Scaler

In no time at all, you can make an efficient little device for removing scales from fish. It requires a short piece of wood suitable for a handle and a bottle cap having sharp, scalloped edges. Tack the cap on one end of the handle, hammering the nail through the underside of the cap. Bend down any extension of the nail on top to attach the cap more securely. You will find this contrivance a very serviceable scaler.

Simple Smoker for Fish

Here is an easy way to make a cheap fish smoker: Take a good-sized, firm cardboard carton. Open one end, and tape or tie the flaps

so that the box can be set upright on them. Pierce the carton, 6 inches below the other end, with metal coat hangers or skewers to form a level grillwork.

Add a little brown sugar to a brine solution so salty as to float a potato. Steep any fish of solid meat in this solution for a minimum of four hours, overnight being preferable.

Take out the fish, pat it with paper towels, and let dry completely in the air. When dry, it will exhibit a slight glaze.

Build a small charcoal fire. When the coals become white, add hardwood chips. Hickory or apple impart a distinctive flavor.

Lay the brined fish on the grill. Set the box on its flap legs over the smoldering chips. Close the flaps on top, and weight them shut with a rock. Fish about 2 inches thick will need to smoke approximately four hours. Less time is required for thinner pieces.

The wood chips should be hindered from flaring up by the lack of oxygen in the closed box. However, if the lower portions of the carton become hot to the touch, sprinkle them with water as a precautionary measure. If the lower edges of the box ignite, quickly douse them with water.

Fire Rack

To keep frying pans and coffee pots from tipping over into your campfire, make a fire rack from hinges. You will need a stove bolt and three 8-inch strap hinges.

Lay one segment of the three hinges on top of one another, and line up their middle holes. Put a stove bolt through them. Now you have the top of your fire rack; the remaining hinge segments will act as legs. When the rack is not in use, it can be conveniently folded for storage or for carrying in a pocket of your camping clothes.

Crow Decoys

You will need one wire coat hanger for each crow decoy.

Straighten the hook with pliers to make the feet for anchoring it in the ground. Bend the rest of the hanger in the outline of a crow. To achieve a realistic shape, compare it as you work with a picture of a crow in profile.

Cut newspaper in strips. Saturate them with a papier-mâché paste of flour and water. Vertically wrap the wire framework with the moist strips. Let dry overnight.

Fasten a wire hook on the bird's back if you plan to hang it in a tree. More papier-mâché may be added on the sides to give the crow a fuller body, if so desired. Finish by applying flat black paint to your decoy.

Decoy Weights

You can make excellent weights for floating decoys with small expenditure in money and effort. Purchase premixed concrete at a hardware store. Add water according to directions. Fill paper cups with the concrete, and insert spread cotter keys for a string eye. Twelve weights can be made from a 1½-pound bucket of cement.

Duck Retriever

To make a lightweight duck retriever that can be carried easily in your hunting coat, cut strong cord or a heavy fishing line to a length of 6 feet. At each end tie a loop. In the center of the cord (or fish line), tie another strong string, from 75 to 150 feet long.

Take a small scrap of wood about 2 by 4 inches in size, and wind the string around it. Start with the free end of the longer length, leaving the cord with the loops to be rolled on last. Tuck it in your pocket.

When the duck you have killed lies far out of reach in the water, look for a stick about 4 feet long. Slide a loop of your duck retriever over each end; draw it tight. Throw the stick out beyond the bird. Pull the triangle over your duck, and haul the fowl in to shore. Toss aside the stick. Roll up your string retriever as before, and put it in your hunting coat.

PART II

HEARTH AND HOMESTEAD

12 | WAYS WITH PAINT AND PAPER

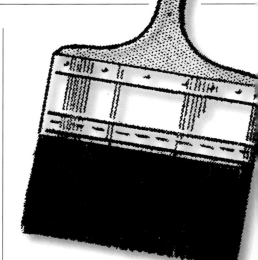

House Painting

Main Tasks

Painting a house consists of four main tasks:

Surface Preparation: Some scraping, sanding, caulking, and priming may be necessary. For paint to adhere properly, underlying areas must be free of dirt and loose paint. Start by hosing down the outside walls of the house to remove soil; then scrape any cracked, chipped, or peeling places. Areas where the bare wood has been exposed need primer. If the patch is not large, however, two coats of paint will suffice. Recaulk doors, window frames, and chimneys when necessary.

Window and Trim: Save time by painting windows with care to avoid the job of scraping panes later. When doing trim on a house with overhanging eaves, you will be painting overhead, so wear a hat.

Main Body of House: Using a wide brush, take long strokes, but don't overextend your reach when standing on a ladder.

Cleaning Up: Pick up and dispose of any old caulking material, putty, or paint chips. Look over your work, and touch up places you have missed or failed to cover well.

Requirements for House Painting

Paint: Buy the best quality paint you can afford. The results of your labor will last longer and look better than when a cheaper product is used. Available types of paint are oil-based and water-based (latex). Water-based paint dries in roughly one hour so that two coats can be applied on the same day. Brushes can be cleaned with soap and water. Allow a drying time of forty-eight hours between coats of oil-based paint. Clean the brushes in spirits of oleum.

Brushes: Some painters like a wide brush because of its extensive coverage. Others prefer one 2½ inches in width with a rounded handle. It easily covers narrow siding while its length permits reaching a wide swath. As time wears on, brushes of larger width tend to feel heavy. The better the brush, the better the results. One of nylon retains its shape and is easy to clean.

Spirits of Oleum: Use it for cleaning brushes and thinning paint.

Ladders: Generally a 6- to 8-foot ladder and a 12- to 14-foot extension are sufficient.

Dropcloths: Protect shrubs and bushes from paint by draping them with old sheets or dropcloths of light canvas or plastic.

Scrapers: Prepare surfaces with a 2-inch scraper that's been maintained in sharp condition with a file. A razor-blade scraper and putty knife will also come in handy.

Rags: For cleanup.

Nylon Stockings: Paint that becomes scummy can be

satisfactorily filtered through a piece of old nylon stocking. To prevent this condition in the first place, splash a small amount of oleum on the contents of the paint can before covering it at day's end.

Wire: Hang paint buckets on the ladder with the aid of coathanger wire. Suspend the pail on the side nearest your painting arm.

Painting Clothes: Hat, shirt, and overalls (or pants) can be purchased cheaply at thrift stores. Overalls provide room for stowing cloths and tools. When working in warm weather, choose white garb to minimize the heat.

Shoes: Footwear with steel shanks will make perching on a ladder more comfortable. Your feet won't tend to wrap around the rungs.

Massage (optional): At the end of a day's painting, you may welcome a massage to assuage aching muscles.

Paint Estimate

Here are some guidelines for estimating the amount of paint needed for a house:

Figure the number of square feet of surface to be painted by finding the distance, in feet, around the outside of your house. Next, determine the average height to the eaves. (If there are gables, add 2 feet to this number.) Now multiply the first number (the distance around the house) by the second (the height to the eaves).

Ask your paint dealer for the approximate coverage in square feet of each gallon of undercoat. Divide the total surface area by this number.

Ascertain how many square feet are covered by 1 gallon of top coat; divide as indicated above.

If the surface condition is uncommonly dry, porous, rough, or heavily textured, 20 percent more paint may be needed for the first coat.

Application of Paint

Begin painting under the eaves at the highest point and work downward. Guard against lap marks, the buildups where ending and beginning areas meet. Whenever possible, avoid painting in direct sunlight, which dries the coat too rapidly and can cause lap marks. If you do encounter a sunny spot, feather the ends of your brush strokes and draw the paint out to a thin, gradually fading streak.

When approached by flying, stinging insects (bees, hornets, etc.), yield ground. If the creature persists, have a knotted rag handy to flick at it in self-defense. The insect will be dazed long enough for you to make a safe retreat. It may be of some solace to know that you are less likely to be bothered by such pests in the morning. During the early hours of the day, flying insects are more sluggish in their activities.

Making Paper

Paper from Plants

Paper can be made from all fibrous vegetation. One can prepare a wide assortment of paper, differing in texture and quality, from the various plants that grow in woods and meadows.

The most favorable time to gather your plants is toward summer's end or at the beginning

of fall. Place them on a floor of stone, and keep them moist until they decompose.

Chop the rotted material into ½-inch-long pieces. Put them into a large vessel filled with water and add a good amount of caustic soda. Rub a thumb and forefinger together in the water. If enough soda is present, the water should feel greasy. Immediately after this test, wash your hand well, or the caustic soda can cause burns.

Paper intended for writing or painting has to be sized. Slowly heat the pulp. Use a thermometer to check the temperature. When it reaches 98° F, add gelatin for sizing. (Sizing—any thin, viscous substance—serves as a filler for porous materials, such as paper.) Boil for a minimum of three hours; be careful that the container does not boil dry.

Transfer the pulp to a pail. Wash the material until the water is clear, and pound it with your hands to press out the water. Put bleaching powder (chlorinated lime, available through building supply and hardware stores) into a large jug for mixing; then add

water and stir. Allow to settle. Pour the bleach solution on the fibrous pulp. Let it stand for twelve hours, and stir now and then with a stick. When the material has become a pale fawn color, it has bleached sufficiently.

Once more, wash the material well and squeeze out the water. Cut the fibrous pulp into ½-inch pieces with scissors. In a large mortar, crush the pulp with a pestle until the fibers split lengthwise. You may pound the pulp on a stone slab with a heavy mallet if mortar and pestle are not available. Continue this procedure until the desired consistency is achieved. The longer the pulp is crushed, the smoother the paper will be.

To make but one sheet of paper at a time, put a nylon sieve, 10 inches in diameter, into a shallow pan of warm water. Place 3 cups of pulp in the sieve. Using your hand, spread it evenly on the sieve. Take the sieve from the pan and let any water drain off. Place it in a warm spot to dry.

Lift the dry sheet by slipping the tip of a knife beneath the edges of the paper. Its thickness will depend on the amount of pulp used. Repeat the process to make more sheets.

To prepare a greater number of sheets in a shorter time, make a wooden frame and nail a sheet of perforated zinc to it. Spread pulp

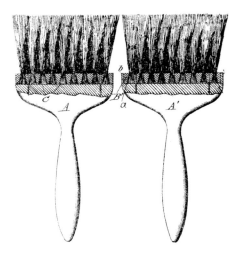

evenly on the piece of zinc. Have some old blankets handy. Invert the frame and press the paper onto a wet blanket. Place another wet blanket on top in readiness to receive the next sheet. Continue alternating layers of blankets and paper sheets. Finally, place large, heavy stones atop the pile to press out the water. Now unstack the blankets, letting each sheet of paper dry on its blanket.

Paper from Paper Scraps

Paper can also be made from odds and ends of gift-wrapping paper, old magazines, junk mail, and newspaper. For equipment you will need an electric blender, a 5- by 7-inch picture frame (one that's 8 by 10 inches may also be used, but no larger), window screening the size of the frame, thumbtacks, a pile of newspapers, a 14½- by 10½- by 2-inch glass baking pan, two desk-sized white blotters, one wooden spoon, paper towels, and an iron.

Tear or cut the old paper in slender strips; loosely fill one-third of the blender with them. Pour water into the machine until it is two-thirds full. Blend the contents for four or five seconds. In the next step you can control the shade of your paper by introducing a preferred color; for example, if pink paper is desired, add strips of red. Blend once more. Produce texture by mixing in bits of colored thread, parsley, or even chili-pepper flakes.

Fashion a sieve by tacking the piece of screening to the frame. Place three stacks of newspapers in a row. Set the baking pan on one and a desk blotter on the next.

Pour the pulp into the baking pan, and add about 1 inch of water. Mix thoroughly with the wooden spoon. Holding the screen side of the frame uppermost and over the pan at a slight angle, spoon the pulp evenly on the sieve. Let excess water drip back into the pan.

Put a long edge of the sieve on the blotter, and quickly flip it over, pulp side down. With paper towels, blot up excess moisture, particularly at the edges of the frame, and carefully lift away the sieve. Immediately cover the soggy paper with the remaining blotter. Transfer the blotters protecting the moist paper to the last stack of newspapers.

Heat the iron at its wool setting, and press the blotter "sandwich" on both sides. Take away the top blotter; peel off the sheet of paper. If difficult to remove, it is still too damp. Iron directly on the paper until it is dry. Then lift it from the blotter.

Your tinted paper is ready for use.

Wallpaper and Wall Stenciling

Preparing Walls for Paper
Stretched on his deathbed, Oscar Wilde quipped, "My wallpaper is killing me—one of us must go!" If you have long felt that your wallpaper "must go," but have postponed replacing it to avoid the cost, consider making and hanging your own paper. The job is not difficult or expensive and the results are rewarding.

First, judge whether it is necessary to remove old paper before putting up new. Your decision depends on whether the present covering is firmly attached to the wall. Examine it closely. If no bulges exist and the seams are securely in place, new paper quite probably will adhere well. Should there be a few pieces of loose paper, snip them off and sand the edges. Unanchored seams can often be re-glued.

When old paper is in an overall loose condition, it must be removed. Heavy types of wallpaper generally peel away with ease. Other kinds require sufficient moistening to soften the glue beneath. At that moment, scraping (use a wide-blade putty knife, large case knife, or handscraper) or stripping should commence immediately, for it will quickly dry. Wetting and stripping but one section at a time is the most efficient procedure. To permeate the paper and soften the glue, use a wet sponge. You can also use a liquid wallpaper remover (available at paint dealers and hardware stores).

Once the paper has been taken off, wash the walls with vinegar and water or soda and water applied with a brush or large sponge. Then let the walls dry thoroughly. Prepare whitewashed walls by wetting them with a solution of 1 pound of alum to 2 gallons of water. Allow them to dry before papering.

Fill any holes or seams in the plaster or wallboard with patching plaster. When patching wallboard, it is advisable to use a primer-sealer over repaired places. The walls are now ready to receive your homemade paper.

Making Wallpaper

Wallpaper is believed to have been a Chinese invention. Europeans next adopted it, and by the seventeenth century the practice of covering walls with decorative paper became popular in North America.

Early wallpapers were designed by woodblock printing, handstamping, and the letterpress method. They were sometimes made to resemble fabrics that were the valuable wall coverings of the period.

To decorate your wallpaper with the simplest or the more complicated designs, use the rubbing technique described under "Gravestone Rubbings." Produce them on lining paper, which comes in the same width and length as ordinary wallpaper. Detail paper (used in architectural firms) will also serve. The motifs can overlap or be spaced in a chessboard, stripe, or diamond arrangement.

For your design to be most effective, rub it with varying amounts of pressure—lightly in some areas, heavily in others, sometimes using a mixture of the two. By such selective rubbing, you can develop certain areas of the design to greater prominence. Either one color or a pleasing combination of colors may be employed throughout.

Preparing Papering Paste

Prepare papering paste the day before it is needed so that it will be cold when applied. For fourteen rolls of wallpaper, 5 quarts of paste are required. Mix a bit more than 2 cups of wheat flour (rice flour or cornstarch can be substituted) with enough water to form a thin dough. Thin it down to avoid lumps. Heat 4 quarts of water. At the boiling point, pour in the thin hot batter. Stir constantly to prevent burning until the boiling point is reached once more. Then empty the vessel into a tin pail, and allow the paste to stand until the following day. To insure a lump-free paste, strain and press it through coarse muslin.

Hanging Wallpaper

Hang your wallpaper in the customary manner. Climb a ladder, and hold plain lining paper up to the ceiling while a helper below marks it along the baseboard with any blunt instrument. Cut along this mark. Use it as a pattern, cutting a sufficient number of decorated strips for walls that have no doors or windows.

Lay some boards, a sheet of scrap plywood, or an old door across widely spaced sawhorses, chair backs, or barrels. Place a wallpaper strip face down on this work surface, and evenly apply the papering paste with a whitewash brush. When the paper is sticky rather than wet, press the upper end just up to the ceiling, beginning at a corner, and work downward. Smooth out any wrinkles and large bubbles by moving a clean cloth from the center outward to the sides. Don't be concerned about smaller bubbles; they will dry smooth. Place the next strip so that its edge abuts on the first piece but does not overlap it.

Do not attempt to cut paper to fit around windows and doors prior to putting it up. Hang it in the usual way, and upon reaching the obstruction, paper right over the edge. Then trim around doors and windows by cutting diagonally up to and a little beyond their corners, which you can indicate with your finger as you feel them through the paper. Fold back the excess paper, mark the edge, and cut it off.

Remove light fixtures, switch plates, thermostat covers, etc. Papering under instead of around them makes a much simpler and neater job. Mark the paper in these

areas; then trim out the holes and replace the items.

Old-time paperhangers advise brushing an even coat of paste on walls instead of wallpaper, moistening the backs of strips with a water-soaked sponge, and then hanging them.

Preparing Walls for Stenciling

If you prefer painted walls to wallpaper but want them decorated, employ the technique of stenciling.

First, prepare walls with a coat of latex paint. Those that have been whitewashed will require scraping with a blunt-edged tool to remove any loose lime. You will find a hoe handy for this job. Next, go over the walls with sandpaper tacked to a large piece of wood that has a handle attached to it. Wash them down with a sponge. After they are dry, fill all cracks and breaks with plaster of Paris. Then apply the latex in white or in some pastel shade as the background for your stenciled pattern. Latex is preferable to oil-based paint. With its use, any necessary touching up will not be as evident as it would be with oil-based paint.

Stencil Designs

Select your stencil designs. You will find books containing patterns at the library or in art supply stores. You may enjoy creating original designs of your own. Using carbon paper, trace your motifs on waxed stencil paper or yellow stencil paper

(available at paint and art stores).

Cut the stencils with a single-edged razor blade. Work on a glass surface. This step requires great care, for any errors will show up when you apply pigments to the wall.

Plan the layout of your stencils by measuring the design and the wall space it will occupy. Position it according to the number of times it will occur in that area.

More than one color may be incorporated in a design. Use oil-based, semi-gloss paints for the stenciling work. If you intend to mix your own paints, be sure to prepare enough for the whole room, thus insuring uniformity of tone.

Methods for Applying Stencils

Choose either of the following methods for applying wall stencils:

Stencil-Brush Method: Cut your stencils from waxed stencil paper. As they must be cleaned with turpentine between each application of pigments, it is

convenient to make more than one set. Hold the stencil on the wall with masking tape. Apply pigments with round stencil brushes. Dip the brush into the paint; wipe off any excess on a rag or newspaper. Very little paint is needed. More can be added if necessary, but too much cannot be removed. Painting from the outside of the hole toward the center, rub the paint on the wall through each stencil opening. Make certain that the opening is completely filled with color before going on to another. Smudges, fuzzy edges, or other imperfections should be corrected with the background paint with a watercolor brush. Old-time stencilers generally used this method.

Watercolor-Brush Method: Cut stencils from inexpensive yellow stencil paper. This method will require no more than one set of stencils, and you won't need to tape them on the wall. Using one as a guide, hold it in place as you lightly but clearly outline the design with a hard lead pencil. You may want to sketch the designs throughout the room before beginning to paint. Set the stencils aside, and carefully paint in the drawn motifs with small watercolor brushes. This simplified

method of stenciling was used during the fifteenth and sixteenth centuries in France.

Wall stenciling adapts to any decor, from Early American to modern.

If you intend to cover plaster walls in oil-based paint without stenciling, first brush them with a thin glue sizing (prepared by dissolving 4 ounces of glue in 1 gallon of boiling water over low heat). When wall surfaces are covered with several coats of whitewash, make and apply the following glue sizing:

In 2½ gallons of water, dissolve 10 ounces of glue. In another vessel, mix 9 pounds of bole—a reddish-colored, easily pulverized clay available in paint stores—with sufficient water to produce a creamlike consistency, and strain it through cheesecloth. Add the moist bole to the glue sizing, and stir in 2 pounds of gypsum. Strain the mixture through cheesecloth. Dilute it with water for brushing on walls. When it is dry, apply the oil-based paint.

Gravestone Rubbings

History of Rubbing Technique

The technique of rubbing is thought to have originated in China around 300 B.C. The practice spread throughout the Chinese empire and eventually the entire Far East.

In the beginning, it served as a means to disseminate the written word prior to the invention of the printing press. Literature and edicts of emperors were incised on stone tablets and then reproduced on paper by rubbing. Eventually, pictures were carved in stone expressly for the purpose of being copied in this way. Later, archaeologists employed the method to record early tomb carvings.

Choice of Gravestones

You can use this ancient technique to create decorative pictures for your walls. Surfaces or objects to rub are almost limitless: brasses, architectural reliefs, medals, coins, any incised designs, bark, leaves, flowers, etc.

Perhaps some of the most unusual and interesting rubbings can be made on gravestones in old burial grounds. Those dating before 1800 are hand carved and represent the first sculpture of colonial settlers. As such, they are a unique expression of primitive American art. The stone slabs with their carved motifs and religious symbols were intended for instruction of the generally illiterate public in matters of man's mortality, his relation to God, and the blessings of heaven, thus reflecting religious attitudes of the times. Gradually, as Puritan faith became less strict, religious symbols were replaced by stylized portraiture. Details of dress currently in vogue and often the occupation or social status of the deceased were depicted by the stonecutter. These early craftsmen displayed an instinctive sense of design and expert workmanship. So, rubbings of tombstones several centuries old are both historically and artistically valuable.

While the philosophy of Puritans was revealed in symbols, views of the Old West were expressed in pithy epitaphs, always informative and sometimes amusing. Epitaphs in southern burial grounds often exceeded a single statement; they related a complete story of the circumstances leading to death in colorful local dialect, many times with primitive spellings.

Stonecutters, much in demand in more densely populated areas of colonial life, were master craftsmen. However, smaller towns throughout the country had to depend on woodcarvers or even shoemakers for tombstone carving. Their inexperience left us markers with entire words deleted or letters squeezed in at the end of a line, giving them a quaint appeal.

If you want to create and display such samples of your national heritage, follow these guidelines.

Essential Materials

The essential materials for making rubbings are few:

- *Cleaning Aid:* piece of styrofoam, a soft hairbrush, or a rubber school eraser
- *Paper:* butcher paper (long sheets are available at meat markets), detail paper (used by architects), rice paper, or any kind of thin, strong, linen-base paper
- *Masking Tape*
- *Rubbing Medium:* black lumber-marking crayon or primary crayons (used in primary grades, they have a flat side to prevent their rolling off desks)
- *Kneeling Pad (optional):* carpet sample or foam-rubber pad

Surface Preparation

The time of year when you can work most comfortably and efficiently is early spring. By then winter has killed the weeds, and the sun and showers of a warmer season have not yet prodded the growth of grasses, briars, and branches, or roused snakes from their hibernation. The rains and snow of winter will have removed at least some moss from the surface of old gravestones.

If you find a heavy accumulation of moss or lichen on the stone's face, clean the surface gently but effectively with a small block of styrofoam, a child's nylon hairbrush,

or a rubber eraser. (Never use a wire brush or harsh abrasives; old, weather-beaten markers are soft in texture and will erode easily.) By gently rubbing across the stone, most of the moss or other foreign matter will be removed. Where moss clings stubbornly, rub the area with a rag or sponge saturated with vinegar.

Rubbing Technique

After preparing the stone's surface, attach a large sheet of white or light-colored paper with masking tape in the center of all four sides, smoothing the paper from the middle outward before applying each strip. If more pieces are needed to make the sheet adhere tightly, position them midway between the original tape.

Remove the paper wrapper from the crayon (brown or black is most effective) and, using the flat side, work from the center outward. Establish the entire design lightly. The inscription and decorative motifs will spring into relief on your paper. Raised areas beneath the sheet will be registered by the crayon; depressed areas will remain white. Then, using firmer pressure

and working from the edges inward, repeat the procedure.

Check your reproduction at a distance for uniformity of color. Correct weaker areas.

Now that your print is complete, remove it by peeling the tape from the paper toward the stone. To reproduce other surfaces, from coins to manhole covers, follow essentially the same method.

Framing the Rubbing

Set off your rubbing to best advantage with a rustic picture frame. An abandoned, weather-beaten farm building will provide appropriate material (with the owner's permission, of course). Usually, you can have a few rough-textured boards for very little or nothing at all. Select boards that are relatively straight. Don't be concerned about nail holes; they will only enhance the rustic look of the finished product.

Before making the frame, dry any wet wood for several days or more. You may want to add to the frame's weather-beaten appearance with the application of a light gray, semi-transparent shingle stain. Brush in the direction of the grain.

Plant Dyes and Dyeing Fibers

Plants offer an almost infinite source of pigments for dyeing fibers, yarns, and fabrics. Wool has traditionally been the most common textile in Europe and North America, where large areas are suited to sheep raising. Thus, over the centuries, plant dyes were developed chiefly for that fiber.

You should first experiment with wool, which is easier to color than other natural fibers because of its greater compatibility with plant dyes. However, you can toss samples of any kinds of material into the dye bath along with the wool in order to observe their reaction to a specific dye.

The beginner should start by dyeing fibers or yarns, not cloth. Dyeing a quantity of cloth requires greater skill. Through the use of fibers and yarns, you will learn which plants give dye and amass a repertory of colors.

For initial experiments, we recommend unraveling some discarded, white knitted garment, washing the wool well, and winding it into skeins. If no such garment is available, a hank of white wool from the five-and-ten-cent store will do. Check to see that no man-made fibers have been incorporated with it.

General Information for Dyeing

Use steel or unchipped enamel vessels of 1½-gallon capacity for dyeing and plastic pails for rinsing.

Use soft water for the dye bath and rinses.

Stir with a glass or stainless-steel rod. A peeled stick (be sure it is smooth) may be used. Since wood absorbs some dye, use a different stick for each color.

You may want to wear rubber gloves while working.

Wash all plants before use to eliminate dirt or chemical sprays.

Loosely tie the wool in skeins with string so that the dye can reach all areas.

Thoroughly wet yarn or wool fibers before immersing them in the dye bath lest the dye take unevenly.

Use a dairy thermometer to check the temperature of the dye bath.

Never dry fibers or yarn in direct sunshine.

Certain plants will dye well only in the presence of a mordant—metallic salts that fix the coloring. The following dye recipes for beginners use substances generally available in any locality and in any season. They all produce dyes that do not require mordants. However, you probably have

Bring to a simmer; continue simmering for thirty minutes.

Strain the vessel's contents into a plastic pail, discarding the berries. Pour the liquor back into the dye pot. When it is comfortable to the touch (100°–120° F), immerse the clean and completely wetted wool. Bring to a simmer and continue simmering for thirty minutes, gently moving the wool around with a peeled stick.

Lift a skein from the pot, and allow it to drip into the bath for a few seconds. First rinse it in hot water and gently squeeze out excess water. Then give it a cooler rinse, again squeezing gently. Dry it on a rod suspended on hooks. Now and then turn the skein during drying, and give it a gentle pull to stretch it. Clip or tie on a label indicating the dye source, number of the recipe, and the mordant used, if any. This skein will probably be pink.

Simmer the wool remaining in the pot for thirty minutes longer. Remove another skein. Rinse, label, and hang to dry.

Simmer the rest of the skeins for another hour. Take out a skein. It will be considerably darker than the previous two.

Continue the same procedure until all skeins have been dyed.

some mordants on hand in your home—vinegar, salt, and cream of tartar. Though not essential to the success of these dyes, a very small pinch of cream of tartar added to the dye pot before introducing the wool will enliven the color.

Dye Sources and Shades
Dye Source: Blueberries
Shades: Pink to Purple

  1 ounce wool, separated into
  5 skeins and tied with string
  ¾ pound blueberries
  ½ gallon soft water

Crush about ¾ pound of blueberries (they may be fresh, dried, or canned) in an unchipped enamel pan or one of steel. Since the berries will yield juice, add something less than ½ gallon of soft water. Rainwater is preferable, but hard water can be softened with 1 tablespoon of vinegar or a commercial water softener.

Dye Source:
Yellow Onionskins
Shades:
Gradations of Yellow

    1 ounce wool, divided into
      5 skeins
    2 handfuls yellow onionskins
      (outer skins)
    ½ to 1 gallon soft water

Put 2 handfuls of yellow onionskins in ½ to 1 gallon of soft water. Bring to a simmer; simmer for thirty to sixty minutes. Cover to confine the odor. Add water to compensate for whatever amount boils away.

Strain the dye bath, discarding the onionskins. Return the liquid to the vessel. When it is cool enough to touch comfortably, put in the clean, completely wetted wool. Slowly bring to a simmer. Gently stirring the wool about, simmer for fifteen minutes.

Remove a skein and allow it to drain over the pot for a few seconds. Rinse it in hot water and squeeze. Then give it a cooler rinse and squeeze again. Label and hang to dry.

Simmer the remaining wool for fifteen minutes more. Remove another skein. Rinse, label, and hang to dry.

Simmer the rest of the wool for an additional fifteen minutes. Remove a skein. It should be much stronger in color than the other two.

Continue as already directed until all the skeins have been dyed.

Dye Source:
Turmeric Powder
Shades:
Yellow to Brilliant Yellow

    1 ounce wool, separated into
      5 skeins
    1½ teaspoons turmeric powder
    ½ to 1 gallon soft water

To develop a yellow to brilliant yellow color, accompanied by less aroma than the previous recipe, use 1½ teaspoons of turmeric powder, commonly found on most kitchen spice shelves. Bring ½ to 1 gallon of soft water to hand heat (100°–120° F.) as you stir in the powder. Introduce the completely wetted wool. Gradually bring to a simmer. Simmering for two minutes, gently stir the wool around.

Lift out a skein, and let it drip over the pot a few seconds.

Rinse the wool in hot water and gently squeeze it. Then squeeze it again in cooler water. Label and dry the skein.

Simmer the wool remaining in the pot for two minutes more. Remove another skein. Rinse, label, and hang to dry.

Continue simmering the rest of the wool for a few minutes more, and follow the same procedure. A brilliant yellow can be achieved in ten minutes.

Uses for Dyed Fibers

After a number of dyed skeins have accumulated, they can be used in many interesting ways: for decorative embroidery, for crocheting small individual squares that can be sewed or crocheted together, in appliqué, patchwork, samplers, free hangings, cushions, clothes, and in macramé.

The experienced dyer will probably wish to plan a project in advance and dye the necessary quantity of yarn.

Perhaps these first attempts at dyeing yarn will instill you with the desire to try your hand at dyeing cloth and to experiment further with dyes requiring mordants.

An intriguing number of substances provide dyes—bark, pine cones and needles, nut hulls, berries, flowers, roots, cactus fruit, leaves, lichens, mollusk shells, and even insects. To learn more about natural dyes and the process of dyeing, enjoy the thrill of experimentation with these substances or any others that are available to you.

Quilts

A quilt is a bedcover consisting of two layers of cloth with a filler of batting in between. The three layers are stitched together in patterns or lines.

Simple Quilt Frame

For a finished quilt to lie smoothly, it should be stretched on a wooden frame while its layers are being stitched together.

Construct a simple frame with the following materials:

4 boards suggested dimensions:
1 inch by 4 inches by about
8½ feet in length
4 C-clamps
4 chairs of the same height

Scrap lumber would be suitable for this project, since the thickness and width of the wood are not crucial. Sand the boards until smooth to avoid splinters during quilting.

Place two boards parallel to one another on the floor. Lay the remaining two across them to form a square. Use the C-clamps to hold the frame together. Raise the frame and rest it on the tops of the chair backs at each corner. Securely fasten the corners to their supports with strips of cloth or rope.

In the middle of each board, make a permanent ink mark to use as a guide when attaching quilting material. Use thumbtacks to fasten the quilt fabric to the frame.

Tied Quilt

Covers with an underside of satin, nylon, or other slick fabrics tend to slide from the bed. Choose a non-slippery, closely woven material for the backing of a tied quilt. Sheets, cottons, and flannels are appropriate for the purpose. An old blanket (if it is thin, use two) provides a good filler. Scraps of fabric sewn together as patchwork or a colored sheet can be used for the top.

Check to see that the measurements of the top and backing are identical. Indicate the center of all four edges with a straight pin.

Now, match the center points on the fabric edges with those on the boards and fasten the backing to the frame. Working from the middle of the edges to their ends, tack the material to the stretcher.

Spread the filler smoothly on the taut backing. Then lay the top over the filler, and pin it to the backing. Adjust the C-clamps to keep the quilt taut.

Now begin tying. Space the ties evenly, with no more than two inches between each. Either stagger them or arrange them in rows. If the fabric pattern is geometric, it can serve as a guide for spacing your ties. To space them evenly on a scattered print, make a 9- by 12-inch grid of cardboard. Punch holes in it at regular intervals. Place the grid on the fabric, and through each hole put a pencil dot to indicate the spot for tying.

Thread your needle with a 3-foot length of string or yarn.

Adjust the ends evenly to form a double strand, but do not make a knot.

Begin at the first pencil mark in an end row. When tying, work through the top of the quilt; have one hand beneath to insure that the needle penetrates all layers. Make a stitch as small as possible down and back up through the thicknesses of cloth, and leave a tail of thread 2 inches in length on the quilt's surface. Take another stitch directly over the first one. Then tie a firm square knot. Do not snip the thread. Continue to the next pencil mark and repeat the tying method until all the needle's yarn is used. Now go back and cut the thread midway between the pairs of ties. Leave the tails, which should be the same length if you have snipped the thread precisely halfway between ties. Trim any that are uneven.

After you have tied as far as you can reach from one end, work from the other as far as possible. Then free an end of the wooden stretcher. Removing tacks as necessary, roll the tied section around that board until you arrive at the untied area. Replace the clamps and be sure that the material is again pulled taut. Continue in this manner until the tying is completed.

Finish your tied quilt by turning raw edges of both top and bottom to the inside and blind-stitching all sides.

Crazy Quilt

To make a crazy quilt, empty all the fabric scraps from your ragbag. The scraps may be of any color or size. If you prefer that your quilt be washable, choose pieces that are colorfast and will shrink minimally. Iron them so that they are smooth and wrinkle free. Then group the scraps as to light and dark shades.

From some soft, loosely woven material, like muslin or cambric, cut a block sixteen inches square for a foundation. A full-sized quilt will require twenty such foundation blocks.

For sewing, use a short needle 1⅛ inches in length and white thread (# 50 or #60), which is stronger than colored thread and tends to knot less.

Baste a 16-inch-square block of cotton or dacron batting to the foundation block. Dacron will make a fluffy quilt filling. Bulky to work with when fine stitching is required, it is particularly suitable for a crazy quilt, which does not call for delicate sewing. Batting can be bought in sheets.

Start by laying a fabric scrap on the batting in one corner. Fold under the edges on the sides bordering the edges of the block, and baste them in place. Repeat this procedure in the other three corners. Complete the block by placing patches with two basted edges on the unbasted edges of those patches already in the block. Begin in a corner. Working from left to right, use a hemming stitch to sew the patches in place. Produce a pleasing effect by choosing colors that harmonize or make an interesting contrast of light and dark hues. When the entire block is filled in, cover all patch seams with yarn. Use a simple embroidery stitch.

After all twenty blocks have been completed with patches of varying shapes and colors, it is time to "set" your quilt. First, sew the blocks in rows. Since your quilt will be four blocks wide and five long, you may make either four rows of five blocks each or five rows of four blocks each. Now sew the rows together. Make sure that all seams match. Tack the backing in the middle of alternate blocks with decorative stitches.

Finish your quilt by binding the three layers—patches, batting, and foundation—with bias tape purchased in a store or with bias strips you have cut yourself. You may make the bias strips from material that contrasts with the quilt or repeats a predominant color in it. Homemade binding is usually sturdier than store-bought tape.

Puffed Quilt

Making a puffed quilt is simple. Each puff is a square of velvet (you will find cotton velvet easier to use than slippery rayon velvet) or silk sewn to a muslin square and stuffed with batting. The puffs are then sewn together. A quilt of any size can be made by this method.

Cut 3-inch squares of velvet or silk (here's a chance to put those discarded or out-of-date silk ties to use) and 2¼-inch squares of muslin. Putting the wrong sides of the material together, pin the corners of the velvet or silk squares to those of the muslin squares. Pleat the excess velvet or silk on three of the square's sides and pin in place to the muslin. Through the fourth

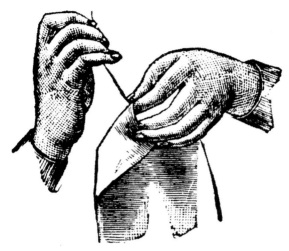

side, fill the puff with batting. Pleat this side and pin it in place. Baste around all sides. Stitch close to the edge.

Keeping the velvet-silk sides facing, and allowing for a ¼-inch seam, sew the puffs together. Then iron the seams open and make rows of either the desired width or length of the quilt.

Line the puffed quilt with some plain soft material. Finally, tack it on the back at regular intervals and catch the seams under the squares so that no tacking shows on top.

Rugs

Braided Cloth Rug

Before attempting to make a braided cloth rug, try a small sample one. In this way you will learn to do even work and to properly calculate the amount of needed materials. A larger rug may then be designed more accurately, ensuring satisfactory results.

Assemble the following equipment and materials:

- 12 (or more) straight pins
- a few large safety pins
- 1 large needle for stitching braids or a bodkin—a thick, blunt needle—for lacing them
- 1 smaller needle for splicing strips
- scissors
- cloth strips, from 1 to 6 inches wide, the width depending upon the weight of the material and the intended rug design

Be sure all cloth is clean and well ironed. Roughly nine ounces of fabric are needed for each square foot of a braided rug. Do not mix materials that have different degrees of shrinkage or varying rates of wear. If you are using old cloth, remove any weak areas.

Cut the material into even strips. When the material is of different weights, the width of strips should be relative to the thickness of the cloth. (Best results are obtained, however, when all the cloth is of uniform weight.) Cut thin cloth in 6-inch widths, medium cloth in 3-inch widths, and heavy cloth in 2½-inch widths. It is wise to use woven, rather than knitted, material. Because the warp is sturdier than the weft, strips should be cut lengthwise on the material. For easy handling, make the strips between 1 and 1½ yards long. Fold the strips in half lengthwise,

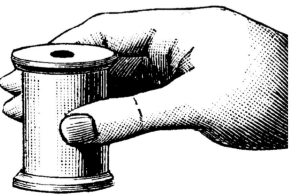

and iron them with their raw edges turned in.

To obtain a pleasing proportion of colors in a rug, arrange and rearrange the bundles of materials on the floor until the desired effect is reached.

Put three or more cloth strips on a safety pin—or fasten them to something stationary—for braiding. You could anchor the strips by closing a window on them. Begin with the left-hand strip. Bring it over the second one and under the third. If your braid is composed of more than three strips, continue in the same manner, placing the strip over the fourth strand and under the fifth. Eventually, you will learn to braid from both sides. Maintain an even braid by folding the outer strip as it is brought back rather than pulling it around as you would with a round cord. When nearly at the end of a strand, attach another by opening it out, cutting a bias at its end and the end of the new one, and sewing a smooth seam. Avoid having two

joinings parallel to each other in the same braid.

Your first braid is the central one. Its length should equal the difference between the width and length of the completed rug. For example, a rug that's 36 inches by 48 inches would have a central braid of 12 inches. Indicate the center of your rug by attaching a safety pin at the starting point. In this way you can gauge whether you have an identical number of braided rows on each side and at each end.

In an oval rug, turn the end of the central braiding by easing it around and along its side. Avoid cupping. You can do this by pulling the inside strip a bit at the turn and stretching the outside one. When the opposite end is arrived at, the tips of the braid should be fastened in place

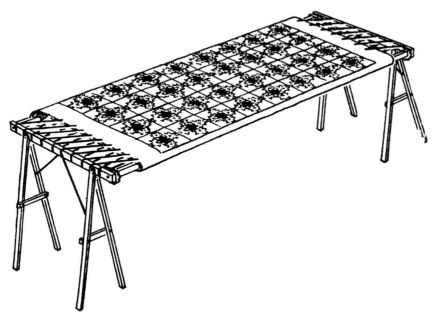

each series of a braid color forms a complete circle in an oval rug and a complete, rectangular stripe in an oblong rug. The border may be composed of colors located in the middle of the rug, but will be more interesting if they are of either brighter or darker hues. The size of the border will vary in proportion to the size of the rug's center according to the vividness of its color.

As your rug nears completion, especially when it is a large one, you may want to transfer it to the floor to keep it perfectly flat as you work.

When the rug has reached its planned dimensions, check for an even number of braids on all sides. Now snip the final braid at the rug's curve. Insert the ends of the braid beneath the last braiding row and pull it into shape, making the two oval rug ends match. Cut the ends of the last braid at uneven lengths so

with pins. The lengths of the parallel braids may then be sewed together.

In an oblong rug, the corners must be turned at each round. When flat strips are used, a good corner can be made by bringing the last strip of a braid to the point of turning back, over, and then under the other strips parallel to it. Follow the same procedure with the other strips; then commence braiding as for the straight braid. In the case of round strips, turn corners by easing the tension of the outside ones and drawing up the inside ones.

Sew the contiguous sides of the braids together with a slip stitch or blind stitch; the stitching should not be visible on either side. While sewing, keep the rug flat on a table top to maintain its proper shape. After sewing one side of the rug, braid as far as the next turn. Then sew the braid in place.

By alternately sewing and braiding for only short distances, you'll find it easier to prevent cupping and make the braids fit smoothly together.

Add new color while working by fastening a new color, one strip at a time, to the braid. The most favorable effect is achieved when

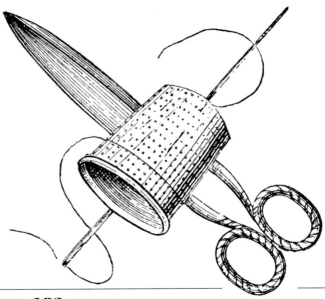

that they terminate at different places. Sew the ends of the strands firmly to the rug's edge.

For a stronger rug, you may fasten the braids together by lacing instead of stitching. Use a bodkin or safety pin for lacing. Thread the bodkin with a strip of material, or fasten the strip to a safety pin. Starting at the turn, lace the braids together. Do this by first sewing the tip of the lacing material to the braid. Now push the threaded bodkin or safety pin through the first loop on the side of the braid on the left, then over to the adjacent braid, and through the first loop on its side. Keep the lacing strand flat by folding it as it turns from loop to loop.

After aligning the braid loops, push the bodkin downward through the left loop, fold it back, and push it up through the right loop. Fold back once more and again pass the bodkin down through the left and up through the right side, thus lacing the two braid lengths together. Continue to braid and lace until the rug is completed. At the turns, extra lacing stitches will be required to avoid cupping. Instead of a strip of material for lacing, you may use a strong thin cord for a different effect.

Crocheted Rug

Crochet a low-cost rug quickly and easily by using fabric from cheap, secondhand clothing and a large crochet needle.

Explore re-sell shops and rummage sales for bathrobes, coats, and wide-skirted dresses with plenty of material in them. Whittle your crochet needle from a ¾-inch-thick wooden dowel, and smooth it with sandpaper.

Rip the garments into strips. Avoid having to sew short strips together by tearing the cloth one way to within ½ inch of the end; then reverse your direction and tear the opposite way. The kind of cloth determines the width of the strips. Those of cotton should be at least 2 inches wide; wool strips can be 1 inch in width. You won't need to hem them if you turn under the raw edges as you work.

Begin the rug with three chain stitches, and continue with a single crochet stitch in concentric circles. Occasionally, when the rug's edges start to curl up, make two single crochets in one stitch. When the end of one strip is reached, sew or tie on another. Keep loose ends on the underside.

14 | WAYS WITH CLAY

Adobe Bricks

Adobe is derived from a wide variety of clay soils, heavy in texture and composed of very fine grained material. The name designates the sun-dried bricks, the clay of which they are composed, and structures built of the stuff.

The word *adobe* comes from the Spanish *adobar*, to plaster. Its use as building material is said to have originated in northern Africa centuries ago. From there it was introduced into Spain. Not long after the discovery of America, Spanish conquerors brought the method to dry areas of the New World. Indians of Arizona and New Mexico began making adobe as early as the 1500s.

Adobe making is an uncomplicated procedure. Put simply, correct proportions of sand and suitable clay are combined and wet down, a small quantity of some fibrous material is added, and the whole is mixed thoroughly either in a machine or with bare feet.

Ingredients of Adobe Brick Mix

The chief components of adobe bricks are sand, clay, and a waterproofing substance. The sand acts as filler; the clay is the binder. Adobe brick mix generally contains more sand than clay. Clay content should be greater than 25 percent but less than 45 percent. Too little clay makes the dry bricks weak and crumbly; too

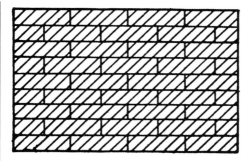

much clay causes cracking as the bricks dry.

Sand: Use sharp, coarse sand. If no natural sources of such sand are available, it can be purchased from a building supply company. (Avoid sand from ocean shores because of its salt content.)

Clay: Although many types of clay are usable in making adobe, one of high kaolin content is preferable. Such material not only is less sticky to handle than others, but also results in stronger bricks. To learn the location of kaolin clay deposits, consult local geologists or those connected with government offices, such as the Division of Mines and Geology.

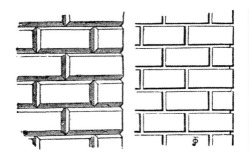

Straw: The incorporation of straw in the mix causes the drying brick to shrink as a unit, thus preventing a considerable amount of cracking in the finished product. Cut the material in four-inch lengths. Straw can be bought at feed stores. Avoid using hay, if possible.

Stabilizer (waterproofing substance): Use emulsified asphalt as a waterproofing agent, or stabilizer, so that the bricks will absorb only a small, safe percentage of water. (A stabilizer is required by the Uniform Building Code when adobe bricks are intended for construction of any type of building.) The liquid is available from road-paving companies or oil dealers.

If your bricks are to be used for outdoor walkways, garden walls, porch floors, and the like, Portland cement added to soil will produce strong bricks that will not be harmed by water. They will be very hard but not waterproof. (Bricks of this type would not comply with building code requirements and must not be used for inhabited structures.) Use 15 percent cement, and insure that it cures properly by keeping the bricks damp for several days.

Soil Testing

Test the suitability of soil for adobe-brick making in the following manner:

Shovel away leaf mold, sod, and other organic matter from a small area of the test site.

Dig a hole as deeply as you intend to go when excavating for soil. Mix the dirt removed from the hole so that all layers of earth are well blended.

Put 8 ounces of the soil sample in a one-quart jar, and fill it with water. Add a teaspoon of table salt to speed settling of the clay. Shake the jar well, and let the contents settle for one hour or until the water is clear.

Examine the jar's solid contents. You will see successive layers: lowermost will be small bits of rock; next will be sand, varying from coarse at the bottom to particles of silt size; the top layer will be clay, characterized by no perceptible particles. Rub some clay between your fingers. It should feel rather like soap and be free of grit.

To determine clay-sand proportions, measure the height of the clay layer and estimate its percentage of the combined layers and the percentage occupied by the coarser layers. Clay material must range between 25 and 45 percent. When the soil test indicates an excess in either clay or sand, you can procure high-clay soil or sand at a building materials outlet. Mix in the proper amount to correct whichever is deficient.

Making Test Bricks

If the soil tests properly, make a stiff mud with some of it and form several bricks of full size. Dry a few in the sun; dry others in shade.

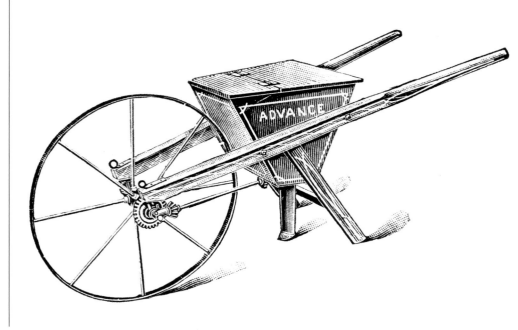

By so doing, you can determine which drying conditions are most favorable. Cracks will appear within the first few days if they are going to occur. A high degree of cracking can be remedied by shading the bricks or by adding more straw or sand.

Once the adobe drying test proves satisfactory, shape bricks that include emulsified asphalt to judge how much of it will be required.

Testing to Stabilize Bricks

Fill a 1-cubic-foot box with loose soil that has already been tested and found acceptable for use. Record the number of shovelfuls required to fill the box.

Empty the soil into a wheelbarrow. Hoe in sufficient water to form stiff mud.

Gradually pour in ½ gallon of emulsified asphalt while continually blending it with the mud. Mix the whole thoroughly until you can no longer discern any asphalt. (A half-gallon of asphalt to 1 cubic foot of soil is a good ratio.)

Shape the test bricks from the mud by hand. Make them some convenient size, perhaps 2 by 3 by 4 inches.

Dry these bricks in a warm oven to shorten the drying time, which would be much longer in the sun.

Immerse one of the dry bricks in water for a few hours. No softening should result, even at the edges. If softening does occur, repeat the test but this time use more stabilizer. Even though test results are good, follow the procedure

again to determine if using less emulsified asphalt will bring equally satisfactory results.

After determining the stabilizer-soil ratio, you can estimate what amount is needed for each mixer load according to the soil capacity of the machine in cubic feet. It's a good idea to use a bit more emulsified asphalt than the minimum required in testing, since conditions may alter somewhat during production. Always allow sufficient time for the stabilizer to thoroughly mix with the mud.

Molds

Make your molds from Douglas fir lumber. Besides being a strong wood, it holds screws and nails better than redwood or pine. Use fine-grained, finished wood. Rough lumber is difficult to separate from the wet bricks.

Molds range in size from 8 inches square and 2 inches thick to 2 yards long, 1 foot wide, and 6 to 8 inches thick. However, the standard dimensions for an adobe brick are 4 by 7½ by 16 inches. So that the finished brick will be 4 inches thick, make the mold depth 4¼ inches to compensate for slight sagging of the mud as the mold is removed and to allow for some shrinkage during drying.

Cut four boards of the proper size and waterproof them.

For a stronger mold, fasten the boards with wood screws instead of nails. Reinforce each mold with two corner braces located diagonally from one another. Countersink them so that they are flush with the wood's surface.

At each end of the form, add wooden rectangles of a convenient size to serve as handles.

Tack a thin metal strip on the top edges of the form to prevent wear as your trowel scrapes away excess mud after the mold has been filled. For ease in separating the mold from the mud, either line the form with a thin sheet of tin or make the mold's bottom 1⁄16 inch wider on each side.

Making Adobe Bricks
Necessary Equipment:
- rectangular mason's trowel
- wooden molds
- pick (for hard earth)
- two shovels: a pointed one for digging soil; a square one for shoveling mud
- deep wheelbarrow
- containers for the stabilizer

- buckets
- large drum for storing water
- mechanical mud mixer equipped with paddles (A dough, plaster, or pug mixer works well; a concrete mixer is not satisfactory.)

This piece of equipment is essential if your bricks are intended for any type of building and will, therefore, require emulsified asphalt. For other purposes not requiring a stabilizer, the ingredients can be deposited in a pit and trampled and mixed with your bare feet.

Casting surfaces: You can cast bricks on flat ground, but a smooth surface is preferable. Use boards or scrap plywood supported on a framework of two-by-fours.

Shading material: If you plan to dry bricks out of the sun, provide shade with plywood supported several inches above the bricks.

Mixing

Break up any dirt chunks, and thoroughly mix the soil during excavation to create a homogeneous blend of the various layers of earth. Speed the breakdown of hard, stubborn clay masses by wetting the soil and keeping it covered with a sheet of plastic.

Now multiply the previously noted shovelfuls (required to fill the l-cubic-foot box) by the cubic-foot capacity of the mixer. This quantity will be shoveled into the machine as you charge it.

To mix the mud, turn on the mixer and add most of the estimated amount of water required. Put in the soil and only enough additional water to form a stiff mud. After the paddles have beaten all lumps from the mud, gradually add the correct quantity of emulsified asphalt. Allow several minutes for this to be thoroughly mixed in. Lastly, add the straw. When it has been introduced, the mixer will labor due to the mud clotting and creating more resistance to the paddles. If left in too long, the straw tends to wrap about the paddles; therefore, just as soon as it is evenly dispersed throughout the mud, discharge the mixer's contents into a wheelbarrow.

Casting

Sprinkle the casting surface with sand or straw to keep the mud from adhering to it. Immerse the mold in water to avoid sticking; place it on the prepared casting surface. Fill the form with mud, making sure the corners are completely filled. Press the mud in with your hands. Using your trowel, strike the mold's contents even with its top. Now slowly and evenly lift the form from the fresh adobe brick. It is not necessary to let the mud set in the form before lifting it away.

After creating each adobe brick, plunge the mold into a tub of water to clear off any bits of clinging mud. Then proceed with making the next brick.

Drying and Curing Bricks

Freshly created adobe bricks must be allowed to dry evenly. During the initial four days, protect them from rain or foggy, cold weather with a sheet of scrap plywood supported several inches over them. Leave the ends open to the wind for further drying. Mild spring days are most favorable for the drying process. When the weather is hot, dry, and windy, however, hang burlap bags over the edges of the plywood protectors to avoid cracking caused by dry winds.

After four days set the bricks on one side to promote rapid, even drying. From this time on, the plywood protector will not be needed. Let the bricks dry in the sun for six weeks.

The molds, when not in use, should be kept in a container of water to prevent their drying out, warping, and separating at the joints.

External Treatment of Adobe Bricks

A good protective covering for adobe walls, both inside and out, is linseed oil. Apply three brush coats. These may be followed by two coats of household paint for interior walls.

Inside walls can also be treated by first applying waterproof glue. Make it of one part quicklime, six parts cottage cheese, and enough water to create a smooth-flowing mixture. Over this primer coat of glue, apply buttermilk paint: 1 gallon of buttermilk to 4½ pounds of white cement.

Pottery

Clay Sources

The amateur potter may buy commercial clay directly from a pottery supplier. He will advise you on the clay best suited to your purpose. It will have proper consistency and texture and already have been subjected to necessary tests, particularly firing.

An alternative is to dig and prepare the clay yourself. Clay so obtained will be just as good as commercial clay, cost nothing, and provide you with adventure while seeking it plus satisfaction in literally creating your pottery from start to finish. Likely sources are pond or stream banks, road or railway cuttings, excavation sites, and brick or pottery works. If you fail to find clay through your own efforts, consult a surveyor or local builder. In most states a published geological survey is available that offers tips on locations of clays.

Preparation of Clay

Two kinds of commercial clay may be bought, either of dry body or plastic body. Clay of dry body comes in powder form and has to be mixed with water for a very considerable time. Clay of plastic body has already been prepared and is ready for use.

Clay you have dug yourself will probably require preparation, though some can be used as is. Others, being too soft, too hard, or full of vegetable matter, stones, and other impurities, will require special treatment:

First, let the clay dry thoroughly.

Then break it into walnut-sized pieces.

Soak them in a pail of water.

Let the clay soak for one to two days until it becomes a thick slop. The slop will remain as a sediment on the bottom of the pail, with the water on top.

Blend the clay and water in the pail to make a thin slop.

With your hands or a stiff brush, pass the material through a fine garden sieve into a second pail to eliminate undesirable impurities.

Let the slop settle once more. During the settling, water can be poured off little by little, and the thickening clay will stay on the pail's bottom. If the clay is needed urgently, it can be spread on a cloth to dry more quickly outdoors. When clay is not needed immediately, however, the ideal way is to let it dry naturally through evaporation until the proper consistency for modeling is reached. This would require several weeks. If the clay lacks sufficient plasticity, combine it with some bought clay by making alternate layers of both and kneading them together.

Storing Clay

Clay of ideal consistency, neither so soft as to stick to the hands nor so hard as to be unyielding to the touch, should be stored to maintain it in this condition. Keep it in airtight containers. Plastic ones are preferable to those of metal, which develop rust, although the rust has no adverse effect on the clay. To ensure that the clay is kept free from air, cover it with a plastic sheet or damp sack. Check it often for drying. If suitable containers are not available, closely wrap the clay in a plastic sheet. Unfinished clay work must also be kept free from air to prevent hardening. Wrap objects in plastic bags or sheets

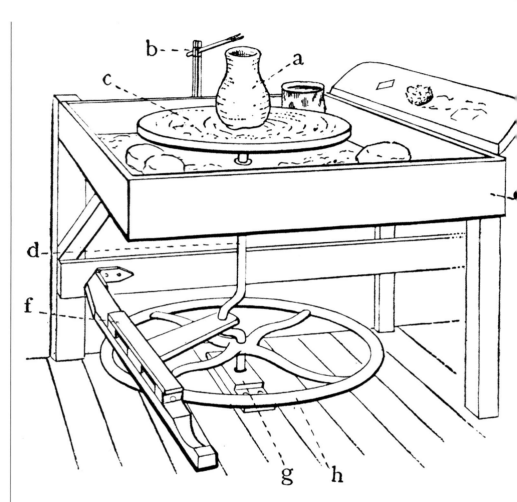

Slip

Slip is clay thinned to the consistency of cream. It is used for binding sections or coils of clay together. Make it by soaking pieces of clay in water until they become refined slop. Sieve it through an 80- or 100-mesh sieve, obtainable from a pottery supplier or lumberyard.

Wedging and Kneading

To prevent the explosion of clay articles during firing, trapped air must be expelled from the clay. This is done through wedging and kneading home-prepared clay. Bought clay will not require such treatment.

Wedge the clay by cutting it into thick slices and forcefully slamming them down on your work table, one after the other. Form them into a mass again, and repeat the procedure ten to twenty times.

Knead the clay by pressing down on it with the base of your palms and pushing it from the body. Lifting the farthest edge of the clay, bring it over and toward you, and then press down again with the palms. The clay has been sufficiently kneaded when a cross section, cut by a wire, shows close, even texture without air pockets.

Clay that is to be fired in a primitive kiln must be strengthened with sand. Slice the clay, and make alternate layers of it and the sand. Then knead them together. Since sand tends to dry clay, you may need to put a thin layer of slop between each clay slice. Use one part sand to two or three of clay.

Techniques of Pottery Making

Pinch Technique: Shape a chunk of clay (the size of a small orange) in your hands as if shaping a snowball. When a smooth ball is formed, cup it in one hand while pressing the thumb of your other hand into its center, thus making a deep hole. Now you have the beginnings of a pot with thick walls. Still cupping the clay in your palm, pinch the wall between thumb and fingers, with the thumb inside and the fingers outside. Slowly rotating the pot in your hand, very gradually pinch out all sides of the pot and gently ease the clay. If cracks begin to appear as you are working, smooth over them with a wet finger.

Coil Technique: Roll clay backward and forward beneath your fingers to form long coils. A beginner should make the coils somewhat thick—approximately

the diameter of a fountain pen. Although it is not essential, try to keep them fairly uniform in length and thickness.

Flatten a sphere of clay into a disc roughly as thick as the coils. This is the pot's base. Now start the coiling. Shape the first coil around the inner edge of the disc, and press the coil's inner edge down on the base. When the coil completes the circle, guide it around on the top of the primary coil, pressing it firmly in place by smearing the inner edge down on

the coil under it. Continue this procedure, coil upon coil, until the pot is finished. Control its shape by the placement of the coils. If you want the pot to swell out, place the coils on the outer edge of the coil below. If the pot is to be narrower, place the coils on the inner circumference. To join the ends of coils, simply smear one against the other.

After a wall of seven to ten coils has been built up, permit the clay to become a bit firm in order to prevent sagging when the weight of more coils is added. Generally, one hour is needed for the clay to firm up sufficiently. If the clay overhardens, soften the top coil by scoring it and applying thick slip until it acquires the same consistency as the new coils.

Slab Technique: With the slab technique, the object is constructed from sheets of clay. Using a rolling pin (or a section of broom handle, a bottle, or a metal pipe), roll out a lump of clay into a flat sheet or slab of the desired thickness. Rolling should be done on a piece of cloth or paper to keep the clay from sticking to the work surface. Clay for the slab technique should be just a bit firmer than that for pinch or coiling work. If it is too soft, allow time for it to harden slightly.

Slabs can be cut into tiles with a knife and decorated with pictures that are incised or impressed on their surfaces. Containers can also be made. For example, to make a round pot, first cut out the base. Then mark it by outlining on the clay some circular object of suitable size. Holding a table knife vertically, cut around the outline. Then cut a long, narrow strip to form the side. Score all edges to be joined with a matchstick or modeling tool. Paint the scored edges with thick slip. Very soft clay can be bonded together securely without scoring and slipping. Stand the narrow strip on its side around the inside circumference of the base; attach it by firmly pressing the pieces together and smoothing over the joinings with a tool. Clay slabs may be wrapped around cardboard tubes of various lengths. Remove the tube as soon as feasible. A disc of appropriate size cut from a slab forms the base. Make a simple dish by pinching up the edge of a circular slab. Any number of articles found about the house—plates, bowls, cardboard boxes, etc.—can be utilized as molds in slab work. Roll out a slab of clay a little larger than the selected mold. Using a damp sponge, gently press the clay, still on its cloth (to prevent sticking), into the mold. Cut away excess clay. Hold the clay down in the mold while cutting in case it should stick to the knife and be pulled out. With a damp sponge, smooth off the rim of the receptacle. Remove it when the clay is hard and pull away the cloth.

Decorating

While a finished clay article is yet in its soft, plastic stage, it can be decorated by impressing. Experiment by pressing small objects on the clay to make interesting patterns. In slab work, the design may be pressed on with the clay still in sheet form, prior to building up the final shape.

Relief decorations—small clay pieces applied to the object's surface—are pressed on while the clay is soft. If the clay is not soft enough, score and coat the surfaces to be bonded together with slip (a small brush is handy for this).

Clay surfaces can be decorated by incising. The clay should be almost completely dry. Experiment with simple tools to scratch, score, or carve.

Kilns and Firing

The beginner can fire his pots in a simple, homemade sawdust kiln. Select a kiln site where the ground is free of vegetation and well away from buildings. Collect dry fuel—wood shavings, twigs, wood—the amount depending on the kiln's size.

For the kiln floor, lay a groundwork of shavings and twigs.

Cover this with a 3- to 4-inch layer of sawdust.

Fill the articles to be fired with sawdust. Place a layer of pots, 2 inches apart, in the bed of sawdust. Be sure the articles do not touch each other and are not too close to the edge of the foundation. Cover the pots with a layer of sawdust. Continue to build alternating layers of pots and sawdust.

The complete mound should then be thickly covered with sawdust, followed by shavings, twigs, and wood. The purpose of the foundation of shavings and twigs and the outer layer of the same materials is to ignite the sawdust. The firewood will burn strongly for about ten minutes and then die out. The sawdust, once lit, will smolder for quite some time. Sudden changes in temperature would cause the pots to explode. However, the temperature within your kiln will rise gradually because of the slowly burning covering of sawdust.

As the sawdust is consumed, more can be added. Leave the kiln until thoroughly burnt out. Depending on the kiln's size, firing time will last anywhere from twelve to twenty-four hours.

When the pots are cool enough to be lifted from the kiln, wash or brush them clean.

Firing of clay articles can also be done in a metal drum with holes pierced around its sides. Fill it completely with dry sawdust. The articles should be dispersed throughout the sawdust. Light the fire from the top. It will slowly smolder downward and require no additional attention.

There are small electric kilns on the market that have been designed for testing purposes. If firing out of doors is not feasible, small objects can be fired indoors in such a kiln.

Should these first attempts at pottery-making spur you to work on a larger scale, a more sophisticated kiln may be constructed.

15 | WAYS WITH LEATHER

Tanning Hides and Fur Skins

Time and patience are the initial requirements for tanning hides and furs. Choose the hide and fur of deer and squirrel for your first attempts. They are more easily readied for tanning than those of some other animals having thin skins, which require greater skill in preparation to avoid damage.

For all soaking and tanning operations, use a wooden, earthenware, or plastic container. Metal containers react with the salt and tanning chemicals.

Preparations
After skinning the animal, flesh the hide; that is, remove all meat remaining on it. Be sure it is also free of blood and mud. Cutting from the skin side, trim any ragged edges.

The hide is now ready for the tanning process, unless you plan to tan a deerskin into buckskin. In that case, the hair must first be removed. In 5 gallons of water, mix 5 quarts of hydrated lime. Leave the hide in this solution until the hair is easily pushed from the skin with your hand, generally between six and ten days. Spread the hide on a board, and push off the remaining hair with the blunt side of a knife. Then work over both sides of the skin with the back edge of a knife. Hold it nearly flat to remove any fleshy material, grease, or lime. (This is known as *cudding*.)

The remains of the liming process—fleshings, limewater sludge, and lime—can be put to good use as fertilizer because they are particularly suitable for acid soil.

The hair, collected as it is removed from the hide and rinsed several times, can be utilized in plastering. After being washed thoroughly in repeated changes of water and dried completely, it is useful in padding, upholstery, and in the insulation of pipes. The body hair of deer is valuable for making the bodies of fishing flies. By adding a water-repellent dressing to the already naturally buoyant deer hair, dry flies can be fashioned that will remain afloat almost indefinitely. Without the protective dressing, a fly of deer hair will become soaked after a time and will serve only as a wet fly.

Now soak the hide in clean water for five hours. Scud again. Fill a 10-gallon container with water. Stir in 1 pint of vinegar with a wooden

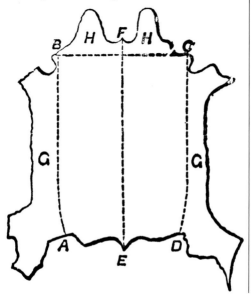

paddle. (You may substitute 1 ounce of lactic acid for the vinegar.) Leave the hide in this mixture for twenty-four hours to halt the action of the lime. Then proceed with tanning.

Tannage Procedures
Salt and Alum Tannage: Prepare the salt-alum solution by dissolving 1 pound of ammonia alum (or potash alum) in 1 gallon of water. In another container, dissolve 8 ounces of salt and 4 ounces of washing soda in ½ gallon of water. Slowly empty the salt-soda solution into the alum solution, while stirring rapidly. Immerse a clean skin in this solution for two to five days, according to its thickness.

Due to the effect of alum on certain furs, it might be advisable, in general, to apply the tanning solution in paste form, and only on the flesh side. Gradually, add flour mixed with a little water to the tanning solution until a thin paste forms. Blend well to avoid lumps.

Spread the skin smoothly and tack it, flesh side out. Completely coat the skin with the paste to a thickness of approximately ⅛ inch. The following day, scrape off the paste. Apply a second coat. Thick skins will require an additional coating on the third day. The final coating should be left on for four days. Then scrape away the paste, wash the skin in 1 gallon of water with 1 ounce of borax, and rinse in fresh water.

Lay the skin out on the board and, using a dull edge, press out much of the water. Proceed with oiling and finishing.

Alcohol and Turpentine Tannage: Tannage with alcohol and turpentine is easiest for a small fur skin. Mix ½ pint each of wood alcohol and turpentine in a wide-mouthed gallon jar having a screw-on lid. Put in the small fur skin. Since alcohol and turpentine tend to separate, shake or stir the solution daily.

After a week to ten days, take out the skin. Wash it in detergent water, removing grease, alcohol, and turpentine. Rinse thoroughly several times to get rid of the detergent. Squeeze water from the skin without wringing. When it is partially dry, begin the oiling and finishing operation.

Oiling and Finishing

Allow the tanned, wet leather to dry somewhat. While it is yet fairly damp, apply a coat of sulfated neat's-foot oil. The amount of oil will vary according to the natural oiliness of the skin. For example, a raccoon skin, being normally more fatty than a deerskin, would require less oil. For a 10-pound deer-hide, the following solution is recommended: In 3½ ounces of warm water, mix a like amount of sulfated neat's-foot oil with 1 ounce of ammonia.

Lay the skin, hair side down, on a smooth surface. Evenly spread one half of the mixture over the hide with your hand or a paint brush. Wait thirty minutes. Then apply the remainder in the same manner. Cover the hide with a plastic sheet. Keep it covered overnight. If several skins have been coated, stack them, flesh sides together, overnight.

The next morning hang the skin, fur side out, over a sawhorse to permit drying of the hair. Then nail the skin, hair side down, on a plywood board and stretch it slightly. Hammer the nails (no. 6 finish) ½ inch in from the edge, spaced about 6 inches apart. The flesh side should be dried at room temperature.

While the skin is still slightly damp, stretch it from corner to corner. Work the flesh side over some wooden edge, such as a chair back. Achieving a soft skin depends on repeatedly working it while it is in the process of drying.

When softening and drying are complete, give the skin a quick bath in unleaded or white gasoline to deodorize it and remove any excess grease. (Do this outdoors, away from flame or fire.)

Clean and brighten the pelt by tumbling it again and again in warm, dry, hardwood sawdust. Shaking, beating, and brushing will clean sawdust particles from the fur.

If need be, you may smooth the flesh side with a sandpaper block. Also, this will further soften the skin.

Preservation of Pelts

Unless tanning is to take place within twenty-four hours, hides or pelts should be treated or cured to avoid deterioration.

Preserve a small animal pelt by air-drying it. Tack it flat, hair side down, on a board.

A large pelt must be salted immediately. Place it, flesh side up, on a smooth surface. Sprinkle the hide thoroughly with salt and work it into wrinkles, neck, legs, and cut edges. For every pound of hide, use 1 pound of salt. If you are curing more than one hide, lay one on top of another, hair side down, and thoroughly salt the flesh side of each. The surface on which the pelts are stacked should have a slight incline to aid drainage of any liquid from the pile.

In two weeks you may hang the hides for complete drying. If salted a second time, they may be stored as late as May, but no longer.

A cured skin must be softened prior to tanning by soaking it several times in a 5- to 10-gallon container of cool water. Renew

the water for each soaking. The soaking time is relative to the skin's condition. Some may require two hours; others, more.

As the skin starts to soften, spread it on a flat board. Begin scraping the flesh side with an old hacksaw blade to break up tissue and fat. To do a thorough job of removing the adhering tissue, you may need to alternately scrape and soak the hides. While scraping, take care not to damage the true skin.

Now mix a solution of 1 ounce of borax or soda to every gallon of lukewarm water. You may also add soap. Put in the skin when it is just short of being soft. Stir it about with a paddle. This procedure cleanses the skin, cuts grease, and induces the final softening.

Again place the skin on a board, and scud it. Then rinse it well in lukewarm water. Press out the water without wringing the skin. Unless

you intend to de-hair it, proceed with the tanning operation as previously described.

American Indians removed the hair from hides with wood ashes. Their tanning agent was deer's brains. To make buckskin soft, weary-jawed squaws laboriously chewed the hides. Though these methods are of interest, we feel sure you will prefer those already set forth.

Making Rawhide

Hide that has been taken as quickly as possible after the death of an animal is called "green hide;" from it the best rawhide is made.

First, stake out a green hide on the ground in some shaded spot for roughly two hours. To stake it properly, pull outward from the center before fastening it down.

After two hours Nature will have changed it from green hide to rawhide, which should be sufficiently stiff to work with. Cut off any bits of hanging flesh. Using heavy shears, cut the hide in an oval or round shape, and remove legs, neck, and other projecting portions.

Now cut the oval or disc into one continuous strip about 2½ inches in width by scissoring around the circle until you reach its center. In thinner areas (such as the belly), cut the strip a bit wider, for after it has thoroughly

dried it will shrink to approximately two-thirds of its original width. When rawhide is neither too dry nor too damp, it can be cut with ease. If the strip becomes difficult to cut due to excess dryness, dampen the hide somewhat.

Attach one end of the long strip to a post, pull taut a section at a time, and grain off the hair with a keen-edged knife. Hold the blade almost flat. Guard against cutting the top skin (scarf skin), which gives strength to the rawhide string.

Once the hair has been removed, stretch the rawhide strip between posts or trees in complete shade. Leave it for five days to dry thoroughly. Then it will be ready for cutting into strings.

Bevel rawhide strings on the hair side to prevent the sharp edges from curling up. If the rawhide strip or strings are to be softened, rub them well with saddle soap (yellow laundry soap is also effective) and work them back and forth against a piece of wood, such as a post or sawhorse.

Sewing Needle for Leathers

Fabricate a needle for sewing leather articles from the "key" used to open sardine cans. Straighten the handle end, and hammer and file—or grind—it to a point. Thread sewing material through the slot at the opposite end.

Preserving and Mounting Snakeskins

Carefully skin the snake by centrally slitting the underside of the skin from top to bottom. If the snake is a rattler, take care not to disjoin the rattles. Using steel wool and borax, scrub the skin to remove all meat.

Leave the skin overnight. The following day, paint both sides with a mixture of one-half wood alcohol and one-half glycerin. After twenty-four hours, paint on a second coat. The skin will now be pliable as well as durable.

Select a board of interesting grain, saw it to the correct length, and finish it. Fasten the snakeskin on the board with any good glue.

Shoe Repairs

In olden times the shoemaker was itinerant, as were tinkers and other tradesmen. His kit consisted of a leather apron, a lap stone on which to work, an awl, knives, pincers, hand-forged nails, a hammer, wax filched from beehives along the way, and sturdy, bark-tanned leather heavily impregnated with whale oil.

The shoemaker was welcome in every home not only for his craft, but also for the "news" he dispensed. Ensconced in a chimney corner with his last, he would fashion new boots and shoes or repair old ones.

However, a good many rural folks were often obliged to tan hides and make their own rough footwear, either for the sake of frugality or because the shoemaker's calls were too infrequent. Whether for purposes of economy or the pure satisfaction involved, you can repair your own boots and shoes by using these guidelines.

Ripped Seams

The repairing of ripped seams in shoe and boot uppers requires a very small outlay for tools and materials. You will need a kit of hand-sewing needles, which can be purchased inexpensively at any dime store or shop selling sewing supplies. The packet contains five different needles, each about 4 inches in length and designed for a specific purpose. You will

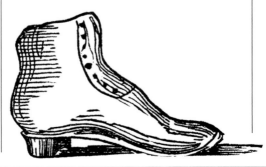

also need extra-strong thread, either the kind used over the years for sewing carpets and buttons or the more recently manufactured polyester-cotton-wrapped thread.

Follow these steps to repair the seams in footwear:

Pull apart the seam until you meet with resistance. Stop at this point. Remove all old stitching with the help of a penknife.

Choose the proper needle from the kit. If your hand will fit behind the seam, a straight needle will be appropriate. If the seam is located close to the shoe's toe, select the curved needle.

To sew a fine seam, use single thread. Use double or even triple strands of thread when the original holes in the leather are large enough. For a more water-resistant seam, first coat the thread with the wax from a beeswax candle. If beeswax is unavailable, ordinary candle wax will do.

Close the seam by sewing through the original holes. Take care not to enlarge them. Make the stitching taut.

Secure the finished seam by repeating the final stitch several times; a knot is unnecessary. To achieve a smooth finish, pound or rub the stitching into the leather.

Attaching Leather Half Soles

Sewing on new half soles will require a last, an item not as easily come by today as in the 1930s and 1940s, but nonetheless available to the adventurous of spirit. Search

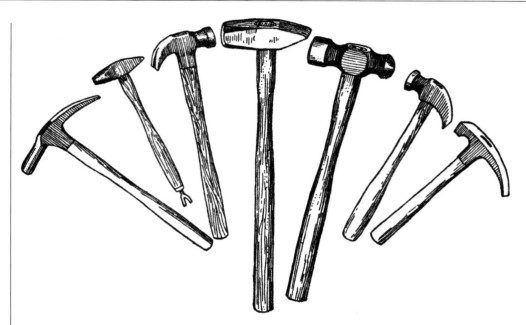

secondhand stores and you may find one for a dollar or two. Antique shops are sometimes a source, but there a last would sell for considerably more. Made of metal, it resembles an inverted leg with a foot (for holding a shoe) and is attached to a wooden base.

In addition to a last, you will need clinching nails and an awl for making new holes in leather. Fashion one from a hardwood dowel of a size that fits comfortably in your grip. Drive a long, heavy nail perpendicularly through the center of the dowel, allowing a portion of the point to extend beyond the wood. Hammer this extension flat against the wood to secure the spike in the dowel. Flatten the nail head with a hammer, and grind it to a smooth point with a coarse file.

Follow this procedure for stitching on leather half soles:

Buy precut half soles, or purchase leather and cut your own.

Soak the half sole or leather piece for ten minutes in tepid water. This step will make cutting and sewing easier. Then wrap newspaper around the leather to absorb excess water.

If you're making a sole, place the sole of the shoe on the new leather and trace around it. Carefully cut along the outline with a sharp knife.

Place the shoe on the last. With a penknife or razor blade, cut the old threads on the original half sole. Lift the sole and separate it from the shoe with a somewhat diagonal cut at the arch.

Bevel the half sole so that it slightly extends over what remains of the old sole.

Clinching-shoe nails range from ⅜ inch to ⅞ inch in length. Choose one a half size longer than the total thickness of both new sole and shoe. Hammer in about nine nails along the juncture of the new and old half soles. Next nail down the tip and sides of the half sole.

Using a sharp knife, trim the edge of the sole for neatness.

Cut a shallow depression or trough on the sole's bottom where the stitching will be. Having the stitches slightly recessed protects them from wear.

With the old holes of the shoe welt (a strip of leather sewn in the seam between the upper of a shoe and the sole to reinforce their joining) to guide you, use the awl to make holes from the topside in the half sole. Every other hole will be enough.

Take a waxed strand of thread 3 feet long and thread two needles, one at each end of the thread. Begin at the first hole closest to the arch. Run the needles consecutively through the same opening, one needle in one direction and the second needle in the other direction. Sew such opposing stitches all around the sole. To secure the final stitch, either sew the last stitch several times or make a knot. Snip off excess thread.

Complete your work by pounding down the depression made for the stitches in the sole. Rub all the needle holes, stitches, and cracks with beeswax or shoe polish.

16 | WAYS WITH WAX

Candles

Materials and Equipment

For simple candlemaking, assemble the following materials and equipment:

Paraffin Flakes: They can be bought in bags by the pound from a candlemakers' supply shop. Paraffin wax is quite hard and makes a smooth-burning candle.

Beeswax: When a small amount of beeswax is added to the paraffin, the candle has a smooth finish, gives off the aroma of honey while burning, and drips only minimally. Small beeswax discs can be purchased as an addition.

Stearin (sometimes known as sterene or stearic acid): This flaky white substance, when melted separately and added to the melted paraffin, facilitates the removal of the candle from the mold, gives it a harder finish, and prevents guttering. As a general rule, you should use 10 percent stearin to 90 percent paraffin-beeswax mixture. It can be bought by weight at a candlemakers' supply shop.

Common White String: Use ordinary white string to make your wicks. Closely braid it in two or more strands according to the thickness desired. To achieve a smoothly burning wick, it is necessary to correlate the wick size with the candle size, particularly with its diameter. The bigger the candle, the bigger the wick. Experience will teach you to gauge the wick size correctly.

Now make a solution of 8 ounces of water, 1 tablespoon of salt, and 2 tablespoons of borax. Soak the wicks in this mixture for about six hours. Then hang them up. Once they are completely dry, they will be ready for use. (You may purchase ready-made wicks very reasonably. Most have a label indicating the diameter of the candle for which they are suited.)

Wax-Based Dye: If you care to color your candles, use commercial wax dyes. Buy them in either powder or liquid form.

Wax Perfume: Scenting your candles is optional. Oil-based perfumes for wax are available at your supplier.

Two Old Saucepans: One pan should be small enough to fit into the other.

Sugar Thermometer: Measure the temperature of the wax with it.

Scissors: You will need a pair of scissors to cut and trim wicks.

Plasticine: Use this to keep melted wax from leaking through

the wick hole in the bottom of the candle mold and to attach bases on bottomless molds.

Knife: Have a sharp one handy for evening the bottoms of candles and doing other small jobs.

Candle Mold: Almost any container can serve as a candle mold as long as it has straight sides and a mouth with at least the same width as its base. You can probably find many appropriate containers in your kitchen vases, cups, mugs, and jugs. By exploring secondhand stores, you can often turn up interesting and inexpensive containers to use as candle molds, and various types can be bought at a candlemakers' supply shop.

Be sure that the molds will allow for easy removal of the finished candle. Check this by oiling their interior and compactly filling them with Plasticine. If the "candle" of Plasticine slips out easily, the chosen container is acceptable as a mold.

Copper and plastic piping provide excellent molds. Purchase off-cuts from a builders' supply center. Making certain that they are perfectly level when standing on end, saw them to the desired length. Smooth the edges with fine sandpaper. Make notches opposite one another on the rim of the top to hold a skewer or pencil from which to hang the wick. Find a jar lid the size of the mold's bottom (or cut one from cardboard, plastic, etc.). Make a central hole in it for the wick, and seal its edges to the bottom of the mold with Plasticine.

Wick Retainers: These are metal discs for candle molds lacking wick holes. Fasten the wick to one and lower it into the bottom of the container. Wick retainers can be bought at a candlemakers' supply shop.

Procedure

Fill the larger of your saucepans one quarter full of water, and place it on a lighted stove burner. Bring the water to the boiling point. Put the required amount of paraffin wax in the smaller saucepan, and lower it into the hot water. Reduce the heat so that the water barely simmers, and let the wax melt.

Cut wicking to correct lengths, somewhat longer than the molds' height, and knot one end of each. Dip them in the melted wax and hang them until dry.

Make sure your molds are absolutely clean. Then insert wicks in their bases, pulling the unknotted ends through the holes until the knot is firmly against the bottom. Carefully seal the hole with Plasticine. For molds without wick holes, use a wick retainer by attaching the wick to it and lowering it into the middle of the bottom.

Now tie or tape the free end of a wick around a metal skewer or pencil placed horizontally and centrally across the opening of the mold. Be sure that the wick is taut

and precisely centered.

If the base of the mold is not recessed, the wick knot will cause imbalance. Remedy this by placing your mold on an improvised platform made of two slightly spaced wood blocks, bricks, or any objects of exactly the same height.

When the paraffin has melted, add a small amount of the beeswax. Gently introduce it into the molten paraffin; let it melt. In a separate pan, melt stearin in an amount equaling 10 percent of the total of the paraffin wax plus beeswax. Add the dye immediately if you desire tinted candles. When melted simultaneously with the wax dye, stearin imparts a more vivid color to the finished product. Tint the mixture a slightly lighter shade than is desired, since the finished candle, being denser, will

be darker in color. Carefully spoon the tinted stearin into the paraffin-beeswax mixture.

Insert the sugar thermometer into the saucepan of wax. Check for the temperature to reach 180° F. At this point, take the container from the stove.

Using a spoon or soup ladle (you may prefer to empty the wax mixture into a warm metal jug with a long spout), pour the wax very carefully into the candle mold at its center. Be sure to avoid wax drips on inner side surfaces. Then tap the mold to release air, thus preventing air bubbles from forming on the surface.

Now let your candle set. Depending upon its size, this may require as many as twenty-four hours. During the setting period, "top up" the candle. As the candle sets, the wax will contract and a depression will appear around the wick. Fill in this hollow with

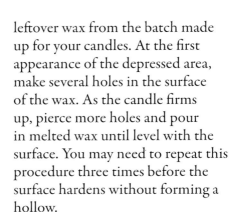

leftover wax from the batch made up for your candles. At the first appearance of the depressed area, make several holes in the surface of the wax. As the candle firms up, pierce more holes and pour in melted wax until level with the surface. You may need to repeat this procedure three times before the surface hardens without forming a hollow.

When your candle has shrunk from the mold's sides, it is set and ready for removal. First, free the wick from the skewer or pencil. Then, holding your hand over its mouth, invert the mold. Remove the Plasticine seal around the wicking knot. Cut off the knot with a sharp knife. Handling the candle delicately in order not to mar its surface, gently shake the candle from the mold. If the surface does not appear sufficiently smooth and shiny, hold on to the wick and dip the candle in boiling water and then ice water.

Stand your candle upright. You may need to trim the wick with scissors. It should be about ¼ inch in height.

Cure the finished candle in a cool, dry place for three days before using it.

Candle in a Glass

To make a candle that will remain in its glass container requires but one item in addition to the supplies already mentioned—glue.

Select some transparent glass container that is eye-catching. Make sure it is thoroughly clean.

Wax a wick somewhat beyond the usual size appropriate for the container's diameter. (The whole surface of a candle in a permanent holder becomes molten; therefore, a too-small wick would fall over and be extinguished.) Turn a short span of the wick at a right angle, and glue it in the middle of the container's bottom. Fasten it at the top in the customary way.

Pour in melted wax that does not exceed 180° F, or you will risk cracking the glass.

Let the candle set, and top up in the usual manner. Try to achieve as smooth a surface as possible. Trim the wick to ¼ inch.

Your dripless candle in glass will need no other holder.

Dipped Candles

Fill a vessel with a prepared candle-wax mixture. Choose one that is somewhat taller than the length of candle intended.

Cut a wick about 3 inches longer than necessary. Completely soak the wick in the melted wax, and hang it to dry, keeping it as straight as possible. Tie the dry wick on the horizontal bar of a wooden coat hanger.

Now add stearin to the wax— about 20 percent for dipped candles—along with dye (optional). When the temperature of the wax is 160° F, dip the suspended wick slowly into the wax. Be careful to hold the coat hanger as nearly on a level as possible. Leave the wick

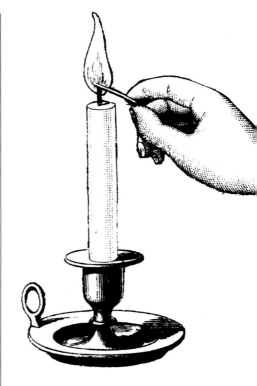

in the wax for approximately five seconds; then slowly lift it out. Suspend the hanger from a hook located away from a wall, and let the taper dry for roughly two minutes.

Continue dipping and drying until the taper reaches the desired thickness. Allow the candle to set hard, an hour or more, before cutting it from the hanger. Trim the base evenly with a sharp knife.

More than one taper can be made at a time by using a vessel with a wider mouth to hold the wax and by hanging more wicks on a longer rod which, after the dipping process, can be suspended across the backs of spaced chairs. Remember to place newspapers beneath the tapers to catch drips.

17 | SPIC-AND-SPAN

Cleaning Methods

Old-fashioned procedures for removing spots, stains, and odors are as effective today as they were in times gone by. Here are some cleaning methods that were used generations ago to maintain spic-and-span households.

Acid Stains

Wrap the stained area around some pearlash (potash) and tie with twine. Boil the cloth in soapy water until the stain is gone.

Baked-On Foods

Scour baked-on foods from pans by using a paste of ½ flour moistened with a little vinegar and ½ salt.

Barrels

Dissolve 2 pounds of baking soda in 4 quarts of hot water. Pour this into a barrel of water and let stand for 12 hours. Empty the liquid and let the barrel stand for 2 hours, and it will be free of odor. All wooden vessels can be treated in this way.

Beds

A good way to shine unvarnished brass beds is to rub them with half a lemon dipped in table salt. After washing them in hot water and drying them well, rub the brass with rottenstone.

Boots and Shoes

For a fast shine, cut a lemon and rub it over your leather boots or shoes; wipe off quickly with a soft cloth.

Bottles and Jars

To remove odor from bottles and jars, fill them with a solution of water and dry mustard. Let stand for several hours and rinse in hot water.

Brasses

Crush onion with a little damp earth for cleaning brasses.

Breadboard

Using a piece of pumice, scrub breadboards and carving boards clean with a mixture of borax and salt.

Carpets

Cut the heart of a cabbage in half. Using it like a brush, go over the entire carpet to clean and renovate it.

Cocoa Stains

Soak the article stained with cocoa in a mixture of water and borax to remove discoloration.

Copper

To remove the tarnish from copperware, clean it with half a lemon dipped in a mixture of 1 tablespoon of salt and 1 tablespoon of vinegar.

Crust

To prevent a crust from forming in water kettles, keep a large marble or an oyster shell in them.

Dust Mop

Clean a dust mop by boiling it in water to which have been added 2 tablespoons of paraffin and 1 tablespoon of baking soda.

Faucets

Lime deposits around faucets can be removed by rubbing with a cloth dipped in vinegar.

Feather Beds

To satisfactorily clean feather beds, spread them on tall grass during a heavy shower. Be sure to turn them so that both sides will be soaked. Place them on slats across chairs in the full sun to dry. Beat them with a stick to fluff up the feathers.

Fireplace

When the fire is burning strongly, toss in a handful of salt. It will act as a cleaning agent and aid in preventing chimney fires.

Flatiron

Wrap a piece of beeswax in a coarse rag. When the iron is almost hot enough to use, rub it with the beeswax cloth to remove starch or rust.

Floors

Clean varnished floors and woodwork with cold tea to bring out their shine.

Flyspecks

Soak a bunch of chopped leeks in a half bucket of water for a week. Strain the resulting infusion and use for washing paintings, mirrors, lampshades, etc. to protect them from being dirtied by flies. To remove flyspecks from varnished furniture, clean with a mixture of half cold water and half skimmed milk.

Fruit Stains

Hold cloth stained by fruit over a piece of burning sulphur. Wash thoroughly.

Glue

Use a cloth dipped in vinegar to remove glue from fabrics.

Gold Articles

Make a paste of cigar ashes and water to polish gold articles.

Grease Spots

Stale grease can best be removed with wood alcohol. Rinse the garment, scrub it with yellow soap, then give it a thorough rinsing in hot water.

Greasy Pots and Pans

Wipe out greasy pots and pans with paper; then scour them with corn meal.

Grindstone

When your grindstone gets coated with dirt and oil and will barely sharpen an axe or knife, clean it easily by holding a piece of ice to the stone while you slowly turn it.

Ink on Cloth

To remove ink stains from white cloth, rub them with freshly picked sorrel. Wash with soap and water, and if necessary repeat the procedure.

Ink on Paper

To remove writing in ink from paper, add 2½ drams of muriate of tin to 4 drams of water and apply with a camel's-hair brush. When the writing has disappeared, dip the paper in water and allow to dry.

Iron Stains

Soak the cloth with iron stains in buttermilk. Dry it in the hot sun. Then launder in cold water.

Kid Gloves

Clean kid gloves by rubbing them with cream of tartar.

Knives

To clean rusty knives, insert the blades in an onion and let stand for a half hour. Rust will quickly disappear when this is followed by washing and polishing.

Lace

Put 1 rounded teaspoon of borax in 1 pint of warm soapsuds. Let soiled lace soak in this for 1 hour. Rinse 3 times, adding 1 teaspoon of sugar to the last rinse water.

Lamp Globes

To remove smoke stain from lamp globes, soak them in hot water in which washing soda has been dissolved. Then wash the globes with a good stiff brush in a pan of warm water to which has been added 1 teaspoon of powdered carbonate of ammonia. Rinse them in cold water and dry.

Lamps

To prevent a lamp from smoking, soak the wick in vinegar; allow it to dry thoroughly before using it.

Leather Articles

Clean leather articles by rubbing them with equal parts of vinegar

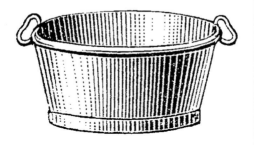

and boiled linseed oil. Then polish with a soft cloth.

Leather Bookbindings
Brighten leather bookbindings by rubbing them with egg white.

Linoleum
To clean and preserve new linoleum, wash it with beer, and wipe it dry. Do this daily for the first week. Then clean it weekly with warm, clear water. When it is dry, sponge with beer. Washing linoleum with milk will also help to preserve it.

Mildew
Rub soap on mildew; then apply salt and lemon juice to both sides of the material. Wash and hang in the open air to dry.

Mud Stains
Remove mud stains from black cloth by first brushing the garment well and then rubbing the stains with half of a raw potato.

Odor
If clothing has a musty odor, restore it to freshness by placing charcoal in the folds.

Paint Brushes
To soften and clean hardened paint brushes, insert them for a few minutes into boiling vinegar. Then wash them in warm soapy water.

Paint Odor
A pailful of water placed in a freshly painted room will eliminate the offensive paint smell.

Piano Keys
Clean piano keys by using a piece of silk cloth barely moistened with alcohol.

Picture Frames
To bring luster to the gold leaf of picture frames, rub them with boiled onion juice and wipe dry. Gilt frames can be cleaned and brightened by washing with a mixture of 2 egg whites and 1 ounce of soda.

Pots and Pans
Boil apple peelings in aluminum pots and pans to brighten the metal.

Privies
Three spoonfuls of spirits of turpentine in a pail of water is an effective cleaner for eliminating odors in privies.

Rugs
Sprinkle a generous amount of corn meal on a rug where there are grease spots. Gently brush it into· the rug, and leave it for 24 hours before removal.

Rust on Cloth
To remove rust stains from white cloth, put a slice of lemon between two layers of cloth on the stain; apply a very hot iron. Repeat until the stain has disappeared.

Rusty Pots
Remove rust stains from iron pots by boiling water and clean hay in them. Allow to stand for 10 hours and boil again with fresh water.

Saucepans
Boil a few pieces of rhubarb in water to remove lime in saucepans.

Scorches
Clothing that has been scorched during ironing should be laid in the bright sunshine.

Shades
Dirty window shades can be cleaned with a piece of rough flannel dipped in flour.

Shawls
Spread a clean cloth on the table and sift dry white corn meal over it. Place the soiled shawl on this and sprinkle more corn meal on top. Roll it up tight. After seven days dust away the meal, and the shawl will be clean.

Silver

Clean tarnished silver by soaking it in potato water for 2 hours. Use a soft brush and silver polish to remove any lingering tarnish.

Sink Drains

To keep sink drains free of unpleasant odors, pour into them 1 gallon of water to which has been added ⅓ pound of calcium chloride.

Skunk Odor

Soak clothing in milk, vinegar, or tomato juice to remove the odor of skunk. If this fails, bury the garments.

Smoke

Put vinegar in an open vessel to eliminate the odor of smoke.

Stains

Apply glycerin to wine and fruit stains. Let it remain for 5 minutes and rinse.

Steel Machinery

Heat 1 pound of lard. Dissolve 12 ounces of powdered gum in it. Add enough black lead to make the mixture the color of iron. Rub this on steel or iron machinery, and leave it for 24 hours. Then rub with a soft rag. This method will prevent rust from forming on sewing machines, coffee grinders, etc.

Sticky Iron

Run a hot iron over salt sprinkled on a piece of paper to remove sticky spots from its sole.

Stovepipes

The best way to clean stovepipes is to put a piece of zinc on the coals in the fire.

Tar on Clothing

To remove tar, rub the clothing with lard, and leave it for an hour or more. Scrape off the lard, and scrub the garment with hot water and soap. If this is not completely successful, apply turpentine.

Tar on Skin

Take tar from your hands by rubbing them with lemon or orange peel and then wiping them off.

Tea Stains

Mix 1 tablespoon of salt with 1 cup of soft soap. Use it to rub the tea stains. Spread the cloth on the grass in a sunny spot. Leave it for two days and then launder.

Vases

Put soapy water and crushed eggshells into vases or bottles that are difficult to clean because of narrow openings. Shake well and rinse.

Wallpaper

To remove grease spots from wallpaper, rub them lightly with a piece of flannel dampened with spirits of wine.

Wax

To remove candle-wax drippings, place a blotter on the spot and hold a hot iron over the blotter.

Windows

Add 1 tablespoon of kerosene to 1 gallon of water for washing windows. This solution will prevent the glass from streaking. To make windows shine, add a little vinegar, or rub them with newspaper.

Wood

Remove stains from wood surfaces with ½ ounce of vitriol in 4 ounces of water. Use a cork instead of a cloth for rubbing.

Woodwork

To clean oak woodwork, wash it with warm beer. Next boil 2 quarts of beer, 1 tablespoon of sugar, and a piece of beeswax about the size of a walnut. Brush the wainscoting with this mixture. When it is dry, polish it with flannel.

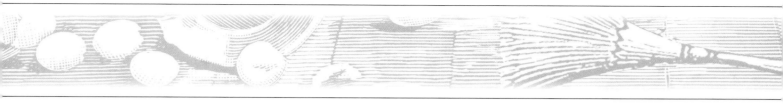

Woolens

Remove stains from black or colored woolens by soaking them in water in which a handful of ivy leaves has been boiled for 15 minutes.

Wrought Iron

Clean wrought iron with a drop of paraffin on a soft cloth.

Cleaning Aids

Laundry Soap

Put 1 pound of quicklime into 1 gallon of very hot water. Stir occasionally over the next 2 hours. Allow it to settle. Pour off the clear liquid into a large vessel, and add 5 gallons of soft water, 4 pounds of bar soap, and 3 pounds of washing soda. When the soap and soda are dissolved, stir in 2 ounces of salt. After the mixture has cooled a bit, pour it into jars or half-barrels. Store covered for use. This amount of half-solid soap will wash four times as much laundry as the bar soap alone would do.

Hard Soap

Put 6 pounds of washing soda, 3½ pounds of quicklime, and 4 gallons of soft water into a kettle. Boil. Stir until the soda is dissolved and the quicklime slaked. Allow it to settle; then pour off the clear liquid. Rinse the kettle, and boil in it 6 pounds of liquid grease (during the winter save drippings from ham, mutton, etc. for soapmaking) and ½ pound of borax until soap begins to form. Empty it into a tub to cool.

When hard enough, it can be cut into bars and placed on boards to dry. This is a good laundry soap; with the addition of a little perfume, it becomes a nice complexion soap. Scent it with oil of sassafras or oil of caraway, using 1 ounce to 10 gallons of soap. Stir it in well when the soap is fairly cool.

Scouring Soap

Put 1 pound of borax and 3 pounds of washing soda into 3 gallons of soft water. When they are dissolved, add 10 pounds of yellow soap shaved fine and 1 pound of tallow. Heat to melt. Then sift a quantity of lime to remove the lumps, slake it, and add as much to the mixture as you can stir in well. This soap is good for difficult cleaning jobs, such as removing grease or tar from the hands.

Renovation Soap

Put 3 drams of camphor gum into 1 ounce of alcohol and reserve. Put 1 dram of powdered pipe clay into 2 ounces of beef gall and reserve. Reduce ¼ ounce of saltpeter and ¼ ounce of borax to powder; mix them and 1 teaspoon of common salt with ¼ ounce of honey and reserve. After 3 hours shave ¼ pound of good soap (such as used by barbers) into a porcelain vessel. Add the gall

mixture and stir over a low fire until the soap is dissolved. Remove from the stove and allow to cool somewhat. Put in the other ingredients, stirring well. Quickly pour the mixture into glass jars, where it will harden. Store them covered in a dark closet until needed for renovating soiled garments. To use, spoon out ½ ounce, and dissolve it in 1 quart of boiling soft water. Scrub soiled areas of jackets, trousers, etc. with a scouring brush dipped in this solution.

Washing Fluid

Dissolve concentrated lye (potash) in 1 gallon of rain water. Put 2 ounces each of muriate of ammonia and salts of tartar into another gallon of soft water. Combine both solutions in a 2-gallon stone jug. Cork and shake. Use ½ cup of the fluid for each boiler of dirty clothes.

Washing Powder

Pulverize 1 pound of borax, 2 pounds of washing soda, and 2 ounces of salts of tartar. Mix them, and add 1½ ounces of muriate of ammonia. Bottle and cork. Use 1 rounded tablespoon of the powder in each boiler of laundry.

Homemade Lye

Here is how to make lye the old-fashioned way. Save fireplace ashes from hickory or oak logs. Find a fallen hardwood tree trunk, and burn it out hollow. Put in the ashes, and set it over an inclined

wooden trough, with a bucket at its lower end. Due to the corrosive effect of lye, the bucket should be of enamel, pottery, or iron. Pour a considerable amount of water on the ashes. It will filter through them, run down the trough, and drip into the bucket as a lye solution.

Soap (yield: 9 pounds)

The making of soap is thought to have developed accidentally through early Roman sacrifices. After animals were burned to appease a god or win divine favor, ashes and a little fat remained. Rain added the final ingredient that produced suds.

Homemade soap is very inexpensive and will efficiently whiten your laundry. Here are the requirements:

6 pounds grease (drippings or drippings mixed with half suet for a whiter soap)
1 can lye (13 ounces)
5 cups cold water

Whenever you trim meat, save the fat. Keep bacon fat, beef fat, or pork fat in the refrigerator. After several cupfuls have accumulated, cook it slowly, rendering out the liquid fat. Strain the grease through cheesecloth. You will need 6 pounds of drippings to make a good batch of white soap.

If you failed to strain the drippings after rendering the fat, prepare the grease the day before making soap. Melt each 3 pounds of grease in 2 quarts of water. While it is heating, stir. Allow it to cool. The following day, remove the cold grease from the surface of the water. The salt and cracklings should remain at the bottom of the vessel.

Put a large stainless-steel pan or glass jar in the sink. Fill it with 5 cups of water. Wearing rubber gloves (remember that lye is caustic), carefully and slowly stir in 1 can of lye with a steel or wooden spoon. Reheat the grease, and cool it until tepid (130° F). Stir it into the lye and water. Continue stirring for twenty minutes, when the soap should have the consistency of honey. Pour it into a granite or heavy metal pan. Allow to set overnight.

The next day, cut the soap into large practical bars or small, personal-sized cakes. However, do not remove them from the pan for several more days. After that, let them season from six weeks to two months.

One-quart milk cartons provide good soap forms. After fourteen to eighteen hours, cut away the

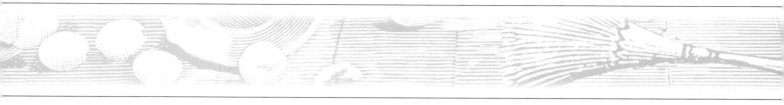

cardboard and slice the blocks. Allow the soap to dry further.

You may shave and melt down larger bars for such household tasks as washing woodwork.

If you like, scent the personal-sized soap by adding a few drops of any essential oils before it becomes cool enough to set. Should perfume be added while the soap is too hot, it will escape with the steam; if the soap is too cold, the fragrance cannot be easily incorporated. Try almond oil, attar of roses, lemon, wintergreen, or whatever you prefer. Another method is to wait until the soap hardens, run it through a meat grinder, and melt it in a double boiler with orange-flower water, rose water, or various other scented waters and common salt. Use 1 pint of scented water and 2 ounces of salt to each 6 pounds of soap. After boiling it, let the mixture cool. Cut it into small cakes with a wire, and dry them away from direct sunlight. Allow to season.

A small bottle of inexpensive hand lotion can be added to hand or bath soap as both emollient and perfume. To make floating bath soap, fold in air (as you would eggs into batter) when the mixture thickens.

Glycerin soap can be made by adding 6 ounces of glycerin to the soap mixture after pouring in the lye solution. This is a good complexion soap.

For saddle soap, use 1 can of lye,

2¾ pints of water, and 6 pounds of tallow. It is excellent for cleaning and preserving leather.

To make tar soap, prepare tallow soap and let it stand, stirring now and then until thickening occurs. Then work in 8 ounces of wood tar. Stir the mixture thoroughly to prevent lumps. Use the soap for shampooing hair.

Water Softener
Thoroughly mix 4 cups of soda ash (found in hardware stores) with 8 cups of waterglass (sodium silicate, available in drugstores). Store the mixture in glass containers.

To soften 5 gallons of water, stir in approximately ½ teaspoon of the concentrate. This ratio is a general recommendation and subject to adjustment according to the water hardness in your particular locale.

Bluing
In 1 quart of soft water, dissolve 1 ounce of Prussian blue powder and ½ ounce of powdered oxalic acid to make a good bluing. It should be added to the last rinse water.

Cleaners for Carpets, Tile, Copper, Glass, and Leather
Carpet Cleaner
Blend equal amounts of salt and baking soda. Add several drops of white vinegar to each 8 ounces of the dry mixture. Stir in sufficient water to form a paste.

Spread the paste on the soiled area, and let it dry completely. Then brush away the powdery cleanser along with the dirt. In the case of stubborn stains, gently scrub the rug when the cleanser is first applied.

Ceramic Tile Cleaner
An inexpensive cleaner for ceramic tile can be made by dissolving 1 tablespoon of trisodium phosphate (found in hardware stores) in ½ gallon of water. Store in a glass container.

To use, moisten a sponge with the cleaner. Always wear rubber gloves when preparing or applying the solution.

Copper Cleaner
Combine vinegar and salt. Apply the mixture to copper surfaces with a rag, and rub clean.

Glass Cleaners
Mix a handful of cornstarch in a pail of lukewarm water. Wash windows and mirrors with the solution, and wipe them dry. They will be clean and shiny.

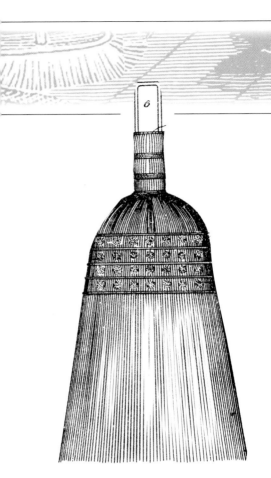

Or mix 1 cup of isopropyl alcohol in 2 cups of water. Add 5 drops of lactic acid (found in paint and hardware stores). Transfer the mixture to a spray bottle for cleaning glass and windows.

Another excellent window cleaner is made by stirring 2 tablespoons of ethylene glycol into 3 cups of water. (Ethylene glycol can be bought at service stations.) Put the solution in a spray bottle for use.

Leather Cleaner

To maintain leather articles in a clean, supple condition, combine these ingredients: ¾ cup of isopropyl alcohol, ½ cup of white vinegar, and 1½ cups of water. Stir to blend. Keep the cleaner in a glass container. Rub it on leather with a damp sponge or cloth.

Air Deodorants

Air Deodorant Spray

Mix 4 teaspoons of baking soda in 4 cups of water. Fill a convenient-sized spray bottle. To dissipate offensive odors, spray the solution in a fine mist.

Herbal Deodorant Vinegar

Fill a 1-pint jar with an aromatic material (flower blossoms, leaves, dried herbs, etc.). Heat 2 cups of white vinegar. When it reaches the boiling point, add it to the jar. Put on the lid, and allow the mixture to stand for several weeks, shaking it daily.

After two weeks, check the scent. If it is satisfactory, strain the jar's contents into a decorative container. Set it wherever odors are a problem.

Refurbishing Aids

Creamy Furniture Polish

Grate 2½ ounces of beeswax into a tin can. Melt the wax by placing the can in a pan of preheated water. Blend 1 cup of turpentine with the melted wax. Using a separate vessel, dissolve 2 tablespoons of powdered rosin and 1 ounce of Castile soap in 2 cups of water. Add this to the turpentine mixture. Store the creamy polish in a glass jar.

For use, rub a little at a time on furniture and polish with a dry, soft cloth.

Lemon Oil Furniture Polish

In 1 quart of mineral oil, mix 1 tablespoon of lemon oil (available at drugstores). Use a spray bottle to apply the polish. Wipe clean.

Rust Preventive

Combine raw linseed oil and about 30 percent turpentine. Coat steel tools—spades, chisels, etc.—with the mixture. It will dry quickly, forming a long-lasting, waterproof finish. When the coating eventually wears off, smear on another. Make sure that the steel is completely dry before applying the mixture, which should never be used on wood.

Whitewash

In 3 gallons of water, soak 25 pounds of slaked lime until a paste forms. You will have roughly 4 gallons of lime paste.

Dissolve 3 pounds of salt in 1½ gallons of boiling water. Allow the solution to cool. Then add it to the lime paste, and stir in 1½ pounds of white Portland cement.

Apply the whitewash to a slightly damp wall for best results.

Another good whitewash can be made by adding ½ pound of salt, dissolved in 3 gallons water, and 1 pound of sulphate of zinc to 8 quarts of slaked lime. This combination produces a firm, hard wash that will not crack. The salt makes the whitewash stick better. For a clearer white, add a little bluing.

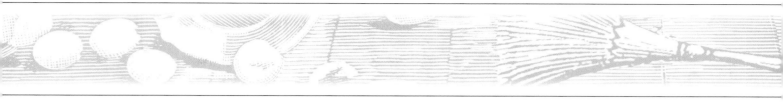

Adhesives

Ordinary paste is made by mixing rice flour or wheat flour in water, with or without boiling. To improve it, various adhesives, such as glue, gum arabic, and rosin, may be added along with alum.

Simple Flour Paste

Make simple cold flour paste by mixing 1 tablespoon of flour with 1 cup of cold water. Add several drops of carbolic acid as a preservative.

Library Paste

Dissolve ½ ounce of alum in 2 cups of warm water. Stir in flour until the consistency of cream is reached. Break up all lumps. Add a few drops of oil of cloves and 1 teaspoon of powdered resin. Boil until thick. If the mixture becomes too thick, thin it with a small amount of hot water. Put it in a glass jar and close it tightly. Keep it in a cool place. When necessary,

soften the paste with several drops of warm water, and melt it over very low heat.

Gum Arabic Paste

Dissolve 2 ounces of gum arabic in 2 cups of water in the top of a double boiler. Combine ½ ounce of white sugar and ½ ounce of laundry starch. Stir the mixture into a little cold water until it reaches the consistency of thick paste, free of lumps. Add this to the contents of the double boiler and boil until the starch is clear. Put in several whole cloves or a few drops of any essential oils, such as oil of cloves, lavender, etc., for a preservative. A little alcohol will also serve as a preservative.

Isinglass Glue

Isinglass—not to be confused with mica, which is often so named—is an animal tissue mainly derived from the air bladders of some fish. It dissolves easily in water and is a strong adhesive.

Dissolve 1 pound of isinglass in 2 cups of soft water in a double boiler. Slowly add ¼ cup of nitric acid, and stir continuously. Bottle the liquid glue and close tightly to prevent evaporation. It is excellent for paper, leather, wood, and many other materials.

Cement for Broken China and Glass

Beat egg whites until frothy. When they have settled, beat in quicklime and grated cheese. Mend china

or crockery by applying it to the broken edges.

In boiling water (enough to fill a wineglass) dissolve gum acacia. Add sufficient plaster of Paris to produce a thick paste. Use this almost-colorless mixture to cement broken china.

Combine 1 pint each of vinegar and milk. Remove the whey, and beat it well with 5 egg whites. Add enough finely powdered quicklime (you may substitute burned oyster shells for the lime) to form a thick paste. It is excellent for mending glass or china.

Cement for Labels on Tins

Boil glue in vinegar. Thicken the liquid with flour to make a paste for sticking labels on tin boxes.

Cement for Paper

To make a white, almost transparent paste for fancy paper work that calls for a strong but colorless cement, mix a little cold water into powdered rice. While stirring constantly, slowly add boiling water until the proper consistency is reached. Then boil for 1 minute.

Cement for Boots and Shoes

Combine 1½ ounces of sulphide of carbon and ¼ ounce of gutta-percha. Bottle it for use in applying patches to boots and shoes.

Paste for Stamps, Labels, etc.

Put 5 ounces of glue into 20 ounces of water to soak for 1 day. Dissolve 9 ounces of rock candy and 3 ounces of gum arabic in this liquid. It makes a particularly good mucilage for the labeling on bottles to be stored in damp cellars.

Wallpaper Paste

Add enough water to 2 cups of flour to make a thin dough, without lumps. Stir it into 1 gallon of boiling water. When it again reaches the boiling point, pour the hot batter into a tin bucket. Let it stand for 24 hours. Strain it through some coarse muslin. Use the paste as an adhesive for wallpaper.

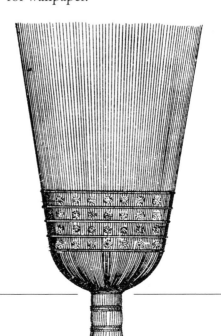

Fire Control

Fire-Extinguishing Powder

Make a low-cost, effective fire-extinguishing powder by combining 6 pounds of fine silica mason sand (available from a dealer in building supplies) and 2 pounds of sodium bicarbonate (available at grocery stores). Mix them thoroughly, and keep the powder in 1-pound glass or metal containers. Locate them in strategic places.

When extinguishing flames, scatter the mixture on the base of the fire.

Pest Control

Here are some old-time means, passed on from generation to generation, for ridding both house and garden of various pests.

Ants

Save cucumber peelings and mix them with salt. Place the mixture wherever ants are a problem.

Place small sponges soaked in sweetened water wherever in the house ants have been seen; the ant-covered sponges can be collected periodically and plunged into hot water.

Paint the floor with paraffin oil in areas that ants most frequent.

Mix 3 ounces of powdered fennel, 3 ounces of chrysanthemum urns, and 1 ounce of powdered sassafras bark with equal parts of red pepper and borax. Spread where ants have been seen.

Boil 1 cup of tar in 1 quart of water. Put this in shallow containers to destroy ants.

To rid the home of red ants, put slices of raw onion in the closets.

If you can locate ants' nests outside the home, put quicklime into the openings and wash it in with boiling water.

Dissolve camphor in spirits of wine, mix it with water, and pour it into the nests of ants.

Pouring a solution strong with tobacco into their holes is an effective means of destroying ants.

A little carbolic acid in boiling water washed down their holes will kill ants.

Aphids

Dissolve 1 ounce of shaved soap in 1 quart of water. Separately, boil 3 pounds of elder leaves in 3 quarts of water for 30 minutes. Cool and strain. Blend this solution with the soapy water and pour or spray on plants to combat aphids in your garden.

Bedbugs

To exterminate bedbugs apply kerosene, benzine, or corrosive sublimate and turpentine on a small brush to the crevices of a bedstead.

Fill a quart bottle with equal amounts of spirits of turpentine and alcohol; add 1 ounce of camphor gum. Shake well before using. Apply the solution with a feather to all recesses in the bedstead to rid it of bedbugs.

Tansy leaves sprinkled between sheets and mattresses will keep bedbugs away.

Centipedes

Though useful for keeping households free of insects, centipedes are not very welcome in most homes. Use pyrethrum powder (made from certain chrysanthemums) to drive them away, putting it freely around pipes.

Cockroaches

Mash ⅔ pound of plaster of Paris, add a little sugar, and mix with 1 pound of oatmeal. Place in areas most frequented by cockroaches.

Fill jars partly full of stale beer. Prop sticks against their sides. The roaches, attracted to the beer, will mount the sticks and fall into the jars.

To rid the premises of cockroaches, mix equal amounts of borax and brown sugar in a dish.

Place it where they are most frequently seen.

Bruise the roots of freshly dug black hellebore. Put them where cockroaches have been observed. Hellebore is poisonous, and they will eat it greedily. The plant can be found growing in marshy places.

Crawling Insects

Add ½ pound of alum to a pail of hot water. Sprinkle it boiling hot in areas of the house where crawling insects have been seen. This solution is effective against roaches, ants, chintz bugs, and other pests.

To discourage crawling insects, spread walls and cracks with a solution of 2 pounds of alum boiled in 3 quarts of water.

Cayenne pepper will keep your pantry free of roaches, ants, and other pests.

Crickets

To destroy crickets, put Scotch snuff into their holes.

Fleas

Tansy leaves, fresh or dried, will keep away fleas.

You can eradicate fleas in the kennel by mixing dried walnut leaves with the straw.

To free your cat or dog from fleas, saturate a string with oil of pennyroyal, and tie it about the animal's neck.

Flies

To keep the house free of flies, put dishes containing oil of bay leaves on window sills. Alternatively, mix equal amounts of bay leaf pieces, coarsely ground cloves, broken eucalyptus leaves, and clover blossoms. Put this blend in small bags of mesh or some loosely woven material. Hang them just inside entrance doors to repel flies. Or, paint door and window casings with paint to which 4 percent of bay oil has been added.

Melt 6 ounces of rosin, and add 2 ounces of shortening. When cold, this mixture will have the consistency of molasses. Spread it on small pieces of wood, and place them about the house. Flies are

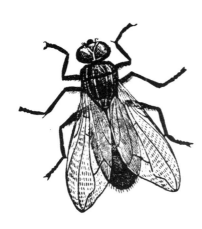

attracted to it and will be held fast. To make flypaper, mix equal amounts of castor oil and melted resin. Spread the gooey mixture on nonporous paper (for example, magazine and catalog covers) with a warm knife. Leave the edges clear so that you can fasten the paper down wherever flies are a nuisance.

Garden Insects

Steep ¾ pound of tobacco leaves in 1 gallon of boiling water. Strain it after 15 minutes. Pour this solution over your garden plants to drive away harmful insects.

Several bugs that are attracted to roses and some vegetable plants can be lured away to marigolds planted near them.

If you have a little kitchen garden in the back yard, plant hot peppers among tomatoes and other vine crops to protect them against insects.

Grasshoppers

Make traps for destructive garden grasshoppers by half-filling deep jars with a solution of water and molasses.

House-Plant Parasites

To effectively destroy parasites on house plants, place containers of steaming soapsuds close to them 3 times a week. Once a week wash the leaves to keep them free of insects.

Insect Eggs

Wash corners of drawers and closets with scalding potash water, 1 teaspoon of potash to 12 gallon of water, to destroy insect eggs.

Lice

Sprinkle sulfur under the wings of your chickens and pet canary to rid them of lice.

Mice

Mix tartar emetic with any favorite mouse food. After eating it, mice will sicken and leave.

Mint, particularly pennyroyal, strewn on floors and placed in beds, in sacks, and near cheeses will keep mice away because of its odor.

Mix corn meal and cement, half-and-half. Place in shallow containers where mice run.

Mites

To rid a pantry of mites, empty it and fumigate it with sulfur. Afterward, scrub it thoroughly with kerosene emulsion.

Mosquitoes

To keep mosquitoes off your person, apply hemlock oil to the hands and face.

Burning pyrethrum powder in the house will discourage mosquitoes.

Make traps for mosquitoes in the form of boxes that can be easily closed. Line them with black or dark blue cloth, to which these insects will be attracted.

A freshly cut sprig of pennyroyal placed in the room will keep away mosquitoes.

Moths

Clean garments before storing, and wrap them in linen with lumps of camphor to protect them from moths.

Combine cloves, lavender, tansy, and wormwood as a substitute for camphor to discourage moths.

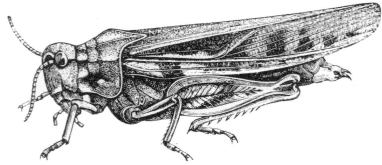

To protect clothes from moths, hang bunches of woodruff in closets. The herb will also serve to scent the linens.

Steep walnut leaves in cold water for 2 hours. Bring gently to a boil and continue boiling for 2 minutes. Then allow the leaves to steep for 15 minutes. Wash cupboards with this solution, and moths will stay away.

As protection against moths place small muslin bags filled with cedar shavings or camphorwood shavings among the clothing, or sprinkle the clothes with allspice berries.

Hang sachets of dried lemon peel inside cupboards and closets to keep moths away.

To safely store fur or hair wraps against moths, add a quantity of black pepper to powdered camphor.

Thoroughly mix 1 dram of flour of hops, 4 ounces of cedar sawdust, 2 ounces of Scotch snuff, and 1 ounce each of black pepper and powdered gum camphor. When scattered among stored woolens and furs, it will keep moths away.

Grind the following to a fine powder: 3 ounces of orrisroot and ½ ounce each of tanguine leaves, caraway seeds, cinnamon, cloves, mace, and nutmeg. Blend them thoroughly, and put the powdered mixture into small cloth bags. Place these among clothing to protect them from moths.

Sprinkle salt around the edges and over the entire surface of the rug while sweeping as a preventive against moths.

Rats

Put powdered potash near the holes of rats. It will encourage them to go elsewhere.

To exterminate rats, mix 2½ ounces of carbonate of barites with 1 pound of grease. Since this mixture produces intense thirst, put some water close by. (It is a deadly poison; be sure all other animals are kept away from it.)

Spread slices of bread and butter, and sprinkle them with arsenic and sugar. Press the arsenic and sugar into the bread with a knife to prevent their falling off. Cut the bread into small squares, and put them in rat holes. As soon as some rats begin to die, others will depart.

Lure rats to one particular spot by leaving quantities of cheese there for some days. When they are accustomed to gathering at this place, affix a piece of cheese to a fishhook suspended about 12 inches from the floor. The first rat to leap at it will be left hanging; his example will put the other rodents to flight.

Mix well equal amounts of unslaked powdered lime and rye meal. Put this on pieces of board where rats are most frequently seen.

Place containers of water close by. When they have eaten the mixture, thirst will drive them to the water, which slakes the lime. The resulting gas will kill them.

Add 2 parts of bruised squills (squill is the dried bulb of a plant belonging to the lily family) and 3 parts of chopped bacon to enough meal to make a firm mass. Form into small cakes and bake. Put them about the premises as food to exterminate rats. It is thought that the action of the squills is responsible for their death.

Using a piece of lead pipe as a conduit, introduce 2 ounces of sulphite of potassium into holes occupied by rats outside the house.

Roaches

Place shallow pans or fruit jar lids containing powdered borax in dark corners of the house, especially around the kitchen sink and cabinets. Replace with fresh borax once a week. Do not allow any food waste or pet food to accumulate in infested areas.

Silverfish

Mix boric acid and sugar. Sprinkle it in areas affected by silverfish.

Slugs and Snails

Pour several inches of stale beer into a shallow vessel. Place it where slugs and snails are damaging garden plants. These pests will be attracted to the beer and drown.

Hair Care

Shampoos and After-Shampoo Rinse
Old-Time Shampoo

Prepare a shampoo by dissolving 1 ounce of salts of tartar in 2½ cups of soft water. To this add 4 ounces of bay rum and 1 ounce of Castile soap shavings. The salts of tartar will remove dandruff; the bay rum will cut oil and act as a preservative for the shampoo; and the soap will cleanse scalp and hair.

Rosemary-Lavender Shampoo

1 cup rosemary leaves
½ ounce lavender oil
⅛ ounce Castile soap

Sprinkle 1 cup rosemary leaves into a vessel holding 4 cups of water; simmer for fifteen minutes. Strain the contents, returning the liquid to the vessel. Put in the soap; heat until dissolved. Take the pot from the stove, and add the lavender oil, beating it in until well blended. Bottle for use.

Natural Shampoo Rinse

Churn the following ingredients in a blender:

1 ounce olive oil
1 egg
1 tablespoon lemon juice
½ teaspoon apple cider vinegar

Wash your hair with this natural shampoo. Rinse.

After-Shampoo Rinse

Steep 2 teaspoons of dried nettles in

boiling water. When the solution is lukewarm, strain it for use as the final rinse after shampooing your hair.

Natural Hair Dyes and Styling Products
Blond

To lighten blond hair that has begun to darken, prepare a safe vegetable rinse. Put ½ cup of chopped rhubarb roots into 3 cups of water. Leave the saucepan uncovered, and simmer its contents for thirty minutes. Steep overnight; then strain the liquid.

Towel dry the freshly shampooed hair. Pour the plant bleach through it several times, and squeeze out the excess liquid. Drying your hair in the sun will heighten its color.

Light Brown

If gray or white hair doesn't become you, mix the following formula to achieve a light-brown color: In separate saucepans, boil onionskins and black walnut skins in enough water to cover them. Combine the resulting juices, using ¼ onionskin juice to ¾ walnut-skin juice. When a deeper shade of brown is desired, use more walnut juice; for a redder color, add more onion juice.

An old-time treatment for coloring gray hair light shades of brown is tag alder bark. It can be purchased from botanical supply houses. Simmer 2 ounces of the chips in 1 quart of water for sixty minutes. When the liquid cools, strain it.

Use the whole quart to shampoo and rinse your hair. Usually, you will need to apply the coloring once a week for a few weeks before desired results are apparent.

Dark Brown

Gather black walnuts during the summer while the hulls are still soft and green. Pry the hulls from the nuts, and press their juice into a jar. Wear rubber gloves to prevent staining your hands. If a walnut tree doesn't grow close by, the hulls can be purchased at health food stores or herbalist shops.

Stir in a small amount of powdered cloves and a little purified alcohol. Close the jar, and let the mixture steep for a week. Occasionally shake it.

At the end of a week, pour the jar's contents through porous cloth to filter out any solid particles. Bottle the dye, and add a bit of salt as a preservative. Store it in a cool place.

Wear rubber gloves to avoid staining hands and scalp. Apply this harmless dye to the hair only.

Black

Blend the juice of green walnut hulls with neat's-foot oil. Add one part of oil to four parts of juice. For very oily hair, reduce the amount of oil a bit; for exceptionally dry hair, add a little more oil.

Natural Hair Spray

Chop a whole lemon. Put the pieces in a saucepan and cover them with hot water. Boil the mixture until the liquid is reduced to one half. Let it cool; then squeeze the lemon and liquid through cheesecloth. If the resulting lemon solution is too thick, mix in a little water. Preserve the hair spray by adding lavender water or cologne. You may prefer to prepare a smaller amount at one time, using half a lemon, and to eliminate the need for a preservative by storing the grooming aid in the refrigerator.

To use, lightly spray it on your hair from a pump-valve bottle.

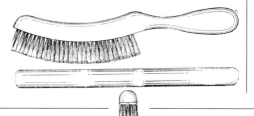

Hair Tonic

Into 1 pint of good alcohol put 4 ounces of oil of sweet almonds, 2 drams of oil of bergamot, and 1 dram of oil of citronella. Then add 8 ounces of rye whiskey, 4 ounces of aqua ammonia, and ½ ounce of gum camphor. Mix well. Shake before using as an excellent hair tonic.

Pomade

Melt 1 ounce of spermaceti in 4 ounces of oil of sweet almonds. When it is cool, perfume it by stirring in oil of neroli (the oil of orange blossoms) or oil of lemongrass. Put the pomade in a large-mouthed bottle for easy access by the fingers. Keep it corked. It is a fine pomade for hair or for chapped hands and lips.

Skin Care

Skin Lotions and Paste
Almond Milk

Shell enough sweet almonds to amount to an ounce. Put them in a strainer, and dip it first in boiling water, then in cold to blanch the nuts. Slip off their skins.

After drying the almonds, reduce them to a powder with mortar and pestle. (A bowl and old china doorknob can substitute for the mortar and pestle.) To achieve speedier results, first grind the nuts in your blender at its highest speed. Then pour the resultant coarse powder into your mortar to further refine the powder, or you can pour it on a piece of clean muslin, producing the desired fine powder with a rolling pin.

Return the powder to a bowl or mortar, and blend in, several drops at a time, 1 cup of distilled water. Grind the almond powder until a milky, smooth liquid forms. Strain it through cheesecloth to eliminate any coarse particles. Bottle for use.

Almond milk has been used for generations to smooth and protect the complexion.

Almond Complexion Paste

Crush 4 ounces of bleached sweet almonds with a rolling pin. Then pulverize them in a marble or earthenware mortar. Almonds may more easily be reduced to paste in a mortar by moistening them with rose water before grinding with a pestle.

Or the almonds may be heated in a saucepan of water until they become a granular mass, similar to cooked oatmeal.

Now add one egg white and equal portions of alcohol and rose water to make a smooth paste.

Sweet almonds contain about 50 percent almond oil. The oil is a gentle emollient that softens and feeds the skin.

CUCUMBER

BOSTON PICKLING

CARD SEED.CO.

· FREDONIA, N.Y. ·

Cucumber Milk

Finely mince one cucumber. Cover it with ⅓ cup of boiling water in a saucepan. Put on the lid, and simmer the contents for thirty minutes, using minimal heat.

Strain the mixture into a bowl, and add tincture of benzoin in drops until the liquid takes on a milky appearance. Add ⅓ cup of boiling water. Put the lotion in a small jar. Close it securely, and shake the contents to blend them thoroughly.

Cucumber milk provides a cooling, soothing lotion for various skin conditions.

Honey-Whey Lotion

Beat ½ teaspoon of rose water into 1 teaspoon of whey. Continue beating until the whey dissolves into the rose water. Stir in 1 teaspoon of honey. Thoroughly blend the mixture.

Apply this soothing facial lotion to troubled skin, leaving it on for ½ hour. Then wash it off with tepid water followed by a cold rinse.

Watercress Lotion

Wash a handful of cress. Simmer it for ten minutes in 2 cups of water. Strain the solution into a bottle.

To smooth rough skin, bathe the face with this soothing lotion. Allow it to dry; rinse with warm water followed by cool.

Lettuce Lotion

Remove the deep green outer leaves from a head of any type of lettuce but the iceberg variety. Wash them well. Put the leaves in a saucepan (do not use an aluminum one). Pour in enough boiling water to cover them. Then put on the lid, and let the contents simmer for about forty minutes.

Beat the leaves in the water, and strain the liquid into a jar. Add several drops of tincture of benzoin. After the addition of each drop, beat the liquid to blend it thoroughly. The lotion will now have a milky appearance.

Apply this cooling facial lotion to help your skin retain moisture.

Sesame Milk

Ladies of an earlier era found that sesame seed milk, applied externally, could soften, nourish, and cleanse their skin. Today, used as a substitute for commercial suntan oil, it can also help to protect the skin from burning or too rapid tanning.

Make this skin aid by grinding one handful of sesame seeds in your blender. Add sufficient water to cover them, and blend for about sixty seconds. Strain the resulting milk into an appropriate container.

Use it to revitalize your complexion or for overall body care. When you wish to remove the milk, rinse your skin with warm water, followed by cool. Blot dry.

Since a little of the sesame seed milk goes a long way, it is not an extravagance. Keep it in the refrigerator.

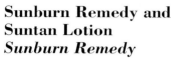

Sunburn Remedy and Suntan Lotion

Sunburn Remedy

Whip one egg white; then beat in 1 teaspoon of castor oil until the mixture is well blended.

Apply it to sunburned areas on face and body.

Suntan Lotion

Beat one egg yolk until it becomes lemon-colored. Gradually beat in 8 ounces of vegetable oil. Whip until thick. Add 1 tablespoon of vinegar and 1 tablespoon of wheat germ. Thoroughly beat the mixture.

Apply the preparation to all skin areas that will be exposed to sunshine. This speeds the tanning process, reducing the time necessary to acquire a tan and thus limiting exposure to ultraviolet rays.

Mouth Care

Preparation for Chapped Lips

Melt 1 ounce of spermeceti and 2 ounces of beeswax in a glass double boiler (a glass bowl set in a saucepan of hot water will also do). Keep the heat very low. Add ¼ cup of honey, and blend it in well. Slowly pour in ½ cup of sweet almond oil.

Take the upper part of the double boiler from the stove, and stir the contents until cool. Before the mixture solidifies, pour it into a small, shallow jar and put on the lid.

Use this preparation as a remedy for chapped lips.

Toothpowders and Paste

Charcoal-Sage Tooth Powder

Scrape the charcoal from burnt toast, and crush it to fine powder. Reduce an equal amount of dried sage leaves to a powder. Blend both ingredients well.

Dip a moistened toothbrush in the mixture to clean teeth.

Soda-Salt Tooth Powder

Make an effective tooth powder by mixing well baking soda and salt, in a proportion of three parts to one. If you prefer flavored tooth powder, add several drops of wintergreen or peppermint oil. Keep the compound in a small-mouthed container.

Toothpaste

To make toothpaste, add 3 teaspoons of glycerin and about 15 drops of some flavoring (cinnamon, peppermint, wintergreen, etc.) to each 4 ounces of homemade tooth powder. Blend the ingredients thoroughly in a bowl, and then add only enough water to turn the mixture into paste form. Spoon the toothpaste into a plastic squeeze bottle for use.

Bath Enhancers

Old-Fashioned Beauty Bath

1 pound barley
1 pound bran
1 pound oatmeal
1 pound brown rice
½ pound bay leaves
½ pound dried lavender
    flowers
Boil all of these ingredients in 4 quarts of rainwater for sixty minutes. Then strain the mixture.

Use 2 quarts of the liquid for each tub of bath water. An extra rinse after this herbal bath is unnecessary and would deprive you of some of its benefits. Follow it with a vigorous towel drying.

Bubble Bath

Make effervescent salts for your bath by mixing well these materials: 4 tablespoons of cornstarch, 15 tablespoons of cream of tartar, and 18 tablespoons of bicarbonate of soda. You may want to add several drops of water-soluble perfume.

About 2 tablespoons of the mixture will give you a tub full of bubbles. Store it in a tightly closed glass or metal container.

Bath Vinegars

Put 1 cup of some fragrant plant material—lavender flowers, rose petals, violet leaves and blossoms, etc.—or a combination of your choice in a 1-pint jar. Heat 8 ounces of white vinegar until it just begins to boil. Pour it into the

jar and put on the lid. Then let it stand for two weeks, shaking it several times each day. After two weeks, strain the contents and bottle in attractive containers.

For a spicy bath vinegar, try blending ½ cup of lavender, ½ cup of dried rosemary, a pinch of sage, and 3 teaspoons of bruised, whole cloves.

One cup of perfumed bath vinegar will scent your bath water and leave your body clean, refreshed, and free of soap film.

Afterbath Powder

You will need a shoe box, 2 ounces of orrisroot powder, and a 1-pound box of cornstarch. Mix the orrisroot and cornstarch. Line the box with aluminum foil. Put in the powdered mixture, and directly over it lay a section of cheesecloth somewhat bigger than the bottom of the box.

Collect fragrant, fresh materials: bark, blossoms, flower petals, leaves, roots, seeds, and stems. Shake them lightly to remove any moisture, and place them right on the piece of cheesecloth. Cover the box snugly. Every two or three days, examine the plants for mold. If any are so affected, discard them. Whenever you find new petals or other aromatic materials, put them in the mix. Continue adding to the box in this way, occasionally stirring its contents. The orrisroot will absorb and hold the combined fragrances.

When a pleasing scent is achieved, take out the plant material. Allow the powder to dry if it has soaked up any moisture. Then package it in attractive containers, and close them tightly.

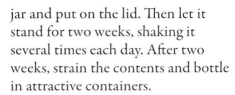

Hand Care

Fingernail Paste

  1½ ounces spermaceti
  ¼ ounce white wax
  2 ounces alkanet root
    (powdered)
  12 ounces oil of sweet almond
  ½ teaspoon rose oil

Melt the spermaceti and the wax in the top portion of a double boiler. Mix in the alkanet root and almond oil. Beat the ingredients until well blended. As the mixture is cooling, stir in the rose oil.

For best results, buff clean, unpolished nails with an old-fashioned chamois buffer before applying the rose paste. Then rub in the paste, and gently buff again to develop a rosy sheen. Daily treatment will increase the health, luster, and beauty of your nails.

Hand Paste

An easily prepared paste to soften hands requires these ingredients:
  2 egg yolks
  ¼ pound honey
  ¼ pound sweet almond oil
  2 ounces blanched almond meal

Beat together the egg yolks and honey until a smooth paste is formed. As you continue to beat the mixture, gradually add the sweet almond oil. Then slowly mix in the almond meal. Store the unused portion in the refrigerator.

Hand Lotion

Warm 4 ounces of honey in a double boiler. Thoroughly blend in 8 ounces of lanolin. Take the pot from the stove, and allow the contents to cool somewhat. Then beat in 4 ounces of sweet almond oil.

Bottle the preparation, and use it for good hand care.

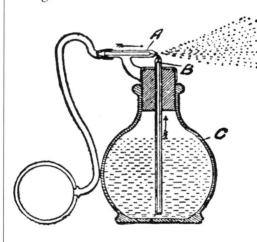

Scents and Salts

Toilet Water

Long ago the famous mineral baths of Budapest found favor with the Queen of Hungary. The Queen herself was renowned for a perfumed toilet water she had concocted for use after bathing. This preparation, known as Hungary Water, has been passed down from mothers to daughters for generations.

To prepare old-fashioned Hungary Water, put 1 dram (¹⁄₁₆ ounce) of essence of ambergris and ½ ounce of oil of rosemary into a pint jar. Add 2 cups of deodorized 95 percent alcohol. Close the jar tightly and shake thoroughly. Open it and allow to stand for twenty-four hours. Again close the jar tightly and let stand for six weeks, shaking it every five days. Transfer the contents to a suitable tightly stoppered bottle for use.

Solid Perfume

Melt 2 ounces of beeswax chips in the top of a double boiler. Using a wire whisk, slowly blend in ¼ cup of sweet almond oil. As you continue stirring, add 2 tablespoons of distilled water. Take the pot from the stove. Add 8 dropperfuls of your favorite cologne, and blend thoroughly with the whisk.

Pour the mixture, while still warm, into 4-ounce pimento jars or other suitable small containers that can be closed tightly. You may divide this recipe in half, perfuming each portion with a different scent.

Pomanders

Scent your linen and clothes closets with pomanders. To make them you will need large, well-shaped oranges, a few boxes of whole cloves, ground cinnamon, a roll of ¼-inch-wide cellophane tape, colored ribbon, a nutpick, and some silver foil.

Let the fruit dry for several weeks. Then fasten a strip of cellophane tape around the center of each orange. With the nutpick, pierce holes in the skin about ¼ inch apart, avoiding the tape. (Since the oranges will shrink more as they continue to dry, a small space should remain between each hole.) Push a clove into each hole. Now dust the oranges lightly with powdered cinnamon. You may use ground allspice or orrisroot for dusting, if you prefer. Wrap them in silver foil, and store them in a dry spot for about seven weeks.

Take the pomanders from the foil, remove the tape, and substitute a length of bright ribbon, tied in a bow, for hanging them in your closets.

Spiced Potpourri

Mix ½ ounce of each of the following in a bowl: allspice, borax, ground cinnamon, whole cloves, ground nutmeg, and ground orrisroot. Blend a cupful of lemon, orange, or tangerine peel with the spices.

Put the spicy mixture into an open china jar, or one with holes in its lid to allow the scent to escape.

Rose Potpourri

On a fair morning, collect unblemished rose petals. Spread them in single layers on paper in a

dry, cool spot. Turn them daily for about two weeks until dry.

Put some of the petals in a glass jar to a depth of two inches, covering them lightly with salt. Continue to alternate layers of petals and salt until the jar is full. Close it tightly. Put it in a dark, cool spot for seven days.

Blend these ingredients: ½ teaspoon of ground cinnamon, ½ teaspoon of ground cloves, ½ teaspoon of ground mace, 1 ounce of orrisroot, 10 drops of oil of bergamot, 20 drops of oil of eucalyptus, and 6 drops of oil of geranium. Mix the petals thoroughly into this blend, and put the mixture back into the jar, closing the lid tightly. After a period of two weeks, the potpourri is ready for use.

Smelling Salts

To make smelling salts, put 8 ounces of true carbonate of ammonia (a volatile salt of lasting pungency) and 1 ounce of oil of lavender (or any other essential oil) in a glass bottle. Close the bottle tightly.

19 | RURAL REMEDIES

When the nearest doctor lived many miles away folks were forced to rely on their own knowledge to treat a wide variety of ailments. Most families had a "doctor book" of some fashion, often handwritten, that contained instructions for home treatment. The treatments and medications were handed down from family to family. This important book often took its place beside the family Bible. Ethel Rogers of South Carolina said years ago that "the Bible shows *how* to live and the doctor book shows how to *live*."

Here are some of the choice home remedies from Ethel's "doctor book" and from others over the country.

(Please note that these "health cures" are intended as a historical reference only. They are not recommended by the editors or publisher of this book.)

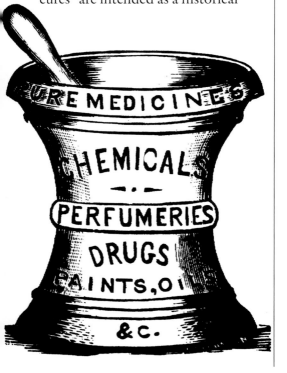

Abscess

Dip a cabbage leaf into hot water and apply to the abscess.

Cut open a fresh fig. Soak it for 1 minute in warm water. Apply it as a poultice to inflamed abscesses and boils.

Alcoholism

Have the patient eat an owl's egg without his knowing what kind of egg it is.

Place a live minnow in his bottle of spirits, and let it die there.

Arthritis

Take a teaspoon of chopped garlic twice a day with water for relief from the pain and swelling of arthritis.

To cure arthritis eat ½ pound of fresh cherries daily.

Asthma

Simmer a bit of skunk cabbage root in ½ cup of hen's grease. Take 1 teaspoon three times each day to relieve asthma symptoms.

For relief of asthma a muskrat skin should be worn over the lungs, the fur side against the body.

Simmer 1 heaping teaspoon of dried, ground okra leaves in 1 quart of hot water until but 1½ pints of liquid remain. Add 1 teaspoon of freshly chopped onion. Cover and let stand until cool. Stir and strain.

Drink equal portions during the day as an asthmatic remedy.

Fasten a live frog on the throat of one suffering from asthma. When the frog dies, the patient will be cured.

Athlete's Foot

To remedy athlete's foot, anoint the feet with whale oil mixed with a little oil of cloves.

Baldness

Blend ½ ounce of castor oil and 5 drops of oil of rosemary into ½ ounce of goose fat. Massage the scalp with this preparation three times daily to combat baldness.

Pound peach kernels, and boil them gently in vinegar until a thick paste forms. Apply three times a day to bald spots on the scalp to regenerate hair growth.

Bed-Wetting

To cure bed-wetting use 1 spoon of corn silk every day to make a tea or in salad.

Make a plaster of vinegar and the root of the herb tormentil. Apply it against the kidneys.

Bleeding

Apply a mixture of flour and salt and wrap with cloth or common paper; or press cobwebs and brown sugar over the cut.

To stop the bleeding from a cut, sprinkle the fungus spore of the puffball on it.

Black tea in powdered form bandaged over a cut will stop the bleeding.

To arrest bleeding and relieve the pain and swelling of a cut, pour lamp oil over it.

Bleeding due to tooth extraction can be checked if the cavity is packed with cotton soaked in alum water.

Blisters

Boil the bark from an oak tree in a small amount of water and apply to blisters.

Blood

To purify the blood take a small glass of the following mixture three times daily: 1 quart of hard cider, ½ ounce of horseradish, 1 ounce of yellow dock.

Combine equal amounts of blueberries, sassafras bark, thyme, and watercress. Make a tea of 1 spoonful of the mixture to 1 cup of hot water. Cover and let stand until cool. Stir and strain. Take 1 cupful four times daily to purify the blood.

Bone Felon

Saturate a piece of turnip in turpentine and apply to the felon.

Breath

To make the breath pleasing, rub the gums with wool coated with honey.

In 1 cup of hot water, steep ⅓ teaspoon each of anise, mint, and rosemary. Cover and allow to stand for 10 minutes. Strain. Rinse the mouth daily with this solution to combat bad breath.

Bronchitis

Mix ½ pint of cider vinegar; ½ pint of water; 1 ounce each of elecampane root, licorice extract, and coltsfoot; and ½ ounce of bloodroot. Steep in a covered pot in a warn place for 5 to 6 hours. Strain and sweeten with honey. Take 1 teaspoonful four times a day for bronchitis.

Simmer 1 teaspoonful of each of the following spices in spirits of turpentine for ½ hour: cinnamon, cloves, mustard, pepper. Strain. Stir ¼ teaspoon of pure, powdered camphor into 1 ounce of the liquid. Blend into 4 ounces of goose grease. Rub on the chest to relieve congestion due to coughs and colds. Cover with flannel.

Bruises

Wash with warm water and anoint with tallow or candle grease.

Apply a paste of butter and chopped parsley to bruises.

Use the skin of a freshly peeled banana to reduce the pain and discoloration of a bruise. Place the inner side of the peel on the bruise and hold in place with wet cold bandages.

Make a brew of the roots of bouncing Bet. Use it in poultice form to relieve the discoloration of a bruised eye.

Treat a bruise by applying brown paper coated with molasses.

Mix 1 part oatmeal and 2 parts of flaxseed, blending in sufficient water to make a thick poultice for bruises.

Burns

The juice from the succulent plant aloe vera applied often is very good. Apply ice directly to burn.

Mix 4 ounces of lard with 1 ounce of powdered wood soot. Apply the mixture to burns and scalds on a dab of cotton.

Honey applied to burns will relieve the pain and prevent blisters from forming.

Thoroughly blend 1 egg yolk with 2 ounces of flaxseed oil. Apply to a burn.

Soak soft linen in cod-liver oil and leave on a burn for 48 hours. Apply fresh oil as needed.

Make a poultice of cold water and oatmeal to benefit a burn.

Mix 2 portions of corn meal with 1 of powdered charcoal. Add milk to make a paste. Use this as a poultice for burns.

Mix the freshly squeezed juice of pokeberries with a little glycerine as an application for burns.

Canker Sores

Several times a day apply ashes from a burned corn cob to canker sores.

Boil 2 tablespoons of dried pomegranate rind in 3 cups of water until the liquid is reduced to 2 cups. Strain and let cool. Use as a mouthwash for canker sores.

Chapped Hands and Lips

Apply castor oil or equal parts of glycerin and lemon juice often to area. Ointment used on cows' teats is a fast cure for chapped hands. Rubbing hands regularly in sheep's wool will work too.

Boil flakes of tragacanth, 1 inch in size, with a few quince seeds. Strain when cool. Thin the solution with some glycerin. Use as a soothing lotion for chapped hands.

To benefit chapped hands, wash them in sugar and water.

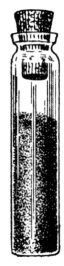

Chicken Pox

Tie bran in a cheesecloth bag. Steep it in boiling water for 2 minutes before applying it to chicken pox sores.

To treat chicken pox externally, apply witch hazel to the sores.

Chilblains

As a cure for chilblains, mix ¼ ounce of each of the following: ammonia, turpentine, olive oil, oil of peppermint. Apply mornings and evenings.

Boil parsnips until soft, and bandage them on affected areas to treat chilblains.

Childbirth

When labor is prolonged in childbirth, blow snuff, held on a goose feather, up the mother's nose. This will induce a sneezing fit, resulting in delivery.

If complications occur during childbirth, give a strong tea of raspberry leaves.

Chills

Mix ginger and pepper in very hot water and drink.

Mix 1 teaspoon of grated jack-in-the-pulpit with milk and sugar. It causes sweating and will cure chills or a cold.

Make a tea of smartweed. Drink it very hot. Go to bed and keep well covered when suffering from chills.

Choking

Into a cup break an egg. Have the choking patient swallow it whole.

When something is stuck in the throat causing choking, blow forcefully into the sufferer's ear.

Colds and Flu

Mix and drink a mixture of cinnamon, sage, and bay leaves, and add a little lemon juice. Drink warm. Drink hot ginger tea freely. Take a dose of quinine every six hours. Drink juice of citrus fruits often.

As a head-cold remedy, put 2 drops of spirits of camphor on a sugar cube; dissolve it in ½ glass of water. A teaspoonful should be taken every 2 hours. Grease the nostrils with a mixture of lard, mutton suet, and sweet oil.

Eating a hot roasted onion before retiring can be helpful in curing a cold.

To overcome a cold with its accompanying miseries of sore throat and fever, drink a tea made from the white flowers of the elderberry shrub.

To relieve congestion due to a cold, rub throat and chest with skunk's oil.

Colic

Put sliced green walnuts into enough whiskey to cover them. Let them soak for ten days. Take 1 teaspoonful of the liquid every ½ hour as a remedy for bilious colic.

To cure colic in children, give a dose of 1 drop of camphor in 1 teaspoon of water.

Constipation

Eat freely of preserves, drink plenty of water; eat garlic.

Stir 2 teaspoons of flaxseed into 1 cup of cold water. Allow to stand for ½ hour. Drink both seeds and liquid to relieve constipation.

Boil for 15 minutes 2 ounces each of barley, figs, and raisins. Put in ½ ounce of licorice root and let steep. Allow to cool, strain out the water, and mash together. Take a dose of 4 ounces, night and morning, as a laxative.

Convalescence

A nourishing drink for those convalescing is barley coffee. Roast barley until brown. Boil 1 tablespoon of it in 2 cups of water for 5 minutes. Strain. If desired, add a bit of sugar.

Put 1 tablespoon of grated garlic into ⅔ glass of red wine. Take 1 teaspoonful five times daily as a strengthening tonic following illness.

Corns

To remove corns easily, bind on bread soaked in vinegar. Renew the application mornings and evenings.

Burn willow bark. Mix the ashes with vinegar and apply to the corn.

Mix and warm 1 teaspoon of brown sugar, 1 teaspoon of pine tar, and 1 teaspoon of saltpeter. Apply to corns on a plaster.

Insert the toe in a lemon. Keep it on during the night. The corn can then be removed with ease. If not, repeat the procedure.

Cough

Make a tea of wild cherry bark; mix with honey. Take a teaspoonful as needed.

For a cough, chop 2 large turnip roots into small pieces, and boil them in 1 quart of water. Cool and strain the liquid. Add an amount of honey equal to whatever portion is taken.

Simmer ⅜ ounce of senna leaf, ⅜ ounce of licorice root, and 1 ounce of anise seed in 2 cups of water until but 1 cup of liquid remains. Strain and cool. Add

½ pint of syrup. Take when necessary to relieve a cough.

Beat together 3 egg yolks, 3 tablespoons of honey, and 1 teaspoon of pine tar, adding 2 ounces of wine. Take 1 teaspoonful three times daily before meals as a cough remedy.

Scoop out a hollow in the middle of a good-sized beet; fill it with honey. Bake. Eat a little when needed to relieve a cough.

Chew a piece of ginger root, swallowing the juice to benefit a cough.

Mix 1 teaspoon of oil of sesame and 1 teaspoon of honey in 1 cup of warm milk. Slowly sip the beverage to relieve a cough.

Cramps

Cramps in neck or legs can be relieved by an application of whiskey and red pepper.

To 1 gallon of denatured alcohol add 1 ounce of monarda oil, 1 ounce of cajaput oil, 1 ounce of oil of thyme, ½ ounce of oil of peppermint, and 1 ounce of camphor gum. Shake thoroughly. Allow to stand for 24 hours. This is a good rub for cramps in the muscles of men or animals.

Croup

Administer 1 teaspoon of goose oil and one teaspoon of molasses to a child suffering from croup.

Boil pig's feet in a vessel of water. Allow to stand overnight. Skim off the fat, put it in a pot, and boil until all moisture has

evaporated. To cure croup, give a teaspoonful every ¼ hour and also rub well on throat and chest.

Cuts and Scratches

Rub with a sliced clove of garlic or apply raw honey.

Crush the leaves of the blackberry bush between your fingers, and rub them on a scratch to immediately check the bleeding.

Remove the inside skin, or coating, from the shell of an uncooked egg. Place its moist side on a cut to promote healing with no scarring.

Bathe the cut in a weak solution of water and baking soda. Sprinkle it, while still wet, with black pepper.

Dandruff

Dissolve 1 ounce of borax in 1 pint of water. Wash the head with this mixture once a week to prevent dandruff.

To cure dandruff make a mixture of 1 ounce of water, 2 ounces of bay rum, 2 ounces of glycerine, and 2½ ounces of tincture of cantharides. Rub this mixture into the scalp once a day.

Make a tea from dried peach leaves and apply to the scalp as a treatment for dandruff.

Deafness

To cure deafness, drop a mixture of onion juice and ant eggs into the ear.

Combine ½ ounce of olive oil, 15 drops of sassafras oil, and 1½ drams of glycerin. Put a few drops into the ear several times a day to reduce excess wax accumulation that is causing deafness.

Melt hedgehog fat, and drop a little into the ear to dissolve hard earwax that can cause temporary deafness.

Diarrhea

Brown a little flour over the fire, add two teaspoonfuls of vinegar and one teaspoonful of salt, mix and drink. Mixing a tablespoonful of warm vinegar and a teaspoonful of salt will cure most severe cases. Do not eat fruit. A hot drink of ginger tea is often good. Repeat any of the above every few hours. Take sips of water often.

For mild diarrhea eat burned rhubarb.

Combine 3 tablespoons of vinegar with the same amount of hardwood ashes. Cover with hot water. Stir and allow to settle. Take 1 teaspoonful of the solution every now and then to check diarrhea.

Earache

A piece of cotton sprinkled with pepper and moistened with oil or fat will give almost instant relief.

Wash with warm water. Place small piece of garlic in ear.

To alleviate the pain of an earache that is not too severe, blow pipe or cigarette smoke into the ear.

For a very painful earache, drop mutton juice, as hot as can be tolerated, into the ear.

Place a brass button in the mouth of one suffering from an earache. Surprise him by discharging a gun at his back. This will cure the pain.

Eye Inflammation

Bind on hot tea leaves or raw fresh meat, leave on for several hours then wash well with warm water.

Mix 3 whole eggs with 4 cups of cold rainwater. Bring to a boil, stirring frequently. Add ½ ounce of zinc sulfate and boil for 2 minutes more. Remove from heat. Take the curd that forms at the bottom of the vessel and apply it to inflamed eyes, using a bandage. Filter the liquid through cloth and use as an excellent eyewash.

To soothe sore eyes, boil black mesquite gum. Dilute the liquid and apply to afflicted areas.

Steep ⅛ teaspoon of eyebright and ⅛ teaspoon of fennel in 8 ounces of hot boiled water. Stir and strain through cloth. Use as an eyewash every 3 hours or when required.

Chew ground ivy leaves, and apply the pulp to an inflamed eye.

Feet

To combat offensive odor of the feet, soak them in water in which the green bark of oak has been boiled.

For excessive perspiration of the feet, put bran or oatmeal into the socks.

Make a powder of equal amounts of

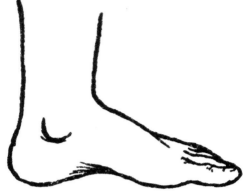

powdered starch; fuller's earth, and powdered zinc. Sprinkle this mixture in the socks as a remedy for perspiring feet.

Fever

Pound horseradish leaves until they are of the consistency of pulp. Apply them as a poultice to the soles of the feet to draw out fever.

Simmer 4 cups of water containing a handful of cockleburs until 2 cups of liquid remain. Drink a small glassful of the solution every ½ hour until the fever dissipates.

Fits

To arrest fits, throw a teaspoonful of salt as far back into the mouth as possible.

Relieve fits by splashing water on the patient's hands and face. Plunging the feet into cold water will prove particularly beneficial.

Flatulence

To alleviate wind in the stomach, chew saffron flowers and swallow the juice.

Into 2 cups of boiling water put 1 teaspoon of dried orange or lemon peel, 1 teaspoon of coriander, and 1 teaspoon of gentian. Simmer for 10 minutes, strain when cool, and reserve the liquid. Slowly sip a small glassful three to four times a day to relieve flatulence.

Frozen Ears, Fingers, Nose, Etc.

Never rub snow on these tender members. Use warmth of hand to rub, thaw, and restore circulation. Dip affected areas in cold water, then add warm water gradually until water reaches blood heat, and massage area.

Hair

Check hair from falling by washing the head each day with a strong sage tea. For best results use pure spring water.

To make hair thicker, massage the juice of water cress into the scalp.

Hay Fever

Use the following mixture as a snuff to cure hay fever: 10 grains of ammonium carbonate, 15 grains of capsicum, 20 grains of sodium borate.

Steep several rose petals in a cup of hot water. Filter the liquid. To relieve eye irritation due to hay fever, apply 1 or 2 drops to each eye five times a day.

Crush fresh milkweed in cheesecloth, and inhale it to combat hay fever.

Mix the leaves and flowers of goldenrod and ragweed. Put ½ ounce of the herb mixture in 2 cups of boiling water and allow to steep for 10 minutes. Drink a small glassful four times a day to cure hay fever.

Headache

Inhale fumes of boiling vinegar.

Moisten a cloth with camphor spirits. Sprinkle black pepper on it and apply to the forehead to relieve a headache.

Apply the fresh leaves of burdock or the fresh roots of pokeweed to the bottoms of the feet to assuage a headache.

Mix 3 ounces of Castile soap, 1 ounce of camphor, and 2 ounces of ammonia in 2 quarts of alcohol. Bathe the forehead with this solution to relieve a sick headache.

To dispel a headache, apply a poultice of grated uncooked potato to the forehead.

For migraine headache, swallow a tablespoonful of honey.

Hemorrhoids

Simmer 2 parts of fresh butter with 1 part of tobacco. Strain, and use as a poultice three times daily to relieve inflamed hemorrhoids.

Remove the outer shell of 4 fresh horse chestnuts. Slice the chestnuts fine. Place them in a tin cup and cover with melted lard. Allow to steep for 1 hour in a warm place. Strain and squeeze out the lard. Apply the salve, when cool, twice daily to hemorrhoids.

Mix equal amounts of horsemint oil, oil of fireweed, and pumpkin-seed oil. Apply twice a day to hemorrhoids.

Hiccups

Eat a tablespoonful of peanut butter.

Make a mint tea, adding 5 drops of oil of amber. Drink the brew every 10 minutes until the hiccups are arrested.

To cure hiccups, eat a sugar cube that has been dunked in vinegar.

Work the jaws as though chewing food while pressing the fingers in the ears. This procedure will speedily cure hiccups.

High Blood Pressure

With mortar and pestle crush 2 teaspoons of dried watermelon seeds. Steep them for 1 hour in 1 cup of hot water. Stir and strain out the seeds. To relieve high blood pressure, drink 1 cupful four times each day.

Forsake salty foods and partake of honey.

Hives

Bathe with rubbing alcohol and follow with a strong solution of baking soda and water over the affected area. Do not drink anything cold.

Cure hives by rubbing them with buckwheat flour.

Make a tea of ground ivy, using 1 teaspoon of the herb to 1 cup of boiling water. Take 1 cupful three times daily to cure hives.

Hoarseness

Dry nettle roots in the oven. Powder, and add them to the same amount of molasses. A dose of 1 teaspoon three times a day will cure hoarseness.

Drink milk and red pepper every

so often, and hoarseness will disappear.

Hunger

To allay the feeling of hunger, chew beechnut leaves.

Chewing elm leaves will quickly dissipate the sensation of hunger.

Indigestion

Stir 1 teaspoon of each of the following into 1 cup of hot water: fennel seeds, peppermint, caraway seeds, spearmint. Cover and allow to stand for 10 minutes. Mix and strain. Take 1 cupful four times a day to counteract excess stomach acid and resulting indigestion.

To prevent indigestion, take 1 teaspoon of whole white mustard seeds before meals.

Take 1 ounce of Peruvian bark and the same amount of gentian root and ½ ounce each of coriander seed and orange peel. Steep them in 4 cups of brandy. Allow to stand for five days. An hour before eating take 1 teaspoonful in a wineglass of water to prevent indigestion.

Stir ¼ teaspoon of ground cinnamon into 1 cup of hot water. Cover for 15 minutes and stir again. Strain. Take 1 tablespoonful for chronic indigestion. Repeat if necessary.

Take an infusion of horehound to remedy stomach distress.

Dry and powder peach leaves. Mix 1 teaspoon of this powder and

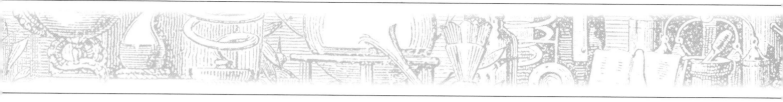

the same amount of chalk into a glass of hot water. Take after meals to prevent stomach upset.

Ingrown Toenail

Apply mutton tallow to an ingrown toenail for several days. The nail can then be cut without harm.

Cut a notch in the center of the toenail's edge. In attempting to grow together, the nail will pull away from the skin on either side, providing relief from the pain and swelling of ingrown toenail.

Insect Bites

Apply common mud, a slice of onion, garlic juice, lemon juice, baking soda, tobacco, or honey.

Dissolve 1 heaping teaspoonful of sodium bicarbonate in 1 cup of cold vinegar. Apply as a compress to insect bites.

Apply a poultice of plantain leaves to insect bites.

Insomnia

Drink a glass of warm milk; or mix equal parts of apple cider vinegar and honey, take two teaspoonsful each hour.

Make a medicinal tea of ¼ teaspoon of celery seed, ¼ teaspoon of valerian, ½ teaspoon of catnip, and ½ teaspoon of skullcap in 4 ounces of hot water. Keep the brew covered for 10 minutes. Mix and strain. Take the tea 1 hour before retiring.

To overcome sleeplessness eat a dish of baked onions before retiring.

Mix lettuce juice with oil of roses and apply to the forehead and temples to induce sleep.

Irritable Infant

Onion tea will cure a baby of fretfulness.

To arrest postweaning restlessness, put molasses on the baby's hands. Give him chicken feathers to hold. During repeated attempts to remove them from first one hand and then the other, the babe will tire and fall asleep.

Itching

Combat itching by bathing with hot water and soap, scrubbing with a corn cob. Follow this with an application of sulfur and lard.

In a small amount of alcohol, dissolve ½ teaspoon of pure camphor. Add this to 4 ounces of calamine lotion and mix. Shake the solution thoroughly before applying to skin afflicted with itching.

A blend of lard and the powdered root of pokeweed makes a good salve for itching.

Apply mutton tallow to skin affected by itching.

Jaundice

Chop fine a handful of black alder. Boil it in 4 cups of old cider. Allow to cool. Drink it liberally to cure jaundice.

Kidney Disorders

Steep fresh yellow corn silk, cut fine, in 1 cup of hot water. Cover, let stand until cold, and strain. Take 1 cupful four times each day for kidney complaints.

Mix artichoke juice with an equal amount of white wine to increase the discharge of urine.

Steep strawberry and mullein leaves with cleavers in water. Drink the solution to assuage kidney ailments.

Liver Ailments

Mix pure olive oil and lemon juice in warm water and drink once each day.

Lockjaw

To treat lockjaw, place moistened tobacco on the patient's stomach. Remove immediately when a cure is affected.

Measles

Steep ⅓ teaspoon each of catnip, marjoram, and yarrow, adding a pinch of marigold or saffron. Give the warm tea each hour to one afflicted with measles to reduce the fever.

Take a tea of elderberry flowers as a remedy for measles.

Mosquito Bites

Apply ammonia, camphor, tar soap, or crushed pennyroyal weed.

Mustache

For a fine, healthy mustache, apply a mixture of the following:
5 drops of oil of bergamot,
7 drops of tincture of cantharides,
½ ounce of simple cerate.

Nervousness

Chew snakeroot or drink a tea made from dandelion leaf, passion flower, plantain leaf, peppermint, or snakeroot.

Combine equal portions of the following: wood betony, root of valerian, skullcap herb, and mistletoe. Boil 1 ounce of this mixture in 2 cups of water for 5 minutes. Allow to cool, and strain. Take a small glassful three times daily for nervousness.

Nervous Stomach

Drink bottled mineral water or make your own mineral water by buying some powdered slaked lime (be sure it is slaked lime) at the drugstore. Add one teaspoonful to one quart water. Shake well. Put in refrigerator and leave until the lime has settled to the bottom of the jar. Pour off the clear, top liquid and drink a few swallows for stomach relief.

Nettle Sting

Rub the area that has been pricked by nettles with mint, sage leaves, or rosemary.

Neuralgia

In 2 cups of boiling water, steep 1 ounce of burdock seeds for 1 hour. Strain. Take 1 tablespoonful before meals and retiring to relieve neuralgia.

Bind wilted horseradish leaves on the area affected by pain of neuralgia.

Nosebleed

To stop bleeding from the nose, chew paper.

Blood flow from the nose can be stopped by insertion into the nostrils of wool saturated with rose oil.

To arrest nosebleed put grated dried beef into the nostrils.

In cases of nosebleed, soak cotton in nettle juice and insert it into the nostrils.

Overweight

Put 1 teaspoon each of fennel seed and chickweed with ½ teaspoon of sassafras bark, sweet flag root, kelp, and licorice in 1 quart of boiling water. Simmer for 5 minutes. Keep the liquid covered for 15 minutes. Strain. Drink ⅔ cupful, warmed, three times daily to reduce excess weight.

Pain

Sprinkle brown sugar on a pan of burning coals. To alleviate the pain of a wound, hold the injured part over the smoke.

To relieve pain in the back, mix vinegar and beef gall. Apply

the solution to the affected area morning and evening.

Phlegm

Dry the leaves of coltsfoot. Smoke them as you would tobacco to loosen phlegm in the chest.

To remove phlegm from the stomach, make a tea of chicory leaves.

Pleurisy

To cure pleurisy, ingest a tea of catnip or pennyroyal, and then apply a poultice of hot boiled nettles.

Boil 1 ounce of pleurisy root in 2½ cups of water for 10 minutes. Strain. Take a small glassful three times daily to treat pleurisy.

Poison Ivy

Wash area often with a cooling solution of baking soda and water and apply apple cider vinegar, or

squeeze the juice from jimson weed and use as a lotion.

Put 1 tablespoon of carbolic acid and 1 ounce of glycerin in 2 cups of boiling water. Bathe areas affected by poison ivy with this solution.

Apply milk, heavily salted, to skin affected by poison ivy. Allow to dry.

For protection all year from the rash of poison ivy, eat a small amount of either the leaves or roots of the plant at the onset of spring.

Poisoning

Give a strong emetic of warm water, mustard, and salt mixed. Cause vomiting by swallowing small piece of soap or tobacco.

Poultices

Boil grape leaves with barley meal to make a soothing poultice for wounds and inflammations.

Roast pokeweed root in hot ashes. Mash them and use in a poultice for felon.

Thicken yeast with finely powdered elm bark and charcoal. Apply as a poultice to open sores.

Prickly Heat

Dust the skin with browned cornstarch to cure prickly heat.

As a remedy for prickly heat, keep a piece of alum in the pocket.

Add 1 quart of alcohol, 1 ounce of borax in powdered form, and 2 ounces of cologne to 3 quarts of rainwater. Bathe with this

mixture three times daily as a remedy for heat rash.

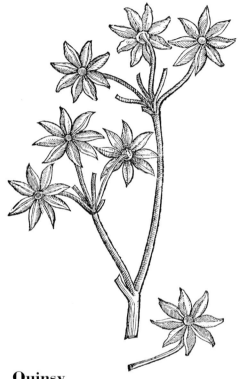

Quinsy

Sprinkle densely with red pepper a rasher of salt pork. Bind it about the throat upon retiring to alleviate quinsy.

A good remedy for tonsillitis is a dose of rattlesnake oil.

Boil 1 quart of water containing 1 tablespoon of tincture of benzoin. Inhale the vapors to soothe tonsillitis.

Rub a combination of turpentine and oil of anise on the throat to relieve the soreness of tonsillitis.

Rheumatism

Powder the following: bloodroot, blue flag root, sweet flag root, prickly ash. Steep in spirits. Take

a dose of from 1 tablespoon to a small glassful three times daily for rheumatism.

Heat a sadiron. Cover the iron with woolen cloth, and moisten it with vinegar. Apply as hot as can be tolerated to parts afflicted with pain of rheumatism.

Put 4 eggs into 2 cups of cider vinegar, dropping in the shells as well. When the vinegar has eaten up the eggs, add 2 cups of turpentine. Bathe on parts affected by rheumatic pain.

Combine 2 cups of bear or coon oil, 2 cups of spirits of turpentine, and 2 cups of spirits of camphor. Rub sore areas with this solution for 25 minutes to relieve the pain of rheumatism.

Simmer 2 ounces of chamomile flowers and 3 ounces of celery seed in 2 quarts of water until the liquid is reduced to 3 pints. Strain. Take 1 small glassful before eating to cure rheumatism.

Steep 1 tablespoon of sulphur and 2 cups of pokeberries in 4 cups of brandy. Let stand for 24 hours. Take 1 tablespoon three times daily as a remedy for rheumatism.

Blend 1 ounce of cream of tartar, 1 ounce of sulfur, ½ ounce of rhubarb, and 1 teaspoon of guaiacum into 2 cups of honey. Stir 1 tablespoon of this into a glass of water and take in the morning and evening.

The miseries of rheumatism can be eased by a massage with goose oil. Follow this with a drink of

calomel mixed with cayenne pepper, gum camphor, and tartarized antimony.

Ringworms

Apply juice from a green walnut hull to area three times each day until ring and redness disappear.

Dissolve 1 teaspoon of borax in 2 ounces of warm cider vinegar. Apply on the scalp to combat ringworm.

Mix vinegar and gunpowder. Apply the paste to ringworm.

Drop a copper coin in vinegar. While it is still wet, place it in the area affected by ringworm.

Wash the root of yellow dock, and chop it into small sections. Simmer in vinegar. Strain. Apply the solution three times daily to cure ringworm.

Scalds

Relieve instantly by using common baking soda applied thickly to wet rags and placed on scalded area. If baking soda is not available flour may be used.

Scalp

Steep ¾ ounce of nettles and ¾ ounce of sage in 2 cups of alcohol for 1 week. Strain, and gradually add 2½ ounces of castor oil. Apply to the scalp to heal irritation.

Scarlet Fever

Steep 1 teaspoon of yarrow, 1 teaspoon of catnip, and ¼ teaspoon of saffron in 1 cup of hot water. Drink 1 cupful each hour to treat scarlet fever.

Scrofula

Cover areas affected by scrofula with codfish skins.

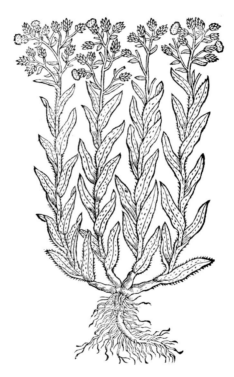

Seasickness

To overcome seasickness, drink great quantities of strong green tea as frequently as possible.

Chew several leaves of sage or mint until they reach the consistency of pulp and no longer have flavor. This is a good remedy for seasickness.

Sinus

To relieve the congestion and pain of sinus trouble, chew honeycomb.

Snake Bite

Incise the snake bite, and apply a mixture of tobacco and salt.

To treat snake bite, cut open a freshly killed chicken and place it on the wound.

Sores

To heal sores apply a poultice of powdered comfrey root.

Boil the following in weak lye: blue vervain, smart weed, wormwood herb. Apply with a feather to sores.

Boil over a low flame for 30 minutes ½ pound of rosin, 1 pound of lard, and 10 ounces of elder bark. Strain and apply to sores.

Sore Breasts

Roast turnips until soft. Mash them with oil of roses. Apply this mixture to sore breasts twice daily and cover them with flannel.

Boil 1 pound each of spikenard root and tobacco and 12 pounds of comfrey root in 3 quarts of lye until nearly dry. Press out the juice, and add beeswax and pitch to it. Simmer over a medium flame. When it becomes salve-like, apply it to sore breasts.

Sore Mouth

Combine ½ teaspoon of tincture of myrrh, ½ teaspoon of borax, and 1 teaspoon of glycerin in sufficient boiled water to equal 1 ounce. Several times a day apply the solution on a camel's hair brush to the inside of the mouth.

Mix the following with honey: burnt alum, burnt leather, powdered sage, roasted egg yolk. Use this mixture to cure a sore mouth.

Sore Throat

Apply fat bacon or pork to outside of throat and hold in place by tying a rag around it. Keep in place until soreness is gone. Swab the throat with diluted tincture of iron. Gargle with warm salt water or apple cider vinegar, repeat often. Hold small piece of garlic in mouth for several minutes, several times during the day.

Combine 1 ounce of honey and 2 teaspoons of borax in 2 cups of hot water. Use while it is yet warm as a gargle for a sore throat.

Boil 2 ounces of apple cider, ½ red pepper pod, and 1 tablespoon each of honey and salt. Add to 1 cup of strong sage tea. Take a teaspoonful when required to relieve a sore throat.

Make a strong brew of equal amounts of hyssop and sage. Add ¼ ounce of borax to each cupful. Gargle often with this solution to ease soreness of the throat.

In 2 cups of water, steep a red pepper. Strain, and add 1 heaping teaspoon each of salt and of powdered alum and ½ cup of vinegar. Gargle with this mixture when necessary to soothe a sore throat.

Spasms of Muscles, Cramps

Eat two teaspoons of honey with each meal.

Speck in Eye

Place flaxseed in eye to absorb particle.

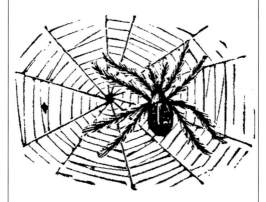

Spider Bite

Combine the beaten white of 1 egg with alum powder. Apply as a poultice to relieve the pain and swelling of a spider's bite.

Treat a spider bite by applying the juice of plantain leaves to the wound. Take 2 ounces of the juice internally.

Splinters

To remove splinters or thorns, apply raw bacon as a poultice.

Mash the freshly picked leaves of marsh mallow. Mix them with niter and apply to splinters and thorns for their easy removal.

Sprains

Mix sea salt and cider vinegar into a paste and apply; or apply Epsom salts with a cloth wet in vinegar.

For 2 hours continually beat a large spoonful of honey and the same amount of salt with 1 egg white. Allow this to stand for 1 hour. Apply to the sprained area the oil which comes from this mixture.

Mix kerosene, cider vinegar, and salt to make a liniment for sprains.

Make a poultice using 2 hen's eggs, 1 ounce of ginger, and 1 teaspoon of salt. Use it on sprains.

Stiff Joints

Simmer 1 pound of hog's grease into which a handful of yellow clover has been dropped. Strain, and add 1 ounce of rattlesnake oil, 10 drops of oil of lavender, and 1 ounce of olive oil. Mix thoroughly. Use it three times daily to massage stiff joints.

Massage stiff joints four times a day with olive oil in which camphor gum has been dissolved.

Stye

Into a small cloth bag, put 1 teaspoon of black tea. Moisten it with boiling water. While the bag is yet warm, place it on the eye during the night. By morning the stye should be gone. Repeat the application if necessary.

Make a poultice of milk and

linseed meal. Apply it warm to a stye. Renew the poultice every 6 hours.

Sunburn

Apply butter or buttermilk, boil tan oak or commercial wet ground tea and apply frequently. Wet dressings of Epsom salts or baking soda also help.

Apply the following ointment for relief of sunburn: Mix 2 tablespoons of almond oil, 2 tablespoons of spermaceti, and ½ teaspoon of honey. Add attar of roses for a pleasant scent.

Mix lime juice in Vaseline to make a soothing salve for sunburn.

Tapeworm

Drink a tea made from pumpkin seeds to be rid of tapeworm.

In 2½ cups of water, boil 1 ounce of fern root until 2 cups of liquid remain. Abstain from eating before going to bed. Upon

arising, take a small glassful of the liquor to combat tapeworm.

Make a tea of 2 ounces of pomegranate root in 2 cups of water. Drink this remedy for tapeworm in three doses before eating breakfast.

Teeth Coming Loose

Dissolve ¼ ounce of myrrh in 1 pint of port wine; add 1 ounce of oil of almonds. Wash the teeth each morning with this solution to make loose teeth more secure.

Toothache

Mix warm vinegar and salt, hold in mouth until pain ceases. For cavities, plug with cotton doused with pepper and ginger.

Mix 1 dram of powdered alum and 3 drams of nitrous spirits of ether. Apply on a dab of cotton to an aching tooth.

Melt 16 parts of beeswax and 4 parts of lard. Cool. Then add 8 parts of oil of cloves and 8 parts of creosote. Thoroughly

soak cotton in the mixture. Roll into small sticks and chew slowly when needed to alleviate a toothache.

To relieve a toothache chew the leaves of catnip.

Roast an onion. Cut it in two and place a half, while still hot, over the pulse of the wrist on the side opposite the painful tooth.

Vomiting

Remove the peel from a good-sized onion and slice it in two. Put a half in each armpit to check vomiting.

Brown field corn, but do not burn it. Immerse it in boiling water. Drink the liquid when necessary to arrest vomiting.

Pound green wheat, and pour boiling water over it. Squeeze out the juice, and sweeten it with sugar. Take 1 tablespoon at 10-minute intervals to stop vomiting.

Skin and clean the gizzard of a freshly dressed chicken. Simmer it in 1 pint of water for 30 minutes. Discard the gizzard. Sipping the broth cures most cases of vomiting.

Warts

The juice from milkweed or castor oil will take away warts when applied regularly.

To remove warts, rub them with green walnuts or bacon rind.

Collect cobwebs to form a mass big enough to cover a wart but not touch the flesh around it. Place the wad of cobwebs on the wart, and ignite it. When the fire has

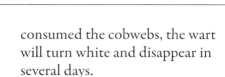

consumed the cobwebs, the wart
will turn white and disappear in
several days.

Remove warts by applying freshly
crushed marigold leaves and
their juice.

Make a paste of vinegar and
hickory-wood ashes. Use as an
application to destroy warts.

To be rid of warts, apply oil
of cinnamon to them four
times daily.

Whooping Cough

Cook 2 ounces of garlic in 2 ounces
of oil. Strain. Mix in 1 ounce of
camphor and 2 ounces of honey.
A dose of 1 teaspoon taken four
times a day, or as required, will
relieve whooping cough.

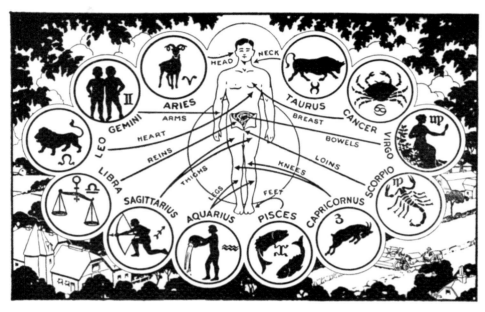

Cut into pieces 3 prickly pear leaves,
and boil them in 1 quart of water
for 30 minutes. Filter the liquid
through a cloth to strain out
all prickles. Add a bit of sugar
to sweeten, and boil for a short
time. Take 2 teaspoonfuls to cure
whooping cough.

Add sweet oil to brandy and simmer
with a slice of onion. To treat
whooping cough externally,
spread the solution, morning and
evening, on the soles of the feet,
the spine, and the chest.

Rub the spine with garlic to cure
whooping cough.

Wounds

To treat wounds apply a mixture of
1 tablespoon of crushed rosemary
and a pinch of salt.

Treat wounds with an application of
fresh warm cow dung.

Sprinkle the dried, powdered
leaves of wild sunflowers on a
wound to arrest blood flow.

To treat the wound from a rusty
nail, apply peach leaves that have
been pounded into pulp.

Moon Sign Medicine

Followers of moon signs in the
treatment of human and animal
ailments say that all procedures
should be in rhythm with the
moon and its various phases.
Most agree that proper timing
should be as follows:

Dental Work

Cavities should be filled during a
waning moon period of the third
and fourth quarter and in a fixed
sign of Aquarius, Taurus, Leo, or
Scorpio. Teeth should be extracted
during a waxing moon period of
the first and second quarters,
but only in the signs of Pisces,

Gemini, Virgo, Sagittarius, or Capricorn. Plates are best made under a decreasing moon of the third and fourth quarters and in a fixed sign of Aquarius, Taurus, Leo, or Scorpio.

Operations

The best time to have operations, pull teeth, remove tonsils, or remove any growth is when the signs are in the knees or feet (the best), such as Capricorn or Pisces.

Removal of Noxious Growths (this includes corns, callouses, superfluous hair, warts, any unwanted growths): Use a barren sign such as Aquarius, Aries, Gemini, Leo, Virgo, or Sagittarius with the moon in the fourth quarter.

Surgical procedures: Choose a time when the moon is on the increase in the first and second quarters. Vitality and thrifty

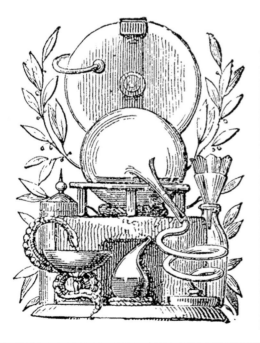

conditions prevail and wounds tend to heal better and faster during this time. An exception is the cutting away of noxious growths, and this should be done on a decreasing moon, third and fourth quarters.

Do not have an operation during the period the moon is in a ruling sign of that part of the body on which the operation is to be performed. Heart operations, for example, should not be performed during the sign of Leo unless absolutely necessary, as Leo rules the heart. If at all possible do not allow an operation on the day the moon is in a ruling sign of that part of the body on which the operation is to be performed as the results are sometimes not good. It is better if the signs are going away from the affected part than approaching it. Consult the table in Chapter 2 for the body parts ruled by the different signs.

Babies and the Signs

To establish the sex of babies divide in half the time between the last day of menstruation to the first day of the next period. If copulation occurs when the moon is in the feminine signs of Pisces, Taurus, Cancer, Virgo, Scorpio, or Capricorn in the first half of the menstrual cycle as

noted above, the child is most apt to be female. If copulation occurs when the moon is in the masculine signs of Aquarius, Aries, Gemini, Leo, Libra, or Sagittarius in the last half of the menstrual cycle, except for the last seventy-two hours before menstruation starts again, the child is most likely to be a boy. The seventy-two hours of the last half plus the first half of the new cycle again produces females.

Hazel Berry of Texas says she practically "cut her teeth" on moon signs. Her father farmed by them and her mother always raised her garden by the signs. Hazel believes babies are born "by the moon." For example, if a baby is thought to be due on April 23 and the next change of the moon phase is April 26 then that's when the baby will be born.

Proper weaning is done when the moon is in a zodiac sign that does not rule a vital organ. These signs are Aquarius, Pisces, Sagittarius, and Capricorn. Weaning should not be done when the moon is in any other sign. The last nursing of the child should be done in a fruitful sign.

20 | COUNTRY PASTIMES

Chautauqua Circuit

When the faded red of barns and the windows of small-town emporiums were enlivened by brightly colored posters announcing the coming of Chautauqua, the pulse of the countryside quickened. Anticipation of this yearly occurrence was savored as much as the actual event.

Men and boys lingered about the local railroad station, awaiting the arrival of the traveling tent company. Country lads, eager for a summer job providing excitement as well as remuneration, labored to set up the great brown tent, acted as ticket takers, or strove to protect audiences and performers from inclement weather. Armed with long poles, they gingerly elevated sagging canvas, dangerously heavy with collected rain, in an attempt to drain away the water. Failure would oftentimes result in a drenching as rents developed, but the enthusiasm of both troupers and viewers was never diluted.

Circuit Chautauqua arose independently of the Chautauqua Institution which germinated in southwestern New York State, a stationary center providing cultural nourishment for those who came from far and wide to attend. Adopting the name and idea from this source, traveling Chautauquas carried lectures, drama, and music to well over nine thousand towns throughout the country, their sojourn in any one community lasting from five days to a week or more.

When Chautauqua was in its prime, radio had not yet become common. So it was the Chautauqua circuit that satisfied the hankering of rural townsfolk for enlightenment and diversion.

From the darkness of a summer night, one stepped into the blazing interior of the huge brown tent. Golden straw, its satiny polish glinting under the bright illumination from naked bulbs strung between tent poles, softened the continual tread of new arrivals and deliciously scented the atmosphere. Seats were usually folding wooden chairs of questionable comfort. Sometimes benches were improvised from planks supported on nail kegs. Children were generally assigned to these, for their restless wriggling during "cultural features" too often set the folding chairs to creaking. After what seemed an interminable but pleasurably tantalizing wait, the tent was darkened, and coughing, chattering, fanning, and fidgeting magically stopped as if on cue. The hushed audience strained to glimpse the first performer to appear on stage, his rouged cheeks and heavily penciled brows dramatically accentuated by the footlights' glare.

Participants in scheduled programs were a varied lot, ranging from explorers to elecutionists; monologists to magicians; pianists to politicians; singers to scientists; teachers to preachers; xylophonists to yodelers—naming but a few. The diversified offerings included lectures on a wide range of subjects by the prominent and not so prominent, Punch and Judy shows,

banjo players in blackface, bell ringers, and the barbershop quartet, said to be an innovation of circuit Chautauqua. As early prejudice against theatrical productions dwindled, plays and operas gradually came to lead in popularity. Shakespearean plays were enacted, Gilbert and Sullivan operettas performed, and operatic arias rendered by renowned singers. As time passed, however, fewer cultural events were presented, and Chautauqua became synonymous simply with entertainment.

Many an old-timer relishes his memories of the magical moments of Chautauqua season—vivid moments that enriched his youth and flavor his latter years with pleasant nostalgia.

Harness Racing

Harness racing became a country pastime after originating in the town. Early in the 1700s, trotting in harness was a customary mode of travel. Roads suitable for wheels were limited to the towns. Occasionally, as four-wheeled vehicles passed each other in the street, impromptu races came about. Street matches of this kind were known as "brushing," and their popularity spread throughout the country. Eventually such racing was permitted on tracks.

In states controlled by puritanical principles, thoroughbred racing was regarded with disfavor. Horse racing was defined as a contest of horses at their fastest speed. Because a horse runs faster than he trots, harness racing was accepted by the morally righteous as a harmless diversion.

At the beginning of the 1800s, the two-wheeled sulky was invented for harness racing. The body of this awkward vehicle hung on springs from enormous wheels, densely spoked with fine rods.

Enthusiasm for trotting became so great in many parts of America that local horses could not satisfy the need. Outstanding thoroughbreds began touring in exhibition matches. Fine trotters were developed by farmers who bred their mares to stallions of prominent lines.

The start of country fairs germinated in the early 1800s when a farmer in Massachusetts tethered some imported Merino sheep to a tree and charged people a small sum to view them. A new custom was established which spread rapidly. All types of animals and produce were exhibited and judged, including harness horses. A fair in Philadelphia was the first to include harness racing in its program. From that time on, such races were the star attraction at country fairs, greatly influencing attendance rates. Soon the smallest, most remote villages had their races, which became part of rural tradition.

In the last quarter of the nineteenth century, the ball

bearing and the pneumatic tire were developed. The two were combined in the bicycle. When wheels of this revolutionary design were put on the sulky, the vehicle's appearance was ridiculed by old-timers. But the new sulky was considerably lighter, and the seat lower for less wind resistance. The reinsman was now situated close to his horse. To prevent the tail from whipping its face, it was braided with an extension, which was placed on the sulky's seat.

People enjoyed a day in the country watching the grace of trotters and pacers in action. Trotters with their long-striding, high knee-action trot, heads rhythmically swaying from side to side, were magnificent in their harness. The pacers, too, stepped with precision in synchronized strides, both pairs of side legs moving in unison.

Harness racing was considered a proper event for ladies to witness as well as gentlemen. However, when it became a gambling medium, every sort of criminal was drawn into the sport. Consequently, the social tone deteriorated with the moral tone. After a reform group restored its respectability, ladies could once again attend the affair with impunity.

In recent years, after a period of lagging interest, harness racing has been fast regaining its former popularity.

Hoedown

That typically American rustic diversion known as the square dance is believed to have developed in the 1600s in England. Many of the square-dance tunes were brought to America by English, Scottish, and Irish settlers. From the Eastern Seaboard they spread westward with the pioneers.

The square dance, known also as a barn dance or "hoedown," was regarded with approval or disapproval according to the moral outlook of each community. In some locales it was considered a wholesome social pastime; in others, where dancing and music-making were associated with the Devil, it was frowned upon.

When word of a barn dance got about, people from miles around arrived on horseback. Unfortunately, some brought their own refreshment in the form of hard liquor, and disturbances often resulted. But on the whole, a barn dance meant a night of conviviality and rhythmic movement to the tune of a fiddle.

The chief personage at a barn dance was the caller. To qualify, he had to have a strong, clear voice, a sense of rhythm, and a knack for concocting impromptu rhymes when necessary. His role was to call out directions for the movements of the dancing couples. Four couples composed a set. Besides a good many basic calls, there were songs which indicated action to follow. Some square-dance tunes were without words, and the caller would improvise as he went along.

A hoedown was a simple and satisfying social event, participated in by young and old alike. Those beyond the age of "dosi-doing" could always engage in a little toe-tapping to the tempo of the fiddle's music.

Husking Bee

In times past, a farm chore too big to be managed by one family was turned into a social event. So it was with the husking bee.

Before the onset of winter, farmers gathered in the cornstalks, storing them in the barn. Neighbors from miles around showed up with helping hands and

expectations of a high old time.

Seated on stools around the pyramid of stalks, bushel baskets beside them, they spiritedly worked by lantern light. The crisp autumn air was alive with animated chatter, the rustle of cornhusks, and the snap as ears were wrenched from them. The labor was spiced with excitement by the commonly observed custom concerning the red ear of corn. The fellow who unsheathed one was permitted to kiss the woman of his choice. Some young rascals attended husking bees forearmed, concealing red ears in their clothing to reveal when the time was ripe.

With the last of the stalks stripped of corn, short work was made of refreshments: platters of steaming pork and beans, hot pumpkin pie, doughnuts, and cider.

There was always a fiddler in the group to stir up some dancing. If the cider was hard, the evening was topped off with some pretty lively stepping.

Maple-Sugaring Time

Maple-sugaring time meant a combination of hard work and fun. In late winter with snow still carpeting the ground, country people set off for the woods equipped with freshly washed buckets, tapping irons, and sap spouts.

Choosing the right time and weather was vital. A bright, sunshiny morning with a west wind blowing, following a night of hard freeze, was best for good sap flow. It was important to tap the trees before their buds swelled; otherwise the syrup had a leathery taste and was fit only for sweetening tobacco.

On the side of the tree where the most limbs grew and at a spot showing new bark growth, the tapping iron was driven in at a convenient height and a metal or wooden spout inserted in the hole. Old-time steel spouts were fashioned by the local blacksmith from discarded scythe blades; wooden spouts were whittled from the young shoots of the staghorn sumac. The pails were hung, and soon the rhythmic drip of sap into buckets sounded through the maple groves.

The sap was usually collected twice a day, in the morning and the late afternoon. A team of horses hauled a low sled bearing a large tank into which the buckets were emptied. The contents of the gathering tank were poured into an evaporator in the boiling house. When it had reached the right consistency for syrup, the liquid was drawn off into cans. If sugar was desired, the sap was boiled longer at a higher temperature. The liquid sugar was poured into wooden tubs, where it hardened.

The foaming evaporator pan was watched through the night in an atmosphere of wood-smoke fragrance, sweet-smelling steam, and great expectation. At last "sugaring off" time arrived. Sometimes young folks would have a party. Snow was brought in and hot syrup poured over it, which quickly cooled and thickened into delicious taffy-like strips. Sour pickles or salt were often on hand to counteract the sweetness.

Indians, in the past, collected maple sap in buckets of birch bark. Their evaporator consisted of a hollowed-out segment of tree trunk; they boiled the sap by dropping in heated stones. An easier method employed by the Indians was to let the sap freeze over and over again, the ice being removed each time.

Eventually the sap thickened to become syrup.

Along about February, squirrels will bite twigs from the maple tree to lap the oozing sap. The resulting small squirrel-made spigots sometimes drip for days, the sweet liquid attracting warblers and other birds.

Today, sugar maples are piped for sap gathering, and the maple syrup and sugar are made in modern evaporating apparatus in factories. However, there are still many country folks who have fond memories of the maple-sugaring times of bygone years.

Marble Game

Country boys knuckling down for a brisk game of marbles probably didn't know they were engaging in a pastime popular among the ancient Romans.

Summers were usually filled with farm chores, fishing along a shaded stream bank, or cooling off in the old swimming hole. But come autumn, boys arrived at school with serious pursuit in mind, their pockets bulging with marbles.

Each player selected the marble he judged best for a shooter, whether because of its appeal to the eye or because of the luck it had brought in the past. The shooter was known as a taw, and the fellow who could boast of one made of agate, fondly called an "aggie," was the envy of all. To decide who would shoot first required "lagging" one's taw up to a line. The owner of the taw nearest the line began the game, and so on down the line. Within a small circle drawn in the dirt, each participant placed four or more marbles. The object of the game was to knock as many marbles as possible out of the circle, those marbles becoming the prizes of the shooter, who continued until he missed. When all the marbles had been claimed, the game ended.

In more recent generations, playing for "keeps" became popular, though this was much frowned upon by the school as being in the realm of gambling. However, unhampered by the eye of authority, the game proceeded in earnest, resulting in a good

shooter's lugging home a heavy bag of marbles by day's end.

Winter with its frozen ground and occasional blankets of snow temporarily interrupted the sport, which revived with the first hint of spring warmth. By the end of a season, a serious player displayed quite a set of callused knuckles.

Today the game of marbles is less enthusiastically played among schoolboys. Instead it has been organized as an international sport, played by a few adult professionals, who cannot possibly enjoy the game as much as we did years ago.

Mumblety-Peg

In the old days, standard equipment in the pocket of every country boy was a good, sharp jackknife. One with a long, stout blade and fancy handle for killing a bear or one on a ring attached to a long chain and concealing a variety of useful tools—bottle opener, can opener, screwdriver, and leather punch—had its place. But the knife commonly carried and cherished by every young lad was a plain, solid one with a good-sized sturdy blade plus a smaller blade, having a strong spring and a well-shaped handle harmonious with the owner's grip. It was a kind of symbol that the boy had reached a responsible age. He employed it in a variety of ways— for whittling useful articles, cutting

fishing line, and scraping animal skins. In addition, it was used for sheer amusement.

A popular game in those times was variously known as mumble-the-peg, mumblety-peg, or mumblepeg, depending upon the area from which you hailed. Two players or more could take part, the only prerequisites being their jackknives and soft ground. A starting line was marked, and each player in turn attempted to toss his knife, held in stipulated positions, so that it would stick into the ground. These are the basic holds, often altered or embellished upon at whim, that were required in playing mumblety-peg:

- The knife is held flat on the palm with the point out. It is flipped up, makes one revolution, and, if all goes well, lands point first in the ground.
- The same procedure as above is followed with the knife balanced on the back of the hand.

- This time a fist is made, the knife lying between the fingers and palm. The knife must be tossed three times in succession.
- The knife is held by the tip and flipped.
- The hand is held palm up in the policeman's stop position; the knife point is directed downward in the lower palm.
- The knife point is held between the left thumb and forefinger; the handle is struck smartly with the fingers of the right hand. This position is known as "spank the baby."

A number of others followed, some rather dangerous, such as tossing the knife over the head or through a circle made by the thumb and forefinger. Any position in which it landed was considered fair, no matter how far it inclined to one side, if another could be passed beneath it.

The person first to complete the required throws was the winner. It was the privilege of the victor to drive a 2-inch peg into the ground with three sound whacks from the handle of his knife. Then, with eyes closed, he was entitled to three more blows. He strove desperately to drive in the peg until it was flush with the ground, because the loser, on hands and knees, had to extract the peg from the dirt using his teeth as pincers. This obligatory penance of the vanquished gave the game its title.

Pitching Horseshoes

The clang of a horseshoe landing bestride its mark is a summer sound that evokes memories of good companionship, good exercise, and possibly a good cold drink of well water. Country folk used to say that the best stakes (or stobs, as they are called) for horseshoe pitching are old railroad spikes driven firmly into the ground 40 feet apart. Favored was a 2½-pound shoe, the claim being made that lighter ones don't carry the distance as well.

Rules vary according to the whims of players, but in pitching horseshoes according to standard rules, a ringer gives you 3 points and a leaner, 1 point; otherwise, the shoe closest to the peg gets a point, provided it is not more than 6 inches away. The first player to chalk up 50 points is proclaimed the winner.

The horseshoe itself has a long history dating back to the second century B.C. Prior to that time, horse owners attempted to protect hoofs from wear and breakage by covering them with socks or sandals. Not until the fifth century of our era was horseshoeing widely known in Europe, but by the Middle Ages it was a common practice. The Japanese attached slippers of straw to the horse's feet, replacing them as they wore out. This archaic custom survived until the 1800s, when rimming the hoof with iron was introduced.

An aura of superstition has surrounded the horseshoe for centuries. Ancient Romans attributed magical properties to anything made of iron, and so equine hardware was regarded as a good-luck symbol. Finding a horseshoe meant good fortune, provided the shoe pointed toward, not away from, the finder. Since the horses of many dignitaries in Roman times were shod in gold or silver, chancing upon such a horseshoe, no matter the direction

it faced, was doubtless considered good luck! Sages of the time advised that horseshoes were a dependable defense against witchcraft. In bygone days, owners of race horses were careful to keep a horseshoe in the stable. This practice was supposed to prevent witches from riding the horses all night before a race. Generations ago the belief was widespread that a new moon had the force to counteract the influence of the evil eye. Perhaps because of the horseshoe's resemblance to a

new moon, it became associated with supernatural power.

All manners of hanging a horseshoe are advocated for ensuring the very best of fortune. Some say the open end should point downward; others argue that the open end should be uppermost to prevent the luck from running out; and then there are those who believe that tacking it up in a horizontal position is most favorable. Silas Hubble of Ohio says that your luck depends not so much upon *how* you hang it as on how *well* you hang it up. He avers that the thud of a horseshoe on the head is decidedly not good luck!

Play-Party

In rural areas where square dancing was disapproved of because of its musical accompaniment (some held that the fiddle was an instrument of the Devil), the play-party was accepted as harmless recreation. Popularly called the swinging game, the play-party differed little from the square dance except that the instrumental music was replaced by the singing of the dancers themselves and of enthusiastic onlookers.

Participants in a play-party were generally from the local community. People didn't flock to it from long distances as they did to the square dance. Even hearsay

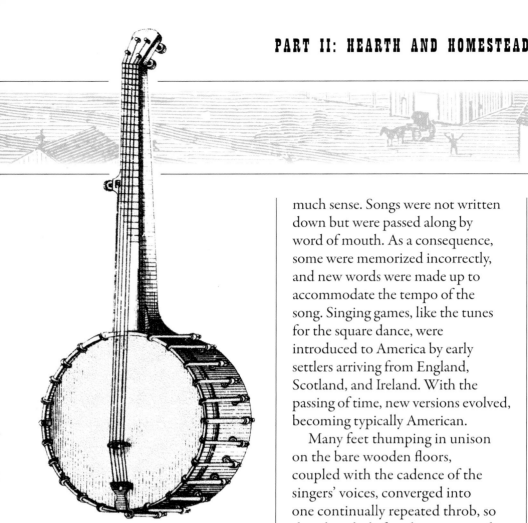

invitations were sufficient to bring folks out for a good time.

Guests usually arrived at sundown, and dancing commenced the moment enough were on hand to dance the figures, which were known as "games." Rugs and most of the furniture were removed from the room set aside for dancing. Along the walls, planks spanning boxes or chairs and covered with homemade quilts served as benches.

The man who could do a fair job of carrying a tune and whose voice could be heard despite the din of the dancers took the lead in the game. As the dance proceeded, newcomers joined in. The figures, or games, were very similar to those of the square dance, but simpler. Words of the play-party song accompanying them were good-natured and seldom made

much sense. Songs were not written down but were passed along by word of mouth. As a consequence, some were memorized incorrectly, and new words were made up to accommodate the tempo of the song. Singing games, like the tunes for the square dance, were introduced to America by early settlers arriving from England, Scotland, and Ireland. With the passing of time, new versions evolved, becoming typically American.

Many feet thumping in unison on the bare wooden floors, coupled with the cadence of the singers' voices, converged into one continually repeated throb, so that the whole farmhouse seemed to pulsate. When the players sometimes became breathless, those watching took up the singing, often clapping their hands or tapping their feet to reinforce the rhythm.

As a general rule, refreshments were not served at a play-party, but the old water bucket was put to good use by guests thirsty from so much singing and exercise.

Washer Game

Though it is rarely heard of today, years ago many a country boy whiled away the hours playing the washer game. Three empty tin cans were sunk into the ground some 20 to 25 feet from the toe line. The cans were spaced about 6 inches apart, forming a row at

a right angle to the toe line. The players each arrived with a large metal washer in hand, usually one snitched from some old, abandoned piece of farm machinery. It was roughly the size of a silver dollar and of sufficient heft to carry the distance. Just as in pitching horseshoes there is a stake at either end of the game area, so in the washer game there were three cans in single file at either end to expedite the playing.

Each player's washer was identifiable by a certain mark scratched on it or perhaps by a paint daub of a particular color. Much was made of the manner in which it was held when being tossed. Some players attributed their good luck to holding the washer with thumb and index finger encircling its perimeter; others preferred grasping an edge and spinning it horizontally to the mark.

The clunk of a washer in the nearest can meant 10 points; a successful landing in the second brought 20 points; and a washer in the third and farthest can earned 30 points for its owner. A player had to chalk up precisely 100 points to win—no more and no fewer. If he exceeded that score, he lost as surely as if he had failed to meet the required number of points.

Sometimes money was bet on the outcome of the game—considerably adding to the excitement and importance of a well-placed washer in an old tin can!

Bean Bag

In times past, a bean bag was generally found in most every child's collection of toys. It was fun to throw back and forth and could be used for playing games of skill, such as tossing it into a receptacle placed at a distance. A bean bag had the advantage of staying put if it failed to be caught or missed its mark, not rolling out of reach like a ball.

Make your bean bag of some heavy material that will stand up well under hard use. Cut two 6-inch squares. With their right sides facing, sew them strongly together, allowing a seam depth of ½ inch. Leave a few inches open through which to fill your bag with dried navy or pinto beans. Turn it on the right side. If there is any chance that the bag might become wet, first heat the beans in a 200° F oven for about one hour to keep them from germinating. Do not overstuff the bag so that it is rigid. It should be somewhat limp and flexible, no more than 1½ inches in thickness. Turn in the raw edges of the gap, and stitch the bean bag closed.

Cloth Ball

Ransack your rag bag for cloth scraps too small for patchwork. These odds and ends can be used to create a safe toy for babies and toddlers: a cloth ball.

The more variety in the color and texture of the fabrics, the more attractive the plaything. Suedes, sailcloth, and other such sturdy materials are especially suitable for cloth balls, but any fabric will do nicely.

You will need a cardboard pattern in the shape of an equilateral pentagon when cutting the cloth remnants. A size 3 inches across between the farthest points is about right; however, you can alter this measurement to suit yourself. The more you increase the pattern size, the bigger will be the completed ball.

Cut twelve pentagons, allowing an extra ⅜ inch for seams as you scissor about the pattern. Sew down the seam allowance on all five sides of each piece. Iron the stitched areas so that the cloth will lie flat.

Now begin assembling the patches. Sew together three pentagons, which will form the top of the ball. First, put two patches together, and whipstitch their common seam line. After fitting the third piece against them, sew one of its sides to each patch. The three pieces will have formed a sort of dome. Fit the points of three more patches against the triangular edges beneath the dome, and stitch them in place. You have finished the top half of the ball. To make the bottom half, repeat the same steps.

Complete the toy by matching up the jogs in the two halves and sewing the remaining seams. Leave an opening in one to insert stuffing. You can fill the ball with batting or old nylon stockings snipped in pieces. Sew the opening shut with the blind stitch.

Just before closing the last seam, tuck a big jingle bell in the center of the stuffing. It won't ring but will rattle as the toy is rolled or tossed.

Disc Top

Cut the disc for your top from a 5-inch square of pine wood, 1 inch thick. In the center of the disc, make a hole having a 1-inch diameter. Saw 3 inches from the tip of an old broom handle. Push the flat end into the hole in the disc until it is flush with the wood's surface. Secure it with glue. Use a slender 5-inch-long dowel for the top's stem. Bore a hole in the middle of the flat end of

the broom handle nub. Insert the stem, and reinforce it with glue. Into the rounded tip of the broom handle section, hammer a domed tack to facilitate the top's spinning smoothly. Paint the toy a bright color.

Drill a small hole about midway in the stem; run a cord or shoelace through it. Thread the other end of the cord through the width of a short dowel to use as a grip, and knot it on the far side of the hole. Make winding the cord or shoelace about the stem easier by placing the top's tip in a hole cut in a wooden block. After winding the cord around the stem, set the toy on the floor, give the cord a quick pull, and let your top spin.

Sock Doll

Use a boy's or man's sock to make a sock doll. Lay it flat, and cut off the upper half of the ankle section. Vertically cut through its double thickness in the center so that you have two folded portions for the arms. Turn the pieces on the wrong side, and sew seams ⅛ inch deep, except on one end. Fill the arms with stuffing through the open ends; then sew them closed.

Vertically cut open the remainder of the ankle section at each side to form the legs. With the heel of the sock at the rear of the body, sew the leg seams on the wrong side, ⅛ inch from the edge. Turn the material right side out again.

Cut off the toe. Through this opening you can stuff the legs, body, and head with cotton. Fill the doll until firm but not stiff. Sew the head closed and stitch on the arms.

To form the neck, tightly tie a piece of string around the doll just below the face area. Shoe buttons make good eyes. For a realistic touch, you might stick on two of the white circles used to reinforce the pages of looseleaf notebooks. Then sew small black shoe buttons in the center of each. Embroider the other features. Use yarn for hair, and dress the sock doll according to whim.

Sock Puppet I

To create a sock puppet, select a size of sock appropriate for the hand that will work it. Lay the sock flat, and cut a slit several inches deep for the mouth, starting from the middle of the toe end. (The length of this slit will depend upon how big or small you want the mouth to be.) For the interior of the mouth, cut a piece from felt to fit the opening, crease the fabric in half across its width, and sew it in place.

Complete the puppet with embroidered or button eyes, yarn hair, ears, and clothing. Let imagination be your guide.

Now put your hand in the sock, the thumb below and four fingers in the upper section above the mouth. By opening and closing your hand, the puppet will speak. The resiliency of the material allows you to make your creation smile, look grumpy, or move its head in any direction.

This type of puppet is particularly adaptable to animal characters.

Sock Puppet II

Turn the sock inside out. The closely knitted sole is just right for the puppet's face. Roll thin cardboard or heavy paper into a tube with a circumference to fit around the index finger and a length of about 5 inches. Glue or tape it together, and insert it in the foot of the sock. Stuff the part intended for the puppet's head with cotton, using enough to give it a round shape. Let the tube extend from the stuffed portion downward, forming a neck. At the point where you judge the head should end, tightly tie string or thread around the tube.

At appropriate places on each side of the body, cut slits for arm holes. Sew on simple arms shaped like glove fingers.

Embroider or paint on features (use poster paint). Add hair and clothing.

To work the puppet, put hand and arm into the sock leg, using thumb and center finger to manipulate the arms and the index finger in the tube to move the head.

Hand Puppet

Design a cloth puppet according to the hand dimensions of the person who will use it. Place the hand flat on a piece of paper with the three middle fingers together and the thumb and little finger spread at a comfortable distance. Trace around the hand, including several inches of the arm. Cut along the outline.

Pin the paper pattern on some heavy cloth (wool, drapery material, etc.), and cut two sides. With the right sides facing, sew them together. Hem the edge of the "sleeve." Turn the puppet back to the right side of the material. It should cover the hand like a glove, but a glove with three fingers: a large middle one for the head area, flanked by two smaller ones for the arms.

You may transform the puppet into any character you wish, human or animal, by adding yarn hair or ears, embroidering facial features, and dressing it.

Insert your middle fingers in the head to move it, using the thumb and little finger for arm actions.

Toy Parachute

A square of lightweight scrap material or a man's old handkerchief can act as the chute. To each corner tie a piece of string 12 inches long. If you use a square of fabric larger than handkerchief size, increase the string length proportionately.

Saw several inches off the rounded end of a discarded broomstick. Line up three metal washers of about the same circumference as the nub of the broom handle, and run a screw eye through their centers and into the flat end of the broomstick tip. Now you have a weight for the parachute. Attach it by knotting the four strings to the eye of the screw.

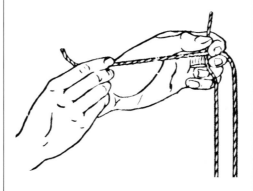

Modeling Clay

To make an excellent modeling clay for children, blend 1 cup of cornstarch with 2 cups of baking soda. Stir in 1½ cups of cold water, and add food coloring, if desired. Heat the mixture over a medium flame. Stir constantly until it reaches a doughlike consistency. Cool the clay, and cover it with a moist cloth until ready for use.

Finished pieces can be preserved by coating them with shellac.

Wooden Block Puzzle

Cut cubes of white pine wood, 1½ by 1½ inches. Select six paper pictures, and cut precisely around each. Next, brush three sides of the cubes with several coats of lacquer. When the sides are dry,

repeat the procedure with the remaining three sides.

The cubes, having six faces, will form six different puzzles when correctly assembled. Using wooden blocks to construct picture puzzles originated long ago in Germany.

Rubberband Boat

Cut a piece of wood 8¼ inches long, 2⅝ inches wide, and 1 inch thick for the hull of your boat. Shape the front in a tapered curve for the bow. Cut out a rectangle at the stern, 2 inches deep and 1⅞ inches across, to accommodate the paddle wheel. Cut notches ⅛ inch deep on the outer edge of the resulting projections, ½ inch in from their ends, to hold a rubber band. Make the four-blade paddle wheel of two lap-joined pieces of thin board, fitted together as in egg-carton construction.

Reinforce the joining with waterproof glue. If you like, you may make a cabin of a block of wood 3½ inches by 1¾ inches by 1 inch, fastening it in place with waterproof glue. Fit the rubberband into the notches in the stem. You may need to test different sizes of rubber bands to find a suitable one. Place the paddle wheel on the rubberband and wind.

Simple Sailboat

Cut a hull about 8 inches long and 2½ inches wide from a sheet of cork. Taper the front of the boat to shape its bow. Sharpen a straight twig somewhat, and drive it into the cork for a mast. Make a sail from paper or thin cardboard. A hole at the bottom and top of the sail will allow you to slip it on the twig mast. If a strong gale is up, the owner of the craft may request that a small hole be punched in the stem for attaching a long string to keep his sailboat from being carried out of sight.

Diamond-Shaped Kite

A diamond-shaped kite is the easiest of all kites to make.

Essential materials are these:
- one straight strip of wood for the vertical piece, ³⁄₁₆ by ⅜ by 36 inches in length
- one straight strip of wood for the cross piece, ³⁄₁₆ by ⅜ by 30 inches in length
- tissue paper or lightweight cloth for the covering material, 30 by 36 inches
- whipcord string
- white glue

At the ends of both sticks, make a ¼-inch deep cut with a saw. Center the cross strip perpendicularly on the vertical strip at a point 9 inches from one end. Bind the strips together using string. Glue the binding. Run a string around the edges of this framework through the slits at the ends of the strips, and tie it. Place the framework on top of the covering material, and cut it 1 inch larger than the kite's framework. Fold the extra 1 inch over the taut string. In the case of tissue paper, glue it down; if cloth is used, sew it. Bow the cross piece to a depth of 4 inches, with the convex curve away from the covering. Keep it in this bowed position by tying a piece of string from one end to the other. Fasten the bridle string to the vertical strip at the kite's top. Then punch a small hole in the paper 10 inches from the bottom, and again tie the string to the vertical piece. Flying conditions will dictate at what point to attach the main string to the bridle.

When the wind is blowing at 12 miles an hour or more, test your kite. If the kite has a tendency to dive downward, add a tail string with rags tied to it at intervals.

22 | ONE THING AND ANOTHER

In the old days few wants were "store bought." Country people supplied themselves with life's essentials by tediously making at home everything from blackboards to shoe polish. Here are some homemade items of the past and their methods of production.

Blackboard

You can make a large blackboard in no time from a sheet of hardboard, which is a thin sheet composed of pressed fibers, one side being hard and glossy brown. One 4 by 8 feet would be a good size. Coat it with blackboard paint. When the paint is dry, nail up your homemade blackboard.

Corncob Pipe

Self-sufficient old-timers seldom spent money for things they could produce themselves. The corncob pipe is an example of such thrift.

To try your hand at making one, select a firm ear of corn having sufficient pith to be properly hollowed out. You will need to break several ears and examine their cross section. In addition, choose one with ends that fit comfortably in your hand. When you have found the right cob, dry it.

Now decide which of the ends better suits your hand. Some people prefer the pointed end. Snap off an appropriate length for the size of bowl you favor. A bowl of 1¾ to 2 inches should be satisfactory. You may trim the break evenly, but this step is not essential.

Using the bigger blade of your pocketknife, dig out the pith to an approximate depth of 2 inches. The next layer will be woody and hard. Because it will give strength to your pipe, be careful not to remove too much of it. The completed hole should have a diameter of ½ to ¾ inch, depending on the cob's size.

Whether or not you believe the claim that a thicker bowl means a cooler smoking pipe, don't shave its outside walls. You'll like the rustic appearance and cushiony feel.

The pipestem can be made from the cornstalk by cutting the most slender part that's close to the top of the plant. An elder twig makes a good pipestem too. Either can be hollowed out with a hot coat-hanger wire. After piercing the stems, blow through them to force out any loose debris. A section of wild rice stalk, being naturally hollow, can provide a convenient stem. Cut the mouthpiece end directly above a joint in the reed. This strong area can be gripped between the teeth without concern about splitting the pipestem. Cut the opposite end directly above a joint in the stalk. The solid joint at the mouthpiece end is the only place you will need to ream out. Prepare the bowl end of the stem by cutting a flat slice, roughly ⅓ inch in length, from one side, forming a U-shaped opening.

Make a hole in the wall of the bowl just above the bottom of the hollowed-out area. This job can best be done with a twist drill having a diameter slightly smaller than that of the prepared pipestem. Maintain the bit at a right angle to the pipe bowl; bore a full twist in one direction followed by a half twist the opposite way. Work cautiously to keep the opening from becoming too large for the stem. After you have drilled clean through the bowl wall, insert the stem with the U-shaped opening uppermost. Firmly press in the pipestem for a snug fit.

Be patient with your pipe for the first few smokes. Any pith remaining in the bowl will have to burn away, and the woody part will need to season a little. Then, too, it's always difficult to keep a new pipe lit. After two or three smokes, however, you should be able to settle back and puff with satisfaction on your homemade corncob pipe.

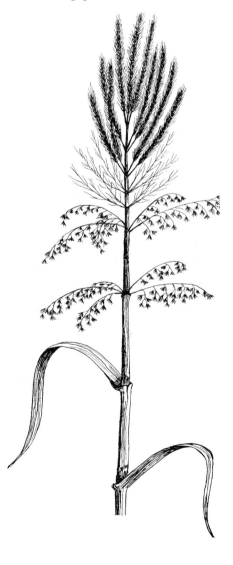

Crystal Garden

If the weather is too cold for outdoor gardening, make a garden indoors—of crystals.

A beautiful crystal garden can be created inexpensively and easily in any glass container, such as a jar or glass bowl. In addition, you will need enough coarse sand to layer the bottom of your container; some water glass, which is a stony powder that forms a colorless, syrupy liquid when dissolved in water (in times past, housewives preserved eggs by coating them with it); and packages of different crystals. The most satisfactory crystals to use are cadmium nitrate, cobalt nitrate, Epsom salts, ferrous sulfate, manganese sulfate, and zinc sulfate. The water glass and crystals can be bought at most drugstores or hobby shops.

Before starting your crystal garden, place the container in its intended location; otherwise, the delicate growths might be damaged in moving. Layer the floor of the container with coarse sand, which can be obtained from a building supply company or from the beach. From Plasticine, available at craft shops, create miniature trees and shrubs, garden seats, and birds, positioning them in the sandy bottom. You might add a few small shells and pebbles. If you want the crystals to grow in specific areas only, put them in place now. For a beautiful effect, try slightly embedding some (not too deeply or they will not grow) in the branches of the Plasticine shrubs and trees.

Mix the water glass by dissolving 3 tablespoons of it in 2 cups of hot water. Prepare sufficient solution to fill the container. Pour it slowly into the glass receptacle until full. The crystals will immediately begin growing.

If you prefer a wild, unplanned garden, pour in the water glass and then drop in enough crystals to cover the bottom of the container.

The crystals will develop into beautiful plantlike forms within about ten minutes.

A crystal garden can also be made with some common household items, but it will require considerably more patience than the first one described.

Assemble these materials: ammonia, liquid bluing, food coloring, table salt (not iodized), water, a 6-inch container, and several lumps of soft coal or a brick.

Wrap the coal or brick in a rag, and pound it with a hammer into chunks about the size of a walnut. Arrange the pieces in the middle of the container.

Mix the following ingredients in the order in which they are mentioned: 4 tablespoons of salt (noniodized), 4 tablespoons of liquid bluing, 4 tablespoons of water, and 1 tablespoon of ammonia. Blend them until the salt liquefies.

Pour the mixture on the chunks of coal or brick. Using

an eyedropper, spot the wet pieces with various shades of food coloring.

You will have to wait patiently for several hours before the interesting shapes of your crystal garden begin to sprout.

Drinking Glasses

The conversion of tall glass bottles into drinking tumblers requires a small amount of new, standard-weight motor oil, a ⅝-inch steel rod about 12 inches long, pliers, and a source of heat.

Decide at what level you want the bottle to break, and mark the spot. Pour in the oil to within ⅛ inch of that mark to allow for a slight rise in fluid when the rod is introduced. Before cutting the glass, let the liquid settle and be sure that none adheres to the bottle's sides above the intended cleavage line. The colder the container and oil, the more successful the operation. Fill bottles, and set them outdoors on a cool night. Complete the task the following morning.

Gripping the rod with pliers, heat the first 3 or 4 inches of the metal until they are visibly red hot. Immediately immerse it about 2 inches into the oil, keeping it there for at least thirty seconds. In approximately that amount of time, the majority of glass will snap off clean. If the method is unsuccessful, however, it may

be that the glass is too thin. In that case, try a thicker-walled container, such as a wine or soda bottle.

Don't touch your newly created drinking tumbler until the oil has cooled. Empty it into a jar to keep for future use. Wash the glass in hot, soapy water. After rinsing and drying it, smooth the cut edges with sandpaper or emery cloth.

Another method for cutting glass containers involves wrapping ordinary cotton cord several times around a bottle at a slightly lower level than the planned severance line. Thoroughly saturate the string with alcohol; light it with a match. After the flame has subsided, pour ice-cold water over the jar or bottle. The glass will separate easily.

Gourd Uses

Gourds, with their variety of colors, shapes, and textures, make an attractive table decoration; hollowed out, they become objects for daily use.

If you are raising your own gourds, train the vines on trellises or fences to prevent the fruit from growing lopsided or rotting on the bottom. Discourage bug attacks by sowing a few radish seeds among the plants.

Soft-shelled gourds serve for ornamentation; the more durable

thick-shelled gourds are good for utilitarian purposes.

After harvesting, clean them in warm, soapy water containing a household disinfectant. Dry the gourds with a cloth, and spread them on newspaper in a warm, dry place. At the end of a week, wipe them with a cloth moistened only in disinfectant. Again spread the gourds to dry in a warm, dark, damp-free spot for about one month. Every other day, turn them. When seeds rattle about inside them, they are properly seasoned. Some thick-shelled gourds may require as much as a six-month drying period.

Now is the time to varnish or shellac thin-shelled gourds to prevent their fading and decaying. Waxing and polishing them will accentuate their lustrous hues.

Select large thick-shelled gourds for making containers.

Using a sharp knife, cut the shell to suit its intended function as bottle, bowl, water dipper, etc. Smooth rough edges with sandpaper or a file. Remove seeds and fiber from the interior.

When creating a bottle, slice a nub from the narrow end of a gourd. In it, wedge a cork long enough to extend into the bottle's neck when stoppered. A bowl can be fashioned quickly from the bottom half of a

gourd. You might like to glue on wooden feet. For a dipper, lay the gourd horizontally, and cut a slice from the top side, leaving the neck to serve as a handle.

If you want to attract birds to your yard, with the added advantage of keeping down the mosquito population, convert gourds into birdhouses. The purple martin likes both mosquitoes and a gourd home.

Choose large, round gourds having short necks. If you are growing your own, let them dry right on the vine until January. After picking them, cut a hole 2 inches in diameter on one side. Sand or file the doorway's edges smooth. Clean out the inside. To permit drainage, drill a few small holes in the gourd's bottom. Bore two more on opposite sides of the neck, and run a thong or nylon cord through them.

In February, suspend a number of gourd birdhouses

1 foot apart on wooden cross pieces fastened to a 20-foot pole. Locate the pole in an area no closer to trees or buildings than 15 feet. A teaspoon of sulfur in each residence will discourage mites and insure satisfied tenants.

Gourds can also be used for Christmas tree ornaments, flowerpots, napkin rings, toys— anything that your ingenuity might suggest.

Even the contents of a gourd are useful. They can provide you with a treatment that enhances well-being.

In Europe, dry bathing has long been famous for its favorable effect on one's skin. The bath, involving not water but a friction glove, stimulates blood circulation while removing any dead skin particles. The French claim that the dry bath is a remedy for insomnia.

The textured fabric of a friction glove is such that the slightest massaging movement tones the body. Friction gloves are

fabricated from various materials: hemp, horsehair, wool, coarse cotton, plastic. You can produce one of the finest kinds of dry bath gloves in your garden by planting old-fashioned dishcloth gourds. Harvest them when they are ripe, and carefully cut the shell away, revealing the web-like interior. Lay it in the sun for seven days to eliminate all moisture. Once completely dry, the web will be stiff and just a few shakes will rid it of seeds. Your friction glove is now ready for use.

Gently massage your body in an upward movement with the glove. This type of bathing should be indulged in no more than once each week. If you find the dry bath a little too severe, accustom yourself to it gradually by using the glove in your water bath the first few times. Its effect will be softened by the water.

Oatmeal-Box Radio

Anyone can build a crystal set with a few simple components: headphones, a crystal, coil, a variable condenser, and a long wire for an antenna. Having no tubes, no transistors, and no amplification, a crystal set has almost no distortion; music and voices are pure in tone.

Cut a rectangle 14 inches long and 12 inches wide from a well-seasoned board to serve as a base for the crystal set.

Use a cylindrical oatmeal or salt box for the coil form. Cut off one end to a depth of 4 inches; immerse it in melted wax.

The wax coating will prevent it from absorbing moisture. The coil consists of about 150 feet of insulated copper wire (of a size ranging between numbers 22 and 28) or enameled wire (A WG number 24). Either fasten on the wire by running it in and out of three pinholes punctured about ¼ inch from one end of the cardboard cylinder, or secure the wire in place with cellophane tape. Wind on 166 turns. Every seventh turn, twist a small loop for a tap until you have a total of eight loops. Then wind forty turns with no taps. After that, make a loop on every tenth turn. Wind the coil tightly so that no space exists between

turns. On each tap, scrape away any insulation to insure a good connection with the short wires leading to the switch points. When all the turns have been wound, attach the wire end with cellophane tape or thread it through pinholes in the cardboard. Bring down the various taps, and secure them beneath screws or brass-headed tacks on the baseboard. When the coil assembly is completed and working satisfactorily, you may give it a coat of varnish or paint it with melted candle wax.

Purchase a variable tuning condenser with the standard value of approximately 365 pF (picofarads). Position it on the board.

Headphones should be the high-impedance kind (at least 2000 ohms). Do not use hi-fi headphones.

In the old days the detector was an open crystal of galena (a lead-gray mineral), lightly touched by a delicate wire known as a "cat's whisker." Since such crystals are not easily found today, buy, instead, a germanium diode (for example, 1 N 34), costing about a quarter.

The longer the antenna the better. One about 200 feet long will give the best results. String it between trees or buildings, and bring a lead-in to your set. To be on the safe side, provide a lightning arrester. When the set is not in use, the lead-in wire can be ground to a water pipe.

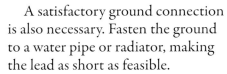

A satisfactory ground connection is also necessary. Fasten the ground to a water pipe or radiator, making the lead as short as feasible.

The diagram will aid you in assembling the set properly.

Your crystal set uses no power and will cost nothing beyond the original small expense of constructing it.

Sawdust Stove

To make a cheap stove that burns either free or low-cost fuel, find a large empty paint can. Remove the top. In the center of the bottom, cut a hole 2 inches in diameter. Place the can on three improvised legs and your stove is finished.

For steady heat over a long period of time without refueling and without smoke, burn sawdust in your stove. Since powdered wood is generally discarded as a waste product, it can often be had

for the asking at lumber yards and sawmills. When there is a charge, it is nominal.

Before loading your stove, be sure the sawdust is absolutely dry. To fuel the burner, you have a piece of water pipe or a smooth, round stick of sufficient length protrude above the can's rim when it has been inserted through the hole in the bottom and rests on the floor. After positioning the pipe or stick in the hole, keep it vertical while pouring sawdust around it. Every so often, press the fuel down firmly as you load the can. Make the sawdust as compact as possible. When the stove is just about full, spread a thin layer of ashes or sand over the sawdust. Then, carefully twisting the pipe and pulling upward, remove it from the packed sawdust. There will be a neat hole directly through the mass.

To light your stove, fold a piece of newspaper accordion style and gently push it through the hole until it appears underneath. Ignite the lower end with a match. The burner will need no further attention until all the fuel has been consumed. Because some fumes are given off by the stove, ventilate the room where it is used.

The rate of burning is approximately 1½ to 2 inches an hour. A sawdust stove 12 inches in diameter will burn for roughly six hours. The degree of heat generated is controlled by the can's depth. The longer the central

hole, the greater the heat. A tall, narrow container will be very hot for a relatively short period of time; a squat, wide container produces gentler heat for longer time; a tall, broad drum burns hot and long. Select a container to meet your requirements.

A sawdust stove is an inexpensive, efficient means of both cooking and heating.

Pet Food

Save all leftover food—meat, vegetables, etc.—and refrigerate it. When about 2 quarts have accumulated, put the scraps in a pot with enough water to cover them. Bring to a boil. Add 1 envelope of active dry yeast, 2 cups of dry beans (any kind), and 3 cups of oats. Cook the mixture over low heat for two hours. Refrigerate. Freeze the excess in containers.

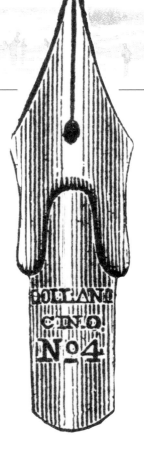

Quill Pen

The use of large, stiff, tailor wing feathers as pens was first recorded in the sixth century; however, quills may well have served as writing implements at a more remote time. They continued in use until the early nineteenth century, when steel pens were introduced.

Pens have been most commonly fashioned from goose feathers. Only the five outer wing feathers are utilized, the second and third being considered best; left-wing quills are more prized than those from the right because they curve outward, away from the writer.

Crow, eagle, hawk, owl, turkey, and swan have also contributed quills for writing instruments. A swan quill is ranked superior to that of a goose, and crow quills are favored when a fine line is required.

The choicest quills are obtained from live birds during the spring. To make a pen, clean an appropriate quill until it is free of fat and oil. Thoroughly dry it in a warm spot to induce brittleness. Then, using a keen-edged knife, slit the tip and sharpen it to a point.

Grafting Wax

Melt 1 pound of rosin, and blend in 4 ounces of mutton tallow and 6 ounces of beeswax. Cool the mixture a bit in cold water; then work it until it is pliable. It not only makes a good grafting wax, but also serves as a salve for cuts you may sustain while climbing and sawing among tree branches.

Sealing Wax for Fruit Jars

Melt 1 pound of beeswax, 4 pounds of rosin, and 1 pound of orange shellac. Dip a brush into this mixture and paint the corks of fruit jars to seal them effectively.

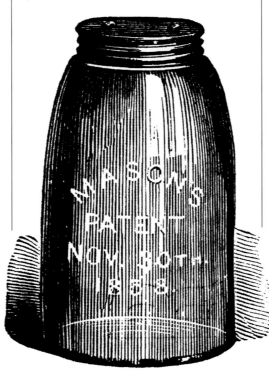

Black Copying Ink

Mix thoroughly ⅛ pound of soft brown sugar, ⅛ pound of gum arabic, ⅜ pound of powdered nutgalls (nut-shaped tumors found on oaks and other trees, formed by irritation due to insects), and ⅛ pound of copperas. Let the mixture steep in 1 gallon of rain water for 2 weeks, shaking it occasionally. This procedure will result in a good black copying ink.

Indelible Ink

Dissolve a strong solution of Prussian blue in water. Add it to a quantity of gall ink. While being used in writing, the ink is green. When dry, it will be black and indelible.

Permanent Black Ink

Boil 1 ounce of logwood chips in 1 gallon of soft water. Cool and strain. Add more hot water to compensate for evaporation, and bring it to a boil. Pound ¾ pound of blue nutgalls into a coarse mash. Put them into the kettle with 3 ounces of purified copperas, ½ ounce of verdigris (acetate of copper), ½ ounce of pulverized sugar, and 4 ounces of gum arabic. Remove the mixture from the fire, and let it stand until it attains the desired blackness. Strain and bottle. This ink will not fade and consequently is excellent for keeping records.

School Ink

Dissolve 10 grams of bichromate of potash and ½ ounce of extract of logwood in 1 quart of hot rain water. When it is cold, bottle it. Leave it uncorked for seven days; it will then be ready for use. It is a good black ink for school purposes, one that will not leave a permanent stain on clothing.

Copying Pad

Soak 2 ounces of glue in a dish of water. When it is soft, drain off the water. Put the dish into a pan of hot water and let stand until the glue melts. Mix in 1½ ounces of hot glycerin. Add a few drops of carbolic acid. Pour the mixture into a shallow square pan to cool. It can be used as a copying pad after 12 hours. Write what you want to reproduce on a sheet of paper with a sharp pen and aniline ink. When the ink dries, put the paper, writing down, on the pad. Press lightly. Remove the paper; an impression will remain on the pad. You can make a duplicate of the original writing by placing another paper on the pad. When the required number of copies have been made, wash the pad with a sponge and cold water.

Whitewash

To make whitewash, slake ½ bushel of lime in a barrel. Add 1 gallon of sweet milk, 1 pound of common salt, and ⅓ pound of sulfate of zinc.

White Paint

You can make a beautiful white paint by mixing the following: 9 ounces of slaked lime, 2 quarts of skimmed milk, 6 ounces of linseed oil, 2½ ounces of Burgundy pitch, and 3 pounds of Spanish white.

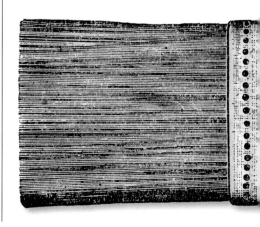

Machine Polish

To make an excellent polish for machinery, blend 3 parts of oil of turpentine, 3 parts of blood coal, and 1 part of stearine oil. Dilute this mixture with alcohol, and brush it onto the machine parts to be cleaned. When the alcohol has evaporated, rub the coaling with crocus (powdered iron oxide) or some other polishing agent.

Piano Polish

To make a good piano polish, mix ⅔ cup of vinegar, 1 cup of turpentine, and 1 cup of boiled linseed oil. Using a flannel cloth, rub the polish well into the wood. Finish by polishing the piano with a chamois skin.

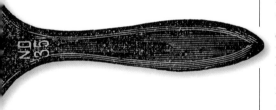

Boot and Shoe Polish

For a good shoe polish, combine the following in a saucepan: 1 pint of soft water, 1 quart of cider vinegar, ¼ pound of clear glue, ½ pound of logwood chips, and 2 teaspoons each of powdered indigo, isinglass, and soft soap. Boil for 10 minutes. Strain when cool. First clean boots or shoes, and then apply the polish with a swab.

Waterproof Blacking

Melt and stir 16 parts of beeswax and 1 part borax to form a jelly. In another pot, stir the following mixture: ⅓ parts of oil of turpentine, 1 part asphalt varnish, 1 part of melted spermaceti. Add to this the contents of the first vessel. For coloring put in 5 parts of ground Berlin blue and 12 parts of vine black. This waterproof blacking may be perfumed with 1 part of nitrobenzole. Store it in boxes. Apply it to boots and shoes with a rag; then brush them.

Harness Blacking

Reduce to powder 1½ ounces of blue nutgalls. Put the powder into a bottle, and add 1 pint of soft water, ½ pint of alcohol, and 2 ounces each of tincture of muriate of iron and extract of logwood. Allow to stand for several days; shake the bottle twice daily. When the extract of logwood is dissolved, the harness blacking is ready for use.

Axle Grease

To make a good axle grease, put 2 pounds each of rosin and tallow, 1 pound of beeswax, and 1 quart each of castor oil and linseed oil into a kettle. Heat well and stir to blend. Continue stirring until the mixture cools.

Ice Chest

Select 2 boxes, one sufficiently smaller than the other so that there is a space of 4 inches on all sides when the smaller box is placed in the larger. Pack the free space between the boxes with sawdust. Make a cover for the larger box that fits snugly inside the top. Insert a small pipe in the bottom of the chest for drainage of waste water. This will make an efficient ice chest.

Making Ice

Into a cylindrical container pour 1⅓ ounces of water, 3½ ounces of sulfuric acid, and 1 ounce of powdered sulfate of soda. Set a vessel of water in the middle of this. The water will freeze. To make more ice, insert another vessel of water.

Fire Extinguishers

Dissolve 5 pounds of salimoniac and 10 pounds of common salt in 3⅓ gallons of water. Pour the liquid into bottles of thin glass that will easily break. Keep one in each room.

When a fire starts, hurl the bottle into the flames forcefully enough to shatter the glass. The contents will extinguish the fire.

Oiled Cloth

Over a low flame mix 2 ounces of lime water with 4 ounces of linseed oil. Beat separately 1 ounce of egg white and 2 ounces of egg yolk. Blend them into the other ingredients. Stretch close-textured white cotton cloth on frames, tacking it well. Apply the mixture with a brush. As each coat dries, brush on another. The oiled cloth will be waterproof after three coats.

Bushel Boxes

Make bushel boxes 17½ inches long, using lath for the length and bottoms. Use common pine wood for the ends, the boards to be 12 inches wide and 14 inches long. Plane the boards on both sides. Cut holes in them for the hands. With an inch bit bore 3 holes, and trim them with a pocketknife. An average wagon bed will accommodate from 32 to 36 of these bushel boxes. Potatoes, apples, and other produce packed in them will be less bruised than those in a loose load.

Mats

Wash a fresh sheepskin in warm water and strong soapsuds to which has been added a tablespoon of kerosene. Scrub it thoroughly on a washboard. Repeat the washing in fresh soapy water. When the wool looks clean and white, submerge it in cold water. Dissolve ½ pound of alum and ½ pound of salt in 3 pints of boiling water. Pour this mixture over the skin, and allow it to soak for 12 hours. Then hang it over a fence to drain. Next nail it on the side of the barn to dry, with the wool side against the wood. When it is almost dry, rub 1 ounce each of saltpeter and powdered alum into the skin for an hour. Rub it daily for three days or until completely dry. Scrape all impurities from the skin with a stick, and rub it with pumice stone. Trim it to a satisfactory shape. It will make a serviceable mat and can be dyed if color is desired.

Scarecrows

A stuffed coat and pants propped upright is customarily used to frighten crows from crops. Another means of keeping off these marauders is to string kernels of corn on long horsehairs and scatter them over the cornfields. Upon swallowing them, the crow will make such a raucous noise as he tries to free his throat of

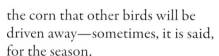

the corn that other birds will be driven away—sometimes, it is said, for the season.

A well-recommended method involves reflected sunlight.

Fasten two small mirrors back to back; hang them on a cord from a pole. As the glass dangles, sunshine is flashed over the field. A crow will leave as quickly as one of the startling flashes strikes him.

The following plan is efficacious in ridding fields not only of crows but of smaller birds and even domestic fowl: Make an imitation hawk, using a large potato and long turkey feathers. Stick the feathers into the potato in such a manner that they resemble the spread tail and wings of a hawk. Suspend it from a tall, bent pole. The wind will lend it realism by agitating it.

Christmas Wreaths

The sight and scent of fresh Christmas wreaths add to holiday pleasures. Wreaths can be fashioned easily with little expense if you have access to fir trees of some type: balsam, Douglas, grand, red, silver, or white. Consult your local nursery or forester to learn what suitable trees grow in your area's woods.

When you know where trees are available, set out on a bough-collecting trip equipped with garden clippers and a carrier for the branches. Take a long strip

of canvas several feet wide and deeply hem its lengths. Run one continuous piece of rope through the resulting tubes, letting it extend beyond both ends of the cloth to serve as handles. Knot the rope ends together, and cut off any excess. (This carrier is also handy for transporting firewood from chopping block to woodpile and from woodpile to hearth. Use nylon rope. Not only is it strong and rotproof, but its elasticity will cushion the jolt when you lift a load of wood.)

Once you have found a good stand of firs, snip off branch ends to a depth of about 18 inches. Stack them on your canvas carrier. Trimming only the tips of boughs in this way will stimulate thicker, fuller growth; it will not damage the tree.

Transforming the greenery into wreaths will require a spool of thin wire (22–24 gauge) and the heavy wire hoops to which the evergreens are fastened. (Wreath frames range from 8 to 24 inches. You'll find a larger size easier to work with for your first attempt.) Both items can be bought at hardware stores.

Now follow these steps:

Place a hoop on a flat work surface, and attach an end of the wire to it.

Break a branch into three roughly equal pieces. Putting their thicker ends together, arrange them in a fan shape.

Lay the fan horizontally along the hoop, right side up.

Holding the twig ends together, bind the wire several times around them and the ring.

Fashion a second fan.

Turn the wire frame over. Lay the fan, right side uppermost, approximately 2 inches along the hoop from the first. Tightly attach it with a few turns of wire.

Continue in this manner, shaping fans and fastening them on alternate sides of the frame. Try to keep all twig bunches the same size. Always attach them right side up and wind the wire tightly.

Make the last two fans a little shorter than the others. Tuck them beneath the first fan to neatly complete the circle. Wrap them with wire, and tie it off. The knot will be invisible, covered by the twigs of the original fan.

If your finished wreath is

somewhat shaggy, use the clippers to even up the central hole and to trim away any pieces elsewhere that protrude too far.

Your fragrant holiday wreath is ready to hang. You might want to brighten it with a fat red bow.

Christmas Tree Ornaments

Use decorative odds and ends and your imagination to create beautiful Christmas ornaments.

Begin with plain silver glass balls. Glue on leftover ribbon scraps of colored grosgrain or velvet and lace ruffles made crisp with spray starch. Apply designs from discarded gift wrapping paper,

cutouts from last year's Christmas cards, or appropriate decals. Before gluing paper decorations on the balls, glue them to a backing of thin, flexible cardboard.

Whenever you prepare a recipe calling for eggs, save the shells. Keep them whole by puncturing both ends with an ice pick and forcefully blowing out the contents. After a good number has accumulated, transform the pale shells into bright Christmas tree ornaments.

Lacquer them in brilliant hues or pastel shades. When they are dry, glue on sparkling sequins, small pearls, and colored beads from broken necklaces. Gold or silver cord can be glued on in a spiral pattern or used to outline four

ovals of vivid velvet spaced around the shells' circumferences. Decorating possibilities are almost limitless.

Finish each ornament by fastening a bead to one end of a thin wire and running the other end through the bottom hole in the shell and out at the top. Fashion a loop in the wire for hanging your shell ornaments on Christmas tree boughs.

Make a whole collection of original Christmas ornaments to enjoy season after season.

Christmas Tree Preserver and Fire Preventive

Dissolve the following ingredients in 1 gallon of hot water: 1 cup of ammonium sulfate (available at drugstores or chemical supply companies), ½ cup of boric acid (found in drugstores), 2 tablespoons of borax (found in hardware or grocery stores), and 8 tablespoons of 3 percent hydrogen peroxide (available in drugstores). If you like, add pine oil emulsion for an appropriate aroma. Store the mixture in a glass container.

For use, fill a spray bottle, and spray your Christmas tree with this fire-retarding solution. To prolong the life of your tree, keep the cup of its stand filled with the liquid. Help the tree absorb the solution by cutting the trunk anew at its base.

PART III

THE COUNTRY TABLE

Many of our commonest farm foods have histories stretching far back in time. In addition to their use in nutrition, they often served in other ways—to remedy bodily ills, to enhance beauty, and to fulfill superstitious beliefs. Here are some uncommon facts about some common foods.

Asparagus

Asparagus was cultivated as food before the Christian era in Persia and Arabia. It is a delicious vegetable rich in vitamins A and B.

The plant has no true leaves. Its so-called foliage consists of a great many slender branchlets, looking like green threads, which emerge from a tiny scale leaf at the tip.

Long ago, people believed that they could grow asparagus by planting the crushed horn of a wild ram. Its stalks were thought to have medicinal value. A broth made of them was said to relieve the pain of toothache and sprains. A drink of the plant's roots boiled in wine was administered to victims of snake bite.

In years past asparagus was known as "looking-glass weed."

Before the use of window screens, its feathery sprays were draped over bedroom mirrors for flies to alight on. Walking very cautiously, one might succeed in reaching an open door or window with a spray still black with flies!

Carrot

All carrots sprang from a common ancestor—that beautiful wildflower Queen Anne's lace.

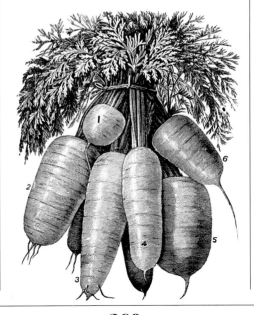

In the early 1500s the English were cultivating carrots in their gardens. Besides providing a delicious vegetable for tables, carrots furnished an adornment for women. In autumn their delicate, feathery foliage takes on a red or purple hue. Ladies used to pick the leaves and wear them on hats or in their hair instead of feathers.

Today a yellow pigment derived from the carrot is sometimes used to give butter a richer color. Furriers use the oil from this orange root on pelts to protect them from moths. Carrots also serve as nutritious food for livestock.

Cheese

A camel is supposed to have been responsible for the world's first cheese. Thousands of years ago, legend has it, a camel driver used a lamb's stomach as a container for fresh milk. The fermenting action of the enzymes remaining in the lamb's stomach, plus the constant swaying motion of the camel's gait, transformed the milk into cheese.

Cheese was said to have provided David with nourishment and strength when he challenged Goliath. It was brought to Europe by Crusaders returning from the Holy Land. Early Britons, in addition to getting subjugation from Caesar, got cheese. The eighteenth-century Italian lover Casanova advocated cheese and

wine as a means of hastening love's blossoming.

Speaking of love, if you are a lover of cheese, you're known as a turophile.

Garlic

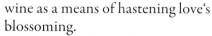

Garlic, that odoriferous member of the lily family, was native to southwest Siberia.

In olden times its odor was considered so intolerable that those guilty of heinous crimes were punished by being forced to eat garlic. Because animals as well as humans were believed to be offended by its strong smell and taste, domestic fowl were sprinkled with garlic juice to keep them safe from weasels and other predators.

The ancients valued garlic for its medicinal qualities. It was prescribed externally as a treatment for the bite of beast or insect and internally as an antidote for poison. Garlic was supposed to improve eyesight. When cattle lost their vision, farmers hung roots of it about their necks. A very ancient use of garlic was as a disinfectant in the cremation of corpses. During the First World War, when antiseptics were scarce, garlic oil was used as an acceptable substitute.

Magical protective powers were attributed to garlic. Throughout ancient times it was considered a sure defense against the influence of the evil eye.

Hung on doors and around windows, it was supposed to provide protection against vampires. Midwives kept garlic cloves handy to place about a baby's neck immediately following birth or after baptism to guard him from harm. Country dwellers fastened garlic around their cows' necks to deter goblins from stealing milk in the night. To prevent a snake from crawling out of its hole, a clove of garlic was laid at the entrance.

A very practical use for garlic was to keep heavy drinkers from becoming intoxicated. Putting a few crushed cloves at the bottom of their sizable wine pitchers was supposed to do the trick. In Europe, garlic accompanied by chunks of coarse dark bread was a standard breakfast for peasants. In the United States, it is used chiefly for flavoring. High in iron content, it may eventually be regarded as a staple food in the American diet.

Meanwhile, rural folks claim that it's a dependable corn cure. Kermit Zog of North Carolina says to rub a pesky corn with a crushed clove of garlic every night before going to bed, or to bind a sliver of it on the corn with a plaster. This procedure should be repeated until the corn drops off, usually within eight to ten days. Kermit cautions that you may find yourself sleeping alone!

By the way, if you're fond of garlic, you're an alliophiliac.

Honey

In olden times honey affected people's lives virtually from cradle to grave. Regarded as pure, it was the first food given to newborn infants. Marriage contracts often specified a quantity of honey that the groom was obliged to give his future wife every year of their married life. Marriage ceremonies were sticky affairs. In addition to honey's being served in food and drink, it was smeared on the bride's ear lobes, forehead, eyelids, and lips. Its purity served as a kind of talisman to protect the couple from evil and ensure their happy future.

Honey became known as an aphrodisiac and was the chief ingredient in love potions designed to increase virility. People believed it could influence fertility in women, cattle, and crops.

Esteemed for its nutritional value, it formed part of the daily diet. The ancients considered it an elixir of youth and predicted longevity for faithful users of honey as nourishment.

Since it was felt to be a magical substance, soothsayers used it in their ceremonies. It was regarded also as sacred and was generally included as a sacrificial offering during religious rites.

Over the centuries honey has been considered a cure-all for internal and external woes: gastric disorders, respiratory troubles, inflammation of the kidneys, epilepsy, labor pains, skin diseases, and inflammation of the eyes and eyelids. It has been used for dressing wounds, to spread on the skin of smallpox victims, and to treat obesity, typhoid fever, pneumonia, rheumatism, and insomnia. Because of its antiseptic quality, it was recommended as a gargle.

Peasants paid their taxes in honey. As a widely accepted medium of barter, it served as purchasing power.

Country folks valued it not only as a stimulant for the appetite and an aid to digestion, but as a supernatural agent to protect their cattle. Honey fed to cows and applied to their eyes were sure to guard them against pestilence. Rural folk added honey to their wells so that the water would not become contaminated. It was regarded as a cure for persons of disagreeable temperament and for those poisoned by mushrooms, bitten by snakes, or attacked by rabid animals. Used externally, it was said to kill lice and nits. Country people maintained that lightning never struck where there were honey and bees.

At life's end honey continued to play a role. Since honey represented eternal bliss, vessels of it were placed near the coffin and later in the tomb. Outstanding members of

society were embalmed in honey. The belief prevailed that the souls of those whose bodies were preserved in it would be reincarnated.

Nowadays honey might be associated with a country breakfast of hot biscuits spread with butter and honey or the aroma of split acorn squash baking in the oven, honey and spices steaming in the hollows. Yet among country dwellers today, honey is often mixed with hot lemon juice and used as a cold remedy or administered, combined with roasted onions, as a poultice for congested lungs.

To all the uses for honey down through the ages there has been added a modern one. Because of its low freezing point, honey mixed with an equal amount of water has been utilized as an emergency substitute for antifreeze.

Jerusalem Artichoke

Though the Jerusalem artichoke is a true native of North America, facts about it are not widely known. It is not an artichoke but a member of the sunflower family, having a thick, fleshy root. North American Indians ate the root raw, boiled, or roasted. In the western part of the country the plant grew wild, but Indians in the East cultivated it along with other crops of beans, maize, and squash.

French explorers carried it back to their homeland, where it was favorably received as table fare and used as feed for livestock. Upon reaching Italy, it was called *girasole*, the Italian word for sunflower. The English mispronunciation of this word brought about the first part of the name "Jerusalem artichoke;" a comparison of the tuber's flavor to that of the artichoke accounts for the latter part. After its introduction to the English, it was looked upon initially as an unusual delicacy. Since the Jerusalem artichoke grows prolifically, it was soon considered common and shunned.

The plant is similar to other small wild sunflowers but grows to a greater height. During the summer months the edible root grows very little, because the lengthening stalk

and maturing flowers consume most of the nourishment. Fortunately, the Jerusalem artichoke is resistant to frost, since its chief growing season extends through the cool months, from October to June. This vegetable is more widely cultivated in Europe than in America, its homeland.

Lettuce

In ancient times travelers from the Mediterranean area eastward were guided by the "compass plant." This plant was wild lettuce. Along its tall stalk climbed upturned leaves whose edges pointed due north and south. One's direction could be determined by it as surely as by the sun. Thirsty journeyers could rely upon its juicy leaves for refreshment, and so it became known as the "water plant."

Not long afterward the leaves, cooked as greens, were found to be a wholesome, palatable food. From then on and that was probably three thousand years ago lettuce was a cultivated plant.

Partaking of lettuce salad at the beginning of a meal, it was believed, would stimulate the appetite; eating it at meal's end would prevent inebriation from the wine imbibed while dining.

Because lettuce has a white juice similar to that of opium poppies, it was thought to have narcotic and sedative properties and was recommended as a treatment for pain, fevers, and insomnia.

Onion

The onion is one of the world's earliest-cultivated plants. The Bible relates that it was a food much craved by the Israelites in the wilderness.

Egyptians were said to have placed their right hand on the onion as they took an oath. They sometimes used it as a sacrificial offering to their deities. Divine honors were bestowed upon one variety, and it was depicted on Egyptian monuments. The nutritional value of the bulb was appreciated by Egyptians, who fed it to slaves erecting the pyramids as a defense against scurvy. In later centuries ships of other lands, destined to be long from home port, put to sea with holds laden with onions for the same purpose.

The onion reached the New World through the West Indies, where it was introduced by the Spanish. It spread throughout the Americas and was grown by early colonists and a little later by the Indians.

According to folklore, the onion was an aphrodisiac. From this belief developed the custom of carrying onion soup to a newly married couple.

In the past it was believed that various ailments could be remedied by the onion. A few drops of onion juice in the ear would cure deafness or ringing. Onion juice applied to bald areas of the head would rejuvenate hair growth. For the relief of gout, the juice mixed in a tea of pennyroyal should be spread with a feather on affected areas. Onion juice blended with capon grease was recommended as a cure for blisters on the feet. Today country people of America use raw onion to draw out the poison from a bee sting.

Parsley

Long ago parsley was used for both the living and the dead.

It was considered a healthful food for man and other creatures. The herb was used in meat dishes, poultry stuffing, omelets, soups, salads, and gravies. Eating parsley was said to benefit the brain and memory, beautify the skin, and counteract the effects of a mad dog's bite. One variety boiled in ale

was a drink prescribed for the bite of a poisonous spider. Ailing fish were cured, it was believed, if parsley leaves were tossed into their ponds.

Victors of athletic games were crowned with chaplets of parsley. As for the dead, their graves were customarily spread with it, for parsley was long regarded as the death herb.

To account for parsley's tendency to germinate slowly, legend said that it is the property of the Devil and must make seven trips to him before sprouting. During the Middle Ages it was believed that an enemy would meet sudden death if one uprooted parsley while repeating his name. To this day there are those who avoid transplanting the herb, fearing it might cause bad luck.

Potato

The potato grown in this country, often called the "Irish" potato, followed a rather circuitous route in reaching us. Though its history is spotted with unauthenticated information, there is general agreement that its original home was Chile.

From Indians in the Andes of South America, potato cultivation spread to other tribes, gradually finding its way to the West Indies and, to what is now Virginia, even before colonial days. Sir Francis Drake's ships, bearing supplies for settlers there, returned

to England with potatoes obtained by barter from the Indians. These curiosities were presented to Sir Walter Raleigh, who planted them on his estate in Ireland. When the English imported them from that country, they became known as "Irish" potatoes.

Grain was the chief crop of Ireland at that period, and it was a long time before the potato was established as a staple food. By many it was regarded as unfit for human consumption. Its denouncers organized the "Society for the Prevention of Unsatisfactory Diets." From the initials of this group came the word "spud," used for the potato.

The potato was rejected in Scotland as a product of the Devil, since no mention of it could be found in the Bible.

Spaniards became acquainted with the vegetable when they invaded South America early in the sixteenth century. They carried it to Spain, from which country it spread to other parts of Europe.

For a considerable time the French would not accept the potato, believing it was poisonous because of its membership in the nightshade family. It was also believed to cause leprosy. Later, however, it was found to be a cure for scurvy on long sea voyages. In Germany it became a chief crop food as a result of a grain failure. Eventually the potato won its way into the hearts and stomachs of most of the civilized world.

The potato is actually the enlarged tip, or tuber, of an underground stem. In addition to their nutritional value for both humans and farm animals, potatoes are utilized in manufacturing potato flour, starch, alcohol, glucose, and syrup. Country dwellers use the potato as a remedy for lumbago by carrying a small one in the pocket, replacing it when it becomes dried out.

The most reliable written record shows that potatoes were first cultivated on a large scale in New Hampshire from a stock of "Irish" potatoes brought from Ireland. To do its ancient lineage justice, the potato should actually be called the "Chilean" potato.

Radish

The radish was cultivated so long ago that it's unclear where it originated. In ancient times it was food for the people of China, Japan, India, and southern Europe.

The plant is believed to have been cultivated at first for its leaves along Mediterranean shores. Constant tending caused its root to enlarge, providing a second vegetable. Possibly its ancestor was the wild radish of Europe, credited with the power of detecting the presence of witches.

Medicinal properties were ascribed to the radish. Taken internally, it was believed to quicken mental capacities; used externally, to cure bruises. Mixed with honey vinegar, it served as a soothing gargle for tonsillitis. The radish was also considered efficacious in the event of snake bite. Cosmetically, it was recommended for renewal of hair growth and the removal of freckles.

In addition to the pleasantness as food of the crisp, pungent root of the radish plant, its pods are enjoyed when pickled.

Raspberry

Old-timers attached much importance to raspberries when hunting season arrived. Bears are particularly fond of them. When the fruit ripened, bears were easily located.

In olden times people believed that vinegar made from raspberries was a good protection against plague. The juice of the berries was used to dissolve tartar on the teeth and to treat scrofula.

Rhubarb

Rhubarb, usually served as a dessert, is a vegetable of the buckwheat family. Its origin was the Mediterranean area.

In ancient China a variety of rhubarb was cultivated for the use of its roots in medicine.

Benjamin Franklin, in the late 1700s, was responsible for introducing rhubarb to America. While in England, he sent a gift of it to a friend in Philadelphia. Its popularity soon spread. Only the stalks were used for pies and wine making; hence rhubarb is often called "pie plant" and "wine plant." The leaves are discarded because of their poisonously high content of oxalic acid, which can cause a skin rash.

Rice

Rice was probably a native crop of India some five thousand years ago. It soon spread and was cultivated throughout Asia.

The Greeks and Romans did not plant this cereal grass but imported it. Rice cultivation was introduced to the Mediterranean area by Arab armies in the seventh and eighth centuries, and by the fifteenth century it was raised in Italy and France.

On his second voyage to North America, Columbus brought rice from Spain, but its growth was not successful. Then late in the seventeenth century, a storm-tossed ship sought safe harbor along the coast of South Carolina. Some of its cargo was unhusked rice from Madagascar. The captain gave a quantity to a plantation owner, who cultivated it with good results. It was the start of a new money crop for the South. Today the states of Arkansas, California, Louisiana, and Texas produce most of America's rice.

Long ago rice was prescribed as a treatment for hemorrhages and lung disease. Powdered and mixed with milk, it was used as a poultice for skin inflammations. Today a standard country cure for diarrhea is rice water.

Soybean

One of the very earliest food crops grown by man was the soybean. It was a common food among the ancient Chinese well before the Christian era; yet not

until the seventeenth century did it find its way to Europe.

In the United States, soybeans were first cultivated to a limited extent in the late nineteenth century, and by the early 1900s home-grown soybeans were processed for the first time.

In China, superstition clings to the soybean. One wearing a concealed necklace of the beans is supposed to be capable of great feats. Diviners are able to predict future events by consulting soybeans that have been soaked in sesame oil for three days.

Besides being a nutritious food containing ten times the protein of milk, soybeans provide oil that is important in the finishing of automobiles.

Spinach

Spinach was first cultivated in ancient Persia and surrounding areas. Not until the Christian era did the plant become widespread. It was introduced to China in the seventh century. Moors were responsible for carrying it to Europe in the twelfth century. For generations a variety of spinach was grown in secluded monastery gardens of Europe.

Finally, in the early part of the sixteenth century, colonists transported the plant to North America. Today Arkansas and Texas produce our major spinach crops.

Nature included an acceptable

amount of oxalic acid in spinach. However, with man's constant hybridization of the plant, the acid content has been substantially increased and can cause formation of small stones of calcium oxalate in the body. Eaten occasionally and in moderate amounts, spinach is a good source of vitamin B_2.

Recently the plant has been processed to form a film of chlorophyll which produces electricity when under the sun's rays. The resulting energy is stored in batteries. So spinach has twofold potential energy: food power and electrical power.

Tomato

Spanish padres are credited with the initial dissemination of the tomato plant. Peace following the conquest of the Aztecs permitted them the leisurely pursuit of examining plants

in Mexico used by the natives for food and medicine. The Indians cultivated tomato plants on their floating gardens and ate the red fruit. Tomato seeds were among the first sent by the monks to Spain for planting in monastery gardens.

Some years later a Moorish visitor to Mexico, intrigued by the plant's beauty, carried seeds to Morocco. It was here that the bright fruit caught the eye of an Italian sailor. He took the pomo dei Mori, the apple of the Moors, to his homeland, where it spread quickly. The French received it from Italy and cleverly changed the name to pomme d'amour the apple of love. The tomato reached England from France and continued being called the "love apple" for centuries.

The tomato plant of those times differed considerably from that of today. The fruit was very much smaller and deeply furrowed. Considered poisonous because it belongs to the nightshade family, it was cultivated not in the vegetable garden but amid flowers, solely as an ornamental plant. Stalks of the shiny red fruit were kept in vases as colorful centerpieces for dining tables or as decorative touches for fireplace mantles. Because of the supposed poisonous quality of tomatoes, they were thrown to marauding wolves, along with poisoned meat chunks.

During the days when tomato plants were relegated to flower

beds, ketchup was made from English walnuts. By the mid-1800s, however, walnut ketchup had lost favor to ketchup made from tomatoes. The Italians extracted an oil from the seeds, which they used in making soap. Today tomato-seed oil, along with other oils, is still incorporated in soaps.

After centuries of cultivation the tomato has developed into the large, smooth-skinned sphere of red we know today, delicious to eat and nutritious as a source of vitamin C. We think of the tomato as a vegetable; actually it is a berry.

The tomato really came into its own as a food in America just about the time that hoop skirts went out of style. Resourceful country housewives used discarded hoop-skirt frames as improvised trellises for training tomato vines.

A Hash of Kitchen Wisdom

Baking
A cup of water placed in the oven when you bake will keep the crust of bread and cake from getting hard.

Baking Powder
To make a good baking powder, thoroughly mix the following: 4 ounces of flour, 5 ounces of bicarbonate of soda, 10 ounces of cream of tartar, and 1 ounce of tartaric acid.

Butter
Butter can be made firm during hot weather in this way: Mix 1 teaspoon of powdered alum with 1 teaspoon of carbonate of soda. At churning time put this mixture into the amount of cream that will produce 20 pounds of butter.

Cabbage
Odorless cabbage cooking is accomplished by adding half a green bell pepper without seeds to the cabbage pot. It flavors the cabbage and kills the odor in the kitchen.

Cake
When cake sticks to the pan, wrap a damp warm cloth around the baking pan. The steam will cause the cake to loosen.

Citrus
Roll an orange, grapefruit, or lemon vigorously on a hard surface before squeezing it and you will get a lot more juice.

Currants
To clean dried currants, shake them about in a sieve with a little flour until only the currants remain. Wash them thoroughly, and remove any twigs. Spread them on a flat surface in some warm spot to dry. Don't use the currants until you are sure that they are completely dry, or else they will sink to the bottom of your puddings and cakes.

Eggs
When boiling eggs, add a little salt to the water and the shells will slip off easily. To boil an egg that is cracked, add a teaspoonful of salt to the water and the egg will stay in the shell.

To keep eggs fresh, follow this procedure: Gather new-laid eggs, and coat each with salt butter so

that the shell is completely sealed. Dry some bran in the oven. Place a layer of the bran in a box, and pack the eggs in it with their small ends down. Continue to fill the box with alternating layers of bran and eggs. Keep the box in a cold, dry place, and the eggs will remain fresh for 10 months.

Fish

Dip fresh fish in hot salt water until the scales curl and they will be a lot easier to clean.

Flavoring Extracts

Homemade flavoring extracts are found to be more delicious than those that are bought. To make lemon extract, put 1 pint of good alcohol in a jar and add 1 ounce of lemon oil and the peel of 2 lemons. Allow it to stand for a week; shake it 3 times each day. Now take out the peel, and bottle the liquid for use. All essences can be made according to, the same proportions as the lemon-flavored extract.

Fruits

Fruits of an acid nature should be cooked in tin, brass, or porcelain vessels.

Herbs

Gather herbs on a sunny day of low humidity. To dry them, you may spread them in the shade on such a day, or hang them near a stove, or place them in an open moderate oven. When the herbs are very dry, powder and sift them. Store them in bottles with snug corks or in air-tight tins to preserve their flavor.

Milk

Raw milk curdles quickly when boiled. This can be corrected by adding a pinch of soda.

A pinch of salt in raw milk will keep it from souring quickly.

Sprinkle table salt on scorched milk and it will help eliminate the bad smell.

When cooking with milk, put a little water in the pan first and heat it to boiling, then add the milk. It will keep the milk from burning or sticking to the bottom of the pan.

Molasses

Molasses and syrup will pour completely out of a cup or any container if you will first grease it with butter or cooking oil.

Nuts

Soak hardshell nuts in salt water overnight. They will break open easily and the kernels will shell-out whole.

Onions

When cooking onions set a cup of vinegar on the stove to kill the odor.

Preserving Apples

First pile them in a heap to sweat. Then pack them in barrels or boxes in hemlock sawdust. In this manner they can be kept fresh until Nature provides new fruit in the spring.

Preserving Root Vegetables

Put root vegetables into a large box. Pack them in such a way as to leave a space of an inch or more around the sides of the box. When it is filled to within 6 inches of the top, shake in sand or dry road dust and cover with a layer of fresh earth. This will nicely keep vegetables—especially beets and turnips—for winter use.

Restoring Tainted Meats

To remove the odor from tainted (not rotten) meat, prepare this solution: Boil 1 quart of water, and allow it to cool. Then add 1 ounce of permanganate of potash. Put the liquid in a tightly closed bottle and shake well.

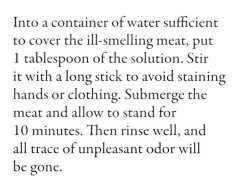

Into a container of water sufficient to cover the ill-smelling meat, put 1 tablespoon of the solution. Stir it with a long stick to avoid staining hands or clothing. Submerge the meat and allow to stand for 10 minutes. Then rinse well, and all trace of unpleasant odor will be gone.

Soup Coloring

To impart an amber color to soup, add finely grated carrot. If a reddish color is desired, use red tomatoes, straining out their skins and seeds. Press the juice from spinach; dry and powder the leaves. To give soup a green color, add both the juice and the powdered leaves. For brown soup a clear stock should be used.

Soup Flavoring

Wash the large leaves of 5 celery stalks. Boil them in 1 quart of water until the liquid is reduced to ½ pint. Allow it to cool, strain out the celery leaves, bottle the liquid, and store it in a cool place. Use it as a flavoring for soups, gravies, and stews.

Substitute Jelly

If jelly is desired and fruits are not available for its making, the following method will produce a satisfactory substitute: Boil ½ ounce of powdered alum in 1 quart of water for 3 minutes. Put in 8 pounds of white sugar; boil for a few minutes, and strain. Add any preferred flavoring.

Tomatoes

To easily slip tomato peels off place the tomatoes in boiling water for one-half minute then place them in cold water until they are cool. The skin will slip off and leave a firm, full, unbroken tomato.

Vinegar Uses

• When cooking rice, add 1 teaspoon of vinegar to the water. This will keep the grains whole.
• You can make lettuce and other greens clean and crisp by soaking them for 5 minutes in water with a little vinegar added.
• Put vinegar in the water for boiling eggs. This will keep the whites from running out if the shells crack.
• Add a few drops of vinegar to uncooked icing during the mixing, and it will remain softer.
• To keep cheese fresh, wrap it in a cloth moistened with vinegar.

Vegetables

The taste of oversalted vegetables can be removed by covering the bowl with a wet cloth for a few minutes.

Whipping Cream

If whipping cream won't whip add the white of an egg.

Moon Signs in the Kitchen

Country women who heed the zodiac signs in their kitchen work agree with these tips:

Baking

Bread prepared when the moon is in the first and second, or waxing quarters tends to "rise" more. Baking is best done when the moon is in Aries, Cancer, Libra, or Capricorn, the movable signs. Some believe this makes the bread lighter.

Brewing and Winemaking

The third and fourth waning moon quarters are usually best, especially when the moon is in the watery and fruitful signs of Pisces, Cancer, or Scorpio.

Canning

Can fruits and vegetables during a waning moon in the third and fourth quarters, preferably in the watery signs of Pisces, Cancer, or Scorpio. Put up jellies and preserves during a waning moon in the third and fourth quarters, but in the fixed signs of Aquarius, Taurus, Leo, or Scorpio (especially Scorpio since it is both a fixed and a water sign).

24 | FROM THE SPRINGHOUSE

Butter

Back in the old days when butter was homemade, the process began with the care of cows. Some farmers, believing that a diet of corn fodder did not result in good butter, advocated a blend of half bran and half cornmeal. Others swore by a twice-daily feeding of early-cut hay and a mixture of scalded cornmeal and wheat bran, moistened with sweet skimmed milk.

The milk produced was strained through a cloth and "set" for cream. It was poured into deep tin pails either standing in vessels of ice or maintained at low temperature by cold spring water running through the milk house, if the building was so favorably situated. Cream setting lasted for a period of twenty-four hours or more, some dairymen claiming that a preliminary heating to a temperature of 130° F would cause the cream to rise more quickly.

The temperature considered ideal for cream at churning time was 57° F. After being skimmed from the pails, the cream was put in a churn and worked for twelve to twenty minutes. The cylindrical dash churn, with a stick handle protruding through the top, was generally made of pottery or stripped cedar banded in brass hoops and powered by hand. Another old-time means of butter making was the dog churn. The sheep or cattle dog was recruited to run the equipment, freeing farm

folks for other duties. Harnessed on a sort of treadmill, the animal set in motion an attached container for cream as it trotted in place. To each 20 pounds of butter, 3 ounces of white sugar and 6 ounces of salt were added.

In the absence of pasturage during the winter months, butter generally lacked sufficient yellow; so country housewives colored it with annatto, a dyeing material prepared from the seeds of a tropical tree. A lump about the size of a hickory nut was dissolved in 8 ounces of water. One tablespoon of the mixture was used to color 5 pounds of butter. Coloring the butter was also done with carrots. For each 3 gallons of cream, 6 large carrots were washed and coarsely grated. Boiling water was poured on them to extract their color. The carrot juice, allowed to cool, was then strained through coarse muslin into the cream prior to churning. Besides improving the

appearance of the butter, the carrot juice gave it a sweet taste, similar to grass butter. Powdered turmeric, too, served as a yellow dye and was said to impart a richer flavor to sweet butter.

Tin pails and other dairy utensils were often scoured with the aid of nettles and plenty of suds from homemade lye soap.

Today, a simpler way of making butter is with your electric mixer. Attach the mixers, set the machine at its lowest speed, and slowly pour in all the cream while the mixer is running.

When pale butter grains appear, drain them in a muslin bag. Then put the substance in a bowl, and wash it thoroughly by spooning cold water over it until the water becomes clear. Finally, press the grains into one mass. If you wish to add salt, use about 1 teaspoon to the pound.

Perhaps the easiest means of making butter is provided by your blender. Put 4 cups of fresh cream into the machine. Let the cream reach close to room temperature (about 68° F). Then run the blender at its slowest speed. After about three minutes, yellowish flecks should appear on the surface. Continue running the blender until the cream turns to butter, within eight minutes or so.

When butter has formed, drain off the buttermilk, reserving it for cooking purposes, and replace it with an equal amount of cold

water. Cap the blender and churn the contents for ten seconds. Strain off the water. Repeat this cleaning method until the water is quite clear.

Drain the butter. Transfer it to a bowl, and press out excess moisture with a spoon. Add salt if desired.

Cheeses

Hard Cheese (yield: 1½ to 2 pounds)

If you have access to milk fresh from a farm, let 4 quarts of the evening's milk stand overnight in a cool place where the temperature ranges between 50° and 60° F. The next morning, mix in 4 quarts of fresh morning milk. Either cow's or goat's milk may be used. The best store-bought milk for cheese is fresh homogenized milk.

Be sure all utensils are completely clean. In a stainless steel pot or enameled or tin pail, heat the milk to 86° F. Use a dairy thermometer. You may add cheese coloring (optional) at this time by dissolving about one eighth of a cheese color tablet in 1 tablespoon of water and stirring it into the milk. In a glass of cold water, thoroughly dissolve one quarter of a cheese rennet tablet by stirring and crushing it with a spoon. Set the pail of milk in a larger container of warm (88°–90° F) water, and place it in a warm spot protected from drafts. Thoroughly stir in the rennet solution for about one minute.

Leave the milk undisturbed for approximately forty minutes while a curd forms. Test the curd's firmness by inserting your finger at an angle and lifting. When it breaks clean over your finger, it is ready for cutting. With a knife long enough for the blade to reach the pail's bottom, cut the curd into small pieces. Cut in all directions so that the pieces will be quite small. Using your well-washed hand or a wooden spoon, gently stir the curd from around the sides and from the bottom upward. Carefully cut any large chunks that rise to the surface into smaller pieces; do not mash them. Try to make the curds of uniform size. To prevent their sticking together, continue the stirring for fifteen minutes.

Gradually raise the temperature of the pail's contents to 102° F at the rate of 1½ degrees every five minutes. Stir frequently with a spoon to prevent the curds from sticking to each other. By this time, the curds should hold their shape and fall apart easily when they are held without being squeezed.

The next step in the process lasts one hour. Take the pail from the heat, and stir the contents often enough (about every five minutes) to prevent the curds from coagulating. Let the curds stay in the warm whey until sufficiently firm so as to shake apart after being pressed together in your hand. Turn the curds into a piece of cheesecloth 4 feet square, spread in a container. Gather up two corners of the cloth

in each hand, and rock it gently for about three minutes so that the curds move about while the whey drains through. (When making cheese with cow's milk, don't discard the whey. It can be used to prepare butter that will taste like the salted variety, but with a delicate cheese flavor.)

Lay the cloth holding the curds in a clean pail. Sprinkle 1 tablespoon of salt over the contents and mix thoroughly. Add another tablespoon of salt and blend well.

Now tie the corners of the cloth together, forming a ball of the curd. Hang it so that it drips for a half hour or more.

Have your cheese press ready. Cheese-making kits are available in stores, complete with a cheese press, dairy thermometer, cheese coloring, and rennet tablets with directions for use. However, you can make your own cheese press by

taking two pieces of wood, 8 by 12 inches, and putting a 1-inch dowel through both at either end. The dowels will keep the boards in place.

Take the cloth away from the sides of the curd ball. Fold a long cloth, such as a dish towel, into a 3-inch-wide strip, and wrap it tightly around the ball. Form the ball into a round, flat wheel. Smooth the surface of the cheese with your hands. Put several thicknesses of cheesecloth under and on top of the wrapped cheese. Set the cheese on the bottom board of your cheese press, and lower the top board to rest on the cheese. Place two bricks on top. That evening turn the cheese over, placing four bricks on top. Allow to stand until morning.

The next day remove the cloth from the cheese. Leave it on a board for half the day, turning it now and then to let the rind dry completely. Or put it on a wire rack; air will circulate around it, making turning unnecessary. Then paint on liquid paraffin with a brush. If you prefer, you can wrap the cheese tightly in plastic wrap. Store it in a clean and cool but frost-free place. Turn it over daily for the first few days and then several times weekly for four weeks. At the end of that time, your homemade cheese should be good to eat. However, you may leave it longer to develop a higher flavor if you like.

Cottage Cheese (yield: 1 cup)

2 quarts skim milk
6 tablespoons homogenized milk
1½ teaspoons vinegar
½ rennet tablet
1 tablespoon cold water
½ to 2 teaspoons salt

Combine milk and vinegar in the top half of a double boiler with water beneath. Gradually warm the milk to a temperature of about 70° F (not more than 75°). Take the top of the double boiler from the heat. Blend into the milk one half of a rennet tablet that has been dissolved in 1 tablespoon of cold water. Cover the mixture, and set it in a warm spot (between 75° and 80° F) for about fourteen hours. Leave it undisturbed.

After twelve hours, examine it. There should be whey on the milk's surface. Tilt the pan a little; the curd should separate. If these signs are not evident, allow it to stand several hours more.

Then place a colander, lined with a towel, in the sink. Pour the mixture into the colander, letting the whey drain off. Occasionally stir it lightly with a fork, and lift the towel, moving the curd about to further the drainage. Add salt to taste when the curd has thoroughly drained.

Creamed cottage cheese can be made by stirring in 1 or 2 tablespoons of cream or milk. Caraway seeds, chopped parsley, chopped olives, and pimentos may be used for flavoring, if desired.

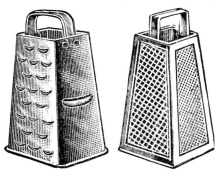

Homemade Rennet

Here are ways to make rennet from four different sources:

- Rennet from Calf Stomach (dated 1887): Ask the butcher for a calf's stomach. Scour it well with salt, both inside and out. Tack it to a wooden frame, and dry it in the sunshine for one or two days.

Cut the stomach into ½-inch squares. Put the pieces in a large jar; pack them in salt. Before using the rennet, soak it in water for thirty minutes and then wash it well. As an alternative to packing the pieces in salt, pour enough alcohol into the jar to cover them. With this method the rennet does not require soaking.

To easily remove the rennet from the curd when making cheese, tie the rennet sections together with a string before immersing them.

- Rennet from Lamb or Kid Stomach: Remove the stomach from a nursing lamb or kid that has eaten no solid food. Tie the opening securely; roll the organ in

ashes until well coated. Hang it to dry out of direct sunlight in a warm, dry, well-ventilated spot. (Old-timers used to hang the stomachs in their grape arbors or from house rafters.) Once it is completely dry, the milk inside will have become brown powder.

When making cheese, pulverize a bit less than ¼ teaspoon of the powder in a mortar. (If you lack mortar and pestle, use a bowl and an old china doorknob instead.) Add enough water to form a paste. Then thin it, using a little more water. With the added water, the total liquid will equal about ¾ cup, enough rennet to help make twelve 2-pound cheeses, each made from 8 quarts of goat's milk plus 1 tablespoon of the solution.

- Whey Rennet: Reserve 1 quart of whey for use as rennet. About ¼ cup cuts 5 gallons of milk. Replace the whey used each day; the quart of rennet will last two weeks before it is too weak to work as it should.

- Nettle Rennet: It is said that a vegetable rennet for cheese making can be prepared from nettles. We haven't been able to learn the particulars concerning this method. You might like to experiment, however, with the idea on your own.

Goat's-Milk Cheese (yield: 1½ pounds)

Pour 1½ gallons of raw goat's milk into an earthenware bowl. Leave it for seven days or until it becomes clabbered, when thick curds will

rise to the surface. Heat the clabbered milk in a vessel until very hot but not boiling. Stir often to separate the curds and whey (the liquid). Continue to cook and stir for thirty minutes. When the curds are tough, drain them in a piece of cheesecloth. Remove as much of the whey as you can by squeezing and wringing. Put the cheese, still wrapped in the cloth, beneath a heavy weight in a pot. Leave it overnight to allow more whey to drain out.

The following morning, add 4 tablespoons of fresh sweet butter and ¾ teaspoon of soda. Mix the ingredients thoroughly, and chop the curd until very fine. Press the mixture flat on a board. Leave it in a warm spot for two hours.

Transfer the cheese to a double boiler over low heat. Put in ⅔ cup of very sour heavy cream and 1¼ teaspoons of salt. Stir until it starts to become a runny mass. Then empty the double boiler into a well-buttered bowl, and allow the cheese to cool. When solid, it is ready for serving.

To cure and store your goat's-milk cheese, take it from the bowl when cool and solid and coat the

surface with melted paraffin, using a brush. Keep it in a cool place.

Clabbered Cheese

These are the necessary ingredients for clabbered cheese:

    3 gallons clabbered, skimmed milk

    1½ teaspoons soda

    ½ cup butter

    1½ cups sour cream

    ¼ teaspoon dandelion-butter coloring

    2 teaspoons salt

Heat the clabbered milk in a vessel until just bearable to the touch. Set the pot on the back of the stove; keep it hot for ½ hour.

Drain the curd through cheesecloth, thoroughly squeezing out the whey. Blend the soda and butter into the curd. Allow to stand for two hours.

Put the mixture in a double boiler, stir in 1 cup of sour cream, and melt it until smooth. In the meantime, blend the salt and dandelion-butter coloring into the remaining ½ cup of sour cream until the color is uniform. Add this to the contents of the double boiler.

Pour the mixture into a buttered pan, preferably one of stainless steel (do not use aluminum). Allow to stand uncovered for five days. Then coat the cheese with paraffin.

Cream Cheese

The best cream for making cream cheese is that skimmed from fresh whole milk. If you buy cream in a store, avoid the kind that has been treated for long shelf life. Allow the cream to sour at room temperature.

After two days put the sour cream into a cheesecloth bag. Suspend it over a bowl to let the whey drip through. Hang it from a cupboard door handle or the kitchen faucet.

A lump of cheese will remain in the bag. If desired, mix in a little salt. Form the cream cheese into a cake; chill it. Should it be too soft to make into a cake, shape it after chilling.

Save the whey; it contains valuable nutrients. Use it as a substitute for water in baking. You'll find potato or spinach soup taking on a new, delicious flavor from its addition.

Ricotta-Style Cheese

Slowly bring 2 quarts of milk to the boiling point, stirring it now and then. Turn off the heat, add 3 tablespoons of lemon juice, and stir twice. Set the vessel in a warm place for twenty-four hours.

Bring the mixture to a boil once more. Allow it to cool, and then strain it through cheesecloth.

If desired, the cheese may be seasoned with salt. To heighten its flavor, you may let it age in an uncovered dish for a few days.

Yogurt

Yogurt, a semisolid, cheeselike food that can be used in a variety of ways, is prepared from milk fermented by a particular bacterium.

All utensils used in making yogurt must be extremely clean. Wash them in hot soapsuds, followed by rinses first in hot and then in boiling water.

Assemble these ingredients:
1 quart skim milk
1 cup nonfat powdered milk
¼ cup plain, unflavored yogurt
Blend the skim milk and powdered milk in a saucepan. Put in a dairy thermometer and heat the liquid to about 180° F over low heat. Be careful not to boil it. Take the pan from the stove, and cool its contents to somewhere between 100° and 115° F. Thoroughly blend in the yogurt.

Warm some containers by rinsing them in hot water. Fill them with the milk mixture and cover tightly. Put the containers in an incubator. You can purchase an electric yogurt maker or improvise one by placing the containers on a heating pad set on low and inverting a cardboard box over all. Maintain the incubator at 90° F for three hours, undisturbed. For a stronger flavor, you may incubate the yogurt longer, checking its taste every thirty minutes.

Put it in the refrigerator. As the yogurt cools, it will thicken. Save ¼ cup of your homemade yogurt to start the next supply. Use yogurt that is no more than five days old for the starter.

Yogurt Dressing (yield: 1 serving)

3 tablespoons yogurt
1 tablespoon homemade mayonnaise
1 teaspoon Dijon mustard
dash garlic powder
salt and pepper to taste
Combine yogurt and mayonnaise. Blend in well the mustard and garlic powder. Chill.

On a bed of chopped lettuce moistened with basic dressing (oil and vinegar), arrange a double row of alternating slices of beets and hard-cooked eggs, slightly overlapping. Spoon yogurt dressing over the beets and eggs; sprinkle lightly with paprika.

This dressing is also excellent on crisp, shredded cabbage.

Or fold diced beets into the yogurt dressing, and fill the hollow of half an avocado with the mixture.

Strawberry Yogurt Mold

1 cup homemade yogurt
4 tablespoons homemade strawberry jam (more or less to taste)
1 cup orange juice
1 envelope unflavored gelatin
¼ cup sugar
Thoroughly blend the strawberry jam with the yogurt. Pour ½ cup of orange juice into a small saucepan, and sprinkle it with the gelatin. Put the pan over low heat, stirring its contents until the gelatin dissolves. Remove the pan from the heat; stir in sugar. Add the

remainder of the orange juice. Using a wire whisk beat in the yogurt.

Pour the mixture into four dessert dishes. Chill until firm.

Yogurt Topping
(yield: 1 cup)
¼ cup light corn syrup
¼ cup mayonnaise
½ cup plain yogurt

Stir together the corn syrup and mayonnaise. Fold in the yogurt. Serve over unfrosted cake.

Miscellaneous

Honey Mayonnaise
(yield: about 1 cup)

Put the following ingredients into a blender: 1 egg, 1 teaspoon of honey, 2 tablespoons of vinegar, 2 tablespoons of lemon juice, ½ teaspoon of dry mustard, ½ teaspoon of salt, and ½ cup of safflower or peanut oil. Churn them until smooth. Now blend in an additional cup of salad oil, pouring it into the center of the mayonnaise. Transfer it to a jar and refrigerate.

Wine Mayonnaise
(yield: about 1¼ cups)
2 egg yolks
1 tablespoon red wine
1 tablespoon white-wine vinegar
1 tablespoon herb-flavored
   vinegar
½ teaspoon lemon juice
¾ teaspoon dry mustard
½ teaspoon salt
½ cup salad oil
½ cup olive oil

Put the egg yolks in an electric blender; run it on high speed until they are frothy (about ten seconds). Blend in vinegar, wine, lemon juice, mustard, and salt at medium speed for slightly longer than one minute, very gradually adding oil in a thin constant stream while the blender is running.

Transfer the mayonnaise to a container, and remove every last bit from the blender with a rubber spatula. Store it in the refrigerator, where it will keep for two weeks. Before blending, you may add various fresh or dried herbs to the egg yolks.

Potato Mayonnaise
3 egg yolks
¾ cup olive oil
1 lemon
salt to taste
1 small potato, boiled and
   mashed

Beat the egg yolks until they are thick. While continuing to beat them, add oil in drops. Slowly pour in the juice of one

lemon. Put in the mashed potato and salt, beating until the blend is very smooth.

Store in a tightly closed jar in the refrigerator. When cooked vegetables and fish are garnished with this mayonnaise, their flavor is enhanced.

Country housewives of bygone days maintained that mayonnaise prepared when a thunderstorm was in the offing wouldn't thicken and emulsify. Whether or not the claim is valid, if your mayonnaise fails to thicken, be the weather foul or fair, remedy the matter by constantly beating one egg yolk while very, very gradually (drop by drop at the start) adding the unsuccessful, thin mayonnaise.

Vanilla Ice Cream
(yield: 1 gallon)
2 quarts light cream (half-and-half)
1 quart milk
3 cups sugar
2 tablespoons pure vanilla
   extract
1 teaspoon salt

Mix all ingredients until the sugar dissolves. Thoroughly chill, overnight if possible.

Wash the dasher, can, and cover of the ice cream freezer in hot, sudsy water. Rinse well in hot, clear water. Dry. Chill them in your freezer or refrigerator. Crush from 20 to 25 pounds of ice in an ice crusher. Return the can and dasher to the freezer bucket. Fill the can from one half to two thirds full with the ice cream

mixture. Cover the can. Follow manufacturer's directions for fitting the crank assembly or motor into the cover and securing it to the bucket. Place the freezer on several layers of newspapers. Allow the motor to warm up for about sixty seconds. During this time, add ice and salt.

Be guided by the instructions accompanying your ice cream freezer. Freezers vary in their required proportions of salt and ice. Put in about 2 inches (6 cups) of crushed ice. Spread ¼ cup of rock salt over the ice. Continue these layers until they surround and cover the can. Keep the hole in the upper side of the bucket free to permit drainage of the brine. Place a plastic container beneath the hole to receive any drips.

A hand freezer should be cranked rapidly and steadily, with an increase in speed as the mixture thickens so as to whip air into it. Beating air into the ice cream gives it a smooth texture. Stop when the mixture becomes so thick that cranking is nearly impossible. When using an electric mixer, disconnect the freezer at once when the motor stops or runs sluggishly. Carefully tip the freezer to drain off the brine. Take out the ice and salt to a depth of two inches below the cover. Remove the cranking assembly or motor. Wipe away ice and salt from the cover, and take out the dasher. Scrape ice cream from the dasher into the can and from the upper sides of the can, using a rubber spatula. Blend it for a few minutes.

Next comes the ripening stage. Place several layers of waxed paper, plastic wrap, or foil over the mouth of the can, and then put on the cover. Fill the hole in the cover with some sort of plug; use wadded foil or paper towels. Add more ice and salt layers, using ½ cup of salt to each 6 cups of crushed ice. Cover the can completely with the layers. Wrap thicknesses of newspaper about the freezer, enclose it with a heavy cloth (an old blanket will do), and set it in a cool spot for three hours. (There are other ways of ripening ice cream. After the machine has been turned off, the can of ice cream can be transferred to your food freezer for ripening. Or you can immediately pack the ice cream in plastic containers and put them in the food freezer for the ripening process.)

Drain away the brine, and remove the ice and salt. Take the can from the freezer. If not eaten immediately, ice cream can be stored in plastic containers in the food freezer.

For a variation of flavor, you may add almost anything to the mixture just prior to freezing.

Grains

Grinding Grain

Whole grains, high in vitamin E, iron, and the B vitamins, are a nearly perfect food. To be eaten at their most nutritious, flavorful stage, they should be ground immediately prior to cooking; vitamins and flavor start to diminish with each hour that grains are exposed to air after grinding. However, if you prefer preparing a larger amount at one time, avoid grinding more grain than will be used within a period of three to four weeks. Store it in clean, airtight containers. Unground grain will keep almost indefinitely in closed containers stored in a dry, cool place.

Unless you are raising your own grain, purchase it (clean or uncleaned) from feed and grain stores, health food stores, or farms. Buy fresh grain that is untreated by chemicals.

You will need to winnow uncleaned grain. Make a frame of convenient holding size, using 1- by 2-inch lumber, and cover it with window screening. Pour uncleaned grain on the winnowing screen. Remove chaff and dust by shaking it. Most of the chaff will be blown away if you winnow on a windy day. Pick out any foreign material, such as heavy grit. To clean grain indoors, pour it back and forth from container to container in the breeze from an electric fan.

Barley, millet, oats, rice, rye, soybeans, and wheat are grain that can be ground successfully at home in a hand (or electric) mill, coffee grinder, or some blenders. Depending on its intended use, grain may be roughly ground or converted to very fine flour. About four grindings will produce fine flour.

Whole or ground grains can be used for all baking purposes and cereals. Cracked wheat imparts a nutlike flavor to breads and waffles. A combination of grains provides a delicious and unusual breakfast cereal.

To prepare a hot cereal, put cleaned, unground wheat in an iron skillet, which will not heat up too quickly and will maintain steady temperature. Spread the grain in a thin layer and stir continuously. It will double in size and turn brown. The kernels will pop but won't burst open. Grind your toasted wheat, and then cook it as you would regular wheat breakfast cereal.

Granola

Mix the following ingredients:
    4 cups rolled oats (or rolled wheat)
    1½ cups unsweetened coconut, shredded
    1 cup wheat germ
    1 cup chopped nuts
    1 cup sunflower seeds, hulled
    1 cup sesame seeds
    ½ cup bran
    1 cup soybeans, ground and toasted
Heat these ingredients:
    ½ cup oil
    ½ cup honey
    1 to 2 teaspoons vanilla
Add the honey-oil-vanilla mixture to the dry ingredients; blend well. Spread on oiled cookie sheets. Bake for twenty to thirty minutes in a 375° F oven. Stir occasionally.

If you would like to prepare freshly shredded coconut but avoid doing so because of the difficulty in opening the coconut shell, here are two tips to make the task an easy one: Either heat the coconut in a 350° F oven or freeze it for about two hours. A blow from a hammer will then quickly crack it.

This recipe may be changed according to your taste. Substitute any suitable, wholesome ingredients that you prefer, but always maintain the same ratio of seven parts dry ingredients to one part wet ingredients for successful granola.

Hominy

To make hominy, first shuck ears of firm, dried corn. (Hominy comes

from an Indian word meaning "parched corn.") Take off the underdeveloped kernels from either end of the cob. Then shell the corn by hand.

Put the kernels into an iron vessel. Cover it with cold water. Add 1½ tablespoons of lye to every gallon of corn. Boil until the husks start to separate from the kernels.

Transfer the corn to another vessel, and wash it seven or eight times in clear, cold water. Rinse out the first pot to prevent sticking when the hominy is boiled again later.

To completely remove the husks, put the kernels in a coarse-meshed sieve. Wearing rubber gloves as protection against the lye, run a forceful stream of water on the corn, at the same time rubbing it over the mesh. The water will carry away the unwanted husks. After husking, return the corn to the iron vessel and boil in fresh water until tender.

Hominy may be canned for future consumption. But if its golden goodness sets you to craving some immediately, try frying it in bacon drippings for a real treat. It can also be eaten just salted, rather like boiled peanuts.

In the old days, hominy was chiefly made during the winter months when country folks had fewer farm chores.

Southern Fried Corn

4 ears corn
¼ cup all-purpose flour
⅛ cup fine bread crumbs
½ teaspoon salt
½ teaspoon paprika
⅛ teaspoon black pepper
1 egg
cooking oil

Husk the corn and remove the silk. In a shallow dish, blend flour, bread crumbs, salt, paprika, and pepper. Lightly beat the egg in another shallow plate. Heat oil in a skillet. Dip the ears of corn in the egg. Drain slightly. Roll them in the flour mixture. Shake off any excess and fry in the hot oil for about four minutes. Turn occasionally. When golden brown, serve with meat, poultry, or seafood.

Sprouts

Essentials for Producing Sprouts

Produce inexpensive, unprocessed fresh food in all seasons by growing seed sprouts. Besides seeds you will need water, air, a few readily available containers, and—in certain cases—some sunlight.

Just about any legume, grain, or seed can be sprouted for nutritious food (potato sprouts should never be eaten): garbanzos, kidney beans, lima beans, mung beans, pinto beans, soybeans, chickpeas, peas, corn, alfalfa, barley, oats, rye, wheat, unhulled sunflower and sesame seeds, the seeds of cress, parsley, radishes, and many more.

Choosing Seeds

Choose whole seeds that have not been treated chemically. They can be purchased from health food stores or through mail-order sources. Wash them thoroughly. Discard seeds that float; they are probably sterile.

Yield

A fairly small amount of seeds yields a considerable quantity of sprouts: 1 tablespoon of alfalfa seeds produces about 30 square inches of sprouts; 3 tablespoons of beans or peas produce a similar quantity. As a general rule, ½ cupful of seeds swells to 1½ cups when soaked, making a quart or more of sprouts.

Put the seeds in a vessel containing three times their volume in warm (70°–80° F) water to soak overnight in some dark, warm spot, such as a kitchen cabinet. The following morning, drain off the water. Reserve this vitamin- and mineral-rich liquid for cooking rice, potatoes, and vegetables, or for adding to soups and fruit or vegetable juice drinks. Rinse the seeds, now double in size, to prevent mold. Put them in a moist (not wet) container. Keep it in a dark place where the temperature ranges between 80° and 90° F. If you prefer, instead of putting the container in a cupboard, you can invert a paper bag over it to keep out light. Rinse the seeds twice a day (three times daily in warm weather) to cleanse them and provide sufficient moisture for their growth. After each cleansing, drain them well to avoid rotting. Utilize the rinse water to feed your plants; they will thrive on it.

Begin a new batch of seeds each night to have a continuously fresh supply on hand. For variety in your menu, have about three containers of different sprouts developing at one time: a grain, a bean, and a seed. Don't crowd larger beans like black-eyed peas, kidney beans, and soybeans. Some folks maintain that garbanzos, lentils, mung beans, and soybeans grow better in the same container than when sprouted separately.

Procedure for Germination

Sprouts can be grown successfully in common kitchen containers: colanders, the strainers of coffee percolators, flour sifters, sink strainers, vegetable steamers, and tea strainers. A wide-mouthed jar can be used by stretching cheesecloth over the opening and fastening it on with a rubber band. A circle of wire mesh secured with a screw-on canning ring can substitute for the cloth. Put the jar in a bowl, top down, at a 45-degree angle to facilitate drainage. An unglazed earthenware flowerpot can serve as a sprout garden. It will absorb moisture, maintaining the sprouts in a moist, not wet, condition. Plug the drain hole with cotton or cheesecloth. Place a saucer on top, and set the pot in a shallow container of water. Regularly rinse the sprouts, as with those in other types of sprouters, to prevent mold from developing. Yet another way to germinate legumes, grains, or seeds is to place a rustproof metal rack in a glass baking pan. Put warm water in the container, but not enough to reach the rack. Spread a wet terry cloth towel (or several thicknesses of cheesecloth) on the rack, letting an end hang into the water beneath. This arrangement will provide the seeds with moisture without wetness.

Harvesting Sprouts

Within three to six days, depending on the type of seed, the sprouts will have greatly increased in volume and be ready for harvesting. If you like, during the last few hours of development, you can place them in indirect sunlight to generate healthful chlorophyll. Be sure to limit the exposure, however, since too much chlorophyll will toughen the shoots.

Seeds	Proper Size of Sprouts for Harvesting
Alfalfa	Two to three inches long
Peas	Two to three inches long
Soybeans	Two to three inches long
Grain	No longer than the length of the kernel
Sunflower	No longer than the seed length
Lentils	One inch
Mung Beans	Three to four inches

Most shoots are at their peak from sixty to eighty hours after germination, but you may wish to use personal preference in taste and texture as a guide for determining the harvest time.

The nutritional value of sprouts produced by the water method is high, but higher still when they are raised by the earth method. Eliminating the necessity to periodically rinse them is an additional benefit.

Soak beans or seeds for twelve hours. Then scatter them evenly on a layer of good soil in a wooden box or large flowerpot. Sprinkle on enough earth to cover them, water lightly, and spread a cloth over the container to retain moisture and exclude light. Several days later, pull out the entire sprout, wash away the soil, and enjoy this extra nutritious harvest in your favorite recipes.

If the sprouts develop before you are ready to use them, put them into a colander and steam them for several minutes. Then immerse them in cold water. Drain and refrigerate the sprouts until they are needed. To preserve them for an extended time, freeze or dry them; their nutritional value will not be diminished.

Sprout Uses

It is unnecessary to remove the seed hulls from sprouts before serving them. Use sprouts as meatloaf filler, as steamed vegetables, in stews, sprinkled on soups, mixed into beverages (with a blender), and raw in salads.

26 | BREADS, SPREADS, PRETZELS, AND CRACKERS

Dough Starters

Some dough starters, kept active for more than 100 years, have been handed down from one generation to the next like family heirlooms.

Buttermilk Yeast Starter

1 quart buttermilk flour
½ cup sugar
1 cup yeast
3 pints water

At midday, heat the buttermilk until it commences to boil. Put in the yeast and sugar. Stir, adding sufficient flour to form a stiff batter. Allow to stand in a warm spot until nightfall. Then add 2½ cups of water and allow to stand until the following morning.

Add the rest of the water. Your buttermilk yeast is ready for bread baking.

Peach-Leaf Yeast Starter

Steep 1 quart of fresh. well-washed peach leaves in 3 cups of boiling water for fifteen minutes. Drain, adding enough water, if necessary, to make 3 cups. The water will have a greenish hue, but this will disappear during fermentation. Bake three medium-sized potatoes. Peel them, and put them through a sieve or food mill. Scald ½ cup of cornmeal in 1 cup of water until it boils and thickens. Stir to prevent lumps from forming.

Put all these ingredients in a bowl with 2 teaspoons of salt and 3 tablespoons of sugar. Cover and allow to ferment in a warm place for twenty-four hours, stirring well every two or three hours.

Pour it into a glass jar, and keep it in the refrigerator. Stir it down several times until foaming ceases. When approximately ½ inch of clear liquid rises to the surface, it will be ready for use. Stir thoroughly each time you use it.

When the starter is reduced to 1 cup, add 3 cups of water, three baked potatoes, the scalded cornmeal, salt, and sugar as you did the first time. Leave it in a warm spot. In about seven hours it should become active.

Peach-leaf starter improves with age. It is advisable to use it about twice each week. If not, stir it every couple of days, adding 1 teaspoon of sugar.

You can make this starter into a dry yeast. Begin by sterilizing 2 quarts of cornmeal for one hour in a low oven. Mix it into the starter. Spread it in flat pans to a thickness of ½ inch. When it is set, cut it into 1½-inch squares. Move them apart to dry and harden. Wrap the cakes. Store them in the refrigerator; they will keep a year or more.

A starter can be made from the dry yeast in this way. In a bowl, mix 1 cake of yeast, ½ cup of warm water, ½ teaspoon of ginger, and 1 teaspoon of sugar. Keep it covered until you see white foam on top. Then stir in ½ cup of water, ½ cup of flour, and 1 teaspoon of sugar. After it foams again, add 1 cup of water, 1 cup of flour, and 1 teaspoon of sugar. Allow to foam, stirring often. Pour it into a jar and refrigerate. Put the lid on loosely until the foaming stops. When ½ inch of clear liquid has risen to the surface, the starter is ready to use.

Potato Yeast Starter

Cook three potatoes, peeled and cubed, until tender. Mash them, blending in the pot liquor, and add sufficient cold water to equal 3 cups. Put in ¼ cup of honey. Cool the mixture to lukewarm. Soak one package of dried yeast in 1 cup of lukewarm water. Add it to the mixture. Allow to stand in a warm spot overnight.

The following day, store 1 cup of the starter in the refrigerator; use the rest to bake four loaves of any recipe.

Sourdough Starter

2 cups all-purpose flour
1 package dry yeast
2 cups warm water

Thoroughly blend all ingredients in a large bowl. Leave it uncovered in a warm spot for forty-eight hours. Stir occasionally.

Just before using the starter, stir it

well. Take out the amount needed; replenish the remainder by blending in 1 cup of flour and 1 cup of warm water.

Leave the starter uncovered in a warm spot for several hours. When it bubbles once more, put it into a nonmetal container, cover loosely, and store in the refrigerator until needed.

The night before you plan to make sourdough bread, remove the starter from the refrigerator so that it can warm and commence working. The starter must be used at least once in a two-week period and be replenished each time. Using it daily is even better.

Sourdough Breads

The oldest of breads may well be sourdough bread. It dates back to 4000 B.C.

Sourdough Bread
3 cups all-purpose or whole
    wheat flour
1 cup sourdough starter
2 cups warm water
2 tablespoons sugar
1 teaspoon salt
1 teaspoon baking soda
3½ cups (about) unbleached
    all-purpose flour
cornmeal
melted butter

Put the first six ingredients into a large bowl; beat until smooth. Cover the dough with waxed paper. Allow to stand in a warm spot (80° to 85° F) for a minimum of eighteen hours.

Stir it down. Blend in the remainder of the flour, making moderately stiff dough. On a lightly floured board, knead the dough until satiny smooth for eight to ten minutes. Divide it in two. Form each equal portion into a ball. Roll them beneath your hands to make long thick ropes, more or less 12 inches in length.

Grease cookie sheets, and sprinkle them with cornmeal.

Place the loaves on the cookie sheets; slash the top of each with a sharp knife and brush with butter. Cover them with transparent wrap. Allow to rise where it is warm for approximately one and a half hours until doubled. Bake from forty to fifty minutes in a preheated 400° F oven.

Remove them from the oven, and brush the tops with melted butter. Place on a rack to cool.

Onion Sourdough Bread (yield: 2 large, long loaves or 4 small, round loaves)
1½ cups sourdough starter
3¾ cups (approximately)
    unsifted all-purpose flour
3 tablespoons sugar
2 teaspoons salt
1 package active dry yeast
1 cup milk
2 tablespoons margarine cornmeal
egg white, beaten
1 tablespoon water
²/₃ cup finely chopped onion
caraway seed

Measure out the sourdough starter, and set it aside. In a large bowl, combine 1 cup of flour, the sugar, salt, and undissolved active dry yeast. Put the milk and margarine in a saucepan and heat over low heat. When the milk is very warm, somewhere around 125° F, slowly add it to the dry ingredients. Beat in a mixer at medium speed for two minutes, scraping the bowl now and then. Add ¼ cup of flour and 1½ cups of starter, beating for two minutes at high speed and scraping the bowl from time to time. Blend in additional flour to make a soft dough. Knead it until elastic and smooth on a lightly floured board for about nine minutes. Put it in a greased bowl. Then turn it over to grease the top. Cover it, and allow it to rise for one hour in a warm spot, away from drafts, until doubled.

Punch down the dough. Turn it out on a lightly floured board, and divide it in two. Cover and allow to stand for fifteen minutes. Shape as preferred. Form large, long loaves by rolling each section of dough into an oblong—8 by 12 inches. Roll the dough tightly from the 12-inch side, pinching the seam. Then pinch the ends and fold them underneath. To form small, round loaves, divide the dough in two again. Shape each into a round ball, and flatten slightly.

Sprinkle cornmeal on greased baking sheets. Place the loaves on them and cover. Allow to rise for one hour in a warm spot, away from drafts, until doubled.

Combine water and egg white.

Brush this mixture on the loaves. Sprinkle them with chopped onion and caraway seed.

Bake in a 400° F oven for twenty-five minutes or until done. Take from the baking sheets and let cool on wire racks.

Sourdough Rolls

1½ cups warm water
1 package active dry yeast
1½ cups sourdough starter
2 tablespoons salad oil
2 tablespoons sugar
2 teaspoons salt
½ teaspoon baking soda
1 cup flour

Into a large mixing bowl, measure 1½ cups of warm water. Blend in one package of active dry yeast. Add the sourdough starter, salad oil, sugar, and salt, stirring vigorously with a wooden spoon for approximately three minutes. Put in a large greased bowl, cover with a towel, and allow to rise for one and a half to two hours in some warm spot until doubled in bulk.

Blend ½ teaspoon of baking soda into 1 cup of flour and stir in, making the dough stiff. Knead it on a floured board, and add 1 cup of flour or an amount needed to control the stickiness. After eight minutes or more, it should be satiny smooth. Separate the dough into two sections. Shape into rolls by rolling the dough between your hands. Place them on a greased pan, cover, and leave in a warm spot. Leave for one to one and a half hours to rise and almost double in bulk.

For a crusty top, brush with water just before baking. If a softer crust is desired, brush with melted butter. Bake for seventeen to twenty minutes in a 400° F oven.

Corn Bread Variations

When preparing your favorite corn bread recipe, try using 8 ounces of cracklings in place of the shortening.

Basic Corn Bread

1 cup flour
1 cup cornmeal
4 tablespoons baking powder
2 eggs
1½ cups sweet milk
1 tablespoon cooking oil
1 teaspoon salt

Blend these ingredients thoroughly. Bake in a greased pan at 400° F for thirty minutes or until crusty and brown.

Buttermilk Corn Bread

1 cup cornmeal
1 cup unbleached white flour
⅓ cup sugar
¼ teaspoon baking powder
¾ teaspoon salt
1 cup buttermilk
2 eggs, well beaten
2 tablespoons oil
1½ teaspoons baking powder

Sift all the dry ingredients into a bowl. Mix in the milk, eggs, and oil. Stir only enough to blend. Empty the batter into a greased cake pan (8 inches square).

Bake it for approximately twenty minutes at 425° F. When the top is nicely browned, take the bread from the oven.

Clabber Corn Bread

1 cup cornmeal
1 cup sifted flour
¼ cup sugar
4 teaspoons baking powder
½ teaspoon salt
1 egg
1 cup curd
1 tablespoon oil

Sift the dry ingredients into a bowl. Put in the eggs, curd, and oil; beat the mixture until smooth. Empty the batter into a greased pan (9 inches square).

Bake for about twenty-five minutes in a 425° F. oven. When a knife inserted in the center of the bread comes out clean, remove your clabber corn bread from the oven.

Honey Corn Bread

Thoroughly mix these ingredients:
1¾ cups yellow cornmeal
½ cup wheat flour, plus
   2 tablespoons
¾ teaspoon salt
3 teaspoons baking powder

Beat well the following ingredients:
2 eggs
2 tablespoons honey
2 tablespoons butter (or margarine)

Stir in 1 cup of milk.
Combine the liquid mixture with the dry mixture. Gently blend until

the whole is moistened. Spread the batter in a greased 9-inch pan. Bake for twenty-five to thirty minutes in a preheated 400° F oven.

Johnnycake

2 cups cornmeal
1½ teaspoons salt
1 teaspoon baking soda
2 tablespoons sugar
2 cups sour milk
2 eggs, beaten
2 tablespoons shortening, melted

Sift together the dry ingredients. Add milk, eggs, and shortening. Blend thoroughly.

Pour the batter into a greased 8- by 10-inch-loaf pan and bake in a 400° F oven for thirty minutes.

Molasses Corn Bread

Mix together these dry ingredients:
3 cups yellow cornmeal
1 cup whole wheat flour
2 tablespoons baking powder
1 teaspoon salt
Mix together the following wet ingredients:
3 eggs
½ cup butter
½ cup sorghum molasses
2 cups buttermilk
Blend the two mixtures until the dry ingredients become moist.

Bake the batter in a greased 12-inch pan for approximately thirty-five minutes in a 350° F oven.

Southern-Style Corn Bread

1 cup yellow cornmeal
1 cup flour (whole wheat or white)
2 to 3 tablespoons powdered milk
4 teaspoons baking powder
1½ teaspoons salt
1 cup milk (or buttermilk)
1 egg
2 tablespoons vegetable oil
2 to 3 tablespoons wheat germ
Sift all the dry items, except the wheat germ, into a bowl. Mix in the remaining ingredients, making a uniformly moist batter. Put it in a well-greased 8-inch-square pan and bake for twenty to twenty-five minutes in a preheated 425° F oven until golden brown.

Spoon Bread

2 cups boiling water
1 cup white cornmeal
1 teaspoon salt
1 tablespoon shortening
1 cup milk
2 eggs, separated
Blend water, cornmeal, salt, and shortening. Cool. Thoroughly mix in the milk and beaten egg yolks. Then fold in stiffly beaten egg whites.

Pour the batter into a greased baking dish. Bake for thirty to forty minutes in a 400° F. oven. Serve the spoon bread directly from its baking dish.

Breads with Honey

To cut easily through freshly baked bread, use a heated knife.

Granola-Yogurt Bread (yield: 2 loaves)

2 envelopes dry yeast
1½ cups very warm water
1 teaspoon honey
8 ounces homemade yogurt
5 cups unbleached flour, sifted
3 teaspoons salt
2 cups homemade granola
Sprinkle the yeast into a 1-cup measuring cup holding ½ cup of the warm water. Add the honey and stir until the yeast dissolves. Let stand for ten minutes, more or less, until it is bubbly and the volume doubles.

Combine the rest of the water, yogurt, and salt in a big bowl. Stir in the yeast mixture. Beat in 4 cups of the flour for two minutes, setting your mixer at medium speed. Mix in the granola. Slowly blend in the remaining flour to form a stiff dough.

Put the dough on a lightly floured board, and knead it for about ten minutes until it is smooth and elastic. Use only enough flour to prevent the dough from adhering to the work surface.

Place it in a large buttered bowl; turn it to bring up the buttered side. Cover with a clean towel. Let rise in a warm, draft-free place for one hour or until double in bulk.

Punch down the dough. Put it on a lightly floured board and knead several times. Invert the bowl over the dough, and let it rest for ten minutes. Divide the dough in two equal portions; knead each half a few times. Shape them into two round loaves. Lay them on a greased baking sheet, about 5 inches apart. Allow them to rise in a warm spot, free from drafts, for forty minutes or until double in volume.

Using a sharp knife, cut a ½-inch-deep cross in the top of each loaf. Bake them in a 375° F oven for thirty-five minutes or until they are golden brown and have a hollow sound when tapped. Cool them completely on wire racks.

Honey-Oatmeal Bread
1½ cups milk
1 cup oatmeal (quick cooking)
2 tablespoons butter
1¼ cups light cream
½ teaspoon salt
½ cup honey
2 yeast cakes
2 cups flour, unbleached
3 cups whole wheat flour

Scald the milk, and put in the oatmeal, cooking it for three minutes. Add the butter. After it melts, put in cream, salt, and honey. Let cool. Add the yeast and the flour and beat well.

Mix in the whole wheat flour to make a soft dough. Knead it until smooth. Allow it to rise until double in volume. Shape the dough into three loaves. Let them rise until double in bulk.

Bake for fifty minutes at 375° F.

Peanut Butter Loaf
2 cups flour
4 teaspoons baking powder
1 teaspoon salt
¼ teaspoon baking soda
¼ cup honey
⅔ cup homemade peanut butter
1¼ cups milk

Sift together the first four ingredients. Thoroughly mix the milk into the peanut butter; blend in the honey. Add the peanut butter mixture to the dry ingredients and beat well.

Turn into a buttered loaf pan. Bake in a 350° F oven for forty-five minutes. Peanut butter bread is even tastier on the second day.

Whole Wheat Honey Bread
Mix the following dry ingredients:
12 cups whole wheat flour
1¾ cups instant dry milk
1 tablespoon salt
2 tablespoons yeast
Mix the following wet ingredients:
½ cup oil

2 beaten eggs
3 cups warm (110°–115° F)
  water
½ cup honey (Dissolve it
  thoroughly.)

Add the wet mixture to the dry, stirring with a wooden spoon. When the dough is well blended, stir it a little about every ten minutes for an hour.

Now knead the dough slightly until it becomes elastic.

Form two large loaves and one small one. Put them in greased bread pans. Allow to rise for one hour.

Bake at 370° F for ten minutes. Reduce the heat to 350° F and bake thirty minutes longer.

Unusual Breads

Harvest Bread
1½ cups sugar
½ cup vegetable oil
2 eggs, beaten
1 cup canned pumpkin
  (or fresh)
1 cup oats
1 cup flour
1¼ teaspoons baking powder
1 teaspoon salt
½ teaspoon allspice
½ teaspoon cinnamon
½ teaspoon ground cloves
½ teaspoon nutmeg
½ cup chopped pecans

Combine sugar, oil, eggs, pumpkin, and oats. Beat well. Sift the dry ingredients, and add them to the pumpkin mixture.

Pour the batter into a greased 9-by 5-inch-loaf pan. Bake at 350° F. for an hour and fifteen minutes.

Tomato Bread
(yield: 1 good-sized loaf)

2 teaspoons dry yeast
¼ cup warm water
1½ cups tomato juice
1 tablespoon sugar
½ teaspoon salt
1 tablespoon cooking oil
½ teaspoon powdered basil
4½ to 5 cups whole wheat flour

Grease a 9- by 5-inch bread pan.

Put the yeast in a big mixing bowl; pour the water on it.

Let the yeast dissolve (about five minutes). Then mix in the tomato juice, sugar, salt, oil, and basil. Gradually add the flour until a stiff dough is formed that no longer adheres to the bowl's sides.

Place the dough on a floured board; knead it until smooth and elastic, about six minutes. Shape the dough, and put it in the loaf pan. Cover it with a clean dish towel. Let it rise until about double in volume.

Preheat the oven to 350° F. Bake the tomato bread for about fifty-five minutes or until done.

Zucchini Bread
(yield: 2 loaves)

3 eggs
2 cups sugar
1 cup oil
¼ teaspoon baking powder
2 teaspoons baking soda
1 teaspoon salt
3 teaspoons cinnamon
3 teaspoons vanilla
2 cups raw, unpeeled, shredded, and packed zucchini
3 cups flour

Beat the eggs until light and fluffy. Add sugar, oil, and vanilla. Blend well. Stir in the zucchini. Add the dry ingredients to the creamed mixture.

Pour the batter into two well-greased 9- by 5-inch loaf pans. Bake at 350° F for one hour.

Unleavened Bread

Hardtack

Make a stiff mixture of the following ingredients:

1½ cups graham flour
3 cups unbleached white flour
½ cup cornmeal
½ cup shortening
1½ cups milk
1 teaspoon sugar
1 tablespoon salt

Lightly grease several cookie sheets, and sprinkle them with flour. Dust a chunk of dough (about the size of an egg) with flour, place it in the middle of the cookie sheet, and slightly flatten it with your hand. Now roll the dough out to cover the surface of the baking sheet, making it as thin as possible. Dust with flour when necessary to prevent sticking. You may want to use a flour sock on your rolling pin. Trim off any excess dough, and return it to the mixing bowl.

Bake the unleavened bread in a 400° F oven. When the edges brown, turn it over; continue baking until the flat bread is almost as stiff as cardboard. Turn it once more, and when the hardtack actually is cardboard-stiff, remove it from the oven.

It may be eaten when freshly baked and hot but will last indefinitely if kept dry. Break it in pieces, and store them in an airtight container.

Bread Spreads

Apple Butter

Fill a kettle with cider, and boil it down to two-thirds of the quantity. Pare, core, and slice sweet apples. Add as many to the cider as the vessel will hold without boiling over. Allow to boil slowly; stir frequently to prevent burning. When the apple butter is smooth and thick, add cinnamon and sugar to taste.

Let cool. Keep it in the refrigerator in tightly closed jars.

Cherry Butter

Boil cherries until soft. Rub them through a sieve. Add 2 cups of sugar to each pint of pulp. Boil gently until a butterlike consistency is reached.

Store the spread in tightly covered jars.

Green Butter

Mash in a mortar two small green onions, one-half clove of garlic, some watercress, six sprigs of parsley, and salt and pepper. Blend these ingredients into softened butter.

Green butter is delicious when spread on toasted bread, fish, or bland vegetables.

Honey Butter

1 cup butter
½ cup honey

Cream the butter. Beat in the honey until uniformly blended. Honey butter is excellent on freshly baked breads.

Keep it in the refrigerator. Store any excess in an airtight container in the freezer.

Lemon Butter

Beat the yolk of one egg; mix it with the whites of three eggs. Stir in 1½ cups of sugar, ½ cup of butter, and the grated rind and juice of two medium-sized lemons. Set the vessel containing the mixture in a pan of water and cook for twenty minutes.

Let cool to serve or store.

Peach Butter

Pare ripe peaches. Boil them in a kettle of enough grape juice to cook them until soft. Rub the fruit through a colander to remove the stones.

Add 1½ pounds of sugar to each quart of peach pulp. Boil slowly for sixty minutes. Stir often to avoid burning.

When the peach butter is smooth and thick, season it with cinnamon or other ground spices to suit your taste.

Peanut Butter

Two tablespoons of peanut butter contain an amount of protein at least equal to that found in 6 ounces of milk or a medium-sized egg. This nourishing food may be prepared in a variety of ways, depending on your preference, all with good results.

Peanuts can be ground raw or given a slightly roasted flavor by first putting them, unshelled, in a 300º F oven for thirty minutes. For a full-roasted taste, leave them in for sixty minutes. Allow them to cool; then remove the shells and skins, or leave the skins on for their nutritional value.

Put 1 cup of peanuts and 1 tablespoon of peanut oil (the amount of oil may be increased for a creamier spread) into a blender. Grind them, periodically turning off the machine to scrape the sides. Add salt to taste.

Refrigerate your homemade peanut butter in clean, tightly closed jars. After some while, the oil may begin to separate out from the peanut butter; stir a few times to blend it in again.

Make other delicious nut butters by the same method. Some nuts—for example, cashews and almonds—require little or no additional oil, having sufficient natural oils of their own.

Pumpkin Butter

8 cups pureed pumpkin
4 cups sugar
1½ teaspoons cinnamon
1 teaspoon ground ginger
¼ teaspoon ground cloves
¼ teaspoon ground nutmeg
4 lemons

Pare and cube a pumpkin. Steam the pieces in a kettle until they are soft. Drain the pumpkin, and rub it through a sieve to produce 8 cups of pumpkin puree.

Squeeze the lemons. Add their juice and the spices to the puree. Cook the mixture in a 300º F oven until it becomes thick and smooth.

Put the pumpkin butter into jars, and allow it to cool. Seal the jars.

Rhubarb Bread Spread

2 cups rhubarb, cut in pieces
⅔ cup brown sugar
1 cup molasses
1 teaspoon cinnamon
1 tablespoon butter (or margarine)

Combine the ingredients in a pan. Cook over moderate heat, stirring continuously until well blended. Boil for ten minutes.

Transfer the pan to the oven. Cook its contents at low temperature until the rhubarb spread reaches the consistency of apple butter.

Tomato Butter

2 pounds tart red apples
5 pounds ripe tomatoes
juice of 1 small lemon
1 cup cider vinegar
3 cups brown sugar
3 cups white sugar
2 blades mace
2 cinnamon sticks
2 slices ginger root
½ teaspoon cloves

Put chopped apples, vinegar, and sugar into a big kettle. Blanch, skin, and chop the tomatoes. Add them to the kettle. Tie the spices in a cheesecloth bag, and place it in the pot. Slowly simmer for three hours or until the mixture is thick and smooth, stirring continuously.

Then take out the spice bag. Cool the tomato butter, and fill wide-mouthed jars with it. Store them in a cool place.

Crackers and Pretzels

Graham Crackers

⅔ cup graham flour
⅓ cup white flour
½ teaspoon soda
¼ teaspoon salt
3 tablespoons shortening
2 tablespoons milk
¼ cup honey

Blend the dry ingredients; cut in the shortening. Thoroughly mix in the milk and honey.

Make a ball of the dough, and roll it out very thin. (Be sure to flour the board.) Cut the dough into squares. Put them on an ungreased cookie sheet and bake at 325° F.

Remove the crackers from the oven when they are crisp and golden brown.

Soda Crackers

4 cups flour
1 cup butter (or margarine)
¾ cup milk
1 teaspoon vinegar
½ teaspoon baking soda
½ teaspoon salt

Work the butter into the flour with a pastry cutter or forks.

Stir the vinegar, baking soda, and salt into the milk; add this to the butter-flour mixture.

Form the dough into a ball. Then roll it out to a thickness of about ⅛ inch. Lightly score the dough in the size of cracker desired, and perforate the lines with a fork. Bake at 375° F for twenty minutes or until crisp.

Pretzels

Make dough as for white bread with the following ingredients:

¼ cup shortening
¼ cup sugar
1 yeast cake
1½ cups milk
4½ cups flour
¾ tablespoons salt

Scald the milk, shortening, sugar, and salt. Cool the mixture to lukewarm (80° F). Crumble the yeast into a little milk, and dissolve it. Then blend it with the rest of the milk and 1½ cups of flour. Beat until smooth.

Cover the sponge, and set it in a warm, draft-free place.

Let it rise for one and a half to two hours until it is full of bubbles.

Slowly add the remaining flour and blend until the dough is elastic and smooth. Put it on a lightly floured bread board, and pound it with a rolling pin to develop a velvety texture. Turn the dough over frequently while beating it.

Lay it in a greased bowl, brush with melted butter, and cover with a clean dish towel. Allow the dough to rise for about one hour until it is double in bulk.

Roll the dough in strips about 3 inches long and the thickness of a pencil. Tie the strips in knots, lapping the ends over each other. Place them on a lightly floured board; cover them with a towel and allow to rise until light.

Fill a large kettle with boiling water. Cook each pretzel in the water, turning it over to cook the other side.

Take the pretzels from the water, and drain them. Lay them on a well-greased, lightly floured baking pan; sprinkle with salt. Bake in a 400° F oven until brown and crisp.

Coffee

Around A.D. 1000, Arab merchants carried home the coffee berry from Abyssinia. Not long after, coffee became the national drink of Arabia.

When Mohammedans were forbidden to use wine, a brew of coffee soon became a substitute. The drug properties of the beverage were recognized when people found themselves remaining alert in the evenings after drinking it. Probably because of this drug effect, it was given the name *kahweh* (from which our word *coffee* stems), meaning "wine and other intoxicating beverages."

In the sixteenth century the Arabs brought coffee to Europe, whence it spread to the New World.

Years ago coffee came in what we always called a tow-sack—some folks call it a gunnysack. The coffee beans were green and had to be roasted. Roasting was generally done in a long-handled cast iron frying pan, called a spider in New England, and a skillet in the

Southwest. A lid was put on this roasting device and the coffee beans would jump like Mexican jumping beans or popcorn. The trick was to roast the beans without scorching them, so a lot of coffee was made from scorched beans instead of the roasted kind.

Then the famous Arbuckle brothers, Charles and John, came into the picture. They got the money-making idea of roasting the beans themselves on a professional basis and packing them in a handy one-pound sack. Their pack became so popular that for a long time coffee wasn't called coffee any more in some parts of the country—it was called Arbuckle. A lot of old-timers

in the country still call it that.

Arbuckle Brothers coffee, even though roasted, was still in the whole bean form and had to be ground. Coffee grinders were listed in the catalogues and were in almost every general store. Every home had to have one, and it took many a turn of the crank to grind a pound of coffee. Even today the best coffee you can pass over your lips is that made from a freshly ground whole roasted coffee bean. Here are a few more pointers on making really good country coffee:

Use the very best water. Alkali water, high mineral content (hard) water, and deep well water *do not* make the best coffee. Rain water,

melted snow water, and sparkling pure mountain spring water make the best coffee by far.

The best coffeepot is one made of cast iron and the gallon size is the best.

Be sure the pot is absolutely clean before making coffee. Modern scouring soaps are not recommended for this cleaning job as they leave a taste that is far worse than the taste of the old coffee.

Fresh mud, wet clay, or caliche mud is the best cleaning agent you can use to scour the inside of a coffeepot. Don't worry too much about the outside as it will get

smoke black again anyway.

When the pot looks and smells clean, fill it about three-quarters full of good, cold water never warm water. Fresh grind about a third of a pound of roasted coffee beans. Dump these into the water and set the pot on the fire. Do not cover the pot but keep your eye on it and when the brew begins to bubble then stir it. It will foam at this point so stir until the foaming stops to keep it from boiling over. When the deep boiling sets in, move the pot away from the fire but still near enough that the heat of the fire keeps the coffee rolling

around the side of the pot. If you keep the coffee plenty hot but just below boiling it will be fine for hours. You can add more water and more fresh ground coffee if needed and it will be good. You must keep the coffee hot, not boiling but very near. If it ever cools it will never be good again and you will need to make a fresh pot. Here is another way good country coffee is made:

To every cup of water add a teaspoon to a tablespoon of ground coffee; then add one for the pot. Put it in cold water and allow to boil just once. Remove from fire. Settle with ¼ cup of cold water and serve piping hot.

Some country folks like it this way: bring water to boil first. Add coffee, boil five minutes, settle, and serve. (You can put your coffee in a small muslin bag tied loose, then boil five minutes longer and your bag of grounds can be removed before serving.)

Economy Coffees
Sometimes it is necessary to find a substitute for coffee when rations are low. Here are three ways to do it:
- Parched barley, beans, rice, and bread crumbs make a fair coffee substitute. Scorch them a bit and grind. An improvised coffee mill can be a bag and a stone, pounding the materials to a fine pulp.
- Wash carrots and slice into pieces about half-inch thick. Dry them in the sun or oven but do not cook. When they are dry, brown them well

and use as coffee. If you have a little real coffee left to mix with the carrots it makes a fine brew.

Okra seeds should be roasted or browned the same as coffee beans. Alone, they make one of the finest coffee substitutes but if you can add just a little coffee with them it is even better.

Chicory Coffee

Coffee should have aroma, flavor, clarity, and strength.

When chicory is blended with it, these characteristics are developed. The first mention of chicory occurred in an ancient papyrus roll dating about 4000 B.C. In the ninth century, monks of Holland cultivated chicory and found that its ground, roasted root enhanced the flavor of their coffee.

The addition of chicory not only results in a more aromatic, richer-tasting coffee; it also cuts by one half the standard measure of coffee required. Besides its use as a coffee adulterant, chicory can serve as a substitute for that beverage.

The plant grows most anywhere—along country roadsides and in city vacant lots. You will know it by the leaves sprouting from its tall, jointed stalk, which resemble dandelion leaves but are somewhat wider and darker green. If ragged blue flowers bloom at the stem joints, you can be fairly certain that you have found chicory.

Dig up the plants; remove the leaves. Peel the roots, and cut them in narrow strips. Roast the root slices for four hours in a 250° F oven. Then grind them.

To prepare chicory coffee, use 1 teaspoon of the ground root for each cup of water. Boil for three minutes.

Barley Coffee

You can brew a delicious coffee drink, while using less of the product, by blending barley grains and coffee beans. First, roast the barley for forty-five minutes in a 400° F oven. Occasionally stir the grains to avoid scorching. Remove the barley when it is a deep brown.

Grind it in a blender or coffee mill. Then mix it with your usual coffee to taste, and brew the blend as you would regular coffee.

A decoction of barley alone makes a pleasing, caffeine-free beverage.

Chickpea Coffee

Chickpea (garbanzo) coffee can be prepared with an economical amount of coffee. Roast garbanzos in a 500° F oven for ½ hour or until they are very dark brown and very dry. Grind them coarsely (like coffee) in your grinder.

Use 1 tablespoon of the ground peas to 6 cups of boiling water. Continue boiling for three minutes, and then put in 2 tablespoons of coffee (regular grind). Let the mixture cool a few minutes before serving. Sweeten with honey or sugar.

A caffeine-free beverage can be made from chick-peas by roasting them in a 300° F oven until dark brown and then grinding them in a coffee mill.

Use 1 teaspoon of ground chickpeas per cup of water.

Prepare the drink in a percolator, or boil it in a saucepan

for five to ten minutes and strain.

Sunflower seed hulls, dandelion roots, bran combined with other ingredients, and almonds all provide good coffee substitutes.

Sunflower Seed Coffee

Shell sunflower seeds easily by first crushing them with a rolling pin. Then drop them into a vessel of water. Kernels will sink; hulls will float.

Reserve the seeds for wholesome eating. Heat the empty sunflower seed hulls in a skillet until just brown. Put them through your grain mill.

Use 1 teaspoon (this amount may be adjusted to suit individual taste) of ground hulls to each cup of water. Steep for three minutes. If desired, sweeten with honey.

Dandelion Root Coffee

Wash dandelion roots thoroughly. Peel off the brown skin.

Roast them in a low oven (300° F) for about four hours or

until they are brittle and stiff. Then reduce them to a powder in your food grinder.

Use 1 heaping teaspoon of the powder for each cup of water. Boil for three minutes.

Bran-Cornmeal Coffee

Thoroughly mix 1 pint of yellow cornmeal with 2 quarts of wheat bran. Stir in three well-beaten eggs and 1 cup of sorghum molasses. Beat the mixture well, and spread it on a flat pan. Dry it in a 300° F oven, stirring it often during browning.

Use the concoction as a coffee substitute, a handful being the right amount for two persons.

Bran-Molasses Coffee

Bran with molasses also makes a delicious caffeine-free drink. Combine 1 cup of bran with 4 tablespoons of unsulphured molasses. Mix the ingredients with your hands.

Spread the mixture in a shallow pan, and put it in a 300° F oven. Stir it now and then until browning takes place, usually in about ½ hour. Then remove it from the oven. Break up any lumps. The toasted granules will resemble freeze-dried coffee. Store bran coffee in an airtight container.

Pour boiling water on a heaping tablespoon of the granules to make each cup of beverage. Honey and cream or milk may be added.

Almond Coffee

Spread almonds on a flat pan, and roast them at 300° F until they are dark brown. Grind them in your coffee mill, and then reduce the ground nuts to a fine meal with mortar and pestle.

To serve, stir the resulting powder—in an amount to suit personal taste—into a cup of hot milk. Almond coffee is a delicious and nourishing drink.

Teas

Black Birch Tea

The black birch is a medium-sized tree, seldom exceeding 2 feet in diameter. Its bark is dark red to black, and the tree's twigs have a strong wintergreen flavor.

To brew a delicious, hearty tea, first gather 1 quart of twigs, and cut them into 1-inch pieces. Put them in a vessel; pour in hot (not boiling) water. Allow to steep until cool.

Remove twigs and impurities by straining the tea. Heat once more. Serve with milk and a little honey.

Strawberry Tea

If you know the location of a wild strawberry patch, you can prepare a good tea to combat winter's chill by digging beneath the snow and collecting tender green strawberry leaves. After they thaw, put two handfuls of them into a teapot; add boiling water. Sweeten with honey to serve.

Juices

Grape Juice

A glimpse of smoky blue amid vines twining through overhead tree branches probably means you've discovered wild grapes. Pick some of the fruit to make juice.

Crush the grapes, and simmer them for twenty minutes.

Keep the water well below the boiling point. Put the fruit in a jelly bag, letting the juice drip into a container overnight.

To store, freeze the juice or warm it to just short of boiling, and transfer it to sterilized jars, closing them tightly.

Because the grape juice tends to be concentrated, you may need to add water before drinking it. Sweeten to taste.

Tomato Juice

Select juicy, ripe tomatoes; wash them thoroughly. After removing the stem ends, chop them into pieces. Simmer the tomato chunks in a pot until soft, stirring frequently. Then strain the vessel's contents.

Hemlock Tea

The hemlock tree is often found in the company of black birches. Chop its needles into lengths of 1 inch. Pour boiling water on them. Allow to steep for a few minutes.

Strain your hemlock tea to remove the needles. Drink it warm.

Mint Tea

Mint is easily identified by its four-sided stalk and the minty aroma of its crushed leaves. Look for it in fields, along streams, or in sunny marshes. Bring home some of the plants, and spread them to dry on newspaper in some warm place away from the sun. The leaves, when thoroughly dry, can be quickly stripped from the stems. Stored in a tightly closed glass or tin container, they provide fragrant tea throughout cold winter months.

Brew the tea by using 1 teaspoon of dried leaves to each cup of boiling water. Allow to steep for a few minutes. You can make mint tea from the plant's green leaves as well; use 2 teaspoons of fresh leaves to 1 cup of boiling water.

To each 1 quart of juice, add 1 teaspoon of salt. Serve chilled.

Preserve any excess by reheating the juice to the boiling point immediately after preparation. Pour it into sterilized jars to within ¼ inch of the rim. Adjust the lids, and process for fifteen minutes.

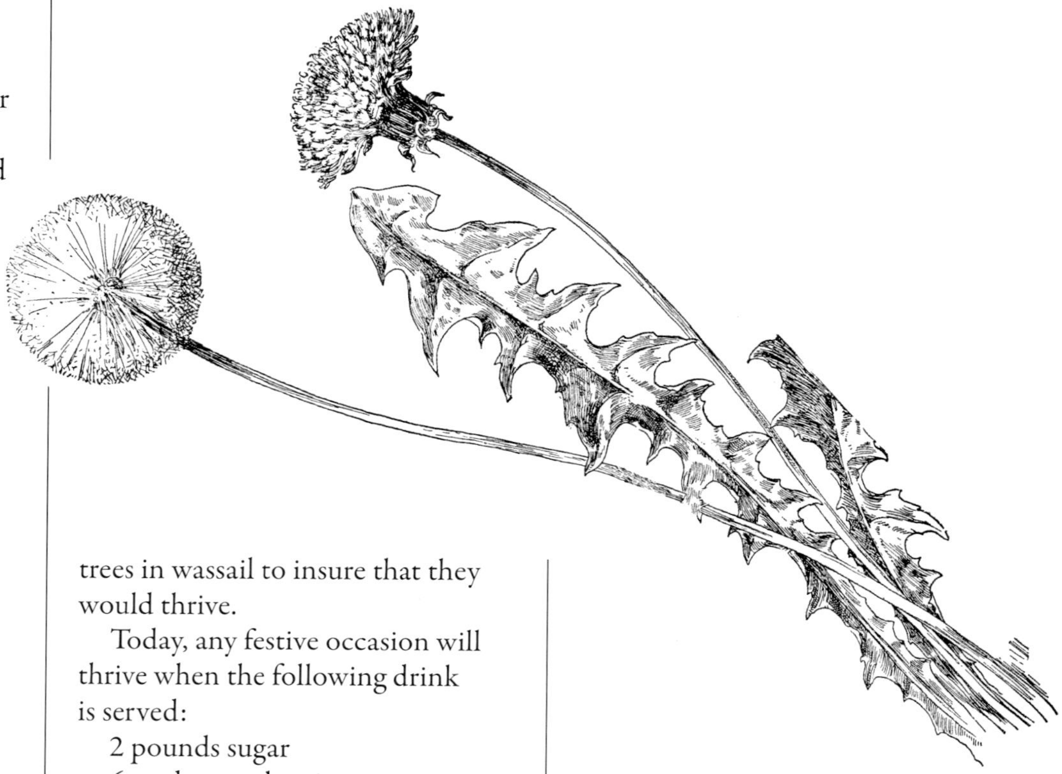

Noncarbonated Drinks

Unique Eggnog (yield: 4½ quarts)

¼ teaspoon cinnamon
¼ teaspoon cloves
¼ teaspoon ginger
¼ cup sugar
6 eggs, well beaten
2 quarts orange juice, chilled
1 quart vanilla ice
    cream, soft
1 quart ginger ale, chilled
    dash nutmeg

Beat the dry ingredients into the eggs. Blend in the orange juice and homemade ice cream. Just before serving, pour in the ginger ale and sprinkle with nutmeg. For extra zest, rum may be added.

Wassail Bowl

The word *wassail* was originally used as a salutation when offering a cup of wine to a guest or toasting the health of someone. It generally meant, "Be in good health." The word applied as well to the liquor in which healths were drunk. Long ago it was the custom to drink to cattle and fruit trees in wassail to insure that they would thrive.

Today, any festive occasion will thrive when the following drink is served:

2 pounds sugar
6 cardamom berries
6 whole cloves
½ teaspoon mace
1 stick cinnamon
1 nutmeg, cracked
1 teaspoon coriander
2 pieces candied ginger
1 cup water
4 bottles Madeira or sherry
12 eggs
½ bottle brandy
6 baked apples

Mix the dry ingredients in 1 cup of water. Add the wine and simmer. Separate the eggs, beating whites and yolks apart. Now combine the eggs, and slowly add them to the hot mixture. Just before serving, blend in ½ bottle of brandy and six baked apples. Put in a stone crock. Keep it hot in front of a glowing hearth.

Cordials

First make a sugar syrup. The recipe you choose may require a sweet or medium strength syrup. To make a sweet syrup, combine 2 cups of white sugar with 1 cup of water, and bring it to the boiling point. To make a medium syrup, combine 1 cup of sugar with ½ cup of water, and bring it to the boiling point. Let it cool for several minutes. Pour the specified amount

of syrup into a clean bottle, and add the indicated amount of extract. Fill the bottle with the required spirits. Close it, and shake the contents until all are thoroughly blended. Allow the cordial to cool before serving.

Apricot Brandy

1 bottle apricot brandy extract
1 fifth (or 1 quart) brandy

This recipe needs no sugar. Follow the steps as already described, omitting the syrup.

Cherry Brandy

1 bottle cherry brandy extract
1 cup medium sugar syrup
1 fifth (or 1 quart) brandy

The amount of spirits you use depends upon the size of the bottle that will hold the cordial. Follow the steps as previously outlined.

Wines

Blackberry Bramble Wine

Gather 4 pounds of blackberry brambles, cut them into small pieces, and put them in a large crock. Using the bottom of a quart bottle or a mallet, mash them to a pulp. Add 2 quarts of boiling water, and cover the crock. Allow to stand for seven days; stir twice each day.

Strain the contents of the crock to remove the pulp. Pour in an additional quart of boiling water and 12 cups of sugar. Blend thoroughly. When the mixture is

lukewarm, sprinkle one package of yeast on it. Cover the vessel, and place it in a warm spot for two weeks.

Strain the mixture into a 1-gallon jug so that the sediment is left behind. Seal the jug by slipping a large balloon over its mouth. This will prevent air from entering while allowing the escape of gases. Occasionally you will need to bleed off the gas that accumulates in the balloon. After ninety days in this container, the wine will be clear and ready to serve. However, it will be even better if strained, poured into bottles, and permitted to age for several months.

Carrot Wine

4 pounds carrots
4 lemons
4 oranges, sliced in ¼-inch
   pieces
2 cups raisins, chopped
8 cups sugar
12 peppercorns
1 ounce yeast, moistened
1 slice whole wheat toast

Thoroughly scrub the carrots; chop them fine. Boil for forty-five minutes in 4 quarts of water. When lukewarm, strain. Return the liquid to the vessel. Mix in the sugar, and add the fruit and peppercorns. Spread the toast with the moistened yeast. Let the toast float on the liquid. Place the container in a warm spot for fourteen days to ferment. Stir each day.

At the end of two weeks, strain the wine. Allow it to settle, then syphon your carrot wine into bottles.

Honey-Dandelion Wine

Put 4 quarts of water and 4 quarts of dandelion heads into a crock. Cover it. Allow to stand for eight to ten days.

Strain the dandelion heads, squeezing out the liquid. Add 3 pounds of honey, three sliced lemons, and one cake of wine yeast to the liquid. Let stand for nine days.

Strain the mixture into a jug. When the wine has ceased working, cork the jug.

Country Dandelion Wine

Pick 1 gallon of dandelion heads in the early morning while they are still fresh from dew. Put them in a 2-gallon crock; pour in boiling water. Spread a piece of cheesecloth over the mouth of the crock, and leave it for three days at room temperature.

Squeeze the juice from the flower blossoms, and discard them, reserving the liquid. Pour it into a large vessel. Add 3 pounds of sugar, three whole lemons, chopped, and four whole oranges, chopped. Cover the pot and boil for ½ hour. Let cool to lukewarm. Empty it into a crock; add 2 tablespoons of yeast. Cover with cheesecloth and allow to stand for two or three weeks.

When the bubbling stops, filter your dandelion wine through cheesecloth to remove the chunks. Bottle.

Honey Wine: Mead

Into a 1-gallon glass jug, put 1½ to 2 pints of honey. The amount depends on individual preference; the greater the quantity of honey, the stronger the wine. Fill the jug with warm water. Shake it vigorously.

Add one cake of yeast. Let the uncapped jug stand in the kitchen sink overnight, where it will foam. When the foaming largely subsides, slip a balloon over the jug's mouth to prevent air from entering and allow the escape of gases. Let sit for two weeks. After bubbles no longer rise to the top, transfer the honey wine to bottles, and seal them with corks so that small amounts of gas can escape.

May Wine

Essential for making May wine is the perennial herb sweet woodruff. It grows in areas of filtered shade and is hardy in every zone. Once planted, it will spread as a ground cover, seeding itself. Sweet woodruff gets along well in the company of other plants, making its appearance in spring. Its dried stems and leaves help to make May wine.

Pick six sprigs of sweet woodruff. Let them dry for several days in a light and airy spot, but away from direct sunlight.

Put them in a punch bowl. Pour two bottles of well-chilled dry white wine over them. Cover the bowl. Allow the herb to steep for two hours. Take out the woodruff. Pour in another bottle of chilled wine.

Blend in 2 cups of crushed, sugared strawberries and 2 tablespoons of simple syrup (one part water to two parts sugar, boiled for five minutes). Put your May wine in the refrigerator to chill.

At serving time you may garnish the wine with mint sprigs and float a few whole strawberries in it.

Rose Hip Wine

Collect 4 pounds of rose hips, those orange-colored fruits that grow behind wild or cultivated rose blossoms. They begin to form in July. Green at first, rose hips become orange by September, developing a red color with the approach of autumn.

When setting out to gather hips from thorny wild rosebushes, wear old clothes. It is advisable, also, to don an old pair of gloves for protection against briars. Snipping off their fingertips will allow you to work with freedom. To remove hips easily, use a twisting motion. Drop them into a bag suspended from your belt to free your hands for picking.

Put the fruits in a crock, pulverize them, and pour 2 quarts of boiling water over the pulp. Allow the mixture to sit for four days, stirring each day.

Strain the liquid to remove the pulp. Thoroughly mix in 2½ pounds of sugar, 6 ounces of orange juice (unsweetened), and 1½ quarts of warm water. Sprinkle in one package of yeast. Put the crock in a warm spot for two weeks.

Strain the wine into a 1-gallon jug. Plug the mouth with a wad of cloth. A seal of this kind allows extra air to enter, giving the wine a flavor somewhat similar to sherry. In ninety days it will be suitable for bottling and ready for drinking.

Raccoonberry Wine

During late summer, mayapples—lemon-shaped fruits—hang half hidden beneath their plant's large, shieldlike leaves. You may know them as mandrake apples, raccoonberries, or hog apples. No matter the name, these yellow fruits can be converted into a delicious golden wine. Search for them in lush woodlands.

Crush the fruit in a good-sized crock. Cover the vessel and let stand for seven days. Strain the contents, squeezing all juice from the pulp. Measure the juice; add water in equal measure. Stir 2½ pounds of sugar into each gallon of the liquid. Sprinkle it with yeast. Cover the

crock, and set it in a warm place for ten days.

Strain the contents into 1-gallon jugs. Seal them with a piece of plastic wrap secured by a rubber band. Let stand for four months to clarify. Then strain and bottle your golden raccoonberry wine.

Clarifying Wine

When homemade wine is not clear, the best remedy is time. However, if your patience wanes before this cure is effective, try these methods for clarifying wine:

• Beechwood chips or shavings can be used to settle the haze in wine without affecting taste. Add several tablespoons per gallon; leave them until clearing takes place.

• Boil oak shavings for several minutes, drain them, and put 2 tablespoons of the wood bits into a gallon jug of wine. They will hasten clearing of the beverage and add a pleasant oak flavor; check the taste every few weeks to be sure the oak flavor doesn't become too strong.

• An old-time remedy for clarifying wine is egg white. Add one whipped egg white to each gallon of wine. Gently shake the container once a day for seven days or until the beverage has cleared.

• As a last resort, filter the wine through cloth.

Remember that haze in no way affects the taste of wine, only its eye appeal.

Carbonated Drinks

Applejack

    5 pounds sugar
    1½ gallons cider (fresh from
        your local cider mill)
    5 pounds raisins, crushed

Put the sugar in a vessel; add sufficient water to dissolve it. Boil the solution for one minute. When the sugar water is lukewarm, mix it thoroughly with the cider in a jug. Add the crushed raisins.

Close the container tightly. Run a narrow hose from a hole in the cap to a pan of water below in order to free the gas during fermentation. Keep the jug where the temperature is maintained at 70° F.

When a few bubbles per minute agitate the water in the pan, the beverage is ready for drinking. Serve your applejack chilled on warm days and piping hot when the weather turns cold.

Birch Beer

Gather 4 quarts of black birch twigs, cut them into short lengths, and put them in a 5-gallon crock. In a large vessel containing 4 gallons of water, stir 8 pounds of brown sugar until dissolved. Heat to the boiling point and continue boiling for ten minutes. Immediately pour the bubbling liquid over the birch twig pieces in the crock.

Dissolve one yeast cake in 4 ounces of warm water. Stir this into the contents of the crock.

Cover and allow to work for ten days or until clear. Ladle into bottles and cap tightly. Birch beer is best when served chilled.

Simple Root Beer (yield: twelve 1-quart bottles)

⅓ ounce root beer extract
4½ cups sugar
3 gallons lukewarm water
½ teaspoon wine yeast

Thoroughly wash and rinse all equipment, bottles, and caps. Dry them.

Shake the bottled extract well. Mix the sugar and extract in the water, blending until the sugar dissolves. Blend the yeast in well until it dissolves. Fill the bottles to within 1 inch of their rim. Close with plastic or crown lids.

When using plastic lids, stand the bottles up in a box. If using crown tops, lay the bottles in the box on their sides. Cover against drafts. Put the box in a warm spot. Where the temperature is approximately 70° F, the root beer will carbonate within one to five days; carbonation will usually take place in one day where the temperature is above 80° F. To check for carbonation, refrigerate a bottle after one day. When it is chilled, slowly open it over the sink. Inspecting and tasting it will tell you whether the root beer is sufficiently carbonated. If it seems a little flat, allow it to stand another day or longer.

Old-Fashioned Root Beer

If certain roots and barks are available to you, make root beer the old-fashioned way from natural ingredients. Here is a good basic recipe:

Mix 1½ gallons of molasses into 5 gallons of boiling water.

Let stand for three hours.

Put in ¼ pound each of wintergreen birch bark, sarsaparilla root, and bruised sassafras bark.

Add 1 cup of fresh yeast, and increase the water content of the vessel to a total of about 16 gallons.

Set the mixture in a spot where the temperature is kept at 65° to 75° F. Leave it for twelve hours to ferment.

Draw off the root beer, using flexible tubing, and bottle it. Secondary carbonation will now take place; maintain the same temperature as before throughout the process.

The percentage of alcohol in the drink depends upon the length of time it ferments before bottling and the depth to which the containers are filled. The lower the level to which the bottles are filled, the longer the period of fermentation and the greater the alcoholic content. By experimenting, you can develop the taste you prefer.

Other ingredients that can be used for flavoring are the bark or root of the following: anise, boxberry, cinnamon, clove, deerberry, spiceberry, teaberry, and vanilla. If they are not available to you, their oils are commercially produced.

Granddad's Home Brew

Home-brewed beer requires these ingredients:

3 pounds malt extract (light or dark)
3½ pounds corn sugar (You may substitute 1 or 2 pounds of honey for part of the sugar.)
1 package brewer' yeast
½ teaspoon powdered gelatin (in case the beer is cloudy)
2 cups corn sugar

To brew beer, follow these steps:

Dissolve the malt extract in 2 gallons of boiling water.

Continue rapid boiling for 1½ hours. Stir frequently to prevent sticking and burning.

Put the corn sugar into a large crock. Pour the malt liquid on it. Add enough water to make 5 gallons of liquid. Allow to cool.

When the liquid is comfortable to the touch, thoroughly stir in one package of brewer's yeast (found at wine supply shops). Place cheesecloth over the mouth of the crock.

After the foam has begun to subside, usually within two or three days, syphon the beer into a 5-gallon glass jug with the aid of a rubber hose. Fill it to within 6 inches from the rim to leave space for gas.

Set the container on a table, and attach a gas lock. One can be purchased in a hardware store, or you can improvise your own. Run

the rubber hose through a hole punched in the jug's cap. Do not let the end of the flexible tubing come in contact with the liquid. The other end should hang into a pan of water placed either on the floor or at least several feet below the level of the table. Rising gas from fermentation will be conducted through the tubing and will bubble in the water. When the action has subsided to about three bubbles each minute, the fermentation process is all but complete. The length of time to reach this stage varies with temperature. In a warm area, fermentation takes place in four to six days; where it is cold, the process takes twice as long.

When bubbling has almost subsided, check for clarity. If the brew is not clear, dissolve ½ teaspoon of powdered gelatin in 8 ounces of water. Add it to the beer.

Return the flat beer to the crock. Insure carbonation and a good head by stirring in 2 cups of corn sugar.

Siphon the beer into bottles. Let your home brew sit for seven to fourteen days before drinking it.

Beer

Put ¼ ounce (one packet) of dry yeast in a cup; add warm water and 1 teaspoon of sugar. Stir.

Heat 2 gallons of water to just short of boiling. Dissolve 3 pounds of malt extract and 5 pounds of sugar in it. Empty the mixture into a 5-gallon jug. Add 1 gallon of cold water. Gently shake the jug. Now put in the yeast mixture. Then fill the jug to within 6 inches of the rim with cold water, and set it on a table or counter top. The 6 inches of space will allow for bubbles and froth as the brew works.

Attach a gas lock—a thin hose running from the air space in the container—through a hole in its cap, and into a vessel of water below. Let stand for four to six days or until only about three bubbles a minute disturb the water in the pan. The beer is then ready for bottling.

If the bottle caps you will use are cork lined, soak them in water on bottling day and they will seal much better.

Utilize your hose to siphon the brew into bottles. Add ¼ teaspoon of sugar to each bottle before capping it to insure a frothy head and proper carbonation.

Store the beverage in a dark, cool place for at least seven days before serving it.

Potato Beer

    5 gallon container
    6 good-sized potatoes
    1 cup of sugar
    3 packages active dry yeast
    1 can malt syrup

Chop the potatoes. Put them in a 5-gallon container; a lard bucket will do nicely. Add the yeast, malt syrup, and sugar. Fill the bucket with water, and stir the contents thoroughly. Allow the mixture to ferment for five days. Do not cover the container.

At the end of five days, stir the brew until no sediment remains on the bottom. Then strain it through cloth. The beverage can be drunk now but will improve with time.

Different vegetables may be substituted for the potatoes to achieve a variety of flavors.

28 | GARDEN TO PANTRY SHELF

Canning Fruits and Vegetables

When I was a boy, canning season in the heat of a West Texas summer was a time to dread. It completely disrupted the rhythm of home life. Mother, weary from long hours in a steaming kitchen, set out only hastily prepared meals at irregular times.

Every member of the family participated in the chores. I was obliged to forego fishing along shady river banks. Endless bushel baskets, filled to brimming with garden and orchard produce, had to be lugged into the scorching kitchen, the twang and sharp slap of the screen door marking each delivered load. Here peaches were peeled, peas shelled, and other work doggedly pursued to keep pace with the maturing fruits and vegetables. No sooner was one crop safely sealed in its glass containers than another reached peak ripeness, necessitating immediate preserving.

With the waning day, and strength and spirits flagging, my only thought was to swim or shoot marbles with my friends. At this moment Mother always seemed to say, "Well, let's do just one more batch."

By summer's end, canning was over at last. Memories of hard work faded at the satisfying sight of pantry shelves gleaming with jar after jar of colorful, mouth-watering fruits and vegetables. As the incomparable taste of wholesome, homegrown foods continued to spark midwinter meals, we were convinced that our canning efforts had been more than worthwhile.

Assembled here are the basic methods for preserving fruits and vegetables as used by home canners for several generations.

Canning Methods

Open Kettle
In this method the food is completely cooked, put into sterilized jars, and sealed. Since the jars are not sterilized after sealing, spoilage is possible. However, the open-kettle method may be safely used for canning preserves in thick syrup and tomatoes.

Oven Steaming
To preserve food by oven steaming, seal jars completely. Then loosen the lids by turning them back ¼ inch. Self-sealing lids must be totally sealed. Space jars 2 inches apart in a shallow container of warm water placed on the middle rack of your oven. Preheat the oven to 275° F. Maintain steady temperature. Seal jars tightly right after their removal from the oven. Tighten the jar tops again during cooling, the exception being self-sealing tops; do not touch them. Set the jars on folded toweling or several thicknesses of cloth. Cool them rapidly and keep them out of drafts. When the jars are cold, test them for leakage.

Cold Pack
The cold-pack method is used for food that must be arranged in the jars and is put into them when cold. By heating the jars in steam or boiling water, the food is cooked and sterilized at the same time. Caution must be taken to seal containers only partially before processing. Expansion of the food during heating may crack the jars if they have been sealed too tightly.

Hot Pack
The hot-pack method involves filling the jars with boiling hot food and processing in steam or boiling water.

When processing is done in water, the jars can be tightly sealed. This method is generally preferred.

Equipment
Either tin cans or glass jars can be used as containers for preserving food.

Tin cans are available plain or lined with enamel. There are two kinds of lined cans: R enamel cans with shiny gold linings are suitable for very acidic foods and those of red color; the C type, having a dull gold lining, is used for vegetables of high protein content. Use plain cans for preserving meat. Lids for tin cans must be replaced each year. The cans themselves can be used three times by reflanging them.

Glass jars may be purchased with a variety of lids: zinc tops lined with porcelain or glass; metal ones with gaskets that melt during processing, automatically sealing the container; and glass lids. All tops, with the exception of those equipped with automatic seals, require rubber rings. Rubber rings and automatic seal lids must be replaced each year.

You can either buy a water-bath canner or substitute a large kettle for it. Use one deep enough for the boiling water to reach at least 1 inch above the jar tops. To keep jars from bumping and to allow water to circulate under them during processing, place a rack in the bottom.

Process nonacidic vegetables and meats in a pressure canner to kill bacteria that form spores. The pressure canner should be equipped with a safety valve, petcock, and pressure indicator. Use one of sturdy construction.

Preliminary Procedures

To insure safe, high-quality results, you must check and clean all equipment. Carefully inspect lids for bent, uneven edges and jars for nicks and cracks. If none are apparent, put a new ring on the jar, fill it partway with water, and seal. Turn the jar upside down, and check for leaks or for tiny bubbles rising as the water cools. An imperfect seal on jars with a wire bail can be remedied by taking off the top bail, bending it in at the ends and down in the center, and replacing it. Check rings by folding them in two. Those that develop cracks should be discarded.

Give cans and jars a thorough washing in hot, soapy water, followed by a rinse in hot water. Fill them with water, and set them upright or sideways, with space between each, in a deep vessel of cold water. Gradually bring the water to a boil, and continue boiling for fifteen minutes. Leave the jars in the hot water until needed; let tin cans drain on a clean cloth.

Wash all tops in soapy water. Leave glass and zinc lids in very hot, clear water for five minutes. Keep them hot until used. Turn them upside down to drain. Pour hot water over lids with a sealing composition. Let them stand until wanted for use. Scald rubber rings quickly; never boil them. Sterilize knives, spoons, funnels, and other utensils by putting them in boiling water after a preliminary washing.

When tin cans are used, a mechanical sealer is a necessity. Test its adjustment each time you employ it by putting 2 tablespoons of water in the can, adjusting the lid, and sealing it. Put it in boiling water, keeping it beneath the surface until steam forms in the can and expands the ends. Air bubbles escaping from the can are evidence of improper

adjustment of the sealer. Readjust it, and repeat the test.

Clean the removable safety valves and petcocks on your pressure canner. Vinegar will remove any corrosion. Clean all openings in the canner lid. A toothpick or pipe cleaner is handy for the job. Be sure the gasket is free of dirt and grease, and examine it for a tight fit. If steam escapes or you have difficulty in removing it, grease with salt-free fat the closing surface of the canner cover that seals metal to metal. Tighten screws on the handle. Eliminate stains and odors with 2 tablespoons of vinegar in 2 quarts of water, processing for five minutes at 5 pounds pressure. With a master gauge tester or a maximum thermometer, check the dial gauge. A weight gauge should be cleaned according to the manufacturer's directions.

Preparation of Food

Select vegetables that are young and tender. Clean them thoroughly, and prepare them as for table use. Do not work with too great a quantity of vegetables at one time, particularly in hot weather. The various canning procedures must be accomplished rapidly to avoid flavor loss, called "flat sour." Large amounts of vegetables cannot be handled quickly enough. Can vegetables immediately after picking them. This applies especially to asparagus, beans, corn, and peas. To thoroughly heat nonacid vegetables, precook them, using the pot liquor to fill the jars. Pack vegetables evenly; do not crowd them. For a good pack, shake the jars. Because shell beans, corn, and peas are likely to swell, leave 1 inch of space between the liquid and the rim. Since spinach and other kinds of greens tend to shrink, pack them down lightly, cutting through them with a knife several times.

Approximate Vegetable Yield

Vegetable	Weight	Yield
Asparagus	3 pounds	1 quart
Beans, Lima	2 pounds	1 quart
Beans, String	1¾ pounds	1 quart
Beets, Baby	2½ to 3 pounds	1 quart
Corn on the Cob	1 quart	7 small ears
Greens	2¾ to 3 pounds	1 quart
Peas, Green, Shelled	4 pounds	1 quart
Tomatoes	3 pounds	1 quart

Choose firm, well-developed fruit that is not overly ripe. Try to can it soon after it has been picked. Prick unseeded plums and cherries a few times with a big pin. When canning fruit without sugar, use fruit juice or boiling water in place of syrup, filling the containers to within ½ inch of their rim. Before serving the fruit, drain it, add sweetening to

the liquid, and bring to a brisk boil. Pour it on the fruit and allow to cool. Then chill it. You may wish to cook berries and fruits in syrup for several minutes to achieve a full pack. Prepare syrups according to the fruit's acidity and the taste preference of those for whom the food is canned. One cup of sugar to 3 cups of fruit juice or water will yield 3½ cups of thin syrup. One cup of sugar to 2 cups of water or fruit juice will yield 2½ cups of medium syrup. One cup of sugar added to 1 cup of fruit juice or water will result in 1½ cups of thick syrup. Blend the sugar and liquid, stirring over heat until the sugar dissolves. Bring the syrup to a boil. Use approximately 2 cupfuls of syrup to each quart of large fruit, such as peaches, pears, and plums. Use 1 cupful of syrup to each quart of small fruit, such as berries and cherries.

To avoid dark fruit, take these precautions:
• Process fruit for the correct amount of time; too-short processing results in dark fruit.
• Maintain sufficiently high temperature. Water should be boiling at the start of processing time and remain at a boil throughout.
• Accurately count the time of processing. Start counting time when a rolling boil commences. Check the timetable, making any adjustments that might be required for altitude.
• The level of boiling water should be between 1 and 2 inches above the lids of the jars during the complete processing time.
• Before packing large raw fruits, such as pears or peaches, treat them with an antioxidant. Put them in a solution of 2 teaspoons of salt to 1 quart of water.

To keep fruit from floating, follow these tips:
• Do not use overripe fruits; use those in their prime.
• Pack fruit closely.
• Don't allow the syrup to get too thick.
• Process for exactly the right length of time.
• Be sure the temperature is not too high.

Sort vegetables and fruits as to size so that each jar's contents will be approximately uniform. To peel foods like tomatoes and peaches, dip them in boiling water, until the skins loosen, and then in cold water for a moment. Once the vegetables and fruits have been heated, work quickly, filling only the number of jars that your canner accommodates. Don't allow the hot foods to stand prior to processing, for harmful bacteria develop between 105° and 150° F. Fill the containers to ½ inch from the top. For vegetables, use boiling water; for fruits, use boiling syrup. To help air bubbles rise to the surface and break, insert a spatula along the sides of the jar. If the contents of the jar are hot and processing is to take place in a water bath, seal the containers completely. Otherwise, seal them partially. If the food in tin cans is not hot at sealing time, rid the containers of air by boiling them for five minutes in 1 inch of water. After adjusting the lids, seal them immediately.

Approximate Fruit Yield

Fruit	Weight	Units	Yield	Bushels	Yield
Apples	2½ pounds	7–8	1 quart	1	28 quarts
Berries	1¼–1½ pounds	5 cups	1 quart	1	24 quarts
Cherries	1¼–1½ pounds	6 cups	1 quart	1	20 quarts
Peaches	2–2½ pounds	8–10	1 quart	1	21 quarts
Pears	2–2½ pounds	5–6	1 quart	1	30 quarts
Pineapples		15			15 quarts
Plums	1½–2½ pounds	24–32	1 quart	1	28 quarts
Tomatoes	2½–3½ pounds	8–10	1 quart		18 quarts

Processing

Hot Water Bath: Put hot, filled cans or jars on the rack in the canner. Cover them with boiling water to a depth of 1 inch above their tops. Heat rapidly to boiling. When bubbles commence breaking over the containers, begin the timing. Make sure that water covers the jars throughout the processing period. When necessary, add boiling water. Take the canner from the heat upon completion of processing.

Pressure Cooker: There should be sufficient boiling water in the cooker to reach the bottom of the rack. Put packed cans or jars on the rack, adjust the cooker lid, and clamp it down firmly. Have the petcock open. After permitting steam to escape for seven minutes, close the petcock, and watch for the pressure to reach the required point. From that moment count to *nine*. Regulate the heat to maintain steady pressure. Changes in pressure generally cause liquid loss in the containers, especially if the pressure builds to the extent of releasing the safety valve, causing an abrupt fall in pressure. Immediately upon termination of processing time, take the canner from the heat. When sufficient cooling has reduced the pressure to zero, slowly open the petcock. Wait until pressure is completely released before opening the canner. When using number 2 cans, open the petcock just as

quickly as processing is completed, permitting the pressure to drop rapidly. Open the canner and take out the cans. Submerge them immediately in cold water to avoid overcooking.

Cooling Containers

Take jars out of the canner. If they are partially sealed, complete the seal. Put them on folded towels. Invert those that do not have an automatic seal. From time to time, examine the jars. Rising bubbles or leakage indicates that the food should be used or immediately recanned. Never invert jars with self-sealing tops. Test them by tapping with a spoon. If the sound is dull instead of a clear-ringing note, the jar is not well sealed. After submerging tin cans in water, check for bubbles escaping from ends or seams. When containers are cold, wash and label them. Store them in a cool, dry spot.

Spoilage

If you detect any evidence of spoilage, dispose of the food.

An odor that is not characteristic of the product is an indication of spoilage. There should be no signs of leakage, bulging of the rubber, spurting of liquid, or expulsions of air with glass jars. Never taste-test a questionable food; destroy it immediately. Always boil all canned vegetables for ten minutes before serving or tasting.

Canning Recipes for Vegetables, Fruits, and Fruit Juices

Vegetables

When seasoning vegetables for canning, use 1 teaspoon of salt for 1 quart of vegetables; for 1 pint, use ½ teaspoonful.

Asparagus

Carefully wash asparagus. Cut it in 1-inch pieces or lengths to fit the containers. Put them into boiling water and boil for five minutes, keeping the tips above water. Pack immediately in hot jars, stem ends down. Pour in seasoned cooking liquid to within ½ inch of the rim. Partially seal jars. Process at once at ten pounds pressure for forty minutes (for pint jars, five minutes less).

Beans, String

Wash beans and remove ends. Cut them into uniform lengths. Cover

with boiling water. When the water commences boiling again, pack loosely in hot jars, adding salt and boiling cooking water to within ½ inch of their rim. Season, partially seal, and process immediately at ten pounds pressure for forty-five minutes (for pint jars, five minutes less).

Beans, Lima

Select small green beans. Wash well, shell, and precook for four minutes. Pack loosely in clean, hot jars to within 1 inch of the rim. Add boiling cooking liquid to the same level. Season, partially seal, and process at ten pounds pressure for sixty minutes (for pint jars, five minutes less).

Beets

Choose very small beets. Wash carefully. Cut off tops. Leave 1 inch of root and stem. Scald until skins slip. Remove skins, and pack the beets in jars at once. Fill with liquid to within ½ inch of the rim. Season. Partially seal jars. Process immediately at ten pounds pressure for forty minutes (for pint jars, five minutes less).

Broccoli, Brussels Sprouts, Cabbage, Cauliflower

Wash vegetables and remove stems. Discard coarse leaves. Precook for three minutes. Pack in hot jars. Fill them with fresh boiling water up to ½ inch from the rim. Season. Seal, and process immediately at ten pounds pressure for forty minutes.

Carrots

Wash young carrots. Precook for five minutes. Skin. Pack at once in hot jars. Fill jars with boiling liquid up to 1 inch from the rim. Season. Partially seal jars. Process immediately at ten pounds pressure for forty minutes (for pint jars, five minutes less).

Corn, Whole Kernel

Cut corn from the cob. Weigh. Add one-half the weight in boiling water. Season each quart with 2 teaspoons of sugar and 1 teaspoon of salt. Heat to a boil. Pack in hot jars, adding boiling liquid to 1 inch from the top. Partially seal jars. Process immediately at ten pounds pressure for seventy-five minutes (for pint jars, ten minutes less).

Corn, Cream Style

Remove uncooked corn from the cob with a shallow cut. Using the back of a knife, scrape the cobs.

Follow directions for whole kernel corn. Process immediately at ten pounds pressure for eighty minutes (for pint jars, the same time).

Greens

Discard imperfect leaves and stems. Wash well. Add water and simmer until thoroughly wilted. Drain, saving liquid. Pack the greens in jars. Cut through their centers several times with a knife. Add boiling cooking liquid up to ½ inch from rim. Season with salt. Partially seal jars. Process immediately at fifteen pounds pressure for sixty-five minutes (for pint jars, five minutes less).

Mushrooms

Wash well. Skin mature mushrooms. Put them in boiling water with 1 teaspoon of salt and 1 tablespoon

of vinegar per quart. Drain. Pack in hot jars. Pour in fresh boiling water to within ½ inch of the rim. Partially seal the jars. Process immediately at ten pounds pressure for thirty-five minutes (for pint jars, ten minutes less).

Okra

Thoroughly wash the okra. Discard the stem ends. Precook for five minutes. Pack hot into hot, clean jars. Pour in boiling cooking water to within ½ inch of the rim. Season. Partially seal and process immediately at ten pounds pressure for forty minutes (for pint jars, five minutes less).

Peas

Shell tender young peas. Precook for four minutes. Pack the hot peas loosely in hot, clean jars. Pour in boiling cooking water to within 1 inch of the rim. Season, and partially seal jars. Process immediately at ten pounds pressure for one hour (for pint jars, ten minutes less).

Potatoes, New White

Wash well. Cook for five minutes. Remove eyes and skin. Pack while hot, adding boiling cooking liquid to within ½ inch of the rim. Season. Partially seal the jars, and process immediately at fifteen pounds pressure for seventy minutes.

Fruits

Rules for processing in boiling water are for an altitude of 1,000 feet or less. Increase processing time by 20 percent for each additional 1,000 feet.

To use the cold-pack, hot-pack, and open-kettle methods, see the procedures under those headings.

These recipes are for quart and pint jars. Consult the directions already given for packing and sealing jars to be processed by the following methods.

Making Preserves

When fruits become plump from absorbing thick sugar syrup and appear bright and clear in color, you have successful preserves. Stew hard fruits before putting them in syrup.

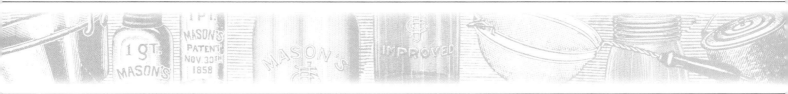

Sweet apples, citrons, hard pears, pineapples, underripe peaches, quinces, and watermelon rinds must be cooked until soft enough to absorb the syrup. Foods that have had this preliminary stewing should be thoroughly drained before being added to the syrup. Use this cooking water to make the syrup. Berries, cherries, ripe peaches, and other tender fruits can be put directly into heavy syrup. Don't cook fruits too long in the syrup, just long enough for them to become filled with it; otherwise a dark, stiff product will result. Bring it quickly to a boil, and continue the rapid cooking until the fruits are shiny and sparkling, indicating that they are saturated with syrup.

For extra-fine preserves, place the fruit in the heavy syrup, and heat it until bubbling begins. Remove from the stove and let stand in a covered enamel preserving pot for a few hours or overnight.

Fruit	Hot Water Bath	Oven	Pressure Canner
Apples: Peel, core, and quarter. Precook or steam for five minutes in thin boiling syrup. Process immediately for	20 minutes	75 minutes at 250° F	10 minutes at 5 pounds
Apricots: Wash. Leave apricots whole, pit them, or halve them. Pack in jars. Pour in thin boiling syrup to cover. Process immediately for	20 minutes	68 minutes at 250° F	10 minutes at 5 pounds
Berries: Pick over berries. Wash and hull them. Fill sterilized jars. Pour in boiling syrup to cover. Process immediately for	20 minutes	68 minutes at 250° F	10 minutes at 5 pounds
Cherries: Wash and stem. Prick with a large pin if unseeded. Fill jars. Cover with thick or medium boiling syrup. Process immediately for	25 minutes	68 minutes at 250° F	10 minutes at 5 pounds
Fruit Juices: Crush (Remove seeds from cherries.) Gradually bring to the simmering point. Strain. Add water and sugar to taste. Heat the juice, and pour it into hot jars. Seal and process at once for	30 minutes		
Peaches: Skin, halve, and pack in jars. Pour in boiling medium syrup to cover. Process immediately for	25 minutes	1 hour at 275° F	10 minutes at 5 pounds
Pears: Remove skins, halve, and core. Boil 1 quart of pears at a time in thin syrup for about six minutes. Pack in hot jars, adding syrup. Process immediately for	30 minutes	1 hour at 275° F	10 minutes at 5 pounds
Pineapple: Peel and remove eyes. Cube the pineapple and pack it in jars, pouring in boiling thin syrup to cover. Process at once for	30 minutes	1 hour at 275° F	10 minutes at 5 pounds
Plums: Wash plums. Prick them with a large pin. Pack jars and cover the contents with boiling medium syrup. Process immediately for	20 minutes	1 hour at 275° F	10 minutes at 5 pounds
Rhubarb: Wash. Cut into· pieces. Pack in jars, pouring in boiling thin syrup to cover. Process at once for	16 minutes	50 minutes at 275° F	10 minutes at 5 pounds
Strawberries: Wash and stem. Add 1 cup of sugar to each quart. Allow to stand for two hours. Simmer for five minutes. Fill the jars. Seal and process immediately for	0 minutes	68 minutes at 250° F	10 minutes at 5 pounds

Then commence the cooking again. In this manner the fruit absorbs more syrup. For an extra fine quality product, repeat the plumping process of heating and cooling a few times. Particularly suited to plumping are citrons, crab apples, green tomatoes, whole tomatoes, peaches, pears, and melon rinds. Always plump fruits that are to be candied.

Seal your preserves in hot, clean jars. Sterilize in boiling water all utensils used in filling the jars with preserves. As a precaution against mold, place the packed jars in boiling water or steam for ten minutes.

Making Jam

Making jam requires mashing or cooking to a pulp small whole fruits with sugar. Ideally, its texture should be tender and soft, its color sparkling bright, and the mixture's consistency uniform.

A jellying substance, pectin, is a necessity for good jam. Broken fruit or pieces remaining from canning may be used for jam making, but part of the fruit must be underripe because pectin is absent in overripe fruit. To develop the pectin, cook the fruit several minutes before adding sugar. When fruit lacks enough juice, add a little water to prevent burning, and cook it in a covered vessel. Porcelain or enamel cooking utensils are best. Use ½ pound of sugar to

1 pound of fruit. After putting in sugar, cook rapidly until the jam takes on a jellylike appearance. To check whether it's done, test it by dropping a bit on a cool dish. If it sets quickly or hangs from the spoon in sheets, it is ready. Keep in mind that upon cooling, jam thickens. Make allowance for this so that the product will not become tough and thick from overcooking. Cooking for too long also darkens the jam.

Because jam is a highly concentrated substance, it will burn easily. To avoid this, always stir from the bottom with a wooden spoon, lifting the jam from the bottom of the kettle. Cook jam rapidly, watching it closely for twenty to thirty minutes.

To protect jams from mold, seal them in hot, clean jars.

Fig Jam (yield: 3 pints)
4 pounds fresh figs
1 lemon
1 cup water
4 cups sugar

Wash figs; peel them. Slice the lemon. Cook water and sugar together for five minutes. Add lemon and figs. Cook briskly until clear.

Seal in hot clean jars.

Grape Jam (yield: 2 pints)
4 pounds Concord grapes
1½ cups water
3 cups sugar

Wash grapes. Remove the skins and seeds. Combine water and sugar; boil for five minutes. Add grape pulp and continue cooking until thick and clear.

Pour into hot, clean jars. Seal immediately.

Peach Jam (yield: eight ½–pint jars)
4¼ cups crushed peaches (about 3½ pounds of the fruit)
¼ cup lemon juice
7 cups sugar
½ bottle liquid pectin

Wash ripe peaches. Remove their stems, skins, and pits. Crush the fruit.

Put the peach pulp in a kettle, and mix in the lemon juice and sugar. Set over high heat, stirring continuously. Quickly bring to a rolling boil and boil hard for one minute, stirring all the while.

Take from the fire, and stir in the pectin. Skim. Fill and seal jars.

Making Marmalade

Generally, marmalades are made from fruits containing both acid and pectin. The fruits are thinly sliced and suspended in a clear jelly. If fruit is used in which the jellying properties of pectin and acid are absent, tart apple juice or slices of lemon or orange can be added to supply them.

The preparation of marmalade is the same as for jams, except that the fruit is in cut pieces or slices, not mashed. Successful marmalade should be of sparkling clarity.

Grapefruit Marmalade

Cut the sections from three grapefruit. Discard seeds and white fiber. Grind the well-washed yellow rind (without the white) of one grapefruit in a food grinder. To the grapefruit sections, add the ground grapefruit peel and the grated rind and strained juice of three lemons. Cover with 6 cups of water; allow to stand overnight.

The following morning, boil the mixture for forty minutes. Repeat for two days more.

Then put in 1 cup of crushed pineapple. Measure the mixture, and add 1½ cups of sugar for each cup of fruit and juice. Cook for thirty minutes or until jellylike.

Seal in sterilized jars.

Tomato-Apple-Ginger Marmalade

Skin enough ripe tomatoes to make 2 cupfuls. Drain. Peel and core enough apples to make 2 cupfuls. Chop. Mince one lemon.

Mix these ingredients, and cook them for fifteen minutes.

Add 3 cups of sugar, and cook until the mixture reaches the consistency of marmalade. For the last ten minutes of cooking, add 4 tablespoons of chopped preserved ginger.

Seal in sterilized jars.

Making Jellies

To make jelly, sugar and fruit juice are combined in proper proportions and cooked until the mixture jells when cool. Jelly of good quality has the natural flavor and color of the fresh fruit, its clarity unmarred by crystals or sediment. It retains its shape when emptied from the jar but is supple enough to quiver. When cut, the jelly does not stick to the knife.

Fruit for jelly must be high in acid and pectin. When fruit is not rich in both of these, it must be combined with a fruit containing whichever substance is absent. The following fruits have pectin and acid in sufficient quantity: crab apples, tart apples, blackberries, gooseberries, loganberries, raspberries, currants, grapes, plums, and quinces. Those with insufficient pectin are as follows: cherries, peaches, pineapples, rhubarb, and strawberries. Fruits lacking enough acid are sweet apples, blueberries, huckleberries, and pears.

Although the flavor isn't as good, fruit that is a bit underripe generally has more pectin and acid than completely ripe fruit. A correct proportion is one-quarter underripe fruit to three-quarters ripe fruit. If either acid or pectin is lacking in a fruit, it can be combined nicely with tart apples, because apple juice has the most minimal affect on the flavor and color of the jelly.

When using commercial pectin, follow exactly the directions

accompanying it. The juice from almost any kind of fruit can be used by adding a large quantity of sugar and the commercial pectin. Jelly is made in less time, but due to the shorter cooking period, the flavor is less rich and full than fruit juice boiled over a longer period. However, success is usually assured with the use of commercial pectin.

Extraction of Fruit Juice

Carefully inspect the fruit, and remove stems and areas of decay. Cut large fruits into pieces. Crush juicy fruits, adding little or no water. Fruits with less juice require adding just enough water until it is visible among the pieces, but not so much that they float. Cook the fruit in a covered vessel until tender and the juice flows liberally. Do not overcook. Apples need approximately fifteen minutes, berries from one to three minutes, and citrus fruits one hour.

Empty the contents into a jelly bag. Use a clean flour sack, or make one of heavy muslin, flannel, or four layers of cheesecloth. Suspend it on a strainer above a bowl to allow the juice to drip through. More juice is extracted by squeezing the bag, but the jelly will not be clear. The first time, let the juice simply drip through; the resulting jelly will be clear and appropriate for special occasions. Squeeze the bag with the second extraction; jelly from this juice will be cloudy, but acceptable for general use. Pulp for a second extraction can be prepared by putting it in a pot, adding water almost to cover, and simmering for about twenty-five minutes. If only one extraction is made, you can press the pulp that remains through a sieve and use it for preparing fruit butter or jam.

Pectin Test

The amount of pectin in a particular fruit juice can be ascertained by combining 1 tablespoon of the juice, 1½ teaspoons of Epsom salts, and 1 teaspoon of sugar. Blend the mixture. When the salts have dissolved, allow to stand for twenty minutes. The formation of large flaky particles or a solid mass means that sufficient pectin is present in the juice to make a good jelly.

Sugar Content

Too much sugar results in weak, syrupy jelly; too small an amount of sugar produces a too-solid jelly. As a general rule, the right proportion is a quantity of sugar equaling two-thirds of the amount of fruit juice. When in doubt, use less sugar instead of more. It is not necessary to heat the sugar.

Cooking Jelly

To produce jelly with the best texture, flavor, and color, cook no more than 2 quarts of juice at one time. Use a 10-quart vessel of large diameter to permit rapid evaporation. When the juice begins to boil, gradually add sugar, stirring slowly. Boil briskly until the jelling point, which can be determined by letting a little juice drip from the spoon. The running together in a continuous strand of the last few drops indicates the jelling stage. Immediately remove the jelly from the heat. Skim and pour into hot, clean glasses. Fill them to within ½ inch of their rims. Seal with paraffin either by pouring melted paraffin on the jelly at once or by covering the jelly with hot paraffin after it has cooled. Put metal covers on the jelly jars after the paraffin cools. Store them in a cool, dry place.

Butter Bean Hull Jelly

5 cups butter bean hull juice
7 cups sugar
2 packages (1¾ ounces each) powdered fruit pectin

Boil butter bean hulls for one hour. Strain them through cheesecloth. Add the pectin to 5 cups of strained juice. Bring the mixture to a boil, and stir in the sugar.

Allow to jell. Pour into clean jars and seal.

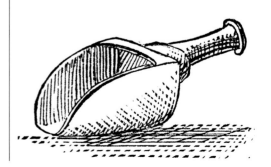

Amounts of Sugar and Fruit Juice for Jelly

Fruit	Juice	Sugar
Apple	1 cup	⅔ cup
Blueberry (with lemon juice)	1 cup	⅔ cup
Crab Apple	1 cup	⅔ cup
Currant	1 cup	¾ to 1 cup
Gooseberry (green)	1 cup	1 cup
Grape (underripe)	1 cup	¾ to 1 cup

Fruit Juice Combinations	Juice	Sugar
Apple	½ cup	⅔ cup
Black Raspberry	½ cup	
Apple	½ cup	¾ cup
Blueberry	½ cup	
Apple	½ cup	⅔ cup
Cherry	½ cup	
Apple	½ cup	⅔ cup
Peach	½ cup	
Apple	½ cup	⅔ cup
Pineapple	½ cup	
Apple	½ cup	⅔ cup
Quince	½ cup	
Blackberry	¾ cup	⅔ cup
Apple	¼ cup	
Cherry	½ cup	¾ cup
Currant	½ cup	
Currant	½ cup	2⅔ cup
Raspberry	½ cup	
Damson Plum	¼ cup	¾ cup
Apple	¾ cup	
Elderberry	½ cup	¾ cup
Apple	½ cup	
Gooseberry (unripe)	½ cup	¾ cup
Cherry	½ cup	

Corn Cob Jelly

12 medium-sized red corn cobs
¼ ounce package
   powdered pectin
2 quarts water
3 cups sugar

Wash cobs. Cut them into fourths. Put them in a vessel of water and bring to the boiling point. Lower the heat. Let boil slowly for about forty minutes.

Strain the juice. Measure 3 cups of it into a large saucepan.

Add pectin; bring to a boil. Add sugar; bring to a boil once more. Continue boiling for five minutes.

Skim the foam from the surface. Pour into sterile jars.

Corn cob jelly is said to taste like mild honey.

Mesquite Bean Jelly

3 quarts mesquite beans
1 box pectin (1¾ ounces)
5 cups sugar

Pick mesquite beans while they are still red. Cover 3 quarts of the beans with enough water to make 5 cups of juice. Add sugar as it simmers until the juice becomes yellow. Strain it.

Follow directions on pectin juice for making jelly, but boil a bit longer than specified. Use the spoon test to check when it has jelled.

Put into sterilized jars. Seal.

Parsley Jelly (yield: six 8-ounce glasses)

3 cups boiling water
4½ cups sugar
4 cups chopped parsley
(2 big bunches)
several drops green food
   coloring (homemade)
2 tablespoons lemon juice
1¾ ounces powdered fruit pectin

Put the chopped parsley in a bowl; pour the boiling water over it. Cover. Allow to stand for twenty minutes.

Strain the liquid through cheesecloth. Put 3 cups of the parsley juice into a good-sized saucepan. Stir in the lemon juice and pectin. Cook over high heat, stirring until the mixture reaches a rolling boil. Put in all the sugar at once and stir. Mix in a few drops of green coloring. Bring to a rolling boil again and boil hard for one minute, stirring continuously.

Take the pan from the heat, and remove the foam with a metal spoon. Quickly pour the liquid into sterilized jelly glasses. Cover immediately with hot paraffin to a depth of ⅛ inch.

Homemade Pectin

Make apple jelly stock-sugar-free pectin-to preserve for future use

or to prepare jams and jellies immediately. (Most commercial pectins contain sugar.)

For your homemade pectin select small, green, immature apples, available in early summer. Being rich in pectin and acid, they make excellent jelly stock and impart a snappy, tart flavor to the finished product. Apples cut or bruised by falling from orchard boughs, and even those damaged by birds and insects, can be utilized by cutting away the imperfect parts.

Wash the fruit thoroughly, retaining only the sound portions and cutting them into thin slices. Put them in a vessel, and add 2 cups of water for each pound of apples. Cover the vessel; boil its contents for fifteen minutes. Strain the juice with pulp through one thickness of cheesecloth; do not squeeze the pulp.

Put the pulp back in the vessel, once more adding the required measure of water. Cook the mixture again for fifteen minutes, but this time over lower heat. Let it stand for ten minutes. Now strain the juice with pulp through cheesecloth, without squeezing the pulp. When the pulp cools sufficiently for handling, press any remaining juice from it. You should have accumulated approximately 1 quart of apple juice for each pound of fruit.

If you don't have immediate plans for blending the pectin with the juice of other fruits to make jam or jellies, prepare it for storage in this way: Heat the jelly stock to the boiling point; then pour it into hot, sterilized canning jars. Seal them. Invert the jars, and allow them to cool. Instead of canning the pectin, you may freeze it by letting the liquid cool and pouring it into freezer containers. Leave 1 inch of headroom to allow for expansion.

To prepare honey jelly, use 2 cups of homemade pectin to each 2½ cups of honey plus ½ cup of water. These amounts will vary a little when fruit juice is used, depending on the kind involved. Remember that the greater the quantity of pectin, the thicker the finished product and the weaker the other fruit's flavor.

Grape Jelly with Homemade Pectin

Blend the following:
2½ cups grape juice (unsweetened and, if possible, homemade)
½ cup honey
2 cups homemade pectin

Rapidly boil the mixture for ten minutes. To prevent its foaming over, stir the jelly but don't lower the heat.

Pour it immediately into hot, sterilized jelly jars. Seal them. Do not disturb the jars until the contents have partially set. To complete the jelling, refrigerate them.

Making Vinegar

In the presence of a particular kind of yeast, the action of oxygen upon a solution of alcohol produces vinegar. The alcoholic liquors from which vinegar can be made result from the fermentation of almost any fruit or vegetable juices. The chief types of vinegar are wine vinegar from grapes; malt vinegar from barley; cider vinegar from apples; sugar and molasses vinegar from sugar cane; beet vinegar; corn vinegar; etc.

Cider Vinegar

Put cider into a jug. For each quart of cider, add ½ cup of molasses and ¼ cup of brewer's yeast. Leave the container partially open to admit air. Fermentation will begin at once.

The cider will become vinegar in about a week's time.

Pour off the clear vinegar into bottles and close tightly. To repeat the process, leave the lees (which provide the necessary yeast) in the jug and 6.ll with fresh cider.

White Wine Vinegar

Crush 1 pound of clean raisins. Add ½ gallon of pure soft or distilled water and put in a l-gallon jug, uncovered. Allow to stand in a warm place. It will turn into white wine vinegar in about a month.

Strain the clear vinegar through cheesecloth. Leave the raisins and sediment in the jug. Add another ½ gallon of water along with ¼ pound of raisins to repeat the process.

Fruit Vinegar

The juice of most fruits, such as currants, gooseberries, and raspberries, contains enough sugar to ferment and produce an alcoholic liquor for making vinegar, with or without adding molasses.

To make vinegar from fruits, extract the juice by boiling the fruit with its equal in water. Press out the juice through several layers of cheesecloth. You can do this by inserting sticks at either end of the cloth and twisting them. To each 2 quarts of fruit juice, add ¼ cup of yeast. Allow to stand in a jar or jug with the top slightly tilted to admit air. Keep it in a spot where the temperature ranges between 70° and 80° F. Or you may let the boiled fruit juice stand for two or three days to ferment before straining it. Add the yeast after the fermented liquor has been removed from the fruit pulp.

Preparing Pickles

Pickling is the process of preserving foods with vinegar or brine. A variation of seasonings and spices results in spiced pickles, sour pickles, and sweet pickles.

Vegetables and fruits can be pickled sliced, quartered, in halves, or whole. The most commonly pickled foods are cabbage, carrots, cauliflower, cucumbers, beets, onions, tomatoes, crab apples, grapes, peaches, and pears.

Preparation of Food for Pickling

Scrub vegetables thoroughly in clear water. Next, soak them in salted water (from ⅛ to ¼ cup of salt for each quart of water)

for a few hours or overnight. The salt extracts moisture from the tissues, crisping the vegetables so that they more readily soak up the pickling solution.

Fruits do not require a preliminary soaking in water and salt. Prepare them as you would for canning, and put them in the pickling solution.

Pickling Pointers

- Lift or stir pickles with a wooden or granite spoon.
- Cool pickles in an aluminum vessel or porcelain-lined graniteware.
- Keep in mind that too much salt will shrivel vegetables and make them tough.
- Vinegar that is too strong can bleach vegetables and cause them to soften after pickling.
- Seal pickles in stone or glass jars.

Bread-and-Butter Pickles

  8 cups sliced cucumbers
  1 tablespoon mustard seed
  5 cups sliced onions
  ½ cup finely chopped
     green pepper
  ½ teaspoon celery seed
  ¼ teaspoon turmeric
  ¼ cup salt
  ¼ teaspoon ginger
  1 quart water
  1½ cups vinegar
  2½ cups sugar
  1 cup water

Put cucumbers, onions, and green peppers in a big bowl.

Dissolve the salt in a quart of water, and pour it on the cucumber mixture. Cover. Allow to stand for four hours at room temperature.

Drain the bowl's contents. Place them in a 6-quart kettle.

Heat the rest of the ingredients in a saucepan to the boiling point, stirring until the sugar dissolves. Pour over the cucumber mixture. Heat to a boil.

Pack in sterilized jars to within ½ inch of the rim. Seal.

Process in boiling water for ten minutes.

Pumpkin Pickles

Cut a pumpkin rind into strips. Peel and cut them in 1-inch pieces. Prepare 4 cupfuls.

Combine the following in a saucepan:

  1 cup sugar
  6 whole cloves
  ¾ cup white vinegar
  2 teaspoons ginger,
     freshly grated
  ¼ cup dark corn syrup
  ½ cinnamon stick, crushed

Bring these ingredients to a boil, and add the pumpkin pieces. Slowly cook the mixture for about forty-five minutes or until tender.

Put the pickles in a quart jar; close it tightly. Store in the refrigerator.

Sauerkraut

  5 pounds cabbage
  5 tablespoons salt

Take off the outer leaves wash and put them aside and any imperfect

parts of the cabbage. Quarter it, removing the core. Slice the cabbage finely with a slaw cutter or sharp knife. Toss cabbage and salt in a large bowl, mixing well.

Solidly pack it into a 1- to 2-gallon crock. Allow to stand for a few minutes. Forcefully press on the cabbage with a wooden pestle (a wooden spoon will serve) until juice makes its appearance. Cover the top with the well-washed outer leaves of the cabbage; place several thicknesses of cheesecloth over them. Lay a plate on the cloth that fits snugly within the crock. To insure that the cabbage remains beneath the liquid and that the cloth stays wet, weight the dish. A heavy stone will do nicely. Let the crock stand in a warm place (65°–68° F) to ferment for about four weeks. When choosing the spot, take into consideration that the contents will give off a very disagreeable odor during the initial stage of fermentation. Check the crock each day. Skim off scum. Remove the cloth cover, rinse in cold water, wring dry, and replace.

After four to five weeks, the sauerkraut is ready for use and should be stored in a cool (below 60° but above 32° F), dark place. Keep the top covered to prevent air from entering. For canning, simmer kraut and juice in a large vessel to heat; avoid boiling. Pack into clean hot jars. Fill them with juice to within ½ inch of the rim. Seal and process.

Watermelon Pickles
General Rules

Cut watermelon rind in long strips. (Leaving on a little pink flesh lends color to the finished product.) Peel them. Cut the rind into 1-inch chunks. Prepare 4 quarts.

In 2 quarts of cold water, dissolve 1 cup of salt. Drop in a few cherry or grape leaves to insure crisp pickles.

Pour this solution on the rind pieces, adding water, if necessary, to cover them. Allow to stand for six hours. (For a shorter soaking period, two to four hours, you may substitute 3 tablespoons of slaked lime for the salt and leaves. Check the bag's label to be sure the lime is intended for pickling.)

After the soaking period, rinse the rind thoroughly, and cover it with cold water. Cook the pieces until just tender. Drain.

Select your favorite watermelon pickle recipe, and tie the indicated spices in a bag of cheesecloth. Put it in a vessel with the rest of the ingredients mentioned in the recipe, except the rind, and simmer for ten minutes. Then add the rind pieces, and simmer them until they become transparent. Should the syrup get too thick, thin it with boiling water.

When the rinds are clear, take out the spice bag. Refrigerate smaller amounts to be used right away. Pack the remainder of the boiling-hot pickles with their syrup into sterilized jars to within ⅛ inch of the rims. Close tightly. Pumpkin, winter squash, and cantaloupe rind can be pickled in the same manner.

Ingredients for Spicy Watermelon Pickles

- 1 tablespoon salt
- 1 teaspoon whole cloves
- 1 teaspoon celery seed
    (Do not put this ingredient in the cheesecloth bag)
- 9 cups sugar
- 2 quarts vinegar

Ingredients for Lemony Watermelon Pickles

- 2 tablespoons whole cloves
- 1 thinly sliced lemon
- 8 cups sugar
- 3 sticks cinnamon
- 1 quart white vinegar
- 2 pieces ginger root
- 1 quart water

Zucchini Pickles (yield: 6–7 pints)

- 5 pounds squash
- 1 quart white vinegar
- 4 to 5 medium onions
- 2 cups sugar
- 8 cloves
- 1 cinnamon stick
- 1 dried red pepper
- ¼ cup salt
- 2 teaspoons ground turmeric
- 2 teaspoons celery seed
- 1 teaspoon dry mustard

Cut the unpeeled zucchini into ¼-inch slices. Thinly slice the onions, enough to make 1 quart. Mix the squash and onions in a big bowl.

Combine the remaining ingredients in a saucepan, mixing them well. Bring to a boil. Pour the bubbling liquid on the vegetables in the bowl. Leave it for one hour;

stir now and then.

Now put the bowl's contents into a vessel. Bring to a boil; simmer for three minutes. Then let the simmering continue as you quickly fill hot sterilized jars to within ½ inch of the rim. Be sure that the zucchini and onion mixture is completely covered by the vinegar solution.

Spiced Crab Apples (yield: 6 pints)

    4 quarts crab apples
    2 sticks cinnamon
    5 cups brown sugar
    1 tablespoon whole allspice
    2 cups vinegar
    1 tablespoon whole cloves

Wash the crab apples, but do not pare them. Prick their skin a few times with the tines of a fork. Remove the blossom ends. Mix the remaining ingredients, and simmer them for twenty minutes. Add several apples at a time; simmer until tender.

Put the apples in hot sterilized jars and cover with syrup.

Seal.

For spicier apples, include a bit of ginger root and one blade of mace with the other spices when preparing the syrup.

Strain the leftover syrup to pour on vanilla ice cream.

Pickled Prunes

    1 pound prunes
    2 cups light brown sugar
    1 lemon
    1 cup tarragon vinegar

Soak the prunes overnight. The following morning, simmer them until plump and tender in just enough water to cover. Add the remaining ingredients, except the red pepper. Cook until glossy; then put in the dried pepper.

Seal the prunes in a 1-quart jar.

Chow Chow (yield: 9–10 pints)

    1 peck (12½ pounds)
        green tomatoes
    1 tablespoon cinnamon
    8 large onions
    1 tablespoon allspice
    10 green bell peppers
    ¼ teaspoon cloves
    3 tablespoons salt
    3 tablespoons mustard
    6 hot peppers, chopped
    several bay leaves
    1¾ cups sugar
    1 quart vinegar
    ½ cup horseradish

Chop tomatoes, onions, and green peppers. Mix them in a bowl and cover with the salt. Allow to stand overnight.

Drain the mixture, and add

the hot peppers (chopped), vinegar, and spices tied in a bag of cheesecloth. Bring the ingredients to a boil.

Pack the chow chow in clean jars and process for fifteen minutes.

Making Mincemeat

Apricot Mincemeat (yield: 3 quarts)

Coarsely grind the following, even the sugar, if need be:

    1 pound dried apricots,
        soaked overnight
    1 pound apples, peeled, cored,
        and chopped
    1 pound pitted dates
    1 pound seedless raisins
    1 pound currants
    2 cups brown sugar
    2 cups suet
    ¼ cup almonds

Add to these ingredients the juice and rind of one lemon and 2 tablespoons of grated nutmeg. Use at once, or can at ten pounds pressure for ten minutes.

Green Tomato Mincemeat

    1 peck green tomatoes,
        finely chopped
    1 tablespoon salt
    ½ peck apples, finely chopped
    2 pounds raisins
    4 pounds brown sugar
    2 tablespoons cinnamon
    1 cup weak vinegar
    2 tablespoons cloves
    1 cup suet, finely chopped
    1 tablespoon nutmeg

Put the finely chopped tomatoes in a large vessel. Cover the contents with cold water; add salt. Heat to boiling. Drain. Cover with cold water; heat to boiling. Repeat the procedure a third time, cooking the tomatoes until tender. Drain.

Add the remaining ingredients. Cook them gently. Once the apples are tender, fill sterilized jars with the mincemeat. Seal at once.

Traditional Mincemeat

4 pounds lean beef, chopped
2 pounds beef suet, chopped
1 peck sour apples, peeled, cored, and sliced
3 pounds sugar
2 quarts cider
4 pounds seeded raisins
5 pounds currants
1½ pounds citron, chopped
½ pound dried orange peel, chopped
½ pound dried lemon peel, chopped
1 lemon, juice and rind
1 tablespoon cinnamon
1 tablespoon mace
1 tablespoon cloves
1 teaspoon pepper
1 teaspoon salt
2 whole nutmegs, grated
1 gallon sour cherries and their juice
2 pounds broken nut meats (if desired)

Slowly cook these ingredients for two hours. Stir them often.

Fill sterilized jars. Seal.

Making Catsup

Apple Catsup

½ bushel sour apples
1 cup sugar
1 teaspoon pepper
1 teaspoon cloves
1 teaspoon mustard
2 teaspoons cinnamon
1 tablespoon salt
2 onions, finely chopped
2 cups cider vinegar

Wash, quarter, pare, and core the apples. Put the apple pieces in a vessel, and cover them with boiling water. Bring to the boiling point, and then simmer the fruit until soft; by this time almost all the water should have evaporated.

Rub the vessel's contents through a sieve, making 4 cups of pulp. Combine the remaining ingredients, and add them to the pulp. Bring the mixture to the boiling point and simmer for sixty minutes.

Bottle and seal the apple catsup while it is hot.

Grape Catsup

20 pounds grapes
5 pounds sugar
2 quarts vinegar
1 tablespoon cinnamon
1 tablespoon allspice
2 tablespoons cloves
1 grated nutmeg

Wash grapes, and remove their stems. Barely cover the fruit with cold water, bring to the boiling point, and simmer until softened. Press it through a sieve; discard seeds and skins.

Put 10 pounds of grape pulp and the other ingredients into a kettle. Bring to the boiling point; simmer until the consistency of catsup is reached.

Fill and seal bottles.

Raspberry Catsup

4 quarts ripe raspberries
4 cups cider vinegar
½ teaspoon white mustard seeds
1 slice ginger root
1 cinnamon stick, in pieces
6 cloves
2 cups sugar

Put the fruit and vinegar in an enameled pot. Simmer gently for sixty minutes. Strain through a fine sieve, pressing the pulp through with the back of a wooden spoon.

Rinse out the pot, and return the puree to it, adding mustard seeds and spices. Cook slowly for twenty-five minutes. Again strain and then measure.

To each quart of berry puree, add 2 cups of sugar. Simmer over a low fire, stirring continuously until the mixture is thick and smooth.

When the raspberry catsup is cool, bottle it.

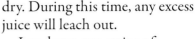

Tomato Catsup
(yield: about 1 quart)

¼ cup cider vinegar
6 large ripe tomatoes (red)
1 3-inch cinnamon stick
    (broken in small
    pieces)
½ cup water
¼ cup minced onion
½ teaspoon whole cloves
3 tablespoons sugar
1 teaspoon salt
½ teaspoon celery seed
dash cayenne pepper

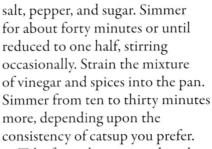

Put the first four ingredients into a saucepan. Boil for one minute. Take from the heat and pour into a container.

Cut tomatoes into quarters, after removing their stems, and place them in the saucepan. Add the onion and water. Heat to the boiling point, using a wooden spoon to stir and mash the tomatoes. Reduce the heat. Simmer about twenty minutes, stirring now and then to avoid sticking. Rub through a sieve. Return the strained juice to the saucepan. Blend in salt, pepper, and sugar. Simmer for about forty minutes or until reduced to one half, stirring occasionally. Strain the mixture of vinegar and spices into the pan. Simmer from ten to thirty minutes more, depending upon the consistency of catsup you prefer.

Take from the stove and cool. Fill a clean container with the catsup, closing it tightly. Store in the refrigerator.

Making Soy Sauce

Prepare soy sauce in autumn after the soybeans have been harvested. Boil them, using any preferred amount, until thoroughly cooked. Put the hot, wet beans through a meat grinder having very fine cutters. Keep the liquid along with the mash. Form the wet pulp into a cone shaped like an inverted flowerpot.

Spread a clean, white towel over a window screen (or fruit-drying rack), and place the mass on it to dry. During this time, any excess juice will leach out.

Lay down two strips of unbleached muslin, about 6 inches wide and 2 feet long, so that they bisect each other. When the cone has dried to a rather hard consistency, set it where the cloth strips meet. Bring up their ends, tie them together, and suspend the bean mass in a warm place while fermentation begins. After several weeks, take it down and put it in a cotton or muslin bag. Store the package in a warm spot through the winter. To avoid damage by insects or mice, it may be hung from a hook.

In spring, break the bean mass into a few chunks; put them in an earthenware crock. Fill it with water, and add salt to taste plus several lumps of charcoal, which will absorb gas and any impurities. (Activated charcoal can be purchased from chemical supply houses or wherever water treatment products are sold.) Set the crock in the sun for a few days to encourage further ripening of the contents. The water will turn black, and moldy pieces of the soybean mass will rise to the surface.

When the few days are up, ladle the liquid into a pot, adding a little garlic. Boil it, skimming off the scum during cooking. Once the liquid becomes sufficiently concentrated, cool, bottle, and store your patiently awaited soy sauce.

29 | FROM THE DRY HOUSE

Drying Foods

Drying vegetables, fruits, and herbs is the cheapest way of preserving food. It also requires little space and fills some needs more readily than frozen or canned foods.

A few generations ago, drying herbs, fruits, and vegetables was a standard way of keeping edibles. Metal racks 3 feet square and equipped with tiers of trays were used for drying sweet corn. The trays could be rotated from top to bottom, hastening the drying process. Corn cut from the cob was spread evenly and thinly on a cloth to prevent the kernels from slipping through the slatted trays. The bottom tray was about 10 inches above a fire or stove, which was used to enhance drying during rainy periods. The procedure was usually carried out in the kitchen or smokehouse. In dry weather, foods were spread or hung outdoors. Pumpkins were cut in circles and the rings hung on stretched lines. Sometimes they were cut in strips and strung on heavy twine. Green beans, snapped into pieces and strung on twine, were called "leather breeches." Folks often constructed small buildings designed for drying fruits. Known as "dry houses," they contained slatted trays attached to the walls, with a small stove for heating the interior.

Sun Drying Method

Sun drying requires time and care. Spread foods on trays, cookie sheets, cake pans, wire racks, or butcher paper; space the pieces for air circulation. Shield them from insects with cheesecloth or wire screening. Most vegetables require about two days to dry properly. Foods should be stirred and inspected frequently during the process. They must be brought in from rain and night dew.

Here are ways to successfully dehydrate certain foods by sun drying them:

Cabbage

Select well-developed heads. Remove the outer leaves. Cut the cabbage in ¼-inch-thick strips. Spread them on trays. For 1 pound of dried cabbage, you will need 18 pounds of fresh.

Corn

Choose corn at its sweet, best-eating stage. Discard the husks. Blanch the vegetable for three to five minutes in boiling water. Cool rapidly in cold water. Remove the kernels from the cob. Spread them on trays to dry in the sun.

Peas

Pick peas in their ripe stage, not too old or too immature. Shell them. Spread the peas on trays placed in the sun for thorough drying. Approximately 3½ pounds of fresh peas make 1 pound of dried.

Pumpkin and Squash

Cut pumpkin and squash into slices ½ inch thick. Since they keep well without processing, you may not want to bother with drying them. However, it's a long time between autumn harvests.

Tomatoes

Bright sunlight is essential for drying tomatoes. Slice them thickly, and spread them on drying trays. To prevent mold from developing, turn them now and then. When leathery dry they can be packed in containers. Sprinkle a bit of salt between each layer.

Storing Sun-Dried Foods

Store dried foods only after they are completely cool.

Package them in plastic or paper bags, and close them securely. Put the bags in insect- and rodent-proof containers. Store them where it is cool and dry. If you live in a humid climate, store them in glass jars. You may keep dried foods in your freezer, particularly if insects are a problem.

Reconstituting Dried Vegetables for Cooking

Prepare dried vegetables for cooking by first soaking them; onions, cabbage, and finely chopped peppers are the exceptions.

To each cupful of cabbage, add about 7 cups of water.

Slowly bring to a boil in an uncovered vessel and boil for thirty minutes. Add salt and preferred seasonings. Dried cabbage in chicken or beef stock with a dollop of margarine makes a hearty, delicious soup.

Corn requires a preliminary soaking of two to four hours.

For 1 cup of corn, use 2 cups of water.

Peas should be soaked for about twenty-four hours. Pumpkins and squash need soaking overnight. Add 10 pints of water to 1 pound. They are then ready for use in breads, cookies, pies, or in any recipe calling for the canned or fresh kinds.

Tomatoes need a period of twenty-four hours or more for softening. Before soaking them, rinse them a few times under cold water to remove any excess salt.

All of these dried vegetables make excellent casserole dishes, either in combination or separately.

Oven-Drying Method

If your area lacks fairly long periods of steady, hot sun, prepare foods by the oven-drying method.

Meticulously pick over all foods to remove blemishes.

Blanch vegetables before drying them. To avoid vitamin loss, blanch by steaming rather than boiling. Use disease-free herbs, and select fruits at their ripest stage when sugar content is highest. Prevent discoloration by treating fruits with ascorbic acid solution.

Spread the food evenly on cookie sheets. Dry them in the oven for twelve to twenty-four hours. (Corn may require more than twenty-four hours.) Use an oven thermometer to maintain the temperature between 90° and 115° F. Do not allow the temperature to exceed 120° F. Stir the food from time to time with a spatula. Turn the pieces over, and transfer those in the center to the outside edges. When done, vegetables should be brittle; the fruit, leathery.

Here are ways to successfully dehydrate certain foods by oven drying them:

Carrots

Wash carrots well. Leave them whole and steam for twenty minutes. Lay them on paper towels to dry. Peel and cut them in slices ⅛ inch thick. Spread the carrots on a cookie sheet. Dry them in the oven until brittle and a deep orange. Don't let the temperature exceed 120° F.

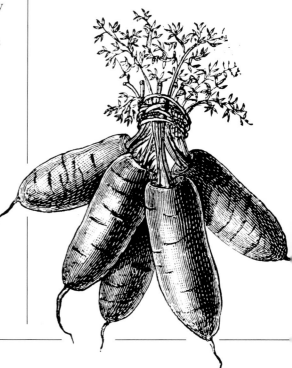

Corn

To avoid the necessity of soaking dried corn prior to cooking it, use this old-time recipe for oven drying the vegetable: Cut enough sweet corn from the cob to equal 16 cupfuls. (Speed the operation by utilizing this handy implement: Take a metal shoehorn and keenly sharpen its wide end. The curve of the shoehorn conforms to the shape of the cob so that its sharpened edge can speedily slice off kernels to just the right depth and over a wider area than a knife.)

Put 4 ounces of cream, 6 tablespoons of sugar, and 4 teaspoons of coarse canning salt into a kettle; add the unblanched corn. Boil these ingredients for twenty minutes. Stir continuously to prevent sticking.

Remove the mixture from the stove, and spread it on shallow pans. Put the corn in an oven set at its lowest temperature. Stir frequently.

Once the corn is dry and somewhat crisp, transfer it to clean paper bags. Close the bags securely, and hang them in a dry place to finish the dehydration process. When the kernels rattle in the bags, they are ready to be stored in tightly closed jars.

At serving time, no presoaking is necessary. Heat the vegetable, using a small amount of milk rather than water to enhance its flavor.

Onions

Onions do not require steam blanching. Peel them and slice thinly. Separate the rings, and spread them on a cookie sheet. Dry in the oven until very crisp at no more than 120° F. Crumble the onions, and put them in airtight containers.

Grapes (Raisins)

Wash grapes; stem them. Lower them in a colander into briskly boiling water just long enough to split their skins. Spread on paper towels to dry. Place on a cookie sheet in an oven set no higher than 120° F. Remove when pliable.

Apples

Pare and core tart cooking apples. Slice them ¼ inch thick. For each 5 quarts of sliced fruit, mix 2½ teaspoons of ascorbic acid in 1 cup of water. Sprinkle this over the fruit slices, completely coating each piece. Spread on a cookie sheet and dry at a temperature not exceeding 120° F. Remove from the oven when springy and pliable.

Herbs

Collect herb leaves for drying just before the plant blooms. Wash the leaves quickly in cold water. Using paper towels, blot them dry. Remove the leaves from the upper two-thirds of the plant. Spread on a cookie sheet. Dry them at an oven temperature not exceeding 120° F. To check to see if they're done, pinch the leaves. If they are brittle and crumble, take them from the oven.

To dry the seeds of herbs, pick the whole plant. Put it upside down in a paper bag. Make holes at the top of the bag to allow air circulation, and hang it up. As the flower heads dry, the seeds will fall into the bag.

Put the seeds in airtight containers. Store them in a dry, dark, cool place.

Storing Oven-Dried Foods

Allow the foods to stand for complete cooling. Then store them in airtight containers. Keep them in a cool, dark, dry place.

30 | MEAT, FOWL, AND FISH

Smoking Meat, Fowl, and Fish

Smoking meat, fowl, and fish converts them into food with a special taste and texture, appealing to the most discriminating gourmet.

The process is a slow one and requires a smoker. Small-scale smokers can be purchased in hardware stores or made at home. Use a semi-enclosed box with some sort of heating element in the bottom, such as a hot plate, to support a pan of wood chips. The chips should be slowly heated and a temperature maintained somewhere between 150° and 200° F, 190° F being considered most favorable. Do not use chips from the wood of evergreen trees. Hardwood chips, such as hickory, keep the flames down and generate more smoke. Soak the chips in water for thirty minutes before use. Dried corncobs can substitute for the chips. As the wood chips smolder, the food gradually absorbs the smoke, which imparts a delectable flavor. Heat and smoke can be controlled by some kind of adjustable vents. To maintain steady temperature, use an oven thermometer. A meat thermometer will help you determine when the meat is done.

Smoked Roasts (Beef, Lamb, or Pork)

The smoker should be preheated to 225° F. Rub the roast with a mixture of salt and your favorite spices, or with seasoned salt alone. Insert a meat thermometer in the middle, away from bone and fat. Smoking time will depend on the size of the roast. Be sure that pork attains an internal temperature of at least 170° F.

Smoked Ribs or Chops

Trim fat from the ribs or chops, and rub them with seasoned salt. Hang the meat or lay it on racks in the smoker. Smoke for about two hours at 80° to 85° F. Slowly raise the temperature to 250° F and smoke for an additional thirty to forty-five minutes. The meat is done when it begins to fall from the bone. During the last fifteen minutes of cooking, baste the ribs or chops with barbecue sauce, if desired.

Smoked Sausage

Any sausage can be smoked; smoking will flavor the meat, not cook it.

Suspend uncooked sausages from hooks in the smoker.

Smoke from one to two hours at 70° F. Then cook according to the recipe.

Put bulk sausage in loaf pans in the middle of the smoker rack. Smoke from one to two hours at 70° F. Then cook according to the recipe.

Jerky (yield: 1 pound)
    4 pounds lean beef
    2 tablespoons lemon juice
    ⅓ cup soy sauce
    3 tablespoons vinegar
    1 teaspoon onion powder
    2 tablespoons sugar
    1 teaspoon seasoned salt

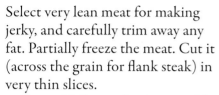

Select very lean meat for making jerky, and carefully trim away any fat. Partially freeze the meat. Cut it (across the grain for flank steak) in very thin slices.

For mild-flavored jerky, sprinkle one teaspoon of pepper and one teaspoon of seasoned salt for each pound of meat.

Smoke it immediately. For a stronger flavor, blend all the other ingredients, and marinate the meat in this mixture either for a few hours or overnight, keeping it in the refrigerator. Turn the meat a few times.

Thoroughly drain the meat, and arrange it on greased racks that are slightly separated to permit circulation of air. Smoke it until brittle and dry for approximately twenty-four hours at 85° to 90° F.

Smoking Pork in a Smokehouse

Preliminary Preparation
Each cut of pork may be wrapped in cheesecloth to protect it from soot, but this measure is not essential. Run wire or string through the meat, and loop it around cross poles in the smokehouse. Hang hams with the hock downward in order to retain juices. Allow free circulation of smoke to all areas of the meat by spacing the pieces.

Fuel
The ideal smoking temperature ranges between 110° and 120° F.

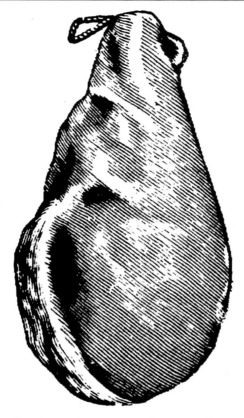

Sawdust, chips, or small pieces of wood from alder, apple, beech, hickory, maple, or oak make good fuel. The wood of all nut and fruit trees is suitable, as are corncobs. Never use resinous wood. Since smoke, not heat, is desired, keep the lit fuel smoldering by lightly sprinkling it with water whenever it flares up.

Smoking Time
The longer the smoking period the better. During prolonged smoking the meat dries slowly, and the acid of the smoke permeates each piece. Quick smoking affects only the ham's exterior; the smoke's acid coats it but does not penetrate its fiber.

Hams may be smoked either for eight to ten hours or for a few weeks, depending on the quality desired. Generally, hams are satisfactory in about five days, bacon in three.

Smoking time can be determined by color. Meat that is mahogany-colored all over, either light or dark in hue, may be removed from the smokehouse. The darker the meat, the longer it will keep.

Storing
Wrap the meat pieces in cheesecloth and then newspaper. Place them in paper bags, tied closed. Store the smoked meat in a cool (43° F), dry place.

Smoked Fowl
Small game birds ducks, pheasants, and quail can be successfully smoked. Smoking will render them tender and succulent. The average pheasant requires about ten hours of cooking time, perhaps a bit longer. You will need to add wood chips three or four times during this period. Smoke should trickle constantly through the vents. If you prefer a heavy smoked flavor, continuously add wood chips to the pan; for moderate flavor, a handful now and then is sufficient.

Some game birds can be put directly into the smoker.

However, for the best results, brine them first. This applies as well to domestic chickens. Place the bird to be smoked in a glass or

⅓ cup of water, ¼ cup of honey, and ½ teaspoon of powdered ginger, all over low heat. Let the mixture cool. Leave the bird whole, or cut it in pieces. Marinate it in the refrigerator for at least eight hours, turning it several times.

When readying a bird for smoking, don't discard the giblets. They can be put to good use as tasty snacks. Prepare livers for smoking by putting them into boiling water and cooking them until all redness disappears. Drain and smoke. Hearts and gizzards do not require this preliminary boiling. Coat the gizzards, hearts, and cooked livers by shaking them in a plastic bag containing a mixture of the following seasonings: pepper, table salt, sugar, and garlic salt. Put the giblets on the racks inside the smoker for forty-five minutes to one hour at 80° F. Then raise the temperature to 225° or 250° for thirty to sixty minutes more.

Take out the giblets; put them in a jar, adding a little vegetable oil. Roll them about in the jar until well coated. Keep the jar refrigerated for twenty-four hours to insure the best flavor.

Smoked Fish
For mildly salty, spiced fish, marinate for several hours; for more spiciness, let it stand in the marinade for at least six hours or overnight.

crockery vessel. Cover it with water. For every 4 quarts of water, put in 4 cups of cider, several dashes of lemon juice, ¼ teaspoon of maple flavoring, 1½ cups of curing salt, ½ teaspoon of ginger, ½ cup of brown sugar, and 3 tablespoons of pepper. You can either cold soak the bird overnight in this brine or simmer it in the solution for approximately five minutes. When it is ready for smoking, dry it in the air for an hour, or wipe it with a towel. Combine brown sugar, garlic powder, and black pepper. Rub the bird generously with this mixture.

Thread a long, heavy string through the body, and truss up the legs, using the excess string to hang the bird in the smoker. Maintain the temperature as close to 190° F as possible. For each pound of bird, allow one and a half hours of cooking time. To determine how well it's done, twist a leg. If it moves easily, the bird is ready for eating.

You might like to give the brine an oriental flavor. Mix ⅓ cup of soy sauce, ⅓ cup of sherry,

lemon slices or
    grated lemon peel
10 fish fillets of firm flesh
½ cup sugar
1 quart water
½ cup salt
one or two of these seasonings:
    garlic or onion salt
    black or white pepper
    leaves of bay, dill, or tarragon
    ground mace or ginger
    hot pepper sauce or dried red
      pepper flakes
    lemon slices or grated lemon peel

Mix the water, sugar, salt, and seasonings in a bowl until the salt and sugar dissolve. Put in the fish. Cover. Then weight the cover down to keep them beneath the brine. Refrigerate the fish either for a few hours or overnight.

Drain the fillets, and thoroughly rinse them in cold water.

Pat dry with paper towels and place on a wire rack to dry in the air for thirty minutes to one hour. Grease the smoker racks, and lay the fish on them, skin down, spaced for air circulation. Smoking should begin at 90° F. After fifteen minutes, slowly raise the heat to 135° to 140° F and smoke for one to two hours.

When the fillets are golden brown and flake at the touch of a fork, they are ready to be eaten; or they can be tightly wrapped and stored in the freezer.

Smoked Oysters

Shuck and wash oysters. Mix 1¼ pounds of salt in 1 gallon of water. Soak the oysters in this brine for five minutes.

Drain them well. Lightly coat the oysters with salad oil.

Lay them on a well-greased rack wide enough apart to permit air circulation. A wire cake rack may be used if the spaces of the smoker rack are too wide. Smoke the oysters for fifteen minutes at 180° F.

If they are not eaten immediately, they can be refrigerated for a few days. They will last for two months when stored in containers in the freezer.

Sausage Making

Sausage comes from the Latin word *salsus*, meaning "salted;" that is, preserved meat. Here is the general procedure for making sausage.

Divide in half the amount of meat required for the recipe you have chosen. Put 3 rounded tablespoons of it in a blender, adding 1 tablespoon of crushed ice. Cover and liquefy at high speed for five seconds. Shut off the blender, uncover it, and move the meat to the blades, using a rubber spatula. Blend five seconds more. Turn off the blender, again moving the meat to the blades if need be, and add a little more ice. Blend five seconds more or until the contents have a peanut butter-like consistency. With the spatula, scoop the meat into a large bowl. Repeat this procedure until you have smoothly blended half of the meat. While allowing the blender to cool, measure all other ingredients into the bowl with the already processed meat. Now process the rest of the meat in your blender, and mix it thoroughly with all the ingredients in the bowl. Use your hands or a spoon (you may also find a potato masher handy for this) to insure that the seasonings are evenly blended.

Tie the end of a sausage casing with a string, and firmly pack in the meat. (Buy synthetic casings. They are easily stored and cannot spoil. The size generally preferred

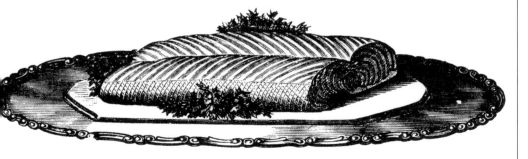

is 24 inches in length and 6 inches in diameter.) Try to squeeze out as much air as possible as you work. Tie the tip close to the meat, and snip off the casing. Cook according to the recipe you have selected. Or, if the recipe indicates, put the mixture into a loaf pan instead of casings and cook as directed.

Pork Sausage

12½ pounds fresh pork
  (approximately 11 pounds lean
  meat and 1½ pounds fat)
¼ cup salt
¼ cup brown sugar, firmly
  packed
1½ tablespoons sage
1 tablespoon black pepper
1 tablespoon red pepper

Trim away excess fat from the pork. Cut the meat into 2-inch cubes. Spread them on a piece of waxed paper. Blend the remaining ingredients, and sprinkle the mixture over the meat. Grind the seasoned meat twice in a meat grinder, and

thoroughly mix it with your hands to help distribute the seasonings and fat. Stuff into casings.

Canned Pork Sausage

Shape the pork sausage into small patties. Bake them for twenty-five to thirty minutes at 350° F.

Then place them in quart jars. Pour in their juice to cover.

Seal the jars and process for fifteen minutes at ten pounds pressure.

Grandma's Cracklings Sausage

The crisp bits of skin and meat remaining after hog fat has been rendered are called cracklings. Grandmother used them as an ingredient in homemade sausage, that is, if she could keep the family from pilfering too many of those crunchy snacks right from the kettle.

Here is her recipe: With each cup of cracklings, mix 1 cup of grated potato. Season the mixture with salt, pepper, and grated onion to taste, adding any preferred

herbs. Grandma favored marjoram and thyme.

When well mixed, the blend should be put in bread pans and baked for one hour at 350° F. Then cool and chill it.

To serve, cut the sausage in slices, and fry them for an old-time country breakfast.

Bologna (Fine-Cut Sausage)

3 pounds ground beef
  (75% lean)
2 pounds ground pork
1 tray ice cubes, crushed
1 cup instant powdered milk
3 tablespoons salt
1 tablespoon white pepper
1½ teaspoons ground coriander
1½ teaspoons ground
  cardamom
1 teaspoon dried sage
¾ teaspoon ground allspice
¾ teaspoon ground mace
1½ teaspoons sugar

Heat the oven to 275° F. Follow the general rules for preparing the meat mixture as already described. Pack the mixture into the casings, tying and cutting them.

Firmly press each stuffed casing into a loaf pan. If the casings fail to fit snugly against the ends of the pan, fill any empty spaces with wadded aluminum foil to keep the sausages tightly in place. Insert a thermometer in the middle of one. Place the pan in the center of the oven. Bake for two hours or until 160° F registers on the thermometer.

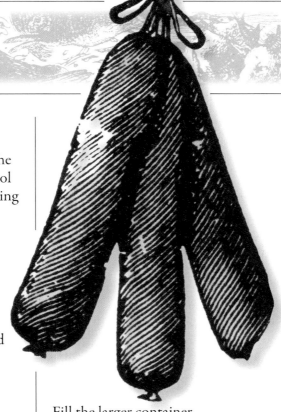

Take the meat from the oven. Remove the thermometer.

Allow cold water to run over the sausages for several minutes to cool them. Refrigerate them until serving time.

Braunschweiger (yield: 1½ pounds)

½ pound ground pork liver
½ pound ground pork
½ pound ground beef
1 medium-sized onion, minced
2 tablespoons powdered milk
½ teaspoon sugar
½ teaspoon pepper
¼ teaspoon ground cardamom
¼ teaspoon ground mace
¼ teaspoon margarine or butter
1 teaspoon salt

When grinding your own meat, use the grinder's fine cutter. If you have your meat man do the job, ask to have all the meats ground together twice.

Heat the oven to 275° F. Follow the general rules for preparing the meat mixture as described previously. Use less seasoning rather than a generous amount. Check the flavor of your sausage meat just before filling the casings by frying well 1 tablespoon of it. Add more seasonings if you find it too bland. Pack the meat into a loaf pan. Place a piece of waxed paper over it, and press down firmly and evenly. Remove the paper, and insert a thermometer in the middle of the mixture.

Set the loaf pan in a larger baking pan in the center of the oven.

Fill the larger container with water to a one-inch depth. Now and then check to see that the water does not boil. If it does, lower the temperature. Bake for one to one and a half hours or until the thermometer reaches 160° F.

Take the loaf out of the oven, and remove the thermometer. Place the pan in a container or sink of ice. Cool it rapidly, and put it in the refrigerator until serving time.

To store the Braunschweiger, remove it from the pan, wrap it in foil or transparent wrap, and keep it in the refrigerator, where it will remain edible for one week. It will keep in the freezer for six months.

Venison Sausage

When making venison sausage, first weigh the venison to determine the amount of pork required. Use two parts venison to one part pork.

The pork will compensate for lost venison fat (which many people dislike), keeping the sausage moist and imparting a pleasant flavor. Your butcher can supply you with pork trimmings, a combination of fat and pork meat, and with casings, if you intend to make link sausage.

After mixing the venison and pork, grind the meat twice to insure a good blend. A hand grinder is adequate unless you are processing more than 100 pounds, in which case a power grinder is practical.

Spread the ground meat on a table or counter top, and flatten it into an immense meat patty, some 4 inches thick. Sprinkle it with 1 tablespoon of black pepper and 2 tablespoons of salt (or garlic salt) for each 5 pounds of meat. If you prefer hot sausage, add 1 tablespoon of chili pequins (very small red peppers), dried and crushed.

Roll the meat into logs, 3 inches thick and 1 foot long.

Wrap them well; freeze for future use.

Bulk sausage may be cooked by cutting it into ½-inch-thick patties and frying them, seven minutes to a side, in an ungreased skillet.

To make link sausage, prepare the casings. Soak them for five minutes in warm water and rinse; turn them inside out and repeat the soaking and rinsing.

Attach the stuffer spout. Gather up a casing (as you would when putting on a sock), and slip it on

the spout. Approximately 3 inches of casing should extend from the spout opening. Tie the lower end of the casing with a string. When 3 to 4 feet have been stuffed, tie the filled casing in individual sausages, using strong cotton cord. Cut the casing in lengths of 24 inches. Tie the ends of each 2-foot length together so that it resembles a loop.

You can broil or barbecue the venison sausage, fifteen minutes to a side. It can also be boiled for twenty to thirty minutes or fried. Before serving the sausage, prick the casings to release pressurized juices.

If smoked meat is desired, keep it in the smokehouse for twenty-four to forty-eight hours. Smoking should be done only in cold weather. Cook the sausage thoroughly before serving it.

Curing Pork

Methods

Meat can be cured by two methods: the wet cure involves immersing the meat in brine; the dry cure entails rubbing the meat with a salt mixture. The wet method is often preferred for smaller cuts, the dry cure for larger pieces.

Whichever method is followed, each piece of meat must first be weighed, rubbed with fine salt, and allowed to drain, flesh side lowermost, for six to twelve hours.

Procedure for Wet-Curing Pork

Pack the meat in earthen or glass crocks (never use metal with brine); fill them up with water. Take out the meat, and empty the water into a vessel. For each 100 pounds of pork, assemble the following: 9 pounds of medium-grain salt (10 pounds in warm weather); 4 pounds of unsulphured molasses (you may substitute 4 pounds of maple syrup or 2½ pounds of brown sugar for the molasses); and 2 ounces of saltpeter. Add these preserving ingredients to the vessel of water, and stir with a wooden spoon.

Fill the crocks with pork, placing the largest pieces on the bottom. Cover them with the curing brine. Put lids on the crocks, and weigh each down with a stone or some heavy object to insure complete submersion of the meat. Store the crocks in a cool place.

Once a week, pour off the brine, remove the meat, and replace it, changing the position of the pieces. Return the brine to the crock. If scum develops on the brine's surface, empty the crocks and wash them and the pork thoroughly.

Repack the meat in fresh brine, if possible. Otherwise, use the original solution by boiling it and skimming off impurities.

Curing Time

Large pieces of meat need four days in the curing solution per pound of pork. Smaller pieces require three days in the brine to each pound. Record on a chart the weight of each cut and its calculated date of removal.

When the meat is taken out, soak it in clean water for thirty minutes.

Procedure for Dry-Curing Pork

Thoroughly mix the following ingredients for each 100 pounds of meat:

6 pounds salt (In warm weather use 8 pounds)
2 pounds molasses, maple syrup, or brown sugar (if the salt content is increased, use 2½ pounds)
2 ounces saltpeter (found in drugstores or meat-packing plants)
5 ounces black pepper

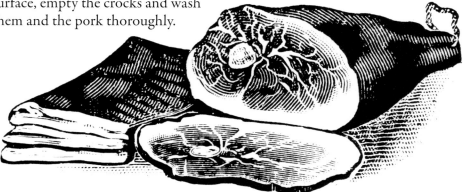

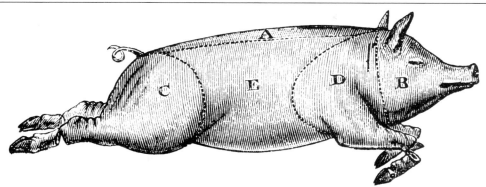

To this blend you may add any preferred seasoning, such as pickling spices, sage, or savory. Using a kneading motion, rub the curing mixture on all meat surfaces. Work it in well around the bones.

Pack the pork in a crock (or barrel) with the larger pieces on the bottom, smaller ones on top. Remove the meat after several days, and repack it. This step insures that the cure completely coats all pieces.

Curing Time

The curing process will require two days per pound of each cut. Keep a chart of weights and the duration of curing periods for individual pieces.

Country Ham

1 ham (10–15 pounds)
4 quarts ginger ale

Place the ham in a very large pot of water heated to just below the boiling point. (If you lack a vessel of adequate size, use a clean lard can.) Allow to boil for ten to fifteen minutes. This will remove excess salt from the exterior of the ham. Take out the ham; discard the water.

Return the ham to the pot, and fill it to the halfway mark with hot water. Pour in 4 quarts of ginger ale and cover loosely. Bring to a rolling boil and continue boiling for thirty minutes. Ginger ale will develop the ham's flavor.

Lay down several thicknesses of newspaper; place the pot containing the ham on them. Cover the pot (or lard can) closely with its lid. Now bring the newspapers up and around the pot's sides and top, and bind them in place with twine. Cover with blankets and quilts. Allow to stand for ten to fourteen hours, depending on the size of ham. A 13-pound ham will need about ten hours.

Remove the skin and cut away fat. Serve your country ham baked or fried.

Country Ham and Grits with Red-Eye Gravy

Cut country ham in slices ¼ to ½ inch thick. To prevent curling, slit the fat around the edges. Cook the ham slices slowly in a heavy skillet, turning them a few times. When the ham is brown, add a little water and simmer for several minutes. Take the ham from the skillet, and keep it warm.

Cook the gravy until it turns red. You may add a small amount of strong coffee to darken the color. Accompany your country ham with grits, serving red-eye gravy over both.

Corned Beef

Put 1 quart of water into an enamel pot with sufficient salt to enable an egg (still in its shell) to float. Remove the egg, and add a bay leaf, 8 peppercorns, and 2 tablespoons of pickling spice mix. Bring the contents of the vessel to a boil; then simmer for ten minutes. Let the liquid cool to room temperature.

Place a 4- to 6-pound beef brisket in a good-sized crock.

Pour the cooled brine into it. Cover the crock with foil topped by a weighted plate. Allow to stand for forty-eight hours. After that, wash the meat, and simmer it again for approximately three hours.

Bake the corned beef in a 300° F oven for one hour. Coat the cooked meat with a glaze of mustard and brown sugar. Serve warm or cold.

Hog Jowl and Black-Eyed Peas

Black-eyed peas are good any old time. But in Texas they are especially good on New Year's Day for luck. Including them in your dinner on the first of January is supposed to ensure a favorable year.

So, for good luck and good eating, prepare your black-eyed peas in this way:

½ pound hog jowl
¾ pound black-eyed peas
salt to taste
1 onion
1 or 2 jalapeno peppers

Cook the hog jowl until partially tender. Add the remaining ingredients. Slowly cook until the peas are just done, being careful not to overcook them.

Headcheese (Pork)

Scrape and clean a hog's head, washing it thoroughly.

Shove a hot poker into the nostrils and ears. Cover the head with lightly salted water in a large vessel. Put in onion and bay leaf. Simmer until the meat comes away from the bones, usually within several hours' time. Then drain the vessel's contents, saving a small amount of the liquid.

Remove all meat from the bones, discarding any gristle, and shred or chop it coarsely. Season it to taste with sage, thyme, salt, and pepper. Press the meat into a crock, and add a little of the pot liquid in which it was simmered. Cover the crock; place a weight on the lid. Allow to stand in a cold spot for three days.

When the headcheese has solidified, slice it for serving cold.

Headcheese (Veal)

Quarter a calf's head. Remove eyes, ears, brains, snout, and the greater part of the fat. Soak the four pieces in cold water to withdraw blood. Then put them in a kettle with enough cold water to cover and simmer until the meat separates from the bones.

Drain setting aside the liquid and dice the meat. Cover it with the stock, adding herbs, salt, and pepper. Cook for thirty minutes. Transfer to a mold. Cover with a cloth, putting a weight on top. Chill.

Cut in slices to serve.

Old-Fashioned Scrapple

Cut a 5- to 6-pound pig's head into four sections. Cover them with water and boil until the meat falls from the bones. Drain, saving the pot liquid.

Eliminate any gristle, and run the pork through a meat cutter. Add water to the stock, making 4 quarts in all. Put in the meat and sausage seasonings. Stir in enough cornmeal or buckwheat to give the consistency of mush. Let the mixture boil for several minutes.

Empty it into greased loaf pans to cool. Cut the scrapple in slices, and fry it without lard until crisp and brown.

Easy Scrapple

Make a thick porridge by cooking 1 cup of rolled oats in 2 cups of water. In another saucepan, cook 1 cup of cornmeal to like consistency in the same way. Then combine the two cereals. Mix in 1 pound of sausage meat plus some additional sausage seasoning.

Pack the blend into a crock and chill. When the scrapple is firm, slice and fry it thoroughly. Serve it plain, or trickle homemade maple syrup over the slices.

Aging Game

Aging tenderizes meat and improves its flavor. Hang game meat in a cool place, such as a garage or a basement, where the temperature remains in the low 40s. Air must be kept circulating around the meat. To create this, hang a small electric fan close by.

Inspect the game two or three times each day. Check for souring, particularly in cracks and folds of the meat. If you detect a sour odor, trim off the area involved, and clean the place with a half-and-half solution of water and vinegar.

The length of aging time ranges from two to fourteen days, depending on personal preference; however, about five days generally suits the taste of most folks.

Venison Mincemeat

Make mincemeat of irregular venison cuts that are not suitable for any particular game recipe.

    3 cups venison, chopped fine or
        ground
    1 cup butter
    1 cup strong coffee
    9 cups apples, chopped fine or
        ground
    3 teaspoons salt
    2 teaspoons cinnamon
    3 cups each of raisins, sugar, cider,
        molasses
    1 teaspoon cloves
    1 teaspoon nutmeg

Blend all ingredients in a large pot. Bring to a boil. Then lower the heat, and simmer the mincemeat for four to five hours.

Put it into hot, sterilized jars. Seal and cool. Venison mincemeat may also be frozen.

Two Small-Game Recipes (yield: 6 to 8 servings)

    2 good-sized squirrels or
        2 rabbits (even better, 1 of
        each)
    2 tablespoons butter
    1 large onion, chopped
    ½ pound smoked ham, diced
    2 quarts water
    1 teaspoon salt
    1 teaspoon pepper
    Tie the following four ingredients
    in a cheesecloth bag:
        1 bay leaf
        1 celery top
        1 hot red pepper pod
        1 parsley sprig
    1 cup corn
    1 cup lima beans
    4 medium-sized potatoes, cubed
    1 cup sliced okra
    1 teaspoon soy sauce
    dash Tabasco sauce
    2 teaspoons Worcestershire sauce

Wash the game, and pat it dry with paper towels. Cut it into serving sizes. Melt the butter in a large stew pot, and cook the chopped onion. When they are soft, put in the meat. Fry it until brown, about three minutes on each side. Mix in the ham. Add the water, salt, and pepper, and the cheesecloth bag containing herbs and vegetables. Cover the pot. Simmer until the meat is tender, for approximately forty-five minutes to an hour, stirring occasionally.

Now put in the vegetables. They may be fresh, canned, or frozen. Fresh vegetables should be added in this order: corn, lima beans, potatoes. After twenty minutes add okra, soy, Tabasco, and Worcestershire sauces. Stir and cook until the potatoes are tender. Take out the cheesecloth bag. Do not add water; the stew should be very thick. It may be served over white rice.

    3–5 pounds small game meat
    ½ cup butter (or margarine)
    1 large garlic clove, minced
    1 large onion, chopped 2 cups
        water
    1 teaspoon sweet basil
    1 cup white wine
    1 28-ounce can whole tomatoes
    2 cups chicken stock or broth
    salt and pepper to taste

Cut the meat into serving pieces; sprinkle it with salt and pepper to taste. Melt the butter in a pot, and brown the meat with garlic and onion. After the meat is nicely browned and the chopped onion is tender, add the white wine, basil, tomatoes and their liquid, chicken stock, and water. Cover. Simmer until the meat is tender, from forty-five to ninety minutes.

During the last twenty to forty-five minutes, put in any desired vegetables, and cook them for the required amount of time, adding liquid if necessary.

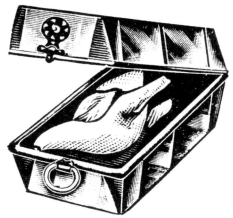

How to Pluck a Duck

For a fast, clean duck-plucking job, follow these steps:

In a bucket of boiling water, melt 1 pound of paraffin wax. Fill a second bucket with ice-cold water.

Cut off the feet and wings of the duck. Use the head as a handle.

Remove the roughest feathers from back and breast. This job should take no more than one minute.

Grasping the head, plunge the body to the bottom of the bucket of hot water and pull it out through the film of wax on the water's surface. Repeat this procedure a total of three times to thoroughly coat the duck.

Immerse the bird in the bucket of cold water to set the wax. Take it from the water to let the wax harden completely in some cool place. When properly hardened, the wax coating should feel cold to the fingers and crack down to the skin when the bird is flexed.

With the duck's back in your palms, split the coating along the breast with your thumbs. It should come away in about six large sections, taking all down, and feathers with it. Around the legs, work your thumb beneath the wax, and separate the skin from the wax. Removing the entire wax coating plus down and feathers should require less than sixty seconds. An essential for success is making certain that the wax coating is thoroughly hard and cold before removal.

Fresh Fish

Try the following recipe with bluefish or your favorite catch.

Grilled Bluefish

    4 pounds bluefish, dressed
    salt and pepper to taste
    lemon juice
    melted butter (or margarine)

Stuffing:
    2 tablespoons chopped onion
    ½ cup chopped celery
    ½ cup butter
    2 cups herb-seasoned bread
        crumbs
    ¼ cup chopped parsley
    4 ounces crumbled blue cheese
    1 tablespoon lemon juice

Rinse the fish; pat it dry. Lightly season the inside with lemon juice, salt, and pepper. Spread butter in the middle of a good-sized sheet of aluminum foil, and place the fish on it.

To prepare the stuffing, saute onion and celery in butter until tender. Put in the crumbs; toss to absorb the butter. Mix in the parsley and blue cheese. Moisten the stuffing with lemon juice and approximately ⅔ cup of water.

Fill the cavity of the fish with the stuffing. Close the opening by drawing the skin together and binding with soft string. Butter the top of the fish. Sprinkle with lemon juice, salt, and pepper.

Bring the sides of the foil over the fish and close them with a double fold. Seal the ends in double folds. Place on a grill over a medium fire for ten minutes on each side; turn a third time and grill for an additional ten minutes.

Serve stuffed bluefish garnished with parsley and lemon slices.

31 | SWEET THINGS

Sugar

Making Sugar from Beets

So highly valued was sugar several centuries ago that it was listed as a wedding present, along with precious gems and jewels, for a future queen of Bohemia and Hungary.

You can produce this once-greatly prized commodity at home from sugar beets. Scrub the vegetable well, and chop it into small pieces. Cook them in water to extract the juice; then strain the juice. Cook down the resulting syrup. Let it cool to crystallize.

Your homemade sugar will not be pure white, and a slight beety flavor will linger. It will be nutritionally superior, however, to treated commercial sugar.

Sugar Substitutes

Each of the following is a sweetening equivalent to 1 cup of white sugar and may be substituted for it when preparing food or drink:

• ½ cup of firmly packed brown sugar

• ¾ of strained honey, minus 3⅓ tablespoons of liquid per cup of added honey

• 1½ cups of molasses or sorghum, minus ¼ cup of liquid for each cup added

• 2 cups of corn syrup, minus ¼ cup of liquid per cup added

• 1½ cups of maple syrup, minus ¼ cup of liquid per cup added

Confections

Granny Barlow's Bran Brittle

    1 cup granulated sugar
    3 tablespoons corn syrup
    ½ cup brown sugar
    ½ cup water
    1 cup bran
    ½ teaspoon lemon extract
    2 tablespoons butter

Cook the sugars, syrup, and water to 290° F on your candy thermometer. Take the pan from the fire, and stir in the butter, bran, and flavoring.

Pour the mixture on a greased slab. Roll it very thin, using a greased rolling pin. When it cools, mark it into bite-sized squares.

Butterscotch Apples

    2 cups sugar
    1 cup corn syrup
    ½ cup water
    ¼ cup butter
    1 teaspoon lemon extract
    ¼ teaspoon salt
    red apples

Combine the sugar, corn syrup, water, and salt in a sauce pan. Cook the mixture until the sugar dissolves, stirring constantly. Then, without stirring, continue to cook the syrup to the hard-crack stage (295° F). Add butter and cook until your candy thermometer reaches 300° F. Stir in the lemon extract.

In the stem end of each well-washed, unpeeled apple, insert a wooden skewer. Dip the fruit in the hot syrup. Stand the apples on a wire cake rack for drainage of excess syrup as they harden.

Cracker Jacks (yield: 2½ quarts)

    2 quarts popped corn
    1 cup molasses
    2 cups shelled peanuts
    ½ cup sugar

Blend the popped corn and peanuts in a pan. Mix the molasses and sugar in a deep saucepan, and cook the syrup until it becomes threadlike when dropped in cold water or

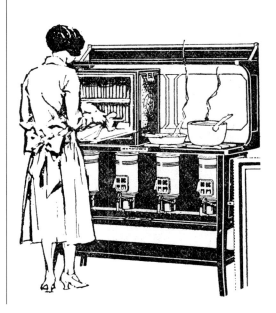

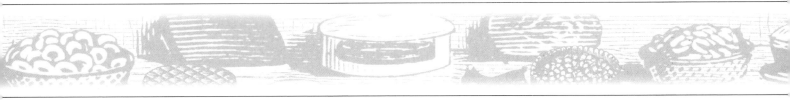

until the candy thermometer registers 234° F.

Pour the hot syrup over the popped corn and peanuts blend, mixing well. When the candy is cold and firm, break it into chunks.

Fruit Leather

Fruit leather, a nutritious, lightweight food, is an excellent addition to the outdoor menus of hikers and campers. Making this old-time confection is a good way to utilize overripe fruit.

Put 5 cups of any ripe fruit (apples, apricots, prunes, persimmons, etc.) in a saucepan. Add 1 tablespoon of lemon or lime juice and sweetening (preferably honey) to taste. Simmer until the mixture has the consistency of thick oatmeal. Stir and mash constantly to prevent burning and promote thickening.

Spread the thick fruit sauce on cookie sheets to a depth of ¼ inch.

Dry in the oven at 120° to 150° F. for about 4½ hours, leaving the door slightly open. If the day is sunny and warm (over 80° F), dry the fruit paste in the sun for about 9 hours, covering it with cheesecloth to screen out insects.

Keep fruit leather in a dry, cool place until ready for use.

It lasts for thirty weeks at a room temperature of no more than 70° F; it can be stored in a refrigerator for months and in a freezer for years.

The idea for preparing food in this manner stems from certain Indian tribes who made plant leather. They cooked the bee plant to a soup, removed the stems, and boiled the mixture until it became a thick paste. It was then sun-dried in sheets and stored for future camp use or on-the-trail consumption.

Fruit leather is not only a staple food for outdoorsmen. By adding five parts water to one part leather and churning the mixture in a blender, you can turn it into a delicious beverage. It can also be used in cooking, and as pie fillings and dessert toppings.

Lemon Gumdrops (yield: 60 pieces)

1 6-ounce bottle liquid pectin
1 teaspoon grated lemon rind
¼ teaspoon baking soda
3 drops homemade yellow food coloring
¾ cup sugar
¾ cup light corn syrup
1½ teaspoons lemon extract

In a one-quart saucepan, mix the pectin and baking soda. Mix the ¾ cup of sugar and the corn syrup in a 2-quart pan. Cook both mixtures simultaneously over high heat until foam leaves the first mix and the second comes to a fast boil within three to five minutes. Stir both vessels often. Continue stirring as you slowly empty the pectin mixture into the sugar mixture in a steady stream. Boil for one minute, stirring constantly.

Take from the stove and add lemon extract, lemon rind, and coloring. Put it in an 8-inch-square pan at once. Allow to stand at room temperature for about two hours. When the candy is cool and set, cut it in 1-inch cubes. Roll them in sugar. Keep gumdrops in the refrigerator.

Lollipops (yield: about 80)

4 cups sugar
2 cups light corn syrup
1 cup hot water
preferred extracts (lemon, orange, etc.)
homemade food coloring
7 dozen wooden lollipop sticks
An old slab of marble is handy for making lollipops. (A baking sheet can substitute.) Coat it with oil.

Line up the sticks on it, about 4 inches apart, with their points all in the same direction.

Combine the sugar, corn syrup, and water in a four-quart pot. Cook them until your candy thermometer registers 270° F (the soft-crack stage). Then reduce the heat and continue cooking until the thermometer reaches 310° F. (the hard-crack stage). Take from the heat; let cool for several minutes. Divide the mixture in half. Add any preferred flavorings and, if desired, the homemade food coloring. Stir to blend thoroughly.

When the candy thermometer falls to 280° F, drop tablespoons of

the syrupy mixture on the points of the lollipop sticks. Let stand until completely cold and hard.

Maple Sugar Candy (yield: about 2 pounds)

    2 pounds homemade maple sugar
    ¼ teaspoon cream of tartar
    1 cup water
Butter the rim of a good-sized, heavy saucepan. (This will keep the contents from boiling over.) Put in all three ingredients, and bring them to a boil, stirring continuously. Cook until your candy thermometer registers 234° F (the soft-ball stage). Let cool.

Now work the mixture with a wooden paddle until it becomes creamy and thick. Turn it into maple sugar molds. (If they are not available, twelve 2-inch cupcake tins will do nicely.)

When the candy is completely cold, invert the molds to remove their contents.

Marshmallows

    2 tablespoons gelatin
    ¼ cup cold water
    ¾ cup boiling water
    2 cups sugar
    ⅛ teaspoon salt
    1 teaspoon vanilla
    powdered sugar
Soak the gelatin in the cold water. When it has absorbed all the moisture, add the salt and vanilla.

Boil the water and sugar to the soft-ball stage (280° F).

Slowly pour this syrup over the gelatin, continually beating the mixture with a wire whisk until it is thick and cool.

Lightly butter a shallow pan; dust it with powdered sugar.

Turn the confection into the pan. Smooth the surface evenly; dust it with powdered sugar. Allow to stand overnight.

The next morning, cut the candy in small squares, and roll them in powdered sugar.

Honey Marshmallows

    1 tablespoon gelatin
    1 cup honey
    ¼ cup cold water
Thoroughly soak the gelatin in cold water. Dissolve it over hot water. Warm the honey, and add it to the gelatin. Beat the mixture for ten minutes in a blender until very fluffy and light. Spread it on a buttered pan. Allow to stand for twenty-four hours or longer.

Cut the confection into squares with a knife that has first been dipped in cold water. Store in airtight jars or tins.

Old-Fashioned Pulled Confection

    2 cups water
    chunk of butter (as big as an egg)
    4 cups sugar
    ¾ cup vinegar
    2 teaspoons vanilla
    1 cup cream
Put all ingredients in a vessel. Boil them until a test sample "cracks" in water. Then pour the mixture out on a buttered platter.

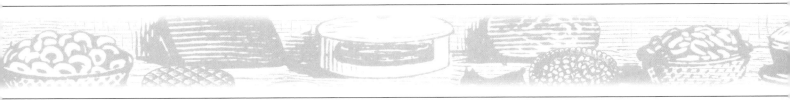

When the candy is cool enough to handle, pull it (as you would for taffy) until white.

Old-Time Sugar Candy

Combine the following ingredients in a pot: 1 cup of water, 6 cups of sugar, and 1 cup of vinegar. Put 1 teaspoon of soda in just enough hot water to dissolve it. Add this solution plus 1 teaspoon of butter to the vessel.

Boil the contents for thirty minutes without stirring. Sugar candy may be flavored to taste.

Popcorn Balls
(yield: 12 to 15)

1½ cups popcorn
1 cup sugar
4 tablespoons butter (or margarine)
⅓ cup corn syrup
1 teaspoon salt
⅓ cup water
1 teaspoon vanilla

Pop the corn, and remove imperfect kernels. Set the popcorn aside in a large bowl.

Mix the butter, water, sugar, and corn syrup in a saucepan.

Cook the blend to the medium-crack stage (280° F on your candy thermometer). Remove from the stove. Add the salt and flavoring.

Slowly pour the syrup over the popped corn, stirring constantly to evenly coat all kernels. As soon as the popcorn is cool enough to handle, shape it lightly into balls with oiled or slightly floured hands. Place them on waxed paper, wrapping them individually.

Potato Candy

Boil and mash a medium-sized potato. Mix in sufficient sugar to make it stiff. On a dough board sprinkled with powdered sugar, roll out the potato mixture. Spread on homemade peanut butter. Roll it up jelly-roll style. Slice in ½-inch pieces to serve.

Spun Carnival Candy

2 cups sugar
⅛ teaspoon cream of tartar
1 cup water

Combine the three ingredients in a saucepan, and boil them without stirring until the candy thermometer reaches 310° F. Immediately put the pan in a larger pan of cold water to halt the boiling; then set it in hot water. Add homemade food coloring if desired.

Lay broom handles across chairs set three feet apart.

Spread newspaper beneath. Dip a sugar spinner into the syrup, and quickly wave it back and forth over the broomsticks. From time to time gather up the spun sugar, and pile it

on a cold platter or shape it into nests. Should the syrup become sugary, melt it over heat for a moment.

Spun sugar candy can be eaten alone or used as a garnish for ice cream.

Taffy (yield: ½ pound)

1 cup light corn syrup
½ cup sugar
1 tablespoon vinegar
1 teaspoon butter flavoring

Lightly butter a platter. Combine the first four ingredients in a saucepan. Boil them until your candy thermometer registers 252° F. The mixture should now be firm.

Pour it on the platter. When it is cool enough to touch, add several drops of any preferred flavoring and pull the taffy with thumbs and forefingers until it is light. Pull away bite-sized pieces; wrap them in squares of waxed paper.

Vinegar Candy

2 cups sugar
2 tablespoons butter
½ cup vinegar

Melt butter in a saucepan. Add the sugar and vinegar. Stir until the sugar is smooth and the mixture starts to boil. When it is bubbly, put a drop in cold water. If it congeals, becoming brittle, empty the mixture onto a buttered pan.

When it is cool enough to pick up, pull it into strands, as you would taffy. Then cut it into bite-sized pieces with scissors or a knife. Place them on buttered plates to cool further.

Cakes, Cookies, and Frosting

Carrot Cake

1½ cups cooking oil
1¾ cups sugar
4 eggs, separated
¼ cup hot water
1 teaspoon nutmeg
1 teaspoon cinnamon
½ teaspoon ground cloves
2 teaspoons baking powder
2½ cups whole wheat flour
1½ cups grated raw carrots
½ cup raisins

Bake carrot cake in a preheated 350-degree oven. Grease and flour a l0-inch tube pan.

Beat the oil, sugar, and egg yolks together. Stir in the hot water until the sugar dissolves. Mix in the spices, baking powder, flour, carrots, and raisins. Blend well.

In another bowl beat the egg whites until they are stiff but not dry. Gently fold them into the batter. Empty the batter into the prepared cake pan, and bake it for seventy minutes or until done.

Grandma's Gingerbread

½ cup shortening
½ cup sugar
1 cup molasses
2 eggs
2½ cups flour
2 teaspoons ground cinnamon
1 teaspoon salt
1½ teaspoons soda
½ teaspoon ground cloves
1 teaspoon ground ginger
1 cup buttermilk

Cream the shortening and sugar; blend in the molasses.

Add the eggs, one at a time, beating after each addition.

Combine the flour, salt, soda, and spices. Alternately add the dry blend and the buttermilk to the creamed mixture.

Grease a 9-inch-square cake pan. Spoon in the batter.

Bake in a 350° F oven for forty minutes or until done. Cool.

Oatmeal Cake

1 cup oats (quick cooking)
1 cup brown sugar
2 eggs
1¼ cups hot water
1⅓ cups flour
1 stick butter (or margarine)
1 teaspoon soda
1 teaspoon cinnamon
1 cup white sugar
1½ teaspoons salt

Pour the hot water over the oats; allow to stand for twenty minutes. Cream the butter and sugar together, and stir in an egg at a time. Add the oatmeal mixture. Sift the dry ingredients. Stir them in, blending thoroughly.

Grease and flour an 8-inch-square pan. Pour in the batter.

Bake in a 350° F oven for thirty to thirty-five minutes until done. Cool and frost.

Sugarless Frosting

Mix 4 tablespoons of cornstarch and 8 tablespoons of cocoa powder. Stir in 8 tablespoons of honey. While stirring continuously, slowly add small amounts of evaporated milk until the frosting reaches the desired consistency.

Country-Boy Ginger Snaps

1 cup molasses
½ teaspoon soda
½ cup butter
1 teaspoon ginger
3 cups flour, sifted
2 scant teaspoons salt

Put the butter and molasses in a saucepan; boil them for two minutes.

Mix and sift the remaining ingredients. Add them to the contents of the saucepan. Beat well.

Chill the mixture overnight. Roll the dough out thin, and cut it with a cookie cutter or knife.

Bake on buttered cookie sheets in a 375° F oven for about ten minutes.

Yogurt Cookies (yield: about 60)

½ cup cooking oil
1 teaspoon baking powder
1 cup sugar
2 eggs
3 cups rye flour

½ teaspoon salt
1 tablespoon grated orange rind
1 cup homemade yogurt
Grease two baking sheets.

Beat oil, sugar, and eggs in a big bowl. Add the rest of the ingredients, stirring and blending well.

Drop dough by the tablespoon on the cookie sheets, spaced roughly 1½ inches apart. Bake in a preheated 350° F oven, until lightly browned, about 10 to 12 minutes.

Puddings

Molasses-Cranberry Pudding

2 cups cranberries
1½ cups flour
½ cup boiling water
1 cup sugar
2 teaspoons soda
½ cup butter
¼ cup molasses
½ cup cream
¼ cup corn syrup
½ teaspoon nutmeg
1 egg, well beaten
½ teaspoon vanilla

Chop the cranberries. Mix the soda into the boiling water; pour it over the berries.

Beat the egg well. Blend it with the molasses and corn syrup. Add the mixture to the cranberries, and stir in the flour. Blend well.

Pour into a well-greased pudding mold. Steam for three hours.

Cream the butter and sugar. When they are of a creamy consistency, add the cream. Cook until fluffy in a double boiler, beating continuously.

Mix in the nutmeg and vanilla. Serve as sauce over the hot pudding.

Persimmon Pudding

1 cup persimmon pulp
½ teaspoon vanilla
1 tablespoon butter, melted
1 lemon
1 orange
1¼ cups flour
1 cup sugar
1 teaspoon soda
1 egg
½ cup milk
2 tablespoons hot water

Sift together the flour and soda. Blend this dry mixture with the milk, persimmon pulp, melted butter, and vanilla.

Pour into a well-greased pudding mold; cover. Steam for 2 hours.

Lightly beat the egg. Cook it in the top of a double boiler along with the grated rind and strained juice of the citrus fruits, the hot water, and sugar until the mixture develops a creamy consistency. Serve the sauce hot over the steaming persimmon pudding.

Chocolate Pudding (yield: 4 servings)

Sift together the following ingredients:
¼ cup flour
dash of salt
6 tablespoons sugar
4 tablespoons cocoa
⅔ cup powdered milk

Store the blend in a tightly closed jar until ready for use. To prepare pudding, empty the mixture into a saucepan.

Gradually add 2 cups of water and 2 tablespoons of margarine, blending thoroughly all the while.

Put over a low flame and stir until the pudding thickens and starts to bubble when stirring is arrested for a moment.

Turn off the heat; blend in 1 teaspoon of vanilla. Cool.

APPENDIX | WEIGHTS AND MEASURES

Most everything you do in the country has a weight or measure associated with it in one way or another; buying and selling, building, planting and harvesting, even counting out the eggs the old hen lays. For this section we have accumulated weights and measures of every kind and description. This is by no means all the measures that exist, but it's a handy reference as almost all of them have a use at one time or another.

Weights

In our modem civilization we find many odd weights and measures, some which indicate a notable need for scales or measuring implements. For many of these, rather fantastic origins have been given. We know that Charlemagne found different, arbitrary measures of distance in every country, and struck his huge foot to earth, ordering that its length should be the sole standard for the world. It is said that the English standard, the "grain," was originally derived from the average weight of a grain of barley. The inch was determined from the length of three barley corns, round and dry. The weight of the English penny, by act of Henry III, in 1266, was to be equal to that of thirty-two

grains of wheat, taken from the middle of the wheat kernel and well dried. Among the nations of the East, we have the "finger's length," from that of the digit, or second joint of the forefinger, the finger's breadth, the palm, the hand, the span, the cubit or length of the forearm, the stretch of the arms, length of the foot, the step or pace, the stone, pack, etc.

Below we give a table showing some of these measures, now only used for special purposes:

A sack of wool is 22 stone, 14 pounds to the stone, or 308 pounds.

A pack of wool is 17 stone, 2 pounds, or 240 pounds, which is considered a pack load for a horse.

A truss of new hay is 60 pounds; old hay, 50 pounds; straw, 40 pounds.

A load of hay is 36 trusses; a bale of hay is 300 pounds; a bale of cotton, 400 pounds; a sack of Sea Island cotton, 300 pounds.

In England, a firkin of butter is 56 pounds. In the United States, a firkin of butter is 50 pounds. Double firkins, 100 pounds.

196 pounds = a barrel of flour
200 pounds = a barrel of beef, pork, or fish
280 pounds = a barrel of salt
3 pounds = 1 stone butcher's meat
7 pounds = 1 clove
2 cloves = 1 stone common articles
2 stone = 1 tod of wool
6½ tods = 1 wey of wool
2 weys = 1 sack of wool
12 sacks = 1 last of wool
240 pounds = 1 pack of wool

Distance

3 inches = 1 palm
4 inches = 1 hand
6 inches = 1 span
18 inches = 1 cubit
21.8 inches = 1 Bible cubit
2½ feet = 1 military pace
3 feet = 1 common pace
3.28 feet = 1 meter

Mariners' Measures

6 feet = 1 fathom
120 fathoms = 1 cable length
7½ cable lengths = 1 mile
5,280 feet = 1 statute mile
6,076.1 feet = 1 nautical mile
880 fathoms = 1 mile
A ship's cable = a chain 120 fathoms, or 720 feet long
A hair's breadth = one forty-eighth part of an inch
A knot, or nautical mile = one-sixtieth of a degree; 3 knots = a marine league; 60 knots, or 69½ statute miles = 1 degree

Dry Measure

2 quarts = 1 pottle
2 bushels = 1 strike
2 strikes = 1 coom
2 cooms = 1 quarter
5 quarters = 1 load
3 bushels = 1 sack
36 bushels = 1 chaldron
1 cup = ½ pint
2 pints = 1 quart
8 quarts = 1 peck
4 pecks = 1 bushel
32 quarts = 1 bushel
1 barrel (cranberries) = 5,826 cubic inches
1 barrel (other fruits, vegetables, and
    dry produce) = 7,056 cubic inches =
    105 dry quarts
1 bushel = a cube measuring
    12.90747 inches on each side.

The Standard Bushel

The standard is the Winchester bushel, which contains 2,150.42 cubic inches, or 77.627 pounds avoirdupois of distilled water at its maximum density. Its dimensions are 18½ inches diameter inside, 19½ inches outside, and 8 inches deep.

The heaped bushel requires six inches in the height of the cone above the top of the struck bushel, and contains 2,748 cubic inches in all.

Dry Measure: A Comparative Scale

Chaldron	Bushels	Peck	Quarts	Pints
1 =	36 =	144 =	1,152 =	2,304
	1 =	4 =	32 =	64
		1 =	8 =	16
			1 =	2

Liquid Measure

1 teaspoon = ⅙ ounce (oz.)
1 tablespoon = ½ ounce
16 ounces = 1 pint (pt.)
2 pints = 1 quart (qt.)
4 quarts = 1 gallon (gal.)
31½ gallons = 1 barrel (br.)
firkin = 9 gallons
liquid barrel = 32.5 gallons
hogshead = 63 gallons
tun = 252 gallons
1 gallon = a cube measuring 6.135792
    on each side.

Wine Measure

18 United States gallons = 1 runlet
25 English gallons, or
    42 United States gallons = 1 tierce
2 tierces = 1 puncheon
52¼ English gallons = 1 hogshead
63 United States gallons = hogshead
2 hogsheads = 1 pipe
2 pipes = 1 tun
7½ English gallons = 1 firkin of beer
4 firkins = 1 barrel

Liquid or Wine Measure

16 fluid ounces = 4 gills
4 gills = 1 pint
2 pints = 1 quart
4 quarts = 1 gallon
31½ gallons = 1 barrel
2 barrels or 63 gallons = 1 hogshead

Can Sizes

Buffet or picnic	1 cup
No. 1	1¾ cup
No. 1, tall	2 cups
No. 2	2½ cups
No. 2½	3½ cups
No. 3	4 cups
No. 5	7 cups
No. 10	13 cups

Liquid Measure: A Comparative Scale

Hogshead	Barrels	Gallons	Quarts	Pints	Gills
1 =	2 =	63 =	252 =	504 =	2016
	1 =	31 ½ =	126 =	252 =	1008
		1 =	4 =	8 =	32
			1 =	2 =	8
				1 =	4

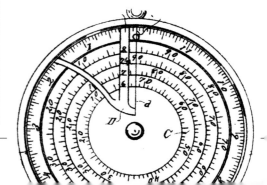

Surveyor's Long Measure

7.92 inches = 1 link
25 links = I rod
4 rods = I chain
100 links (66 ft.) = 1 chain
80 chains = 1 mile

Area or Square Measure

144 square inches = 1 square foot
9 square feet = 1 square yard
30¼ square yards = 1 square rod
272½ square feet =1 square rod
40 square rods = 1 rood, or quarter acre
16o square rods = 1 acre
4 roods = 1 acre
640 acres = 1 square mile or section
43,569 square feet = 1 acre

Surveyor's Square Measure

625 square links = 1 square rod
16 square rods = 1 square chain
10 square chains = 1 acre
640 acres = 1 square mile
36 square miles (six miles square)
   = 1 township

Square Feet and Feet Square

Never make the mistake of supposing that *square feet* and *feet square* are the same; one foot, yard, rod, or mile, etc., square; or one square foot, yard, rod, mile, etc. are the same, but when beyond the unit measure, the difference increases with the square of the surface, thus:

Square Feet and Feet Square

Fractions of an Acre	Square Feet	Feet Square
¹⁄₁₆	2,722½	52½
⅛	5,445	73¾
¼	10,890	104½
½	21,780	147½
1	43,560	208¼
2	87,120	295¼

Note: 43,560 square feet
   = 4,840 square yards = 1 acre
A square 208.71 feet on all sides = 1 acre

How to Compute Capacity of Corn Bins, Cribs, and Piled Corn

- Husked Ear Corn: The formulas below give answers in bushels of husked ear corn.
- Unhusked Ear Corn: Take ⅔ of figure for husked ear corn—unhusked corn varies greatly.
- Shelled Corn: Double the number of bushels of husked ear corn.
- Corn-Cob Mix (Combine run shelled corn and ground cobs): Figure at approximately same volume as husked ear corn.
- Square or Rectangular Cribs: Multiply the length by the width by the depth of grain (all in feet). Multiply this sum by 2 and divide by 5. Result is capacity of bushels of husked ear corn at 70 pounds per bushel (15.5 per cent moisture).
- Round Cribs: Multiply the diameter by the diameter. Multiply this sum by the depth (all in feet). Multiply the sum by .315 for husked ear corn.
- Piled Corn: When heaped in the form of a cone, multiply the diameter by the diameter. Multiply this sum by the depth of the pile at its greatest depth (all in feet). Multiply this sum by .105 for husked ear corn.

Area or Square Measure: A Comparative Scale

Acre	Roods	Rods	Square Yards	Square Feet	Square Inches
1 =	4 =	160 =	4,840 =	43,560 =	6,272,640
	1 =	40 =	1,210 =	10,890 =	1,568,160
		1 =	30¼ =	27½ =	39,204
			1 =	9 =	1,296
				1 =	144

Measuring Crib Contents

Length		10	12	14	16	20	24	28	30 ft.
Breadth in feet	3	135	162	189	216	270	324	378	405 bu.
	4	180	216	252	288	360	432	504	540 bu.
	5	225	270	315	360	450	510	630	675 bu.
	6	270	324	378	432	540	648	756	810 bu.
	7	315	378	441	504	630	756	882	945 bu.
	8	360	432	504	576	720	864	1008	1080 bu.
	10	450	540	589	720	900	1080	1260	1350 bu.
	12	540	648	756	864	1080	1296	1512	1620 bu.

Contents of Cribs

In the West, and wherever dent corn is raised, three heaping half-bushels are roughly estimated to make a bushel of shelled corn of fifty-six pounds. In reality, sixty-eight pounds of ears of sound dent corn, well dried in the crib, will do so. Four heaping half-bushels of flint corn are allowed for a bushel. One rule for finding the contents is to multiply the length, breadth, and height (in feet) together to obtain cubic feet; multiply this product by four, strike off the right-hand figure, and the result will be nearly the number of shelled bushels.

When the crib is flared both ways, multiply half the sum of the bottom breadths in feet by the perpendicular height in feet, and the same again by the length in feet; multiply the last product by .63 for heaped bushels of ears, and by .42 for the number of bushels in shelled corn. This rule is based on the generally accepted estimate that three heaped half-bushels of ears, or four evenly full, form one bushel of shelled corn.

The table above is based on the supposition that the crib is ten feet high, that the breadth is constant, or, if flared, constant half way from the bottom to the top and figuring 3,840 cubic inches of ears to the bushel of shelled corn. Thus a crib 5 feet wide, 10 feet high and 30 feet long will contain 675 bushels of shelled corn.

Contents of Granaries

To find the contents of granaries, multiply length, breadth, and height together to get the cubic feet. Divide this by 56, multiply by 45, and the result will be struck measure. The table below will give the capacities of grain bins, etc. 10 feet high.

Measuring Granary Contents

Width in feet	Bin 6 feet long	Bin 8 feet long	Bin 10 feet long	Bin 12 feet long	Bin 14 feet long	Bin 16 feet long	Bin 20 feet long
	Bu.	Bu.	Bu.	Bu.	Bu.	Bu.	Bu.
3	145	192	241	289	338	386	482
4	193	257	321	386	450	514	643
5	241	321	402	482	563	643	804
6	290	386	482	579	675	771	964
7	338	450	563	675	788	900	1,125
8	386	514	643	771	900	1,029	1,286
9	434	579	723	868	1,013	1,157	1,446
10	482	643	804	964	1,125	1,286	1,607
11	531	707	884	1,061	1,238	1,414	1,768
12	579	771	964	1,157	1,350	1,542	1,920

Contents of Cisterns

Thirty-six inches of rain per year will yield 72 barrels of water for each 10 foot square (100 square feet) of roof. Thus a 30′ by 40′ barn may supply 2 barrels per day throughout the year. In dry areas that is, areas where heavy rains are succeeded by long dry spells the cisterns must be larger than where rains are more constant. When the water is to be used daily a 30′ by 40′ barn should have a cistern 10 feet in diameter and 9 feet deep; this will hold 168 barrels. But if the water is to be drawn from only in time of drouth, it should be three times this capacity.

To determine the contents of a circular cistern of equal size at top and bottom, find the depth and diameter in inches; square the diameter and multiply the square by the decimal .0034, which will find the quantity of gallons for 1 inch in depth. Multiply this by the depth in inches, divide by 31½, and the

result will be the number of barrels the cistern will hold. The following table shows the number of barrels of liquid the following diameters will hold, for each 12 inches in depth:

feet diameter, capacity per foot, in depth,	= barrels.
5	4.66
6	6.71
7	9.13
8	11.93
9	15.10
10	18.65

To find the contents of a square cistern, multiply the length by the breadth, multiply this result by 1,728 and divide the total by 231. The result will be the number of gallons for each foot in depth. The following table shows the barrels for the sizes named for square cisterns:

feet by feet has capacity per foot in depth of	barrels.
5x5	5.92
6x6	8.54
7x7	11.63
8x8	15.19
9x9	19.39
10x10	23.74

Land Measure

Farmers often wish to know the contents of a field. To find the number of acres in any square or rectangular field, multiply the length in rods and breadth in rods together, and divide by 160; or, multiply the length in feet by breadth in feet and divide by 43,560, the number of square feet in an acre. Thus:

10 rods by 16 rods = 1 acre
8 rods by 20 rods = 1 acre
5 rods by 32 rods = 1 acre
4 rods by 40 rods = 1 acre
5 yards by 968 rods = 1 acre
10 yards by 484 yards = 1 acre
20 yards by 242 yards = 1 acre
40 yards by 121 yards = 1 acre
80 yards by 60½ yards = 1 acre
70 yards by 69½ yards =1 acre
220 feet by 198 feet = 1 acre
440 feet by 99 feet = 1 acre
110 feet by 369 feet = 1 acre
60 feet by 726 feet = 1 acre
120 feet by 363 feet = 1 acre
240 feet by 181½ feet = 1 acre
200 feet by 108.9 feet = ½ acre
100 feet by 145.2 feet = ⅓ acre
100 feet by 108.9 feet = ¼ acre
43,560 square feet = 1 acre
4,840 square yards = 1 acre

Useful Rules

- To find the number of gallons in a cylindrical tank: Multiply the square of the diameter in inches by .7854, and multiply this product by the height, in inches, then divide the result by 231.
- To find the number of tons of hay in long square stacks: Multiply the length in yards by the width in yards, and that by half the altitude in yards, and divide the product by 15.
- To find the contents of boards, in square feet: Multiply the length (in feet), by the width (in inches), and divide the product by 12.
- Find contents of a 16-foot board, 9 inches wide: 9 by 16 = 144 ÷ 12 = 12 square feet.
- Of an 18-foot board, 13 inches wide: 13 by 18 = 234 ÷ 12 = 19½ square feet.
- To find the contents of scantlings, joists, sills, etc. in square feet: Multiply the length, width, and thickness together, and divide product by 12.
- To find the contents of granaries, wagon beds in bushels: Multiply the number of cubic feet by .8 (for greater accuracy by .8036). A wagon bed 3 feet wide and 10 feet long will hold 2 bushels for every inch in depth.
- Corn Cribs: Good quality ear corn, measured when settled, will hold out at 274 cubic feet per bushel. Inferior quality, 2% to 212 cubic feet per bushel.
- Hay: The quantity of hay in a mow or stack can only be approximately ascertained by measurement. It takes about 350 cubic feet of well-settled timothy hay to make a ton; from 400 to 450 cubic feet of partly settled hay.
- Haystacks: To find contents of a round stack in cubic feet, multiply the square of the average circumference by the average height, and this product by .08; then divide by 350 if the hay is well settled, by 400 or 450 otherwise.
- For an oblong-shaped stack, multiply the average length, width and height together, and divide by the same figures.
- Coal: Hard coal in the solid state averages about 80 pounds per cubic foot, or 25 cubic feet to a ton. Chestnut-size lumps average about 56 pounds per cubic foot.
- Cord Wood: A cord of wood is a pile 4 feet wide, 4 feet high and 8 feet long, and contains 128 cubic feet. Hence, to find the contents of a pile of wood, in cubic feet and cords, multiply length, width, and thickness together, and divide by 128.
- Stone: A perch of stone masonry is 1½ feet long, 1½ feet high and 1 foot thick, and contains 24¾ cubic feet.
- To find the contents of a wall, in perches, find the number of cubic feet, then divide by 2¾ (or multiply by .0404).

INDEX

About the Author

Jerry Mack Johnson grew up on a ranch in West Texas and worked as a cowboy, rodeo clown, professional bull rider, miner, prospector, merchant seaman, oilfield worker, catfish farmer, salesman, and school teacher. He was the author of numerous books of lore, including *Down Home Ways, Country Wisdom, Country Scrapbook,* and *The Catfish Farming Handbook.*